C0-ATS-179

THE WATCHMAN IN PIECES

DAVID ROSEN AND AARON SANTESSO

THE Watchman in Pieces

SURVEILLANCE, LITERATURE,

AND LIBERAL PERSONHOOD

Yale UNIVERSITY PRESS   NEW HAVEN & LONDON

Copyright © 2013 by Yale University.
All rights reserved.
This book may not be reproduced, in whole or in part, including illustrations, in any form (beyond that copying permitted by Sections 107 and 108 of the U.S. Copyright Law and except by reviewers for the public press), without written permission from the publishers.

Yale University Press books may be purchased in quantity for educational, business, or promotional use. For information, please e-mail sales.press@yale.edu (U.S. office) or sales@yaleup.co.uk (U.K. office).

Set in Scala and Scala Sans types by IDS Infotech, Ltd.
Printed in the United States of America.

Library of Congress Cataloging-in-Publication Data

Rosen, David, 1971–
The watchman in pieces : surveillance, literature, and liberal personhood / David Rosen and Aaron Santesso.
    pages cm
Includes bibliographical references and index.
ISBN 978–0–300-15541-9 (cloth : alk. paper)
1. Self in literature.   2. Privacy in literature.
3. Citizenship in literature.   I. Santesso, Aaron, 1972– II. Title.
   PN56.S46R67 2013
   809'.93353—dc23
                                                                    2012046993
A catalogue record for this book is available from the British Library.

This paper meets the requirements of ANSI/NISOZ39.48–1992 (Permanence of Paper).

10 9 8 7 6 5 4 3 2 1

While Hermes pip'd, and sung, and told his tale,
The Keeper's winking Eyes began to fail;
And drowsie slumber, on the lids to creep,
'Till all the Watchman was, at length, asleep.
Then soon the God, his Voice and Song supprest;
And with his pow'rful Rod confirm'd his rest:
Without delay his crooked Faulchion drew,
And at one fatal stroke the Keeper slew.
Down from the Rock, fell the dissever'd head,
Opening its Eyes in Death; and falling bled:
And mark'd the passage with a crimson trail;
Thus Argus lies in pieces, cold and pale;
And all his hundred Eyes, with all their light,
Are clos'd at once, in one perpetual night.

—*Ovid, Metamorphoses* 1.713–21, *trans.* J O H N   D R Y D E N   1693

CONTENTS

ACKNOWLEDGMENTS

SEVERAL YEARS AGO, we asked a surveillance expert at Scotland Yard what recent technological development posed the most frightening challenge to governments hoping to track criminal activities. His response was instant and unequivocal: Skype. Because the service divided the user's voice into discreet data-bundles, which were then encrypted and sent helter-skelter via servers around the world, before being reassembled on another user's computer, it was practically impossible to monitor in any traditional way. Accordingly, Skype had become a favorite device of terrorists, drug cartels—and, as it happens, ourselves. This book required ten years to research, write, and edit; at no point during this decade were we living less than 900 miles apart. As our research took us across the country and abroad, Skype went with us, ultimately making possible free and lengthy conversations from four different continents. By a happy coincidence, the service entered its beta phase in 2003, just as work on the book was beginning to heat up. Enough time had passed for us to take it for granted—until we were reminded that day of its equivocal role in our very topic. Therefore we begin by acknowledging Niklas Zennström and Janus Friis—and by noting that Skype, now owned by Microsoft, has been restructured to make it more accessible to law enforcement.

One of us received his training in the literature of the eighteenth century, the other in Modernism. It goes without saying that the internal pressures of our profession prohibitively favor continued work in our chosen corners of it. This book, which moves from the early Renaissance to the present day, and which draws selectively from such fields as legal theory, sociology, political science, and art theory, in addition to the two primary disciplines of literary studies and philosophy, runs very much in the other direction. Since we would hope that scholars in those other fields might read this book with interest and profit from it, we have accrued numerous debts in the process of making ourselves (selectively) fluent in those disciplines. We gratefully acknowledge the useful conversations we have had with friends and colleagues working in other areas of English literature—among these, Barbara Benedict, Ciaran Berry, Sarah Bilston, Nihad Farooq, Lucy Ferriss, Sheila Fisher, Ken Knoespel, Dutch Kuyk, Paul Lauter, James Mardock, Steve Monte, James Mulholland, Milla Riggio, Lisa Yaszek and Prakash Younger. Additionally, we have benefited from conversations with colleagues in other disciplines relevant to the project, from mathematics (David Cruz-Uribe), to computer science (Mircea Nicolescu), to political science (Lida Maxwell), to history (Dennis Dworkin, David Randall). Our thanks also go to the library staffs at Trinity College, the University of Nevada, and Georgia Tech, as well as those at Wesleyan University, Emory, Yale, and the University of Georgia. Special acknowledgments to Brandeis University, the British Library, the New York Public Library, and University College, London, for access to their archives.

From the beginning, we meant for this book to be of interest to those outside academia—and accurate in its depiction of the current state of surveillance. This has meant interviewing surveillance professionals, or men and women whose professional lives interact with surveillance in particular ways. Many of those with whom we spoke have requested anonymity, including officers and staff at Covert Policing Command at the Metropolitan Police in London (Scotland Yard); various employees and surveillance operators at the Silver Legacy, Eldorado, Harrah's, Fitzgerald's, and MGM Grand casinos in Reno and Las Vegas, Nevada; and officers working with Homeland Security at the Hartsfield-Jackson Atlanta International Airport. We are also grateful to Joe Navarro, formerly with the FBI, who spoke to us about nonverbal cues and behavioral profiling, and David G. Schwartz, now director of the Center for Gaming Research at the University of Nevada, Las Vegas.

Three anonymous readers at Yale University Press, and one who chose to identify himself (Patrick Brantlinger), had a distinct influence on the form this book finally took. To these we would add readers and editors at the several journals in which parts of chapters have previously appeared—above all Frances Ferguson at *ELH*, who contributed some useful ideas for chapter 2. Because of the book's very broad scope, we profited from readers who were able to identify necessary texts we were ignoring—but just as much from those who called us on the opposite tendency: aware of the territoriality of scholars in each of the fields into which we were venturing, we took care to footnote our research extensively. It was at the gentle suggestion of some readers that we ultimately removed several dozen footnotes from the final text. Our deepest thanks, finally, goes to department colleagues who put in the time and energy to read and comment on all or much of the manuscript as it was being produced; Chloe Wheatley clarified the stakes in our treatment of the early modern period, and Chris Hager was of especial help in making more precise our treatment of American material. It is, finally, a characteristic of our book that it is meant to be read *as* a book: as a through-composed argument with multiple intertwining strands, it cannot be read selectively or quickly. We are grateful to these and other patient and dedicated readers who perceived this ambition and did not try to dissuade us from it.

A final individual, to whom we can only refer as A.F., taught us an early and painful lesson about the perils of dataveillance. We acknowledge him here.

Writing this book would have been much harder without the institutional support each of us received at all stages of the project. Trinity College provided funding for travel to conferences and archives, and for completion of the manuscript, both through the Allan K. Smith bequest and through discretionary funds administered through the Office of the Dean of Faculty. Our thanks go to Associate Deans Tom Mitzel and Melanie Stein and to Dean Rena Fraden. The University of Nevada, through the English Department, Dean's Office, and Provost's Office, funded research and conference trips. Georgia Tech provided a Faculty Foundation Grant; in addition, Ravi Bellamkonda, Associate Vice President for Research, and Dean Jackie Royster not only provided funding but were enthusiastically supportive of the project. We have also been propped up, in more ways than can be counted, by the administrative staffs in our own departments. Grantley Bailey, Christina Bolio, Roberta Rogers-Bednarek, Jocelyn Thomas, and especially Kenya Devalia and Margaret Grasso can take their share of credit for the book appearing as speedily as it did.

We thank Nan and David Skier for their permission to reproduce images from their wonderful collection of Victorian eye portraits, housed at the Birmingham Museum of Art (and which can be viewed in *The Look of Love: Eye Miniatures from the Skier Collection*); we also thank Eric McNeal, registrar at the Birmingham Museum of Art, for his assistance.

Deepest gratitude, finally, to Jennifer Banks at Yale University Press, who saw the potential in this project years ago—and who returned to it in time to see it to fruition. A book is nothing without a smart and committed editor—and we have been truly spoiled. We also appreciate the efficiency that Piyali Bhattacharya, Niamh Cunningham, Heather Gold, Margaret Otzel, Christina Tucker, and especially Eliza Childs have brought to the production of the manuscript.

We additionally have our own personal acknowledgments to make:

DAVID: This is for my friends, colleagues and family, Helen and Joel Rosen above all.

AARON: I would first of all like to thank the taxpayers of the State of Georgia, who supported me while I worked on this project. In addition, I thank Narin Hassan, Chris Coake, Eric Rasmussen, Cody and Kristin Marrs, Kacy and Andrew Tillman, Santiago Echeverry, and Chloe Wigston Smith (for one thoughtful email in particular). Special thanks to Eric Harper for his endless patience and friendship, and of course to my family (my parents Frank and Deirdre, my brother Nathan, and my sister Rachel—as well as Kadri, Nilgün, and Ömer in Istanbul). My greatest debt, one I fear I can never fully express, let alone repay, is to Esra. This book is for her—and for Kaya.

Parts of various chapters have appeared, in substantially altered form, in various venues. Part of chapter 3 was originally published by the Cardozo School of Law of Yeshiva University and the University of California Press as "Inviolate Personality and the Literary Roots of the Right to Privacy," *Law and Literature* 23: 1 (Spring 2011): 1–25. Part of chapter 2 was first printed by the Johns Hopkins University Press as "The Panopticon Reviewed: Sentimentalism and Eighteenth-Century Interiority," *English Literary History (ELH)* 77:4 (Winter 2010): 1041–59. The concluding section of chapter 1 was reconfigured as "Satire and the Afterlife of Allegory," in *Swift's Travels*, ed. Nicholas Hudson and Aaron Santesso (Cambridge University Press, 2008).

Introduction

A MAN DRIVES TO THE AIRPORT. From the moment he leaves his motel to the instant he boards the plane, closed-circuit cameras—at gas stations, stoplights, private businesses—record his every move. Databases register his most trivial purchases and, in turn, supply monitors with information about his personal history. At no point is he truly alone, as GPS tracking systems follow his automobile, and perhaps his very person, indoors and out, with exquisite precision. At no point is he truly anonymous, as voiceprints, thumbprints, retinal scans, facial recognition software, and easily collected bodily fluids instantly lay his identity bare to anonymous observers. If he uses a telephone, or indeed any form of telecommunication, he reveals himself at once to the more than 18 acres of mainframes buried deep beneath Fort Meade, outside Baltimore. Meanwhile, 155 miles overhead, in the airless silence of the ionosphere, satellites capable of detecting a solitary mole on the nape of his neck stare straight down with impersonal accuracy. . . .

To abandon the feverdream for a moment: it is a common cliché that we live in something called a "surveillance society." The seemingly inevitable encroachment on our private lives by corporate data miners or the government (or pick your own bogeyman) is a recurrent topic of Hollywood movies, the news media, and the press, both popular and scholarly. It is a situation conducive to hysteria, and although a great distance separates academic theorists from mass-market authors, most

1

writers who deal with this subject draw on a common core of alarmist premises and imagery.[1] Nineteen eighty-four has finally arrived—George Orwell, as one might expect, being invoked frequently as a prophetic figure or, still more often, as a metonym for opinions and conclusions barely consistent with his stated views. Thus Charles Sykes's observation in *The End of Privacy* (written for a broad audience)—"Big Brother has . . . set up shop at the nearest mall [and] is doing a brisk business"[2]—is echoed, in more solemn tones, by Thomas Levin:

> Not least since Orwell's 1949 vision of an aggressively authoritarian *1984*, our sense of the future—and increasingly of the present—has been marked by the fear of being watched, controlled, and robbed of our privacy. Indeed, one could argue that one of the hallmark characteristics of the early twenty-first century is precisely the realization of Orwell's worst nightmare.[3]

As it happens, most of the elements of *our* opening vignette, including some that are patently fictitious, were taken from a single source: *Enemy of the State*, a film produced by Jerry Bruckheimer, directed by Tony Scott, and starring Will Smith and Gene Hackman.[4] It has become a minor classic of its genre, the paranoid techno-thriller. A successful lawyer (Smith) unwittingly comes into possession of a video depicting the unauthorized assassination of a congressman by the National Security Agency. In short order, his identity is erased (credit cards cancelled, accounts closed, etc.), his character besmirched (he loses his job and nearly his family), and, with GPS devices attached at unawares to various parts of his body and clothing, he finds himself fleeing for his life from assassins who always seem to know exactly where to find him. Things look bleak indeed until he is helped by former NSA spook Hackman; there's a happy ending, but the disturbing issues raised by his experience are anything but resolved. If these details seem familiar, you were perhaps one of the millions who flocked to *Enemy of the State* on its release (over a quarter billion dollars in worldwide box office revenue to date)[5]—but our larger point is that these clichés and topoi, and the assumptions that underlie them, are common currency in the ongoing public discussion about surveillance and privacy.

In the academic world, surveillance studies is at once burgeoning and strangely narrow in focus.[6] The last few years have seen a flood of scholarly publications, and since 2002 the online journal *Surveillance and Society* has provided a quarterly forum for a great quantity—if not great variety—of work. This narrowness is partly methodological, a result of the way the field has constituted itself: it is dominated by a small number of disciplines, pretty much the disciplines one would expect. Political science, communication theory, and sociology are all well represented, but the dominant player, with the deepest institutional support, is legal studies. Perceiving the extension of surveillance activity as a threat to privacy rights, advocacy groups like the ACLU, the Electronic Privacy Information Center, and the Online Privacy Alliance, as well as law schools (for example, Harvard's Berkman Center for Internet and Society) have poured immense resources into studying the problem and proposing courses of action. In all of these endeavors, but especially in current academic discourse, there is more than a whiff of technological determinism, each new advance in data mining or miniaturization understood as producing *inevitable*, harmful results. As one neuroscientist has recently put it, we are on the verge of a "revolution in privacy. Transparency is going to come all the way back to our thoughts."[7] Against such threats, it is perhaps inevitable that much of the rhetoric in the field is reactive or even apocalyptic in tone—thus Levin again: "From the more obvious closed-circuit television (CCTV) observation to the more insidious (because largely unrecognized) digital information tracking known as 'dataveillance' (which covers everything from supermarket purchases to cell-phone usage and internet-surfing patterns)—surveillance has become an issue that is not only increasingly a part of everyone's daily life, but is even embraced as such."

Although the ongoing discussion has attracted fellow-traveling work in art theory, and to some extent literary studies, the distinctive and necessary contribution of the humanities *as such* to this conversation has largely gone unarticulated. Indeed, so long as the effects of scientific or technological advance are taken to be preordained, invariable, or self-explanatory, the questions humanists might raise will go unasked. Let us assume, for example, that surveillance presents a challenge to personal privacy. But what do we mean exactly by "privacy," why do we value it to such a superlative degree—and what, finally, might privacy rights be protecting? The "person," presumably—but what, then, do we mean by *that*? In ways probably unanticipated by our neuroscientist, any account of surveillance must also consider the ultimate target of all surveillance activity: the individual self. Any *history* of surveillance, it follows, must consider the ways that conceptions of selfhood have changed over time: as definitions of the Human have shifted over the centuries, so too have ideas about how to uncover (or dictate) that inner human essence. The reverse is equally true: as means of observation and invasion have become more sophisticated, definitions of personhood have changed. The complex dialectical struggle between surveillance and selfhood is one that the study of literature, with its close interrogation of character, and philosophy, with its central interest in the thinking subject, are well positioned to tackle. These disciplines are indeed the two (in order of importance) on which we draw most heavily in the chapters that follow. It is nevertheless the case, however, that philosophy bears some responsibility for the present state of surveillance studies. The premises and fears that underlie most current work in the field—which speak to a theoretical narrowness in the way key questions about personhood and privacy have been answered—can be traced, finally, to a small group of writers and to three or four big names in particular.

PANOPTICISM

Nearly all contemporary philosophical discussions of surveillance lead back, one way or another, to Jeremy Bentham—or rather, as we shall argue, to a highly tendentious and selective engagement with Bentham's most notorious venture: the panopticon.[8] As Bentham himself recognized, the greatest innovation of his circular prison was not architectural but psychological; it is in this respect that he has had the most influence on successor theorists. In his prospectus for the project, he refers to the plan as "a new mode of obtaining power of mind over mind, in a quantity hitherto without example"; later, he refers to the prison frankly as a machine for producing certain types of behavior and even certain types of human being.[9] While the cells are open (and the prisoners exposed) at all times to inspection from a central guard tower, the reverse is not true: in a crucial innovation, Bentham furnishes the windows of the inspector's "lodge" with Venetian blinds, which are always closed. The prisoners never know whether or not they were being watched, and this, Bentham concludes, will produce certain results:

The more constantly the persons to be inspected are under the eyes of the persons who should inspect them, the more perfectly will the purpose of the establishment have been attained. Ideal perfection, if that were the object, would require that each person should actually be in that predicament, during every instant of time. This being impossible, the next thing to be wished for is, that, at every instance, seeing reason to believe as much, and not being able to satisfy himself to the contrary, he should *conceive* himself to be so. . . . The essence of [the plan] consists, then, in the *centrality* of the inspector's situation, combined with the . . . contrivances for *seeing without being seen*. . . . The greater chance there is, of a given person's being at a given time actually under inspection, the more strong will be the persuasion—the more *intense*, if I may say so, the *feeling*, he has of being so. (40, 44)

This feeling, the conviction of always being watched, abetted by "constant and unremitting pressure" (63), Bentham plausibly concludes, will cause prisoners to behave well at all times, thus fulfilling the "purpose of the establishment."

According to many subsequent readers, Bentham is outlining a psychology of internalization. That is, the inmate of a panopticon, under constant observation, or at least believing himself to be so, gradually absorbs the rules of the prison. Although at first he might conform out of self-preservation, eventually his mind is overwritten by his captors: his feelings of being watched, and the rules of behavior expected of him, become, permanently, part of his very identity. In chapter 2, we will argue that this theory of internalization is fundamentally inaccurate and reexamine Bentham's more basic assumptions about observation and control in the context of Enlightenment philosophy. Be that as it may, the psychology of internalization was the starting point for Michel Foucault, Bentham's most prominent modern interpreter and still, some decades after his death, the key figure in current surveillance theory. Echoing Bentham in *Discipline and Punish* (*Surveiller et Punir*, 1975), Foucault comments that where older prisons aimed to punish the body, new institutions of the sort proposed in the *Panopticon Letters* aimed at the mind: "It [was] no longer the body, with the ritual play of excessive pains. . . . It [was] no longer the body, but the soul."[10] The prisoner's mind was now conceived of as "a surface for the inscription of power" (101), with the final goal of creating an "obedient subject, the individual subjected to habits, rules, orders, an authority that [was] exercised continually around him and upon him, and which he must allow to function automatically in him" (128–29).[11]

Discipline and Punish is perhaps Foucault's most influential entry in a vast, career-long examination of modern discourse; his specific subject here is the emergence of a modern, "disciplinary" state in the nineteenth century out of the older, "sovereign" forms of government that had pertained from the High Middle Ages through the time of Louis XIV (Foucault's frame of reference is almost exclusively French). Where control in sovereign states had streamed downward from the "'super-power' of the monarch" (80), it was more evenly dispersed among the populace in disciplinary societies. This work of dispersion was driven by the spread of human sciences developed or perfected during the Enlightenment—medicine, psychology, criminology (and legal theory more broadly), theology, educational theory, and so on—each of which had the effect of defining the individual more precisely. Where the solitary person had once been part of an undifferentiated mass, and thus relatively invisible to the government, he or she could now be precisely categorized—as, say, "male, homosexual, Catholic, working class, with an I.Q. of 90, [etc.]." In short,

> The disciplines mark the moment when the reversal of the political axis of individualization—as one might call it—takes place. In certain societies, of which the feudal régime is only one example, it may be said that individualization is greatest where sovereignty is exercised and in the higher echelons of power. . . . In a disciplinary régime, on the other hand, individualization is 'descending': as power becomes more anonymous and more functional, those on whom it is exercised tend to be more strongly individualized; it is exercised by surveillance rather than ceremonies, by observation rather than commemorative accounts. (192–93)

These last comments suggest, finally, why Foucault found Bentham's letters so useful. In the older dispensation, the immense prestige of the sovereign coincided with a "constant illegality" on the part of ordinary people; the monarchy had neither the ability, nor any particular desire, to prosecute everyday trespasses (88). With the spread of disciplines, however, which defined and made visible each citizen, the State could now develop powerful mechanisms of observation and measurement. Thus the rise of the police—and the secret police—as well as countless smaller techniques of oversight: "In order to be exercised, this power had to be given the instrument of permanent, exhaustive, omnipresent surveillance, capable of making all visible, as long as it could itself remain invisible. It had to be like a faceless gaze that transformed the whole social body into a field of perception" (214). In short, disciplinary society, with its unseen and thus potentially unremitting watchers, and its citizens, trapped like prisoners in their cells by "hierarchized, continuous and functional surveillance" (176), worked precisely like Bentham's panopticon. The more intense the pressure, Foucault reasoned, the *less* aware citizens would be of its operation, having internalized the conditions of their subjection. Foucault's major revision of Bentham, then, was to expand his model—and his psychology—to fit the entire body politic: a surveillance society.[12]

One of our aims in chapter 2 will be to restore Bentham's thinking on surveillance minus this revision, with an eye towards retheorizing the basic mechanisms of surveillance itself. An obvious strength of Foucault's model, we would acknowledge, and clearly a reason why it has remained dominant in contemporary discussions, is its ability to absorb innovation: each new advance in monitoring technology—from GPS systems, to retinal scans, to supermarket cards—seems to substantiate his vision of total observation and control. Indeed, a good deal of the scholarship on surveillance today consists of little more than applying vaguely Foucauldian conclusions to the latest gadgets.[13] The same may be said of an endless stream of articles and stories in the mass media, with a single proviso: Foucault's assertions, or highly reductive versions of them, have so entered popular consciousness—albeit anonymously—that he is rarely cited or even recognized. Whatever the validity of his theory, Foucault has been internalized, if not quite in his own terms; in the climate of opinion that produced *Enemy of the State*, the wind was blowing from France.[14]

Nevertheless, in the last two decades, some prominent surveillance theorists have begun to question (or complicate) Foucault's more extreme conclusions, even as they have remained in basic agreement with him over premises. In the view of these theorists, the postwar period has been characterized less by centralized, totalizing power (on the analogy of Bentham's inspection tower), than by "networks" and a "space of flows" (Zygmunt Bauman's metaphors).[15] In the new, "Control Societies" (Gilles Deleuze's term), "ultrarapid forms of apparently free-floating control [have taken over] from the old disciplines at work within . . . closed systems."[16] To translate: while Foucault (in their view) saw society as self-contained, with no "outside," and centralized, the world today is far more dispersed, flexible, open, and (another Bauman word) "porous." Competition between rivals (individuals, corporations, governments) is now the name of the game, and everyone, in order to survive constantly monitoring and striving to outdo his opponents, is an active participant. An orthodox Foucauldian might reasonably object that both Deleuze and Bauman at once underestimate the flexibility of Foucault's model and ignore the centralization latent in their own. Beneath the centrifugal energies of the control society, that is, lurks the octopus of international market capitalism. Most pertinently, in the (allegedly) new arrangement, the basic tendencies diagnosed by Foucault—ubiquitous surveillance and internalization—are as powerful and destructive as ever.

These tendencies, finally, are as evident in social ephemera (reality TV, amusement parks, etc.) as in the deep structures of politics and commerce, and for this reason have received equal attention in contemporary aesthetic and cultural theory; indeed, on this front, in chapter 5, we will examine a second, avowedly "postmodern" group of writers influenced by Foucault, who take his revision of Bentham's psychology as the starting point for their theories of art and society. When Bentham ventures into religious speculation, it is with uncharacteristic passive aggression: a "fundamental advantage" of his plan, he writes, is "the *apparent omnipresence* of the inspector (if divines will allow me the expression,) combined with the extreme facility of his *real presence*" (45). These are undoubtedly terms better left to divines, and it seems hardly likely that Bentham is making a serious point about God. All the same, for some of his readers, he is raising a question with profoundly troubling implications: if the panopticon produces desired behaviors as efficiently in the inspector's absence as his presence, why have an inspector at all, so long as he is believed to exist? In the words of one Bentham commentator, "Bentham is less interested in distinguishing fictions from reality, than he is in exploring the effects that fiction has on reality."[17] If one follows Foucault, furthermore, and takes the conditions of panopticism—internalization above all—to be universal, to pervade society, then one is faced with a new kind of existence, in which, to quote Peter Weibel, "Representation [enjoys primacy] over reality, the copy over the original, illusion over truth."[18] The ontic element (the sense of a baseline reality in things) drops away, and one is left only with a play of representations and appearances, with nothing substantial left to guarantee their actuality. Jean Baudrillard's statement of the case enjoys, probably, the widest currency: "All Western faith and good faith become engaged in this wager on representation: that a sign could refer to depth of meaning, that a sign could be exchanged for meaning and that something could guarantee this exchange—God, of course. But what if God himself can be simulated, that is to say can be reduced to the signs that constitute faith? Then the whole system becomes weightless, it is no longer itself anything but a gigantic simulacrum."[19] To summarize: Bentham offers a new way of understanding the relation between observation and behavior; Foucault describes how surveillance and the psychology of internalization can permeate an entire society; the "postmodernists" try to show how this psychology undermines reality itself, with profound (or profoundly superficial) consequences for aesthetics.

SURVEILLANCE AND LITERATURE

Pointedly absent from all considerations is any notion of personal autonomy: that at least a kernel of personality, that a freedom of thought and action, might survive the onslaught of State or social discourses. The advantages of this denial are obvious: it makes for analytical clarity and conforms nicely to an apocalyptic view of the present, in which all political formations—and those of the democratic West in particular—are understood as systems of domination. By reducing to a bare minimum, however, what it means to be human, these lines of inquiry cut off any contributions that the *humanities* might make to the study of surveillance. For all practical purposes, these views foreclose on any possible noncoercive (or even benign) uses for surveillance—of which there are quite a few—or on the ways that surveillance might actually operate in a nonauthoritarian, liberal society (something we believe to exist). In the pages that follow, we will take the idea of personal autonomy as our *starting* point: the individual not merely acted upon, but acting, tactical, and with considerable freedom of mind. These premises, certainly, are hard to square with existing discussions, but even as several near-exhausted lines of inquiry close down, a variety of other, largely unexplored, paths open up—and surveillance itself is revealed as more than one thing. Hardly monolithic, it is a set of genetically related practices, and far more complex and diverse than is usually recognized.

Surveillance, *the monitoring of human activities for the purposes of anticipating or influencing future events*, is not the same thing as literature. It does, however, share some of literature's interests—most notably discovering the truth about other people—and is susceptible to some of the same temptations as literature. This study takes as its foundational premise the idea that surveillance and literature, as kindred practices, have light to shed on each other—on each other's histories, modes of operation, and ways of grappling, as it were, with the reality principle. Each asks what it means to be a person; more than that, each examines how abstract models of personhood—the fictions generated by literature and politics—might relate to the inner lives of real people. The answers each has provided to these questions have been mutually influential—and indeed, in the pages that follow, we will repeatedly observe key developments in surveillance theory first being worked out *in* literature. Far from passively reflecting or responding to developments in surveillance history, poets and novelists have often, for their own self-interested reasons, been the *generators* of that history. The habits of mind, finally, that the reading of literature encourages, and for which the literary corpus serves as a uniquely sensitive register, continue to be of value for anyone negotiating the complexities of modern surveillance. We have no interest, therefore, in latching a literary argument on to observations already made by Foucault or Baudrillard or in noting the effect these theorists have had (often, to repeat, in highly reductive or simplified ways) on literature or the cinema. In the field configured by those theorists, literary study has no position worth occupying. Our contention, however, is that when the field is reconfigured, when the problems of surveillance—and, by implication, questions of privacy, of self-presentation, of social cooperation—are analyzed the way one would analyze literary problems, one is led to a set of conclusions far outside the current discussion. To (begin to) get a sense of what we mean by this, consider the following reimagined vignette:

On the day before Mohamed Atta and Abdulaziz Al-Omari drove to the airport, they enjoyed a fairly ordinary day in South Portland, Maine. They filled up their rental car at the Jetport Gas station, took out money from a local ATM, and spent more than twenty minutes wandering the aisles of the local Wal-Mart. We know all of this because they were captured at each location by closed-circuit cameras. The images have enjoyed a healthy afterlife on the Internet and can be viewed whenever you please.[20] The next day, September 11, 2001, from the moment they left their motel, a Comfort Inn at 90 Maine Mall Road, to the instant they boarded their plane, it is reasonable to assume that most of their movements were similarly captured. Certainly the images of their passing through airport security (in front of some bored-looking guards) have acquired a particular notoriety. Although the second plane to attack the World Trade Center was (inevitably) recorded by numerous observers, it was believed for a while that no film existed of the first attack (Atta's and Al-Omari's plane). Two days later, however, a video, improbably of a fire department training exercise, turned up. Before long, it was possible, using stills, overhead camera shots, and the endless data traces they left behind them (even their last dinner— pizza—left a credit card receipt) to construct a coherent, sequential narrative of Atta's and Al-Omari's last twenty-four hours on earth, from the moment they checked into their motel to the instant they took their own and thousands of other lives.

On the face of it, the September 11 catastrophe was a stunning confirmation of Foucault's argument—and, in a sense, Deleuze's as well: the terrorists were always being watched, not only by the government but by a panoply of independent agents working, unconsciously, in concord. It did not take long for commentators to draw this very conclusion.[21] On sober reflection, however, the implications of the attack amount almost to a complete refutation of the conventional wisdom. In the midst of their future victims, Atta and Al-Omari were nothing but anonymous and alone. The key word, of course, is *narrative*. In the hours immediately following the buildings' collapse, the media response resembled, predictably, the reactions of a trauma victim: a handful of footage, much of it recorded with no intention to surveil, was played and replayed endlessly, in stupid reiteration, as comprehension struggled to catch up with the evidence of the senses. Even the most terrible images—people jumping from towers, billowing clouds of debris—were oddly meaningless, given the lack of any frame in which they could be understood. The same is true, only more so, of ordinary, prosaic images—Atta briefly passing before a surveillance camera at the Portland airport, to the clueless security guard at the time just another commuter on his way to Boston that morning. To state a point that *should* be obvious: a coherent, sequential narrative could be constructed only in retrospect. And yet the conclusion many critics finally reached—that the attack was therefore "unnarrativised [and] unscripted"—is precisely wrong: the attack was scripted to the last detail but lacked an adequate readership.[22]

A dangerous and largely unquestioned assumption lies behind most of Bentham's and Foucault's conclusions: the assumption of interpretive competence. In *Enemy of the State* (but one could cite any pop-culture product in which wicked men dress in well-tailored black suits and are chauffeured about in large, expensive automobiles), the part of infallible interpreter is taken by Jon Voight. Proverbially banal, this evil man understands the hero's actions before the hero himself does and, with a seemingly bottomless budget at his disposal (helicopters, "dedicated satellites," etc.), pursues his victim with single-minded efficiency. In this endeavor he is helped by equally iconic assistants: poorly dressed, socially awkward computer geeks (Jack Black, Jamie Kennedy), whose super-competence is matched only by a complete lack of moral awareness. If Smith ducks into an office building, his GPS signal immediately appears on three-dimensional schematics of the structure; if he uses a random pay phone, murderous goons are sure to appear at the very spot within minutes. To paraphrase Bentham, the watchers, as well as the watched, do not *suspect* but are *assured* of what they're watching.[23] Indeed, if the case were otherwise, if a terrorist looked and acted like just another commuter on his way to Boston, all bets would be off.

Or, to take to take the less momentous case of Hull: in that English city's housing projects, an elaborate network of security cameras was established to stem violent crime. After several months, unfortunately, it became clear that the security guards, with less-than-Voight-like professionalism, were spending most of their time ogling pretty women—streetwalkers especially. When this became known to the prostitutes, they responded by conducting more of their business out-of-doors, correctly surmising that this would protect them from their clients. A tidy symbiosis thus developed, though far from the original "purpose of the establishment"—and probably something less than "Orwell's worst nightmare."[24] The Foucauldian (or, with more restrictions, Benthamite) notion that in a surveillance situation power flows outward from the observer to the (utterly abject) observed is plainly inadequate—and in certain hands conducive to paranoia. Rather, power often lies in the control of narrative—a control frequently in the hands of the person under watch. In Ovid's parable, from which we take our title, Argus Panoptes, the hundred-eyed monster set atop a "hilly height" to guard Io, is lulled into inattention and left abjectly vulnerable by the seductions of Hermes's storytelling. Under such circumstances, even the solitary prisoner in his cell may be hatching plans beyond the grasp of the inspector.[25] Indeed, in a clash of narratives, the observer—playing defense, as it were—is at a natural disadvantage; whatever his intentions, he is thrust into the position of an interpreter—an agent not needed, nor perhaps even present, in the panoptic tower.

Interpretation, narrative, readership; to these one might add *persona, motivation, discourse, character, close reading, empathy, representation*, and the like. But it is not our sole intention to demonstrate how the hermeneutic problems of surveillance are also literary problems and how this complicates existing discussions. We will also explore how the theory and practice of surveillance have developed in close coordination with literary culture over the past three and a half centuries: if surveillance is, on some level, all about reading and authorship, so literature has been deeply engaged with, and transformed by, changing ideas about observation and control. Throughout, our instrument of analysis will be the *mode*, by which we mean a structure of thought and feeling as readily observable in the political and social configurations of a period as in its aesthetic productions. We will speak in chapter 1, for example, of early modern English culture as "allegorical"—meaning not simply that the age produced copious works of literary allegory (the genre), but that allegorical thinking pervaded the age on all levels. For us, the most important feature of allegory, as a way of thinking, lies in its highly problematic equation of social persona and inner self. It was the post-Restoration crumbling of this equation that initiated an intense dialectical struggle between empathy and coercion, as the role of social observation in self-formation was rendered newly problematic. This struggle, which was endemic to a newly liberal and contract-based culture, is the principal subject of chapter 2. The answers the eighteenth century provided to the question of personhood, in turn, gave rise (dialectically) to a new ideology of privacy, the reverberations of which were felt throughout the nineteenth century (chapter 3). Over the course of this study, our selection of literary texts to examine is largely dictated by this question of mode: as we move through nearly five hundred years of social, philosophical, political, and literary history with a seemingly infinite number of texts of potential interest, we are naturally drawn to those works in which the modal energies of the period are most intense or most in flux. In chapter 4, for example, as we examine the return of allegorical thought during the modern period, our attention shifts from the High Literary and towards the popular genres (for example, espionage fiction or fantasy literature) in which this revival is strongest. Because, finally, literature is the natural habitat for the most complex and richly represented modal thinking, this is above all a literary study: to grasp the power dynamics of the Tudor court, one must understand imaginative allegory; to understand the early trials of liberalism, one must pay special attention to those authors most invested in new ideas about the self—Daniel Defoe or Samuel Richardson. This study culminates, in chapter 5, with a new taxonomy of surveillance and with a defense of liberal reading as such.

By locating the genesis of our topic in the mid to late seventeenth century, we concur with numerous theorists who see this moment as the start of something uniquely modern; indeed, like Foucault—but also Max Weber, Adorno and Horkheimer, Jürgen Habermas, and others—we are essentially rethinking the history of modernity, albeit with a new set of tools and conclusions.[26] The confluence of events that occurred during the late seventeenth century (give or take: different things happened at different times in different places) is well known: the growth of truly large cities amidst continuing rural depopulation and the consequent establishment of a powerful and stable middle class; the continuing consolidation of the Protestant Reformation; the foundering of early nation-states and, with them, theories of divine-right monarchy; the Cartesian revolution and the development of empiricism; the founding of the Royal Society and the spread of new methodologies and technologies; the "rise of the novel" and the replacement of the patronage system with the first fully professional writers. For us, the most pertinent of these seismic shifts—which goes together with several of the others—was indeed modal: the collapse of what we will call "social allegory" and the subsequent emergence of contractarianism, parliamentary forms of government, and, most to the point, liberalism. As a political philosophy premised on the autonomous citizen, liberalism was the expression of a crisis in the nature of human identity—identity as something nurtured within rather than imposed from without, as had previously been the case. To put it in terms relevant to literature, liberalism rendered problematic as never before the idea of *character*—as social role, as self—and this shift made possible, or necessary, the modern practice of surveillance.

In Renoir's *La Loge* (1874, figure 1), which hangs at the Courtauld Institute, the consequences of this shift are captured with peculiar clarity. A young, well-dressed woman stares directly at us from her box at the theater while her gentleman companion, just behind her, trains his opera-glasses upward—doubtless at other members of the audience— rather than (downward) at the stage. From the start, the painting has been understood as a parable about modern spectacle and spectatorship, the woman's direct and personal appeal—her eye-to-eye contact with us— contrasting with her companion's somewhat off-putting (and mediated) voyeurism.[27] Any tidy conclusions, however, are upended by Renoir's deft insertion of a balustrade between the woman and her viewer: in fact, it gradually dawns on one, the viewer occupies a physically impossible position. In order to be as proximate to the woman as the painting suggests, the viewer would have to be dangling in mid-air some three or four feet off "la loge." Put plainly, the scene depicted makes sense only as the product of our own voyeurism—the woman captured through our own opera glasses. This somewhat startling conclusion is supported by the painting's curious optics, in which the woman's face is rendered with sharp clarity while the gentleman is more of an impressionistic blur— again suggesting the selective work of a lens. But this, in turn, greatly complicates any notions the painting initially seems to offer about intimacy: whatever the directness of her gaze, the woman *cannot*, in truth, be making eye contact with us. Her own opera glasses rest on the balustrade, unused, while we stare at her from a great distance, perhaps unseen. Who is this woman, then, and what accounts for the personal *effect* of her gaze? Is she, aware that *someone* is watching, engaging in a sort of exhibitionism? Or has something been captured without her knowledge, let alone consent? Or does something about her remain intransigently private? What to make, finally, of the expression on her face, all but buried beneath her heavy makeup: is it a look of resignation, or is she smiling, happy to be watched? A painting that, at first, seemed to offer a neat contrast between surveillance and immediate knowledge turns out to be entirely concerned with the former—and specifically with the way that

FIGURE 1. Auguste Renoir, *La Loge*, oil on canvas, 1874. Courtauld Institute, London / Bridgeman Art Library.

surveillance, in its attempts to grasp something about character, only renders character infinitely troublesome and perhaps unknowable. But perhaps we get ahead of ourselves; for the moment, we may misquote Virginia Woolf to the effect that, in or about May 1660, human nature changed—and, as a result, surveillance shortly became a key problematic of Western (and especially liberal) statecraft.[28] To say, however, that at a certain moment something new happened, is also to make a claim about what passed before. Part of beginning when we do, therefore, necessitates explaining why we *don't* begin earlier. In fact, the problems that took hold at the close of the seventeenth century had deep roots in Tudor-Stuart England—and it is to the Renaissance that we must now turn.

CHAPTER ONE

The Retreat of Allegory

I. ALLEGORICAL CULTURE

> Others there are
> Who, trimm'd in forms and visages of duty,
> Keep yet their hearts attending on themselves,
> And throwing but shows of service on their lords,
> Do well thrive by them; and when they have lin'd their coats,
> Do themselves homage. These fellows have some soul,
> And such a one do I profess myself. For, sir,
> Were I the Moor, I would not be Iago.
> In following him, I follow but myself.
> Heaven is my judge, not I for love and duty,
> But seeming so, for my peculiar end;
> For when my outward action doth demonstrate
> The native act and figure of my heart
> In complement extern, 'tis not long after
> But I will wear my heart upon my sleeve
> For daws to peck at: I am not what I am.[1]

Few passages, even in the vast output of a writer so centrally concerned with questions of role-playing, of performance, and masquerade, suggest a looming crisis in the nature of personality as strongly as this one. Barely fifty lines into *Othello*, Iago is assuring his patsy Roderigo that he means the title character no good: though he appears to serve Othello as a faithful ensign, he follows but himself, for his own "peculiar end." As often in Shakespeare, when a character tries to articulate the split between his own desires and the social role he must play, Iago toys with tropes of interiority and exteriority: in contrast to the "forms and visages of duty," "outward action," and "complement extern," he posits a soul, heart, and self, which only heaven can see and judge. Iago's usual rhetorical strategy, however, is to begin with clear distinctions and then muddy the waters—which is precisely what happens here. In hindsight, his "peculiar end," which he never bothers to explain to Roderigo, turns out to be far more peculiar than his flat understatement would let on. And his comment "were I the Moor, I would not be Iago" sounds logical (not to say obvious) but is sufficiently vague as to support all manner of interpretation: would he rather be Othello than himself? Is he saying he wouldn't need to be duplicitous if he were as well-off (or naïve?) as Othello? Is he making a more banal point about personal identity? Part of Iago's purpose, surely, is to confuse Roderigo (even the *Dramatis Personae* dismisses him as "a gull'd gentleman"), but we would suggest that something additional is happening: a discomfort with the implications of the inner/outer distinction itself, which finally finds expression in pure contradiction: "I am not what I am."

Commentators have always recognized this line as an important moment in the play, an early glimpse into Iago's depravity. Most editions dutifully note that he is blaspheming, revealing himself as a kind of devil figure; in Exodus 3, God defines himself to Moses as follows: "I AM THAT I AM. . . . Thus shalt thou say unto the children of Israel, I AM hath sent me unto you."[2] Beyond that, however, most readers silently translate the line to mean "I am not what I *seem*"—this despite the fact that the word "seem" was fully available to Shakespeare (it appears five lines earlier). By so translating it, we would argue, readers miss the truly uncanny thrill that must have seized Shakespeare's first audiences. That is to say: the two halves of Iago's inner/outer equation—the two iterations of "I am"—are equally true and valid and yet somehow in contradiction to each other. Neither can claim ontological precedence, which would be precisely the effect of substituting "seem" for the second "am." The writer with the largest vocabulary in English has run into a conceptual problem for which his language is inadequate. Critics of early modernism who take interiority and selfhood as their special focus have long understood this moment as a crux, but while we concur with Stephen Greenblatt's comment that " 'I am not what I am' goes beyond social feigning," we cannot endorse his conclusion that Iago in fact possesses no essential self.

> "I am not what I am" suggests that this elusiveness [i.e., at the center] is permanent, that even self-interest, whose transcendental guarantee is the divine "I am what I am," is a mask. Iago's constant recourse to narrative then is both the affirmation of absolute self-interest, and the affirmation of absolute vacancy.[3]

This conclusion fuels a powerful, Lacan-inflected reading of the play as a whole: Iago's inner vacancy makes him particularly adept at entering into the discourses of others. A monster of empathy, he destroys his victims from within. And yet to read Iago as a cipher, we would argue, means underestimating, anachronistically, Shakespeare's deep investment in *both* halves of Iago's line: if anything, Iago suffers from too much selfhood, not the reverse. Behind Iago's seeming self-contradiction lurks neither nihilism nor a Lacanian specter, but rather a confusion over how one should recognize the truth about oneself and other people: a problem in the nature of allegory.

Allegory and Personhood
Proposition: Renaissance culture was allegorical, and (to skip several steps ahead in the argument) this insured that modern surveillance practices would not develop until a new dispensation could take hold. By calling the Renaissance "allegorical" we are not making the obvious point that allegory was the dominant literary option from (confining ourselves to Britain) Langland to Spenser; if that were the case, one could as easily describe Augustan England as "satirical" and the Victorian period as a baggy triple-decker. Nor, for that matter, are we claiming that the Renaissance was particularly conducive (though it most certainly was) to the production of literary allegory. We are not, finally, interested in questions about allegory as a genre per se, but instead are arguing that allegory, as a mode, involves certain habits of thought, observation, and ways of organizing reality that are as operative in everyday life—socially,

politically, ideologically—as in the aesthetic structure of a poem or painting. In the pages that follow, we will examine the ways that an *allegorical state of mind*, as an act of imagination, implied certain ways of understanding the interiority of other people—and by extension provoked certain ways of watching them and of behaving towards them in general. The Renaissance State read and understood its subjects allegorically, as did the subjects themselves—and it is largely in revolt *against* these modes of understanding that modern strategies of observation (and the politics that came with them) took shape.

Our assertion would be tendentious enough were the nature of allegory a matter of general consent—which is hardly the case. On the face of things, this might seem an esoteric concern—but in fact the brief history we are about to offer establishes the premises, and reveals the stakes, for most of the claims (about surveillance, about society, about selfhood) that we will be making in the book. Few definitions are as profoundly adequate and deeply misleading as Angus Fletcher's well-known attempt: "In the simplest terms, allegory says one thing and means another. It destroys the normal expectation we have about language, that our words 'mean what they say.'"[4] In a note, Fletcher explains that he is simply breaking the word down to its Greek roots, "from *allos* + *agoreuein* (other + speak openly, speak in the assembly or market)."[5] The "otherness" of allegory is infinitely complicated, however, by its "didactic function," its basic need for a "common culture of meaning."[6] To take a very simple and famous example from the twentieth century: Orwell's *Animal Farm* is a transparent allegory depicting the course of the Russian Revolution from its idealistic beginnings to its authoritarian conclusion. To be effective, the novel's narrative of rebellious livestock and human owners must be recognized as allegory, and the significance of each character made perfectly clear to the reader (e.g., Napoleon the pig is Joseph Stalin); otherwise it just comes across as the confusing and depressing tale of an extremely dysfunctional barnyard.[7] Without a common culture of meaning, an audience that understands Orwell's point and which is open to his didactic purpose (in this case condemnation), the whole project collapses. At the same time one might ask: if Orwell wishes to write about Soviet Russia, why is he bothering with goats and donkeys? He is saying one thing and meaning something quite different, and it's only natural to wonder what worries or hesitations have prevented him from writing more directly. Even allegories that, unlike *Animal Farm*, succeed aesthetically on the surface level and do not require an awareness of ulterior meaning to give pleasure carry this residue of concealment and anxiety. In short, allegory, as a way of taking in the world, is naturally riven by competing centripetal and centrifugal forces; the basic allegorical unit is a sign/signified dyad, which, at any moment, can either be ripped apart by otherness or collapsed into a monad by the sheer demand for coherence.

Within a broad consensus about the structure of allegory, however, there is little agreement about its purpose or how it functions. Since the allegorical image is always being forced in two directions—pulled towards dissolution and pushed towards collapse, incomprehensibility or reductive simplicity—it is not surprising that critics disagree over which direction is the more important. One side of the debate: allegory appeared in eleventh-century Europe as a naïve, primitive form of psychological writing. Lacking a language of interiority but wishing to depict strong emotions, writers like Chrétien de Troyes were forced to use personified abstractions (e.g., "Reason," "Love"), a process that survives today, in somewhat debased form, as the angel and devil who appear on opposite shoulders every time you find yourself alone with a cookie jar.[8] The angel and devil are comic only because a vocabulary of inwardness exists now to describe what you are feeling ("I am hungry and can get away with it"; "It is wrong to steal cookies from crying four-year-olds")—a language that ostensibly did not exist at the moment allegory appeared in the Christian West. Ultimately, for critics who see allegory as primarily didactic, the *allos*, the otherness inherent in allegory, is almost incidental compared to the genre's requirement to speak openly, vividly, forcefully. For allegory, on this model, to succeed, the relation between sign and signified must be transparent, or better yet, invisible; today the angel and devil fail (or succeed only ironically) precisely because they strike *us* as representations—and grotesquely inadequate ones at that. Allegory may say one thing and mean another, but the *experience* of allegory, as with all powerful metaphor, should be unitary: the sign and signified are *one thing*.[9] With consciousness of difference, allegory dies.

Not unexpectedly, a second (and much more numerous) group of theorists is content to let the metaphor die and admire the exquisite corpse. For this group, allegory is the trope of otherness par excellence, in which meaning is generated precisely out of the disconnect between tenor and vehicle (Joseph Stalin, Napoleon the pig). In Walter Benjamin's classic account of German baroque allegory, the sheer outlandishness and complexity of allegorical imagery is purposely confusing: by steadfastly resisting transparency, it foregrounds its own inadequacy as metaphor, its own brokenness, and points to a transcendent, ineffable reality, a "singularity," as one later critic has put it, beyond human expression.[10] From this viewpoint, however, it is easy enough to plot an even more radical course and dismiss the transcendent altogether. For rhetorical theorists like Paul de Man, allegory is simply the principle underlying a failure in *all* language at *every* moment: the tenor/vehicle disconnect is a spectacular and overt instance of the way all words fail to signify adequately objects in the world.[11] As one might expect, most accounts of allegory finally stake out a position somewhere between the two extremes—or else attempt to explain how both extremes might *simultaneously* be true. That is, in its didactic project, allegory (1) generates meaning by masking the gap between sign and signified, i.e., through profound coherence, *and* (2) generates meaning by foregrounding the very same gap, i.e., through incoherence. To recognize that centripetal and centrifugal forces are always at work in allegory is to acknowledge the mode's complex flexibility and helps explain its persistent appeal, in some quarters, as a way of thinking.

To this conversation, we would add a modest suggestion: while the opposing forces within allegory must, certainly, be understood synchronically (i.e., they are always tugging against each other), they should also be understood diachronically—in short, *historically*. Chrétien worked in the eleventh century, Benjamin focuses on the seventeenth; it is almost banal to conclude that the intervening years saw a gradual process, whereby the centripetal tendencies of allegory gradually weakened (without ever quite disappearing) and the centrifugal forces grew stronger. To give a sense of how this process took place and why it is germane to the history of surveillance in the West, we can offer a just-so story, which probably has the virtue of being true. C. S. Lewis is persuasive in his claim that allegorical personages first emerged as the projections of inner emotions—*Envy, Faith*, and so on—that could not otherwise be articulated, whose interactions could not otherwise be depicted. As psychological entities, they could hardly be called "ideological" in the usual sense of the word, and the

gap between tenor and vehicle would be nearly (or entirely) imperceptible. The act of projecting these emotions, however, also had an
inevitable abstracting, reifying effect: to give these entities a shape and
form outside the mind meant also eventually recognizing them as alien
or other—and, most important, as susceptible to creative reuse. *Reason*,
Love, *Envy*, and *Faith* may first have carried no overt dogmatic charge—
but it would only have been a matter of time (very little time) before their
didactic potential was recognized and allegory put to the service of a belief
system: the Catholic Church, medieval statecraft, etc. A more convenient
and powerful propaganda mechanism could hardly be imagined.[12]

In no time at all, allegory, which had begun as the projection of something internal, would be returned to the self as something external: the
representation of an ideology, as well as a practical way of putting people
in their place. But although this process of alienation and imposition
must have begun almost immediately, its full effects would have taken
centuries to ramify. Indeed, since the process was at least partly unconscious, it would be perfectly logical to expect long periods during which
the nature of the allegorical image (mental figment or didactic emblem?
self or other?) was a matter of sincere confusion. One need only recall
numerous passages in *Piers Plowman* where the characters Will encounters seem at some moments projections of his persona but at others take
on an unnerving and completely autonomous life of their own. It's an
ambiguity that persists as late as Spenser, though by Spenser's time
things have largely shifted towards the alien. Most important, this period
of ambiguity—during which allegory could be strongly didactic and yet
still *seem* unitary, during which, that is, the residue of allegory's origins
effectively masked its increasing tendentiousness and concealed its dual
nature—was also the high point of its true influence as a mode.

It was a situation that could not possibly last, and by the early
Renaissance, dissolution was well underway. The effect can be likened to
a loss of innocence, which is particularly visible in allegorical *writing*: as
the audience became aware of the genre's didactic intentions, as the audience's credulity about the allegorical image turned to skepticism, certain
predictable effects followed. As a performance, allegory became at once
more coercive and spectacular. Faced with increasing resistance, allegory
needed to grow more insistent, thus producing still stronger resistance
and driving a dialectic that could only end in catastrophe. At the same

time, in its hopeless attempt to sustain belief, allegory could not insist overtly: it had to conceal its purposes behind ever more extravagant, and therefore potentially opaque, imagery. To borrow an analogy from psychoanalysis: the more unspeakable the latent desires, the more fantastic and bizarre the manifest display. Thus the intensification of late Renaissance allegory, culminating in *The Faerie Queene*, its conscious perversions of transparent signification, its inclusion of characters who can assume multiple forms and meanings—but with that intensification a plummeting ability to command belief. Meanwhile, an analogous and dialectically related process was occurring beyond the immediate reach of literature, in the realm of individual personality. If allegory first appeared, and was accepted, as a projection of inner states, it was inevitable that the increasingly alien and ideological forms allegory later took, especially when directed by the State towards its citizens, would be experienced as inadequate to the self; indeed, the more strenuously allegory attempted to *impose* a model of selfhood from without, the greater impetus people would naturally feel to *understand* their inmost beings as entirely separate from external forces. Allegory would thus have contributed to two social developments in ironic contrast to its principal goals as a political ideology. First, the development of a new kind of interiority, which critics at least since Burckhardt have seen as a defining characteristic of the Renaissance, and which others have seen as equally pivotal to the Protestant Reformation: a new tendency to see inner identity as something fundamentally different from social persona. Second, a new ability to view Church and State, the key ideological agents in society, critically and with detachment; to view Church and State as the (often hostile) determinants of one's social role, but not one's very selfhood; to view society as something objectively separate from the self.

Burckhardt himself was quick to see that these two transformations went hand in glove:

> In the Middle Ages both sides of human consciousness—that
> which was turned within as that which was turned without—lay
> dreaming or half-awake beneath a common veil. The veil was
> woven of faith, illusion and childish prepossession, through
> which the world and history were seen in strange hues. Man
> was conscious of himself only as a member of a race, people,

party, family or corporation—only through some general
category. In Italy this veil first melted into air; an *objective*
treatment and consideration of the state and of all the things of
this world became possible. The *subjective* side at the same time
asserted itself with corresponding emphasis; man became a
spiritual *individual.*[13]

Without entirely agreeing with Burckhardt's conclusions, we can nonetheless, on returning to *Othello*, better grasp the chill that must have run
through the audience in 1604 when Iago first declared, "I am not what
I am."[14] Two centuries earlier the statement would have seemed nonsensical, not because medieval men and women lacked any sense of
interiority (a silly notion that gets more currency than it deserves, and
which Burckhardt comes close to claiming himself), but because, broadly
speaking, the sense of an inner self (the first "I am") had not yet become
estranged from social persona (the second "I am"). The very idea of split-
ting personal identity, as it were, into tenor and vehicle would have
seemed outlandish. On the other hand, had Shakespeare written fifty
years later, Iago would probably have contented himself with "I am
not what I seem." By the middle of the seventeenth century, the split in
identity would have been accepted as a matter of course, with inner
personhood enjoying obvious ontic priority over outward role-playing.
Shakespeare, however, was writing at a moment of crisis—or, to be more
precise, quite late in a crisis that had been brewing for nearly a century
and which was shortly to end. At this moment, both halves of the equation were felt, at once, to be of equal weight, validity, and priority, and yet
irreconcilable. And thus, finally, the deeper meaning of Iago's blasphemy:
by evoking God's self-identification in Exodus, Iago (and Shakespeare,
we may safely add) is suggesting that, in this world, an uncomplicated,
tautological identification of self and role is possible only for a transcendent being. Iago's little joke is on all of us.

The Renaissance

In the preceding discussion, we have intentionally allowed categories like
politics, psychology, and literary genre to bleed together—our point being
that by the sixteenth century allegory had permeated the social sphere
entirely: its structures of thought, its ways of understanding the State and

the self. Confining ourselves to England: the modal energies that animated and complicated literary allegories like *The Faerie Queene* were also working within the equally elaborate forms of Tudor government and a developing psychology of inwardness. Our most common names for the period—"Renaissance" and still more "early modern"—carry strong connotations of novelty, of a radical break from the immediate past. The ferment of this period, however, is more typical of paradigms in their final stages: as an old dispensation is confronted with increasingly strong challenges to its basic premises, it will respond from within, with ever more elaborate and arcane solutions to those challenges—before finally shifting to a new dispensation, which presents an entirely different and usually simpler set of answers.[15] Thus the epicycles of Ptolemaic astronomy became immensely convoluted before yielding to the relative simplicity of Copernican heliocentrism; thus the Renaissance attempted to solve new challenges of statecraft, psychology, and surveillance through ever more intricate allegory, a medieval instrument stretched far beyond its means before yielding finally to something completely different.

S. K. Heninger's sweeping distinction between a "logocentric" Middle Ages and a "hylocentric" Enlightenment (from the Greek *hyle*: matter)—with the Renaissance as a moment of estuarial flux in between—is of use in filling out the broader implications of this shift. The medieval period, Heninger writes, was "dominated by an idealist ontology defined by [a] Christianized Platonism"—everything rested in the "originary authority" of God. By the eighteenth century, the basic measures of reality had changed completely: "In contrast, the [period] stretching forward into our own day [has been] dominated by a materialist ontology defined by empiricism. The ultimate constituents of its reality, that which provides the source for all truth, are the components of physical nature."[16] Since Bacon, Locke, and the empirical revolution, our faith in the reality of the physical world has rested on the purportedly simplest source: sensory evidence. You trust that the chair on which you are sitting really exists because your nerves tell you that it does. Your knowledge of the world is confined to surfaces: your senses can tell you nothing of the essential—a trivial problem when it comes to chairs, perhaps, but far more serious when dealing with the intentions of other people. During the medieval period, you would have believed in the chair (and in the person next to you) because all corporeal existence was guaranteed and justified by the transcendent Word (*logos*) of God. Above all, God was understood to be everywhere and aware of everything—a truly functional panopticon. "For wisdom is a kindly spirit, yet she acquits not the blasphemer of his guilty lips; Because God is the witness of his inmost self and the sure observer of his heart and the listener to his tongue. For the spirit of the LORD fills the world, is all-embracing, and knows what man says."[17]

In short, the high-water mark of medieval logocentrism and the early period when allegory was perceived to be unitary were the same moment: from God's all-seeing perspective, distinctions between an exterior and inner self would have been meaningless. God does not think in metaphors. Ordinary people lived in a society ordered around a unifying divine gaze. By the same token, the slow *disintegration* of logocentrism was strictly equivalent to allegory's gradual shift into desperation, complexity, and coercion. Such a reading, at all events, is consistent with the common view of medieval society as relatively static and regimented: under the unceasing watch of God, everyone and everything had its own divinely sanctioned place. Under these circumstances, solidarities would still be communal and interpersonal, the king still a baron among barons, each of whom could claim first loyalty from his immediate inferiors—a strict hierarchy that, again, would have an ossifying effect on both social role and the nature of personality.[18] Thomas Greene thus notices in the medieval view of personhood a

> rigidity in the actual representations of human personality . . . a sharply limited belief in man's capacity to alter and especially to alter himself at will. For the literary imagination, the doctrinal conceptions of the personality probably counted for less than sociological factors, such as the social immobility imposed by feudalism, the small extent and prestige of formal education, and a view of personality which depended heavily on the social role which a man was called upon to play.[19]

To return, then, to our main line of inquiry. In a society that actually functioned like a naïve allegory, surveillance, strictly speaking, would be unnecessary: the citizenry would be perfectly legible, and one could gather the inward disposition of a person simply by giving him (or her) the quickest glance. *Everyman*, one recalls, begins with God introducing himself as clear perception incarnate ("I perceyve, here, in My Majeste"), and there is no space between the characters ("Fellowship," Everyman himself) and the values they represent.[20] Indeed, if everyone were an open book (to use the shopworn metaphor almost literally), hidden watchers and informants would be redundant. The inconvenient fact that such a society, in the absence of an omniscient God-king, is impossible seems not to have discouraged the Renaissance mind, which held on to the idea with a tenacity that in retrospect seems remarkable. As the medieval social structure broke down and new forms of instability took root, the conditions for a modern surveillance state were put in place— but the event itself was a long time coming. We have already traced some of the ideological undercurrents that led to this breakdown, but the overt causes are broadly acknowledged: the dwindling prestige of the Holy Roman Empire and the papacy; the loosening of feudal loyalties and the rise of early nation-states under strong kings; the Protestant Reformation; a particular volatility amongst the lesser gentry, whose ambiguous place within feudal hierarchies made them a natural source of unease and obvious candidates for close watching.[21]

The empirical age, beginning at the end of the seventeenth century, would have a response to these new challenges: persistent observation and fact gathering, the concerted development of observational technologies, refinements in social psychology, networks of spies and professional intelligence analysts—in short the vast inductive and coercive apparatus we associate with modern surveillance. Indeed, the rudiments of such a system *had* developed by the end of the sixteenth century, most notably in the operation Sir Francis Walsingham, Elizabeth's Secretary of State, ran during the 1580s to counter Catholic infiltrations from abroad.[22] More broadly, however, nascent empiricism was viewed with distrust; *Othello* itself reads like a skeptical exposé of the inductive method. The hero's dogged demand for the "ocular proof" that Desdemona has been unfaithful to him is perhaps the crudest kind of empirical gesture; yet though the proof is never actually provided, he nonetheless believes by the end that he has seen the evidence of her infidelity. Narrative, in this case Iago's artistry, simply overwhelms what his eyes have told him (or failed to tell him).[23] Most to the point, the Renaissance attempted to solve a burgeoning crisis of personality by adopting allegorical procedures. Confronted with a population that was no longer (in theory at least) legible—and for that reason immensely threatening—the Renaissance state preferred not to use empathizing or invasive procedures, entering into the inmost minds of its potential enemies, but instead attempted, in the old manner, to approach the problem from the outside, which, it was hoped, would restore society to orderliness. If everyone could simply be put in their place—but really *put there* for good—their insides could be safely ignored.

This is the period that saw a material realization of the desire to categorize people. In James Scott's summary,

> processes as disparate as the creation of permanent last names, the standardization of weights and measures, the establishment of cadastral surveys and population registers, the invention of freehold tenure, the standardization of language and legal discourse, the design of cities, and the organization of transportation seemed comprehensible as attempts at legibility and simplification. In each case, officials took exceptionally complex, illegible, and local social practices, such as land tenure customs or naming customs, and created a standard grid whereby it could be centrally recorded and monitored.[24]

To take the seemingly minor example of last names: an immense gap, in fact, lies between "James the baker," as a man might be known during the fourteenth century, and "James Baker," as he would be called in the seventeenth. Scott is mainly concerned with official record keeping, a process made far easier and more efficient by the invention of surnames: James Baker could now be distinguished from the other Jameses of the village (James Palmer and James Chandler, for example), and his relation to other Bakers would be absolutely clear—an immense convenience for the tax man and government bureaucrats in general. But we are more concerned with the anxieties that lay behind the naming process. A century or two earlier, a profession most likely would have remained within a single family or nexus of families for generations—and so, counter-intuitively, from an allegorical perspective, surnames were unnecessary. It was only with the growth of large towns and social destabilization—Jim, the baker's son, might become a carter, or who knows what—that the impulse would have intensified to proclaim *this is what you are and always will be*. A self-evidently futile gesture, but of a piece with countless others at the time, including even proposed Tudor legislation that would have prescribed specific uniforms for each class of society.²⁵ Nor, indeed, were the higher ranks untouched by the prescriptive tendency: the sixteenth century was a golden age for the character book, a genre devoted to the depiction of ideal types; among such books one scholar notes portraits of a model "prince (Pontano and Machiavelli), a courtier (Castiglione), a magistrate (Elyot), a gentleman (Della Casa and Spenser, in their very different versions), a schoolmaster (Ascham), a poet (Minturno . . .), a lover (Ficino, Bembo, Leone Ebreo, and so on)."²⁶ During this time, one critic has observed, self-knowledge had a very different valence from today: " 'Self,' one's inner identity . . . was seen more in terms of the honour and reputation of one's role in life than as something generated out of ego." Education itself was a training in decorum, a Platonism imposed not unconsciously, as during the Middle Ages, but with full awareness.²⁷ If the final aim of literary allegory in its most tendentious phase was, to paraphrase Fletcher, to indoctrinate and put people in their place, allegorical techniques could now be witnessed operating throughout an entire society.²⁸ In a gesture that we will witness recurring in subsequent ages, the Renaissance State, in its authoritarian ambition, attempted to become the allegorical author of its citizenry.

II. IMAGINING ISLANDS: UTOPIAN ALLEGORY

It was an attempt doomed to failure. Indeed, when the Renaissance mind tried to imagine an allegorical state actually functioning, it was forced to invent islands. As a glance at contemporary maps shows, in the early sixteenth century the new world was widely thought to be an archipelago—not the two continental masses of North and South America, but rather a sort of expanded Caribbean, with countless islands of greater and lesser size.²⁹ What better place than a medium-sized island—small and self-contained enough to permit centralized control yet sufficiently large to count as a nation-state, removed from millennia of European politics yet still within the realm of plausibility—to situate one's thought experiment?

Such, in any case, was Thomas More's thinking when he imagined Utopia, the best-known fictional island of the age. And we do mean *fictional* in the etymological sense of the word: something made. This is very much the birth of a certain type of literary island, and perhaps to underscore the virtues of self-containment, More informs us that *his* island is an island by choice:

> They say, though, and one can actually see for oneself, that Utopia was originally not an island but a peninsula. However, it was conquered by somebody called Utopos, who gave it its present name . . . and was responsible for transforming a pack of ignorant savages into what is now, perhaps, the most civilized nation in the world. The moment he landed and got control of the country, he immediately had a channel cut through the fifteen-mile isthmus connecting Utopia with the mainland, so the sea could flow all around it.[30]

More was well aware that his republic was a practical impossibility: his narrator's name ("Hythlodaeus") famously means "dispenser of nonsense" in Greek, and "utopia," of course, means "no place." In his very public role as an MP (he would soon be appointed Henry VIII's privy councilor and subsequently Lord Chancellor) More understood that the early modern nation-state was unmanageable. While the second, and longer, of *Utopia*'s two books is mainly a description of the island, the first begins with a litany of everything amiss in England (and on the continent). In short order, political and mercantile conflict between nations, mass starvation, imbalances of money and power, civil war, barbaric penal codes, the enclosure of arable land and the displacement of agrarian populations, the rapacity of churchmen, and, above all, the necessary toadyism and hypocrisy of life at court are marched out for inspection and, essentially, shrugged off. Shrugging most vigorously is "More" himself, who appears as a character in the dialogue, and as Hythlodaeus's polite but skeptical intellectual adversary—a "More" who finds society's ills deplorable but pragmatically beyond any full solution.

We are not about to resolve, or enter into, the centuries-old debate about where the "real" Thomas More stood in this contest between a nonsensical idealist and an urbane, somewhat cynical alter ego; but even assuming a measure of irony on both sides, the latter voice was certainly one More knew well and whose basic point he would have granted, albeit ruefully. Prior to the following passage, "More" has been comparing state-craft to the theater and suggesting that a "production" should not be abandoned simply because "you happen to think of another [play] that you'd enjoy rather more":

> The same rule applies to politics and life at Court. If you
> can't completely eradicate wrong ideas, or deal with inveterate
> vices as effectively as you could wish, that's no reason for
> turning your back on public life altogether. You wouldn't
> abandon ship in a storm just because you couldn't control
> the winds.
>
> On the other hand, it's no use attempting to put across
> entirely new ideas, which will obviously carry no weight with
> people who are prejudiced against them. You must go to work
> indirectly. You must handle everything as tactfully as you can,
> and what can't be put right you must try to make as little wrong
> as possible. For things will never be perfect, until human
> beings are perfect—which I don't expect them to be for quite a
> number of years! (42)

This pragmatism—which More (the author) must have felt on at least some level—suggests a way to read his depiction of Utopian society: rather than being, primarily, a set of proposals for the reform of the English state—which it may well be in a "tactful" and "indirect" way— Utopia shows us an allegorical mind solving the problems of society unimpeded by the hindrances of everyday, sixteenth-century life. Or, to put it a slightly different way: Utopia is a successful allegorical society in a way Tudor England never could be; the book is an imagining of the conditions that would make a functioning social allegory possible.

Thus, simplification. If the allegorical project of early Tudor statecraft was defeated at every turn by an increasingly diverse and complex social structure, the obvious answer was not—as it would be two centuries later—to perfect and refine the means of inspection and observation, but rather to simplify, and thus render legible, the citizenry itself. Several of the tendencies we have observed in sixteenth-century England are therefore visible in Utopian society as well—only exaggerated. If the English considered imposing different uniforms on different ranks, the Utopians take the next logical step: certain groups can be identified instantly by badges and distinctly colored uniforms. Convicts, for example, all wear "clothes of [a] regulation color," and each slave "is given a badge to show which district he belongs to, and it's a capital crime to take one's badge off, to be seen outside one's own district, or to speak to a slave from another district" (30–31). More is rightly given credit for his principled objection to capital punishment for crimes like burglary, a common sentence as late as the eighteenth century. But he is hardly an opponent of the death penalty, and it is wholly typical of his outlook that a sin against regimentation and order—wearing the wrong color—means the gallows, while mere felons get off relatively lightly. *Regimentation*, however, may be the wrong word: while convicts get special colors, Utopia is otherwise a monoculture. Since "everyone on the island wears the same sort of clothes—except that they vary slightly according to sex and marital status—and the fashion never changes" (55), tailors and dressmakers are unknown. Although, necessarily, different people pursue different trades, everyone is compelled to farm. The cities are identical: "There are fifty-four splendid big towns on the island, all with the same language, laws, customs and institutions. They're all built on the same plan, and, so far as the sites will allow, they all look exactly alike. . . . When you're seen one of them, you've seen them all" (50, 52). If the agrarianism seems to forecast the Great Leap Forward, the towns resemble nothing so much as the eerie Harappan settlements of the Indus valley, with their identical, square layouts, uniform dwellings, and near absence of hierarchical buildings.[31] Diversity is the enemy of transparency, More has intuited, so everyone is more or less the same.

We might observe, in passing, that this intuition seems to lie behind More's espousal of communism, which many take to be his "central innovation."[32] Certainly Lenin read him this way, ordering an obelisk honoring More to be erected in Moscow after the revolution.[33] In addition to the uniformity and agrarianism of Utopian society, "there is no such thing as private property" (53); only useful things are held to be of value, and luxury goods are held in contempt (thus, appropriately, Utopian chamber pots are solid gold). It is possible, however, to give the moral thrust of More's argument too much credit—and more convincingly, Greenblatt has argued for a psycho-economic etiology: if More's life at court necessitated unending hypocrisy and role-playing, Utopian communism, with its erasure of individuality, provided an alternative. In a nascently capitalist society like early sixteenth-century England, "individuals [were] isolated, unattached save where their material interests

[chanced to coincide]. . . . All value depend[ed] upon the admiration or
envy excited by what [was] displayed and consumed."[34] By contrast, the
abolition of private property voided an "ideology of status and custom that
provided a time-honored justification for the unequal distributions of
wealth in society." Utopian communism, Greenblatt concludes, "represents all that More deliberately excluded from the [courtly] personality he
created and played"—and reducing "the scope of the ego" makes possible
a much-desired escape from "individuation" and indeed personality.[35]
And yet to turn More into a Tudor T. S. Eliot has its risks. Both the claim
that More understood himself in strictly dualistic terms (with separate
inner and social selves), and the assertion that the fictiveness of his social
identity was a source of alienation, carry the risk of reading him back
through twentieth-century (or at least seventeenth-century) ideas of
personality that he would have found foreign. We have already offered
reasons to doubt both claims—but whatever the case may be, it is all too
easy, and dangerous, to dismiss the opinions of the "More" who speaks in
the dialogue. A More, for example, who believes sincerely in the value of
a well-advised and powerful king:

> The most effective way of [applying one's talents in the world]
> would be to gain the confidence of some great king or other, and
> give him . . . really good advice. For every king is a sort of
> fountain, from which a constant shower of benefits or injuries
> rains down upon the whole population. (20)

If *this* More is to be taken seriously, it then becomes possible, and perhaps
necessary, not to read Utopian communism and the hierarchical absolutism of Henry's court as contradictory, but rather as essentially sympathetic. That is: communism makes possible the unimpeded exercise of
allegorical power, something the king and his counselors could only
dream about.

Utopia both illustrates the sophistication with which the sixteenth
century thought about surveillance and demonstrates why the modern
practice of surveillance could not develop fully at this time. On the
one hand, monitoring is as pervasive in Utopian society as in Orwell's
Oceania or Zamyatin's OneState. When More describes the social body
as "one big household," he means, essentially, that no one has any
privacy, ever.

> You see how it is—wherever you are, you always have to work.
> There's never any excuse for idleness. There are also no wine-
> taverns, no ale-houses, no brothels, no opportunities for
> seduction, no secret meeting-places. Everyone has his eye on
> you, so you're practically forced to get on with your job and
> make some proper use of your spare time. (65)

At the same time, for all practical purposes, the key target of all surveillance—the inner person, the individual—escapes.[36] The solitary citizen,
who may just be driving to the airport, or who may have other plans, and
whose interiority the State can only perceive as a threat, remains hidden.
Anything that leads to individuation is conspicuously absent on the
island; even the houses are "changed round every ten years" (53), for fear
that habits, attachments, personal feelings may develop. And yet More's
aim is not a "cancellation of identity itself"—not at least if one avoids
using "identity" in the modern sense of the word.[37] Rather, he is staging a
heroic, last-ditch attempt to bring inner and outer identity into concord—
or, more precisely, to preserve the sense that inner and outer identity are
one and the same thing—even if it means paring down individuality
to a degree that most people now would find inhumane. A side effect of
this attitude is a seemingly flippant willingness to accept appearances
at face value:

> There's another type of person . . . who has a passion for
> jewels [but is] so terrified of being taken in by appearances
> that he refuses to buy any jewel until he's stripped off all the
> gold and inspected it in the nude. And even then he won't
> buy it without a solemn guarantee from the jeweler that the
> stone is genuine. But my dear sir, why shouldn't a fake give
> you just as much pleasure, if you can't, with your own eyes,
> distinguish it from a real one? It makes no difference to you
> whether it's genuine or not—any more than it would to a
> blind man! (75)

"Give me the ocular proof." On the island of Cyprus, Othello's demand
can only seem naïve and self-destructive; on More's fictive island, ocular
proof is all the evidence one needs to read one's fellow citizens. So long as
the exterior is genuine, the interior, or what there is of it, can take care of

itself. So long as statesmen held on to this hope—ever so tenuously—the modern surveillance state would have to wait.

Leaving the Island: Prospero and the Divine Right of Kings

> *Miranda.* There's nothing ill can dwell in such a temple.
> If the ill spirit have so fair a house,
> Good things will strive to dwell with't.
>
> —*The Tempest* I.ii.457–59[38]

If you wish to find the nameless island on which Shakespeare set *The Tempest*, simply steer a course directly between Cyprus and Utopia and you will make landfall soon enough. As with More, setting his action at the borders of the known world seems to have liberated Shakespeare to think in the abstract about problems of politics and society; *The Tempest* is as much a thought experiment as *Utopia*, and it covers much the same ground—the limits of allegory and surveillance—albeit in a less self-conscious and systematic way. At the same time, Shakespeare is unwilling or unable to segregate his dream-kingdom, part Caribbean but also clearly Mediterranean, from the complexities of contemporary European politics: they are all too present in the play. His island, in short, is still a Utopia, but in a world increasingly under the shadow of European influence. If, indeed, a sense of claustrophobia fills the drama, it may be an effect of time's passage: *The Tempest* belongs to a later and more desperate moment of allegorical culture than *Utopia*. Although *Utopia* illustrates, finally, the impossibility of a functioning allegorical state, it nevertheless appeared in 1516, at the flood stage of early Tudor prestige; when *The Tempest* was first performed, ninety-five years later, the court was far less stable, with a widely unpopular king, and the fissures of civil war already visible. And thus, perhaps, an explanation for the different approaches More and Shakespeare take to the problem of social allegory: where More investigates the conditions under which an allegorical politics might be possible, Shakespeare offers a direct and brutal critique of the magical thinking that kept a tottering, allegorizing court afloat.

Even more than Elizabeth, James I was a vigorous proponent of monarchy by divine right; as Lacey Baldwin Smith points out, though such claims were integral to new forms of government emerging in the Renaissance, they were also sources of vulnerability:

The early modern nation-state possessed a soft feudal
underbelly, and neither statutes written in blood nor the
doctrine of absolute obedience to an authority ordained by God
and propounded from every pulpit and schoolroom could
entirely dispel the fear on the part of royal magistrates and
administrators that public duty to the Crown might be
corrupted, even replaced, by private loyalty to rank, birth and
religion. . . . From a semi-feudal cluster of highly idiosyncratic
loyalty networks based on kinship, lordship, and an atavistic
attachment to one's immediate locale, sixteenth-century
England was moving into something resembling a nation to
which all subjects gave their undivided loyalty and from which
they derived their status as well as their security. [The monarch
was] no longer . . . a lord among lords, but was now regarded
"not only [as] a king to be obeyed on earth but [also as] a
veritable idol to be worshipped."[39]

To translate the problem into terms we have been using: as medieval
logocentrism disintegrated, an attempt was made to recoup divine prestige in the person of the king. The word of God had underwritten the
decentralized power structure of feudalism; now, in order to justify newly
unified states, the word needed to be made flesh: the *logos* needed to be
relocated in the persons of "kings and emperors, . . . God's attested
leaders among men."[40] From a surveillance angle, however, the new situation presented formidable difficulties. God is, by nature, panoptic: He
sees and understands all. The *logos* carried weight during the Middle Ages
precisely because it was understood to be backed up by an unblinking and
universal divine gaze. Short of declaring themselves gods—a gesture to
which the church might have objected—even the most authoritarian
kings could claim no such power. For the *human* monarch, confronted
with an increasingly illegible and dangerous populace, only a small range
of solutions were open, of which we have already noted two. First, More's
tactic: to simplify the allegory by homogenizing the citizenry, thus making
accurate surveillance possible. Second, Walsingham's approach: the
beginnings of a surveillance bureaucracy, ahead of its time, actually able
to keep potential subversives under efficient watch. The preferred solution, however, was allegory at its most tendentious: an ideology of society

as a divinely ordained array, with everyone in a proper place and the monarch as God's vassal; a cult of personality surrounding the sovereign so intense as to make him or her indeed seem both divine and all-seeing, a master interpreter. The (literally) crowning images of allegorical culture in its last phase, in England and (much later) France, respectively, were Gloriana, the virgin queen, whose body was at once her own and the entirety of her nation, and Louis, the Sun King, who could declare a mystic synonymity between himself and the State.[41]

We do not claim that *The Tempest* is consciously a meditation on the ideology of divine right absolutism, but without question that ideology, a decade into the Stuart monarchy, is everywhere in the play. *What would happen*, Shakespeare seems to ask, if the king—by means of magic, since it could never happen in the real world—truly were the master allegorist, omniscient and all-powerful, perfectly able to define and control all around him? And what would then happen if the world of early seventeenth-century Europe, in its bitter complexity, suddenly washed ashore? Smaller than Utopia, Prospero's island is, if anything, even more profoundly a surveillance state than its predecessor.[42] Caliban, Miranda, and Prospero's enemies are never unwatched: the confounding stage direction "*Enter Ariel, Invisible*" appears throughout the text—Ariel is "invisible/to every eyeball" save Prospero's (I.ii.302–3)—and Prospero's command of the weather, and much else, is evident from the start. With such power, Prospero enjoys, at least initially, a supreme confidence in the legibility of appearances—a habit, interestingly, that he has passed on to his daughter. Having spent her entire conscious existence on the island, Miranda has a naïve trust of surfaces—evident both in her judgment of Caliban and in her declaration that "nothing ill" could possibly dwell in a "temple" as fair as Ferdinand—that might get her in trouble anywhere but here. It is very much to the point, however, that Prospero's allegorical turn of mind predated his exile; his account to Miranda of his overthrow:

> My brother and thy uncle, call'd Antonio . . .
>   . . . he whom next thyself
> Of all the world I lov'd, and to him put
> The manage of my state, as at that time
> Through all the signories it was the first,

And Prospero the prime duke, being so reputed
In dignity, and for the liberal arts
Without a parallel; those being all my study,
The government I cast upon my brother,
And to my state grew stranger, being transported
And rapt in secret studies . . .
I, thus neglecting worldly ends, all dedicated
To closeness and the bettering of my mind
With that which, but by being so retir'd
O'er-priz'd all popular rate, in my false brother
Awak'd an evil nature, and my trust,
Like a good parent, did beget of him
A falsehood in its contrary, as great
As my trust was, which had indeed no limit,
A confidence sans bound. He being thus lorded,
Not only with what my revenue yielded,
But what my power might else exact—like one
Who having into truth, by telling of it,
Made such a sinner of his memory
To credit his own lie—he did believe
He was indeed the Duke, out o' th' substitution,
And executing th'outward face of royalty
With all prerogative. (I.ii.65–66, 69–77, 89–105)

And so, several lines later, a coup d'état. While Prospero's groundless trust in his brother, and inability to read deceit, might be the most striking aspect of his narrative, we are more concerned with the roots of his credulence: Prospero believes that by virtue of holding the title of "Duke," he is indeed the duke of Milan—this despite performing no official duties. By the same token, he assumes that his brother, because he was born second, will be a loyal vassal forever. From Prospero's old-fashioned and disengaged perspective, the social structure is totally transparent—ascribed social roles perfectly predict personal behavior—until he is proven wrong. Antonio, younger and of a more empirical—not to mention self-interested—bent, is content to smash the social allegory and make a case for a different reality principle. Nothing about Prospero's basic habits of mind in fact changes when he goes into exile; to the contrary, the island is changed to fit his habits of mind. His island, like More's, is simply a place where social allegory is possible—not because of utopian simplification but through an unimpeded, godlike exercise of surveillant control by the despot.

Shakespeare leaves no doubts about the kind of society Prospero has left behind: it is even more chaotic and corrupt than the England described by More. Compared to Prospero's odd innocence and naïveté, Antonio offers a brave new world of Machiavellian power struggles and naked ambition, in which all bonds of kinship and personal loyalty are forged only to be broken. Just as More's courtiers are "always prepared to suck up to the king's special favorites by agreeing to the silliest things they say" (20), so Antonio reaps power by working the spoils system:

> Being once perfected how to grant suits,
> How to deny them, who t'advance, and who
> To trash for overtopping, new created
> The creatures that were mine, I say, or changed 'em.
> (I.ii.79–82)

Later, as Alonso sleeps, Antonio and Sebastian discuss regicide (and fratricide) with a chilling casualness, no doubt correctly concluding that the king's retainers will acquiesce at once to the new power arrangement: "They'll take suggestion as a cat laps milk; / They'll tell the clock to any business that /We say befits the hour" (II.ii.288–90). Behind this vision of courtly servility, finally, lies an even deeper fear of plenary social collapse; indeed, we are practically invited to read the eponymous storm as an image of social upheaval. As the ship begins to founder, the sailors rise up against their aristocratic passengers, an image Shakespeare, who had no love for the mob, would have found terrifying:[43]

> BOTSWAIN. What cares these roarers for the name of king? To
>   cabin! Silence! trouble us not.
> GONZALO. Good, yet remember whom thou hast aboard.
> BOATSWAIN. None that I love more than myself. You are a
>   councillor; if you can command these elements to silence,
>   and work the peace of the present, we will not hand a rope
>   more. Use your authority. If you cannot . . . Out of our way, I
>   say. (I.i.16–27)

By implication, the noble passengers, each of whom had a hand in Prospero's fall, are of a piece with the tempest that now threatens to destroy them; certainly none has Prospero's authority to command the elements to silence. And yet, given the clarity with which he depicts anarchy, with which he outlines the worst possible consequences of allegorical collapse, it is all the more striking how little patience Shakespeare has for the utopian ideal. The island is a temptation for would-be social planners, from the drunken Stephano, who declares the place "a brave kingdom" (III.ii.144) and himself king, but whose strategy does not go much further than that, to Gonzalo, who sees the opportunity for something more ambitious:

> GONZALO. Had I plantation of this isle . . .
> And were king on't, what would I do? . . .
> I' th' commonwealth I would, by contraries,
> Execute all things; for no kind of traffic
> Would I admit; no name of magistrate;
> Letters should not be known; riches, poverty,
> And use of service, none; contract, succession,
> Bourn, bound of land, tilth, vineyard, none;
> No use of metal, corn, or wine, or oil;
> No occupation, all men idle, all;
> And women too, but innocent and pure;
> No sovereignty—
> SEBASTIAN. Yet he would be king on't.
> ANTONIO. The latter end of his commonwealth forgets
>   the beginning.
> GONZALO. All things in common nature should produce
> Without sweat or endeavor: treason, felony,
> Sword, pike, knife, gun, or need of any engine,
> Would I not have, but nature should bring forth,
> Of it own kind, all foison, all abundance,
> To feed my innocent people.
> SEBASTIAN. No marrying 'mong his subjects?
> ANTONIO. None, man, all idle—whores and knaves.
> GONZALO. I would with such perfection govern, sir,
> T'excel the golden age. (II.i.144, 146, 148–69)

The immediate source for Gonzalo's kingdom is probably Montaigne, in addition to classical accounts of the golden age—but the echoes of *Utopia* are strong and by no means coincidental.[44] Gonzalo's solution for a society plagued by treason and felony reads like a far less sophisticated version (or a sophisticated send-up) of More's: a radical homogenization of the populace extending beyond More's communism to primitive anarchy; a full rejection of modern technology and even literacy itself. "Innocent," for Gonzalo, means something like "without individuation," and while Shakespeare clearly means his audience to see this vision as fatuous and unrealistic, he also likely wishes us to feel both pain and regret at the ease with which Antonio and Sebastian puncture it. Ninety-five years after More, this kind of utopia is little more than a joke.

Prospero's utopia, on the other hand, is formidable—and so receives the severest critique. Discussing the characters in literary allegories, Fletcher comments that "the perfect allegorical agent is not a man possessed by a daemon, but a robot." By this he means that the constricted significance of, and ideological force behind, such a character will cause him or her "to act somewhat mechanistically."[45] Napoleon the pig is a representation of Stalin as murderous dictator; he is not about to fall in love or compose an opera. More to the point, we have been tracing a similar process of de-realization in imagined social allegories. There is already something robotic about More's utopians, robbed as they are of distinguishing characteristics; indeed, as we have seen, More is relatively unconcerned whether the jewel is true or false, so long as it sparkles. By the time we get to *The Tempest*, Shakespeare is more than concerned: the line between person and simulacrum has nearly blurred. Prospero is never in any real danger from his enemies—this is perhaps the least suspenseful of Shakespeare's plays—but his mastery comes at the expense of turning them into automatons. With Ariel's help, he can dictate when Miranda, Alonso, and Gonzalo fall asleep and when they awaken. Under Ariel's spell, Caliban and his confederates resemble marionettes, and the noble company can only "stand charm'd" like sleepwalkers. This scene comes shortly after the masque Prospero has mounted for Ferdinand and Miranda, and Shakespeare surely intends us to perceive an uncomfortable resemblance between his enchanted Neapolitans and the truly insubstantial figments of the earlier performance. The masque ends with Prospero's famously beautiful speech:

> These our actors
> (As I foretold you) were all spirits, and
> Are melted into air, into thin air,
> And like the baseless fabric of this vision,
> The cloud-capp'd tow'rs, the gorgeous palaces,
> The solemn temples, the great globe itself,
> Yea, all which it inherit, shall dissolve,
> And like this insubstantial pageant faded
> Leave not a rack behind. We are such stuff
> As dreams are made on; and our little life
> Is rounded with a sleep. Sir, I am vex'd;
> Bear with my weakness, my old brain is troubled.
> Be not disturb'd with my infirmity. (IV.i.148–60)

Surely the speech draws its uncanny power from the silent transition between its initial and final referents. When it begins, Prospero is simply discussing the masque, but by the end he is talking about all of us; in the sequence of apposites (from "cloud-capp'd tow'rs" to "insubstantial pageant"), he slides, possibly without noticing, from a parade of shadows to the nature of existence itself. The vexation and "infirmity," we would argue, are indeed his and his alone: Shakespeare is not making a comment about the world so much as the malaise that comes with viewing the world a certain way.

There is never any question about remaining on the island: for all the treachery of courtly life, Prospero's intention, to return to Milan, is simply assumed. In the chapters that follow, we will return to this trope—*leaving the island*—which appears regularly in literature as an image of changing dispensations, at moments, too, when the changing meaning of surveillance, of personhood, of the relation between individual and State is particularly at stake. In *The Tempest*, only Ferdinand, in a gesture that may reflect poorly on his character, expresses a desire to "live here forever," calling the island a "paradise" (IV.i.122, 4); Prospero, pointedly, does not respond. To be a master allegorist, to be able to read perfectly the hearts and minds of one's subjects—a perspective James and Elizabeth could only fantasize about—is finally unsatisfying. Reality—or rather, the lack of it—is as barren for the absolute king as it is for More's utopians. Indeed, Prospero's dream-kingdom begins to come asunder the moment

Ferdinand and Miranda lay eyes on each other: while Prospero can predict the tactics his former associates will take, his control wavers when confronted with powerful human emotion. He confesses to surprise at their mutual attraction (III.ii.92–94) and, his own emotions stirred, allows his oversight of Caliban to slip momentarily during the masque. Though love might conquer all, however, Shakespeare is anything but sentimental about the world to which Prospero is returning or about the kind of person he will need to be when he returns. His first act after regaining his dukedom is to blackmail his brother and Sebastian.

> Welcome, my friends all!
> [*Aside to Sebastian and Antonio*] But you, my brace of lords,
> were I so minded,
> I here could pluck his Highness' frown upon you
> And justify you traitors. At this time
> I will tell no tales.
> *Sebastian*. [*Aside*] The devil speaks in him. (V.i.125–29)

That is: aware that Antonio and Sebastian were plotting to murder the king, Prospero lets them know their lives are in his hands and so ensures their cooperation. In short, the game is won but at the cost of adopting his brother's methods—and Prospero, having left the allegorical, for better or worse, cannot return to it. With a blunt threat, he takes on his brother's paranoia and the "devil" of epistemic doubt. Antonio, like Iago silent to the end, keeping his own, hidden council, is the avatar of the future.

CODA: THE RISE OF MODERN SURVEILLANCE AND THE AFTERLIFE OF ALLEGORY

The Rise of Modern Surveillance

With the passing of allegorical culture, the modern history of surveillance can properly begin; in the four remaining chapters we will follow this history, tracking developments both in the theory and practice of surveillance and in the way literature represents, explores, and at times invades the self. Within the three centuries (and counting) of the post-allegorical dispensation, it is possible to discern a series of major phases. In the first of these, the culture responded rapidly to the crisis given early expression by Iago's "I am not what I am." If inner personhood was acknowledged—conclusively now—to be fundamentally different from social role, this posed challenges both for the State and, less obviously, the individual. The problem faced by the former was palpable: a person's outward demeanor or assigned role in life was no firm predictor of loyalty or political stance; James Baker, on his way to the airport, could be up to anything. In place of the old methods we have already discussed—an attempt to impose from the top down a vision of society as ideal and static—new methods had to be developed, and fast, to pierce the veil of public persona, to observe and interpret everyday activities. The fantastic monitoring devices that Francis Bacon had imagined his scientists producing in *The New Atlantis* would become real before very long.[46] Meanwhile, in a more subtle way, an equally pressing crisis was fomenting on the level of self. Granted the human interior was fundamentally different from social façade, but then what was it, precisely? Centuries of allegorical tradition provided no answer. With an urgency equal to that felt by governments and statesmen, new questions about the nature of authentic character had to be mooted, questions that are still very much with us.

In short, from the very beginning of the new dispensation, we may distinguish two definitional processes intertwined, one "external," concerned with the observation and occasional invasion of self, the other "internal," concerned with self-creation. "Intertwined," however, is not quite precise: the two processes were related dialectically, with developments in one driving changes in the other, a dialectic of observation and privacy. In part it was fueled by technological progress. As new apparatuses from indoor plumbing, to I-beam construction, to the radio, made for increased solitude, new methods had to be devised to penetrate it; contrarily, each new physical incursion was met by new means of escape. The nuts-and-bolts side of the story is seductive—if it wasn't, movies like *Enemy of the State* would not make millions, and a lot of materialist historians would be out of business—but, we argue, only part of the truth. At least as consequentially, the dialectic was conceptual and even spiritual. The threat of constant assault was itself conducive to the creation of a modern sense of self; the idea of privacy, as we now think of it, as a basic human right, as a condition of the soul, could not have come about without an unremitting social pressure perceived as hostile and dangerous. In turn, surveillance, both in practice and in theory, needed to become more sophisticated and complex as its human target matured and deepened. More diverse as well: not so much a single activity as an array of activities and ideas with complex interrelations. A dialectic of observation and privacy: the next two chapters will take up each side of the issue, respectively, with special attention to the way each process occurred in partnership with specific literary genres during the eighteenth and early nineteenth centuries.

Unfortunately, as dialectics go, the one we trace proved to be as mutually destructive as it was fruitful; the fulfillment of one aim could come only at the expense of the other. Behind each of the opposing sides lay an impossible wish: driving the development of ever more sophisticated surveillance techniques, a desire to violate the human interior entirely, to render the human surface utterly transparent; propelling the development of privacy theory, a desire for the soul to be purely autonomous and free from social influences. Both of these quixotic projects may be traced to a foundational error in empiricism, an error that was far from evident—to most people, at least—during the first decades, generations, even centuries of the post-allegorical age. It was only a matter of time, however, before the dialectic must come undone, and the new dispensation—which we may call liberal-contractarian— undergo its own crisis of convictions, leaving itself vulnerable, ultimately, to revivified forms of social allegory.

For the present, it remains only to write the postscript to Renaissance allegorical culture, looking at an author who, writing after the next dispensation had taken hold, both demonstrated the tenacity of the old ways of thinking and exposed flaws in the new that would not become broadly evident until much later. Though Jonathan Swift was not a key player in the debates about surveillance spreading quickly through post-Restoration Britain, he nevertheless, from his alienated position, exposed problems in surveillance theory that would not become obvious until the twentieth century. Though his allegiances were to allegorical culture, he was not a writer of allegories per se; indeed, to reiterate a basic point, our primary concern is not with genre, but mode. To be sure, literary allegories continued to get written during the late seventeenth and eighteenth centuries, by authors from Bunyan (*The Pilgrim's Progress*), to Dryden (*Absalom and Achitophel*), to Pope (*The Temple of Fame*). Yet after the loss of a transcendental verifier (God's eye, manifested as the eye of the monarch) and a waning of the social faith that had made the genre a powerful and plausible representation of reality, the result could only be a hollowed-out form of allegory: allegory as a self-consciously didactic tool. In place of the powerful ambiguities of a Langland or Spenser, allegories now, in a tradition that continues with modern texts like *Animal Farm*, offered the crystalline clarity of mathematical equations, the meaning no longer ineffable and beyond representation but rather explicitly political or intellectual. To appreciate *Absalom and Achitophel*, in which one-to-one matches are drawn with unfailing wit and propriety between biblical characters and English politicians, is also to perceive the loss of power that befalls a genre when the modal energies that once sustained it have disappeared. In *Gulliver's Travels*, on the other hand, the disappearance becomes itself a source of uncanny power; in his hostile critique of early liberal-contractarian culture, Swift found a final relevance for allegorical thinking precisely in its utter social absence.

The Afterlife of Allegory: Swift's Negative Theology

For artists of a traditionalist bent with lingering affiliations to social allegory—especially political loyalties to the monarchy, the landed aristocracy, the High Church, and the prestige of received wisdom—few options would seem to remain open after the Glorious Revolution: neither an outmoded literary allegory nor the novel, the aesthetic embodiment of a despised modernity, would have had much appeal.[47] The surest course was mockery—and it is merely stating the obvious to note that the great Tory genre of the early eighteenth century was satire. Indeed, the decline of allegory (the genre) and the rise of satire were related processes, with satire typically understood as a *continuation* of allegory, not so much a successor genre as a perverse extension: allegorical mechanics, but with the sign/signified relation purposely perverted.[48] Thus, in Pope's *The Dunciad*, the greatest instance of such a text, "a new world to Nature's laws unknown, /Breaks out refulgent, with a heaven its own." As a depiction of perceived social chaos, the simplicity and propriety of post-Restoration allegory is replaced by a surreal world in which "Nature's laws" break down: "The forests dance, the rivers upward rise, / Whales sport in woods, and dolphins in the skies."[49]

Some such strategy certainly lies behind period pieces like *Macflecknoe* and *The Splendid Shilling*; we would argue, however, that

Swiftian satire, satire at its most complex and consequential, cannot be understood in such terms: it is in no simple or direct way a successor genre to Renaissance allegory. In contrast to the mature Pope and Johnson, who both attributed the failure of allegory to a fundamental flaw in the *form*, Swift recognized a fundamental flaw in *society*. To put it in analytic terms we have used already: the *modal* forces that had underpinned Tudor-Stuart culture, and which had made a stable social allegory possible (or at least, as More proved, imaginable), had now given way to a crass materialism embodied, in different ways, by Walpole, Defoe, and Locke. Swift indeed frequently imagined himself as fighting this new society, commenting in a letter to Pope: "Drown the world! I am not content with despising it, but I would anger it, if I could with safety."[50] If social allegory—and, almost in passing, truly potent literary allegory—was no longer feasible, the task of the satirist was to diagnose the modal sickness ravaging the body politic. It is a testament to his success that he uncovered flaws in the new dispensation—and again, in nascent empirical ideas about surveillance—centuries before they were generally acknowledged.

Swift, the eldest of his circle, may well have been the last Augustan to remember what an allegorical society was like; a friend to both Sir William Temple, the cavalier statesman, and Alexander Pope, he bridged two distinct cultural moments. For this reason he was uniquely attuned to the social and literary consequences of a post-allegorical world. Perhaps no passage captures the distance fallen—as Swift would undoubtedly see it—so well as the notorious passage in *Gulliver's Travels*, book 1, in which the Lilliputians rifle the hero's pockets.

> Imprimis, In the right coat-pocket of the Great Man-Mountain
> . . . after the strictest search, we found only one great piece of
> coarse cloth, large enough to be a [room-sized carpet]. In the left
> pocket, we saw a huge silver chest, with a cover of the same
> metal, which we the searchers were not able to lift. We desired it
> should be opened, and one of us, stepping into it, found himself
> up to the mid leg in a sort of dust, some part whereof, flying into
> our faces, set us both sneezing for several times together. (etc.)[51]

As the little folk examine everyday items—a handkerchief, a snuffbox—in microscopic detail, Swift's point is obvious: myopic realism, of the sort engaged in by empiricism (and its literary offspring, the novel), leads to estrangement and a defamiliarizing of the world, not the reverse. When Swift calls Defoe a "stupid illiterate scribbler," he is expressing also a broader disgust at the kind of writing an empirical society has inspired.[52] Behind the parody lies a serious worry, and a question Milton had avoided by ending *Paradise Lost* at the moment Adam and Eve leave Eden: what is the fate of representation in a world where the eye of God no longer has any correlate in the social body, and in which the divine gaze no longer implicitly guarantees the stability of everyday objects? With the severing of the royal connection between divine and human worlds, nonrealistic imagery, of the sort that had abounded, say, in Spenser, could no longer seem *natural*; artists were left with the choice of either self-conscious artifice (the impotent political allegories of the Restoration) or the mimesis of an empirical, secularized world (Defoe and the novel). Swiftian satire remains disturbing and powerful precisely because it disdains both of these alternatives: neither allegorical nor novelistic, it offers a kind of negative theology in which the numinous power of the divine, though still strongly felt, can find no manifestation in the state or indeed in any worldly object. *The world itself*, in consequence, appears distorted, a place where nothing can be recognized clearly; images that *remind* us of an allegorical order abound, but the organizing system is brutally absent.

It is a situation with concrete and quantifiable social consequences—and there is never any question that the object of Swift's (quite rigorous) analysis is contemporary England. Although the age of allegory has passed, he reasons, there nevertheless persist basic human desires and motives—for coherence, for authority, for the knowledge of other people—that allegory had once satisfied and which still cry out for satisfaction. A post-allegorical culture will therefore strive to meet those needs, especially through surveillance, but in the absence of any ontic authority will fail in certain predictable ways. He writes, in short, not of a *deus absconditus* so much as a *civitas abscondita*. His critique reaches its fullest development in book 3, perhaps the least familiar of Gulliver's four journeys, and in particular in Swift's development of two key images: the Academy of Lagado and the Flying Island of Laputa. It is no coincidence that Balnibarbi, the island of which Lagado is the capital and over which Laputa hovers in endless, menacing patrol, is located somewhere in the South Pacific—more or less where Bacon had set his utopia in the

New Atlantis. The Academy, in particular, is a frontal assault on the Royal Society, an attack on the institutional incarnation of the Baconian, empirical worldview. When left solely to human ingenuity, Swift argues, the drive to gain knowledge of the physical universe (and human nature) ends not in mastery but in chaos and incoherence: various academy projects reflect a reversal of cause and effect (e.g., the "Project for extracting Sun-Beams out of Cucumbers," the "Operation to reduce human Excrement to its original Food") or descend into pure idiocy (e.g., attempts "to calcine Ice into Gunpowder").

Because of the desires and motives from which they spring, more-over, the actions and products of a post-allegorical culture will inevitably resemble, morphologically, the most outlandish products of allegory itself. To anticipate a moment much later in our own analysis: when images and structures reminiscent of allegory begin to reappear in twentieth-century culture, it is in ways that Swift predicted in book 3. The Laputans, for example, are addicted to astrology; lacking, however, the master narratives conferred by allegory (and underwritten by the divine word), they create and impose random meanings upon their minute yet uncomprehending stellar observations. The sheer effort required to create artificial coherence is so great that the Laputans lose any ability to comprehend events on earth (leading, most notably, to rampant adultery by the wives of the astronomers). The natural outcome, finally, of this obliviousness (to the very events they hope will be explained by the stars) is paranoia—paranoia, again, of a kind one is more likely to associate with the modern era than the early 1700s. Laputan society is plagued by "Apprehensions . . . of impending Dangers" (151). That their "apprehensions" are commonly wrong does not assuage their terror; rather, the astronomers, good empiricists that they are, simply continue to collect massive amounts of data and speculate wildly as to what disasters they might predict.

In a manner of speaking, the society Swift depicts in book 3 may be seen as the negative image of Utopia. If *Utopia* was a visionary imagining of the conditions under which a social allegory might function, Swift illustrates what a utopian project might look like in his own materialist age, under conditions profoundly hostile to allegorical thinking. Thus, where More had preached a simplification of the social body, a monocul-ture, Laputan and Lagadan society are complex beyond legibility. If the functioning of the Utopian state was made possible by unremitting and omnipresent surveillance, book 3 illustrates what happens when surveillance operates in the absence of divinely supported perspective. It was as obvious to Swift as it had been to More that no one besides God can see into the soul; in Laputa, Swift suggests the consequences—at once despotic and utterly ineffectual—of attempting to create an empirical replacement for the divine eye. The flying island is at once one of great panoptic images in literature and (quite literally) pi in the sky. It is not just a spying device used to discipline the population below but also a weapon to punish and crush them; yet the problems with employing this power are all too apparent: the island might shatter upon hitting the ground, or it might be heated from below by rebels until it cracks, or its magnetic core might be drawn in with lodestones and trapped—all weaknesses that the subjected populace understands and exploits. Though Laputa is a splendid achievement of technology, it is only—like any technology—as effective as the people using it and thus an object lesson on the dangers of placing too much faith in the physical apparatus of surveillance. Unable to comprehend what it sees, unsure even of what to look for, it is Utopia blinded.

CHAPTER TWO

The Liberal Panopticon

A MAN WALKS INTO A CASINO. As soon as he passes through the door, his image is captured by hidden cameras and compared, via an advanced biometric system, to a vast international database. Any resemblance to known cheaters or other undesirables at once alerts a team of security professionals. As he sits at the card table, his mannerisms are observed and recorded, analyzed for signs of stress or abnormality, his various feints and wagers compared to normal patterns of betting and play. At one point, all of this work would have been done manually, by pit bosses or by men standing on walkways above the gaming floor, armed with binoculars. Now, however, the gaming industry has become one of the great laboratories of electronic surveillance; indeed, the world's most advanced digital surveillance system is not to be found in Guantanamo Bay or Langley, Virginia, but Las Vegas.[1] *The goal is to gather and interpret information before cheating can take place; developments in "smart" surveillance hold forth the promise not only of observing the patron but of understanding him, anticipating his every move.*

In contrast to the vignette with which we began our introduction, this scenario is anything but a feverdream—though, again, many of its specific details are the product of Hollywood embellishment. In *Ocean's Thirteen*, to give only one of many recent examples, security at a fictional Las Vegas casino is handled by "Greco," an artificial-intelligence system that instantly analyzes body temperature, facial tics, heart rate, and so on in order to separate the honest gamblers from those up to no good. In point of fact, alas, the efficacy of casino surveillance lags far behind cinematic cliché; indeed, conversations with security experts in Las Vegas or Reno are inevitably punctuated with as many stories of embarrassing failure as success: the man whose suspicious glances turned out to be a nervous reluctance to look at the slot machine he was playing; the gambler whose dangerously erratic bets were actually the result of uncertainty about the rules of the game he was playing.[2] Nevertheless, the casino industry continues to pioneer "smart" systems designed to interpret the finer points of human demeanor—such as, perplexingly enough, the difference between "natural" conduct and conduct that is natural in a casino known to be full of cameras. Few surveillance professionals accept the common premise that knowledge of being observed eliminates erratic or dishonest behavior. Instead, they have learned that an awareness of cameras encourages casino patrons to behave like "casino patrons." The very act of entry is a moment of performative transformation; why, after all, go to Las Vegas if you're going to be your boring everyday self when you get there? When everybody is performing, however, it is exceedingly difficult to determine which performances are hiding illegality—especially when the activities *encouraged* by the management might well be considered sociopathic in the outside world. Far more than theft or debauchery, casino managers fear their patrons' premature return to ordinary fiscal responsibility.

We would suggest that the casino is a figure for the intricate and anarchic world of surveillance-related activities that took hold at the end of the seventeenth century and beginning of the eighteenth, as the allegorical order of English society disintegrated and numerous competing forms of control and evasion sprang up to take its place. Towards the close of the previous chapter, we indicated that the largest consequence of allegorical collapse was a dialectical struggle, at once material and spiritual, between observation and privacy—innovations in the one driving developments in the other, and the reverse, straight through to the present day. The two lines are not easily disentangled, nor do we intend to disentangle them. All the same, in the interest of clarifying the stakes in each history, the next chapter will concern itself largely with the "interior" narrative, the long genesis of the modern concept of privacy, while this one focuses more on externals, and the complex interrelations between observation and behavior. As the casino signifies, surveillance in the modern world comprises a multiplicity of activities and indeed entire systems, some of them coercive but many more of them participatory and connected even to pleasure. "Surveillir et punir" in Foucault's title are treated essentially as synonyms: the panoptic society he envisions is carceral. A casino, on the other hand, though panoptic, is clearly not a prison, nor do the (primarily economic) purposes of the establishment map in any simple way to systems of political oppression: we enter willingly, are encouraged to relax and abandon our usual moral self-policing, and are helped to do so by an environment explicitly bracketed from ordinary reality. Of course, those economic purposes may finally take a sinister turn—the ultimate goal of every casino being to transform "casino patrons" into casino patrons, i.e., persons who (pleasurably) spend each and every weekend blowing their salaries or pensions at the poker tables or dollar slots.

To put it another way: masks have a way of turning, in the fullness of time, into "true" faces—a fact, once again, that the eighteenth century was largely left to discover. As novelists like Defoe and Richardson, poets from Pope to Gray to Wordsworth, and philosophers following in the wake of Locke came to realize, the theory and practice of surveillance, and the unremitting pressure of social observation on the individual, finally had a profound impact on the nature of self, on the idea of personhood. It took the better part of a century fully to work out the consequences of this discovery, a process this chapter will trace through early theories of liberalism, early experiments in the novel, and with reference to modern and Enlightenment theories of social behavior. In this work of discovery, cultural forms like the novel and lyric poem, no less than the courts of law or halls of Parliament, were the engines and laboratories of change.

I. SENTIMENTALISM AND PERFORMANCE

> One can speak of the formation of a disciplinary society that stretches
> from the enclosed disciplines . . . to an indefinitely generalizable
> mechanism of "panopticism." . . . In [Bentham's panoptic principle]
> there was much more . . . than architectural ingenuity: it was an
> event in the "history of the human mind."
>
> —*Michel Foucault, Discipline and Punish*[3]

As we noted in our introduction, the first eighteenth-century figure one associates with surveillance is Jeremy Bentham, proponent of the panopticon and a man whose psychology of incarceration is widely taken to have marked a watershed moment in the history of human interiority.[4] In this view, Bentham's prison, with its abject inmates and unblinking observers, allowed the State to invade and rewrite the very structure of the human mind, where previously it could only exert crude pressure through physical violence. To recall Foucault's formulation, which we have already discussed, the prisoner's mind was now treated as "a surface for the inscription of power," with the final goal of creating an "obedient subject, [an] individual subjected to habits, rules, orders, an authority that [was] exercised continually around him and upon him, and which he must allow to function automatically *in* him" (101, 128–29; our italics). Indeed, the argument continues, in Bentham's prisons, the spread of discursive power, a process that had been under way for most of the eighteenth century, was suddenly made explicit and given overt spatial expression. The modern disciplinary State, made possible by the coupling of newly perfected human sciences with unremitting surveillance, found an early, concrete symbol in the Benthamite penitentiary.

So goes the standard account.[5] As we turn our attention, however, to surveillance practices in the immediate wake of social allegory, we would argue that though the panopticon's importance has not been understated, it has largely been misunderstood, and that Bentham, though certainly a key figure in the history of surveillance, has been made to stand for views that have little or nothing to do with his expressed positions. To read Bentham as a prophet of "internalization" and the modern surveillance State is anachronistic—and over the next few pages, we propose to address two consequent (and related) errors in the way eighteenth-century psychological and social thought is now received. The first is a tendency to read period texts, literary and otherwise, through lenses colored by powerful developments in post-structuralist or late-Marxist philosophy; the most influential interpreters, in this tradition, of Enlightenment Europe, from Foucault to Jürgen Habermas (his early work on the public sphere rather than his later engagement with communicative rationality) to Terry Eagleton, have tended to ignore, or simplify beyond recognition, highly complex thinking about interiority and the development of the self. The idea that eighteenth-century society was "disciplinary" is used to explain the behavior of characters ranging from Robinson Crusoe to Joseph Addison's intrepid man-about-town Mr. Spectator. Blessed with 20–20 hindsight, we commonly read works from the eighteenth century as parables of internalization and mono-directional social control, in ways that anticipate contemporary discourse theory.[6] And yet this position is thoroughly compromised by a typical passage from, say, Shaftesbury:

> There was a time when Men were accountable only for their
> Actions and Behaviour. . . . Every one took the Air and Look
> which was natural to him. But in process of time, it was thought
> decent to mend Mens Countenances, and render their
> intellectual Complexions uniform and of a sort. . . . Imagine
> now, what the Effect of this must needs be; when Men became
> persecuted thus on every side about their *Air* and *Feature*, and
> were put to their shifts how to adjust and compose their *Mein*,
> according to the right Mode; when a thousand Models, a
> thousand Patterns of Dress were current, and alter'd every now
> and then, upon occasion, according to *Fashion* and the Humour
> of the Times. Judg whether Mens Countenances were not like
> to grow constrain'd, and the natural Visage of Mankind, by this
> Habit, distorted, convuls'd, and render'd hardly knowable.[7]

In the manner of our own casino parable, Shaftesbury takes the relation between observation and interiority, or at least between social pressure and personal demeanor, to be dialectical: the more closely people are watched, the more they tend to perform according to the expectations of their viewers. As a result, the more individual behavior is perceived *as* performance, the greater the social anxiety about authenticity. Control of any situation, it follows, is inevitably complicated by the arts of impression management: a person must meet expectations but give no sign of calculation; his or her audience, in turn, must watch constantly for insincerity. Though the community exerts an influence on personal comportment, the individual, at any given moment, is at least as likely to be dictating terms. For reasons we will discuss presently, the modern theorists most helpful in understanding this triangle of observation, interiority, and behavior are not Foucault or Habermas, but rather twentieth-century Anglo-American sociologists like George Herbert Mead, David Riesman, and (especially) Erving Goffman, who analyzed the ways that self-aware, theatrical tactics influence and complicate the development of selfhood.[8] In Goffman's well-known statement of the case:

> In their capacity as performers, individuals will be concerned with maintaining the impression that they are living up to the many standards by which they and their products are judged. ... [As] performers, individuals are concerned not with the moral issue of realizing these standards but with the amoral issue of engineering a convincing impression that these standards are being realized.[9]

Goffman's favored term is "dramaturgy." The thought process that lies behind public actions takes into account social observation but is not controlled by it.

By their own admission, the Anglo-American sociologists were refining and updating Enlightenment thinking about selfhood, its nuanced understanding of human relations and the power of sympathy to shape complex behaviors.[10] Specifically, period thinking about *sentimentality*, both in the work of philosophers like Hume and Adam Smith and in the long, psychologically probing novels of the era, was an overt and acknowledged influence on the work of Goffman, Mead, and Riesman (and others).[11] Admittedly, Habermas's comment that during the early development of the bourgeois public sphere (that is, the period in question) "the innermost core of the private was always oriented towards an audience" seems to accord well with the dialectical view of social persona we are urging.[12] Ultimately, however, as we will have occasion to discuss at length in the next chapter, the particular tradition from which Habermas emerges forecloses on the possibility of taking seriously a personal autonomy that stands (at least partially) outside, and dynamically engages with, the pressures of public expectation; the individual is inevitably overwritten by the prevailing discourses of the era. As Habermas concludes, the individual in his or her most private moments is "only apparently set free from the constraint of society."[13]

Thus the second line of inquiry we intend to pursue: if we can correct the habit of reading Enlightenment texts as anticipatory of (a late twentieth-century) Bentham, might we not also reexamine Bentham himself and recover the way his panopticon writings are a product of their own century, the result of a new and distinctly post-allegorical way of thinking about personality? His concept of the relation between social observation and individual psychology was surely derived, at least in part, from the intellectual culture around him—and not only from philosophy. As it happens, he was a surprisingly avid reader of sentimental literature, with one author in particular standing out:

> When I got hold of a novel, I identified myself with all the
> personages, and thought more of their affairs than of any affairs
> of my own. I have wept for hours over Richardson's "Clarissa."[14]

Bentham the apostle of passionless objectivity is hardly visible in this remark or in his numerous other references to Richardson. He admits to his literary executor John Bowring that as a young man his "interest [in *Pamela*] became extreme. 'Clarissa' kept me day after day incessantly bathed in tears" (10:22). Rather than ask how Bentham (as he is presently understood) sheds light on Clarissa and her literary sisters, we might ask how Clarissa taught Bentham to understand everyday conduct. Could the man committed to the "suffocation of individuality," as one critic puts it, have been deeply affected by sentimentalism and its urbane understanding of sympathy?[15] Might the panopticon itself, and the theories of surveillance underlying it, be sympathetic and respectful of individual autonomy? We will address these questions later in the chapter; our initial focus, however, taking our cue from Bentham himself, will fall on two near contemporaries who, independently and in very different registers, grappled with self and social watching: Adam Smith and Samuel Richardson.

Social Theater

The Richardson text that matters most for us, ultimately, is *Pamela* (1740), his first novel—not because it is his weightiest achievement but because, as the first important epistolary novel in English, it presents his ideas in a more embryonic and uncertain state than in the longer and more intricate *Clarissa* (1748). Indeed, as we will discuss later, Richardson all but backed into his career as a novelist, his initial intention having been to furnish middle-class readers with models of letter-writing style. In its tentative way, the book reveals a surprisingly skeptical and resistant view of behavior under observation, a view that challenged dominant contemporary presumptions about surveillance and self. The two main characters—a servant and the young master, Mr. B., who spends most of the narrative laying siege to her virtue, before abruptly changing course and marrying her—are at all moments conscious of being observed and worry frequently about "the world's censure."[16] Far from being instinctively or unconsciously reactive, however, they imagine themselves as actors able to manipulate the narrative by which they are understood, and behave in certain ways to control how they are perceived. As Goffman might put it, Pamela and Mr. B. are players in an "information game," a

> potentially infinite cycle of concealment, discovery, false
> revelation, and rediscovery. It should be added that since the
> others are likely to be relatively unsuspicious of the presumably
> unguided aspect of the individual's conduct, he can gain much
> by controlling it. The others of course might sense that the
> individual is manipulating the presumably spontaneous aspects
> of his behavior, and seek in this very act of manipulation some
> shading of conduct that the individual has not managed to
> control.[17]

Not a bad description of Richardson's novel—but it's all too easy to see why so many of his early readers responded with shock at the apparent duplicity of his heroine.[18] Pamela's strategic behavior, slowly turning her would-be rapist into a trophy husband, is so pronounced that she was often scorned as a shrewd counterfeiter of emotion and her author accused of a kind of moral idiocy.[19] In *Shamela* (1741), by far the most famous such response, Henry Fielding parodies what he sees as Pamela's cynical performance of the "bashful virgin": "I left off at our sitting down to Supper on our Wedding Night, where I behaved with as much Bashfulness as the purest Virgin in the World could have done. The most difficult Task for me was to blush; however, by holding my Breath, and squeezing my Cheeks with my Handkerchief, I did pretty well."[20] Fielding, with an Augustan's acute awareness, but also distrust, of the performative, focuses his attack on the seeming moral independence of Pamela's physical mannerisms: her affectation of innocence becomes Shamela's "resolv[ing] not to smile" after a fight because "nothing can be more prudent in a Wife, than a sullen Backwardness to Reconciliation" (69).

Fielding's work is often judged to have revealed critical flaws in *Pamela* and indeed in sentimental literature generally—flaws that Richardson himself was forced to admit and which led him to try again with *Clarissa* (written, by happy coincidence, in the year of Bentham's birth). In the most general sense, this account is surely correct; all the same, in order to understand the *terms* of Richardson's response, greater historical specificity is necessary. To take a step back: in their views of character development, both Fielding and Richardson were influenced by the basic empiricist claim that the persistent observation of surface behavior, though profoundly flawed and unreliable, is nonetheless the best source of information about another person's "real," inner self. Their responses to this insight, however, were diametrically opposed, in historically contingent ways. Fielding's intellectual conservatism was essentially *anti-empiricist;* in the world of his novels, reliable old squires are named "Allworthy," Frenchified fops "Didapper," and (naturally) feigning maidens "Shamela." In short, we should by now recognize Fielding's insistence that surface equal depth as a late expression of the allegorical sensibility—or at the very least as the expression of a nostalgia for a time when social allegory of this sort was still possible.[21] When Fielding levels his main charge—inauthenticity—at Pamela, he means that her public role, the virtuous maiden, is at variance with her behavior; the social allegory has been disrupted by the heroine's hypocrisy.

Richardson's view of character, on the other hand, more willingly takes its cues from Locke and Berkeley. In response to empiricism's basic point—that steady observation is our first source of knowledge—it takes precious little insight to gauge the importance of impression management; reality, before long, becomes less a matter of ontological fact than something *made* and then broadly consented to—in short, an information game. In *The Theory of Moral Sentiments* (1759), which appeared little more than a decade after *Clarissa*, we can see Smith working through these problems in the abstract. Beginning with the Lockean (and Humean) premise that because "our senses . . . never carry us beyond our own person," we therefore "have no immediate impression of what other men feel," Smith identifies our imaginative capacity for *sympathy* as the root of all social interaction: "we place ourselves in [the other's] situation . . . changing places in fancy with [him]."[22] This act of identification, in turn, has the perhaps ironic consequence of creating within us a detachment about our *own* behavior:

> As [the observers] are continually placing themselves in [the person under observation's] situation, and thence conceiving emotions similar to what he feels; so he is as constantly placing himself in theirs, and thence conceiving some degree of that coolness about his own fortune, with which he is sensible that they will view it. . . . He is constantly led to imagine in what manner he would be affected if he was only one of the spectators of his own situation . . . [and begins] to view his situation in [a] candid and impartial light. (27–28)

With this "coolness" and impartiality, Smith concludes, we become "masters of ourselves," shaping our own behavior to fit "the particular company we are in" (28). And thus one can observe a process of historical return in the work of writers like Goffman and Mead. In the Anglo-American tradition the purest philosophical expression of this vein of post-empiricism, in which behavior is instrumental and truth is something made, is pragmatism; indeed, the twentieth-century sociologists were consciously extending basic pragmatic insights into the study of culture.[23] It should come as no surprise, however, that a nascently pragmatic testing of empirical claims should have begun almost at once, in the Georgian period; nor, it follows, should the echo of that initial testing in modern sociology be much of a shock. In contrast to the Foucauldian analysis of eighteenth-century culture, in which distinctly modern ideas about discourse and power are applied retroactively to a foreign set of phenomena, Anglo-American sociology, which privileges individual initiative over the power of society, is the natural descendant of sentimentalism and its belief in self-creation.

In the gap between *Pamela* and *Clarissa*, we can witness a growing consciousness on Richardson's part of the complexity of his sentimentalist project, his work of pragmatic testing. When Fielding opened fire with *Shamela*, branding Richardson's first heroine, and by extension Richardson himself, a hypocrite, one can imagine that the charge hit home—Richardson suddenly being confronted, as it were, with his own great subject.[24] Though Fielding's position was profoundly reactionary and based on an outmoded idea of authentic persona that had no appeal to Richardson, *authenticity itself*, and its treacherous relation to person-ality, was now revealed as a problem, perhaps *the* problem of the age. On practically every page of *Clarissa* Richardson asks—now fully aware that he is doing so—what authentic character might mean. Is it something inherent—and if so, can it be observable, or does it lie hidden away from all eyes but God's? Or is it, rather, a matter of performance and consensus? Is personality inborn, or does it grow? If the latter, does it grow in solitude or in the back-and-forth of social interaction? Can mature character be predicted, and will it hold in extreme circumstances or under great stress? Stung by his readers' critiques, Richardson expressed exasperation at a "worse than skeptical age," determined to doubt his characters; as his follow-up novel made clear, social theater is not *necessarily* cynical.[25] The sentimental novel acknowledged that the public *display* of personality was quite possibly a necessary step towards the *development* of personality. To focus on Clarissa's performative behavior, therefore, is not to discount her individuality or "reality" as a character; the danger, instead, lies in assuming a too clear-cut dichotomy between social role and self. *Clarissa* complicates the view of observed behavior that Fielding satirized, and in a way that perhaps explains Bentham's move from "extreme interest" (his reaction to *Pamela*) to incessant tears. If Richardson had been alarmed by the response to *Pamela*, we would suggest that one result was his energetic investigation in *Clarissa* of the ways that behavior is both deliberately executed *and* authentic—and of the moral and personal consequences of this blurring.

There is a temptation in discussing Richardson to read his work as postmodern more than two hundred years before the fact, the idea of authentic selfhood (and reality itself) disappearing down the rabbit hole of discourse. And to be sure, the novel sometimes seems uncannily avant-garde in its gestures: Clarissa is naturally dramatic, perhaps, because she grew up partly in a simulacrum—her nouveau-riche grandfather's "Dairy-House," in which she played at being a commoner—which introduced her early to the advantages of (literally) constructing an artificial public façade. In doing so, she certainly participates in the novel's own reflexivity about action and selfhood.[26] To follow this line of speculation too far, however, is to miss the age-specific complexity of Richardson's engage-ment with the authenticity question. Once again, Goffman provides a terminology to describe what's at stake:

> Ordinarily the definitions of the situation projected by several different participants are sufficiently attuned to one another so that open contradiction will not occur. I do not mean that there will be the kind of consensus that arises when each individual present candidly expresses what he really feels and honestly agrees with the expressed feelings of the others present. This kind of harmony is an optimistic ideal and in any case not necessary for the smooth working of society. Rather, each participant is expected to suppress his immediate heartfelt feelings, conveying a view of the situation which he feels the others will be able to find at least temporarily acceptable. (9)

Even under the best circumstances, consensus is underscored by discontent. Though reality is an artificial projection commonly agreed on, the projection is unlikely to satisfy any one participant fully, and complete harmony is but an "optimistic ideal." Yet where Goffman (pragmatically) cuts his losses (full happiness of all participants is not necessary for society to work), Richardson belonged to an age more likely to worry the issue. In contrast to *Pamela, Clarissa* is notable less for its view of behavior as performative than for the strenuousness with which it tests this view. What happens, *Clarissa* asks, when the projected realities of the protagonists are not merely dissonant, but incompatible—when consensus cannot be realized? When a "rake" and "paragon" are set on a collision course, does a performative reality survive, or does something break? Under the duress of physical assault, does something of the essential self emerge from behind the mask, or does selfhood, having in fact *become* the mask, crumble? Can life still be understood as theater when staged personae come up against brute force—and once this kind of violation has occurred, what is left for a genre, indeed an ethos, premised on natural theatricality?

The results are ambiguous. Lovelace's infamous revelation of his scheme—"the haughty Beauty will not refuse me, when her pride of being corporally inviolate is brought down" (5:283)—might be read as a simple admission of evil or an act of violent desperation; but this misses the way Richardson's characters are themselves entangled in the labyrinth of their own dramaturgy. Lovelace—more than anyone alert to Clarissa's tactics ("Who says, Miss Clarissa Harlowe is the Paragon of

Virtue? . . . Has her Virtue ever been *proved?*—Who has dared to try her Virtue?" [3:80])—seems to conclude that the only way to challenge a performance of virtue is through plain physicality: to remove the physical proof of virtue (through sexual assault) and thus cause Clarissa to drop as futile the mask of chastity. Yet just as Clarissa's performance perhaps creates actual virtue, so Lovelace's strategy has the commensurate effect of transforming staged amorality into real evil. It is on this question of real versus performed ethics, in any case, that the twentieth-century sociologist and eighteenth-century novelist part ways. Goffman is anything but an amoralist when it comes to action; nevertheless, his moral views would be profoundly disturbing to an earlier religious sensibility like Richardson's. Reality, for Goffman, is finally instrumental, a gentlemen's agreement; if getting on in society is a matter of consensus, it is unethical to break form.

> Society is organized on the principle that any individual who possesses certain social characteristics has a moral right to expect that others will value and treat him in an appropriate way. Connected with this principle is a second, namely that an individual who implicitly or explicitly signifies that he has certain social characteristics ought in fact to be what he claims he is. . . . Since the sources of impression used by the observing individual involve a multitude of standards pertaining to politeness and decorum, . . . we can appreciate afresh how daily life is enmeshed in moral lines of discrimination. (13, 250)

It is a conclusion that replaces God with society as the source and judge of proper behavior—a conclusion that, in very different ways, neither the humanist Smith nor the polemically Christian Richardson would ever find satisfying; and yet, disturbingly, it was a natural consequence of each author's post-empirical position.[27]

Thus the unsettled quality of the novel's ending. On the one hand, Clarissa's quasi-suicide can be read as a final affirmation of impression management. In this view, Lovelace underestimates the power of performance, or in any case Clarissa's commitment to performance as self-construction. Her reaction to the rape is to starve herself to death—and in doing so, she chooses a new type of public display (though now of shame rather than chastity), which affects her body more violently than

Lovelace could. Even critics determined to defend Clarissa from charges of hypocrisy recognize the final turn as transforming a private body into the ultimate public stage: those around her are forced to witness her withering away.[28] Virtue, in a manner of speaking, "wins," even as dramaturgy is overtly acknowledged as a necessary condition of modern life. He or she who assumes a role most effectively and convincingly gains power over the surrounding narrative (of the book as well as the life), even if the power gained is self-annihilating. And yet something in this conclusion rankles, seems implausible. Contrarily, we might recognize Richardson's sensitivity to the way that social posturing, wearing masks, is a necessity in which we all engage to control the public meaning of our lives. It is also, however, something that, in extremis, must be surrendered. For Richardson the moralist, this is the way of the world, and the novel necessarily ends with Clarissa's death, the moment when she can finally surrender her mask, confident in the knowledge that the only adequate judge of true personhood is God. For all practical purposes, the inner self, the purported target of observation, is as inaccessible as it ever was.

II. LIBERAL-CONTRACTUAL CULTURE

> To doubt everything or to believe everything are two equally convenient solutions; both dispense with the need for thought.
> —Henri Poincaré, Science and Hypothesis[29]

Instrumental Agreements

Pamela and *Clarissa* give a pretty good idea of the tangled and ambiguous relations between surveillance and selfhood, observation and behavior, during the mid-eighteenth century. To understand fully, however, the vast array of positions on surveillance staked out at this time, we must move further back in the period, to the years when allegorical culture was giving way to something new. An underlying argument of our previous chapter was that *allegory*, understood as a mode, involved certain habits of thought and ways of organizing reality that, while certainly visible in aesthetic production, could also be seen operating in the politics and social structures of the early modern era. Similarities between the aesthetic and the political could not be understood simply as otherwise unrelated emanations of something else—a Zeitgeist, as it were—nor was the relation between the two one-way. Rather, allegorical thinking with profound consequences for politics was first conducted in literary representation— and vice versa. Though it has perhaps been harder to see, not least because its effects have been far more various, we would propose that a similar modal energy has permeated and connected the political, artistic, and social dynamics of the dispensation that has followed allegory—the dispensation, for all intents and purposes, under which we still subsist. The name we would give this modality is the *contract*—or, if that term is too laden with historical baggage, the perhaps more accurate *instrumental agreement*, an expression to which we have already had some recourse.

That various stripes of contractarian thinking were in the air during the seventeenth and eighteenth centuries will astonish precisely no one who has spent any time with the political writing of the era—either British writers or the long line of Continental jurists and philosophers stretching from Grotius and Pufendorf to Rousseau and Kant. This legal and political tradition is but a subset, however, of the vast field of bargaining activities between rivals, ranging from informal or tacit deals to official written covenants, that defined the period, and which we are using the term *contract* or *instrumental agreement* to denote. It is not surprising, perhaps, that the first great contract theorist in England could imagine no better *use* for the contract than the restitution of social allegory after its final disintegration during the English Civil War. The view of human nature Hobbes offers in *Leviathan* (1651) is precisely the nightmare that Shakespeare had anticipated at the end of *The Tempest*. Hobbes takes it for granted that since "Nature hath made men . . . equal in the faculties of body and mind" (this equality newly relevant due to shifting social hierarchies), men are also naturally competitive. This competition turns us all into Antonios and Sebastians (and post-exile Prosperos) and leads inevitably to a *bellum omnium contra omnes:* "without a common Power to keep them all in awe, [men] are in that condition which is called Warre, and such a warre, as is of every man against every man."[30] Where Swift would later see the removal of God's eye (manifested in the absolute monarch) from the body politic as producing intellectual and spiritual disorder, Hobbes predicted anarchy itself—a not unreasonable fear given the times in which he lived. His solution was, in his own terms, to make a "Mortall

God" (227)—that is, reinstitute absolutism on purely secular terms through a contractual agreement on the part of the citizenry to exchange most of their liberties for security. His description of the commonwealth as an "artificiall man" (81) explicitly evoked Elizabeth's claim to have "two bodies," one natural, one comprising the entirety of the nation. The metaphor is even clearer in the frontispiece to *Leviathan* (figure 2), which depicts the State as a single man comprised of countless smaller persons.

Hobbes's influence on subsequent political theory is indisputable, though the extent of his sway over Locke's *Second Treatise of Government* has attracted especially lively debate.[31] Again, however, we would argue that the political tradition from Hobbes to Rousseau and Kant represents only the more formalized strand of contractual thinking that characterized the period. In the absence of a final, legitimizing authority on earth, *everything* was up for grabs and had to be concurred on; the nature of reality itself, as a particularly awkward passage in Locke's *Essay Concerning Human Understanding* makes clear, was little more than an instrumental

Figure 2. Abraham Bosse, frontispiece to Hobbes's *Leviathan* (cropped), 1651.

agreement. Taking up the question of perception, Locke asks whether it can be proven that an individual's experience of the world matches that of any other person. Who is to say (his example) that the color you call *blue* is not what I have been calling *yellow* my whole life? Locke's answer is essentially to shrug his shoulders: since communication is not affected by this problem (when you say "blue" I understand you, whether or not we share the same percept), "we need not trouble ourselves to examine it."[32] Locke's seemingly cavalier attitude towards a fundamental question of epistemology has caused no small discomfort among his staunchest defenders and has given his critics ample ammunition to judge him inferior to subsequent empiricists like Berkeley and (especially) Hume, whose skepticism about the relation between perception and knowledge was, on the face of things, far more rigorous.[33] And yet there is a certain magnificence to Locke's gesture, in which pure philosophy willingly sacrifices itself for something larger. Indeed, it is characteristic of Locke to push a question just to the point where it ceases to be useful ("for the improvement of our knowledge or conveniency of life")—and no further. To insist on the very real difficulties posed by the "blue" problem, Locke recognizes, would mean either falling into the abyss of pure doubt (as Hume would later do) or rebounding into some form of unquestioned dogma—both options ultimately dispensing with the need for thought. The fundamental insight of Locke's empiricism, it might therefore be said, is not epistemological but pragmatic; not that the mind before experience is a blank slate, or that all knowledge comes to us through the senses, but that, when faced with twin perils of nihilism and unquestioning belief, the epistemology he offers is the best conceivable. We *agree*, as it were, that all knowledge comes to us through the senses and that the mind before experience is a blank slate, so as not to slip back into absolutism or forward into anarchy.

The contractual mode, as we are describing it, was active in both political history and the history of literary representation. As theorists of the novel from Georg Lukács and Ian Watt to Michael McKeon have long recognized, the most modern of literary genres "arose" at roughly this moment, its canons of realism closely tied to the empirical revolution.[34] Indeed, we would take the argument a step or two further: the logic underlying "formal realism," as Watt famously dubbed it, was every bit as instrumental as the basis of empiricism itself; realistic conventions were less a way of accurately representing the world than expressive of a tacit understanding between authors and readers about how the world *should be represented*. Unfortunately, as our reading of *Pamela* and *Clarissa* has perhaps begun to indicate, this covenant was particularly susceptible to infringement and bad faith; the history of the novel is a series of author-reader agreements forged, broken, reforged, and broken again. Before we dive into this history, however, we must clarify the broader social implications of the new modality. Locke's "blue" problem (and his epistemology in general) has an ideological shading related to, but not quite congruent with, his best-known political writings. We paired the terms "anarchy" and "absolutism" on purpose: as the subsequent history of empiricism would make all too clear, utter skepticism, far from being the opposite of unquestioning belief, was rather its support and enabler. Beginning with Hume, but continuing into the present, intellectual nihilism has frequently been the justification and prop of an absolutist (or at the very least reactionary) politics.[35] Always testing the limits of useful knowledge, always self-questioning, the path charted by Locke—let's call it liberalism—offered a middle way between pure belief and pure doubt, though its vulnerabilities to attacks from both sides were readily apparent from the start.

A Little Theory of Liberalism

Nearly every serious account of liberalism is also a eulogy for it. In this respect, the political tradition descending from Locke must be unique. From Mill's *On Liberty*, through the work of twentieth-century figures like L. T. Hobhouse and Isaiah Berlin, to the more explicitly funereal diatribes of contemporary analysts, liberalism is typically figured as dying, dead, or perhaps a still-warm corpse, and the author's work presented as an exercise in retrospection: *what was liberalism, and how did we let it give way to X* (X being the corporate State, a resurgent conservatism, atomization, socialism, etc.)?[36] In part, this malaise indicates a genuine fragility in the tradition. At the same time, it surely reflects an ambiguity, traceable back to Locke himself, about what fundamentally constitutes liberalism as a political philosophy: is it rights centered or liberties centered? How does it imagine the relation between the State and the individual: as protective, inimical, or indifferent? What, forgetting the State for the moment, does it signify by the term *individual*, anyway? Something autonomous (whatever that might mean) or socially implicated? Any circus that features such disparate acts as Mill and F. A. Hayek, John Rawls and Ronald Dworkin must have an immeasurably large tent—must exist as an immeasurably "large tendency," as Trilling put it.[37] Given such circumstances, it is all too convenient to cherry-pick some aspect of the tradition, declare it to be central and thus (not uncommonly) doomed. We do not have the space to offer a full-dress account of these problems, nor have we much interest in doomsaying. Nevertheless, we do believe that some aspects of liberalism are unavoidably important—and often selectively ignored.

We would insist, for example, that liberalism begins in violence and bears the scars of violence even in its most abstract and idealistic iterations. It begins in the same circumstances that produced *Leviathan:* the political turmoil of civil war and the ideological chaos of collapsed (or collapsing) social allegory. For this reason, we would suggest that theorists who locate the essence of Locke's political thought in the *Second Treatise of Government* are joining the discussion too late. By the time he writes that work (likely 1680–81), the crucible in which his fundamental ideas were forged has already cooled; indeed, as Richard Ashcraft was probably the first to argue convincingly, the *Second Treatise* was a partisan document in a subsequent life-or-death political struggle and as such (we would add) contains emphases and deflections that ultimately obscure his foundational insights about society and self.[38] Locke's theory of rights and his contractarianism itself (as put forward in the *Second Treatise*) may finally be back-formations: means towards practical ends that were clearer at the start of his career.

To this end, we would nominate as the urtext of Lockean liberalism his *Essay on Toleration* (1667)—not, that is, the far better-known *Letter Concerning Toleration* (1689), which is a product of his triumphant late period, but a relatively obscure piece he wrote shortly after joining the retinue of Lord Ashley (later the first Earl of Shaftesbury) and the first to bear the traces of his employer's radicalism. As is commonly known, Locke had a conservative upbringing, which accrued to him for much of his early life. His papers preserve, for example, a poem very much in the mode of Dryden, celebrating the 1660 restoration of Charles II:

> Kings always are the gifts of Heaven, but you
> Are not its gift alone, but transcript too;
> Your virtues match its stars, which you disclose
> To th' world, as bright, and numberless as those.
> Your motions all as regular, which dispence
> A warmth to all, and quickning influence.[39]

Locke the great opponent of divine right monarchy is nowhere to be found in these lines—quite the opposite—and yet he can perhaps be forgiven his youthful toadyism and hackneyed royalist language. In the wake of civil war and the tumultuous end of the Protectorate, the king's "regular . . . motions" promise a much-desired civil stability. By the time we get to the *Essay on Toleration*, Locke's sympathies and prescriptions have shifted, but the terror of national upheaval is still a vivid memory and the revival of hostilities an abiding fear. It is this apprehension, perhaps, that gives the *Essay* its strikingly dour cast. Unlike the later *Letter*, which couches its argument for toleration in the language of natural rights, the *Essay* more typically presents its case as a matter of security: compulsion never changes people's minds but rather makes them unhappy; unhappy people become restive; large numbers of restive people are dangerous. Therefore the "magistrate ought to . . . meddle with nothing but barely in order to securing the civil peace and [property] of his subjects."[40]

In this manner, Locke exposes the roots of toleration in aggression. That is to say: we tolerate only people or beliefs of which we do not *approve* but cannot justify attacking or destroying. In the pithy reduction of one critic, "toleration is only required for what seems intolerable."[41] To be sure, less sinister interpretations of the topic are possible. In a recent essay, Slavoj Žižek has traced the origins of the European tolerationist tradition to the Thirty Years' War, a period when the brutal conflict between Protestants and Catholics forced right-minded persons from both sides to view their own lifeworlds as contingent and thus to entertain the thought of peaceful coexistence with their erstwhile enemies.[42] Locke himself, we know, was deeply impressed by the relative ease with which people of different faiths got along in the Brandenburg capital of Cleves— an experience that was later echoed (to a lesser degree) during his years of exile in Holland; something of this high-mindedness does indeed find its way into the 1689 *Letter*.[43] In the 1667 *Essay*, however, his approach is unsentimental—the English Civil War having had no leavening effect on his suspicion of political or religious blocs: "Most men, at least factions of men, when they have power sufficient, make use of it, right or wrong, for their own advantage and establishment of themselves in authority, few men forbearing to grasp at dominion that have the power to seize and hold it" (*Essay*, 147).

It is this dim view of humanity, so near, it would seem, to Hobbes's, that explains ultimately why surveillance is a pervasive theme in Locke's early work, whereas it vanishes in his better-known later writings. "When men [adopt] a stricter confederacy with those of their own denomination and party than other [of] their fellow subjects," Locke reasons, the more they should be "suspected and the more heedfully . . . watched." Should they at last "*visibly* . . . threaten the peace of the State," the magistrate shouldn't hesitate to "lessen, break, and suppress [them]" (*Essay*, 147; our emphasis). As late as 1679, Locke was half-seriously toying with a utopian scheme overtly influenced by More and Bacon. Or perhaps we should say half-influenced: Locke's "Atlantis" papers envision a nearly pure surveillance state, with few of More's perceived benefits but plenty of security.

> Every ten neighboring houses shall have a tithingman who shall inform the judge of the colony in writing of the faults or suspected course of life of anyone living in his tithing. . . . If [a citizen's] manner of life shall be such as [the judge] finds suspicious, he shall [set a watch over him] or else commit him to some public workhouse. . . . Every man being a watch upon his neighbour, faults will be prevented, which is better than that they should be punished.[44]

It almost beggars belief that the Locke of the *Second Treatise* was just around the corner when he wrote these lines so suggestive of contemporary surveillance—from the Stasi to the gulag—at its most coercive and paranoid. A natural place to look for Orwellian precedents—and yet it's the 1667 *Essay*, finally, that shows Locke's thinking about observation and control at its most subtle. Toleration, he concludes, does not merely *prevent* subversion from happening: administered wisely, it can also *expose* existing unrest. Practically speaking, he reasons, "whispering" is far more dangerous and likely to "foment a conspiracy" than open dissent.[45] It therefore behooves the magistrate not to drive dissenters into secrecy but rather to use "gentler remedies"; "factions," in short, "are best secured by toleration" (150, 157). Locke's insight (which he never again takes up explicitly), that the seemingly benign forces of an open society are in fact more conducive to control and monitoring than outright repression, is the moment in his work *most* anticipatory of the course surveillance theory took over the next three centuries.

For the purposes of articulating a comprehensive political theory, the early Locke is at once more realistic and less grounded than Hobbes had been. Hobbes's vision of a war of all versus all is terrifying (and memorable) and probably the inevitable way a late Renaissance mind would imagine the aftermath of exploded allegory. In the end, however, his predictions are also rather implausible. As the experience of collapsed states has shown time and again, pure, literal anarchy ("no leader") of the sort evoked by Hobbes's catchphrase rarely if ever happens—and if it *did* happen could hardly be the deadly threat Hobbes had imagined. Roving gangs, organized mobs, and local warlords, on the other hand, are relatively common and legitimately dangerous—and Locke, we notice, shifts his unit of analysis from the atomized individual to the group, the *faction*. With the experience of the civil war before him, Locke understands that while individuals by themselves are usually powerless, the natural tendency of splinter groups, when they become large enough, is to undermine the State (or, if they can manage it, *become* the State, which is quite possibly worse). When it comes, however, to moving beyond the practical insights of the 1667 *Essay* and extrapolating from his basic tolerationist insights to a more abstract and applicable political theory, Locke finds himself at an impasse: it is far easier to talk in the abstract about the relation between the State and the individual than between the State and various subgroups.[46] The problem continues to haunt writers from Montesquieu to Madison: can factions be said to have rights—or "natural rights," for that matter? How should a State be organized, precisely, if its most significant subunits are fluctuating and unstable political or religious aggregations?[47] It is our contention that Locke's perception about toleration—about the *need* for toleration as a precondition for a stable society organized around formal and informal contracts—*precedes* his theory of rights, precedes his (explicit) contractarianism in the *Second Treatise*, and precedes even his epistemology; that it, indeed, may be understood as the *motive* for all of them. As presented in the 1667 *Essay*, unfortunately, it is useless for all practical applications; contrarily, the model offered by Hobbes in *Leviathan*, in which the key elements are the State and the individual, however preposterous in many ways it may be, *does* make possible broader claims about natural law, natural rights, and the organization of society by covenants. While we would suggest, therefore, that it is incorrect to locate the wellsprings of Lockean liberalism in the key works of his last two decades (the *Treatises*, the *Letter Concerning Toleration*), it is certainly the case that Locke returned to Hobbesian ideas of the social contract (via Grotius and Pufendorf) in order to make his liberalism work.

Whether he succeeded or not is another question. In addition to the overtly fictive aspects of the *Second Treatise* (both his conception of the State of Nature and his premise of an original social contract have been criticized over and over again as fanciful inventions), Locke gives little indication of how a State composed of autonomous individuals might emerge from the still highly authoritarian and factionalized politics of his own day.[48] In the 1667 *Essay*, on the other hand, he *had* floated a fascinating suggestion about how this could happen. If repression, he reasoned, caused people to band together, a regimen of toleration might have the opposite effect: infinite fragmentation, turning each person, in a manner of speaking, into a party of one.[49] A highly Protestant fantasy, it is worth pointing out, and one that helps explain his hostility (and intolerance) in 1667 towards Catholics (who, sharing a common loyalty to the pope, were unlikely to splinter). When, in the 1689 *Letter*, he revisited the subject of toleration, presenting the problem as one of individual freedoms, that hostility had largely vanished. Be that as it may, Locke's key failure, for our purposes, was terminological. Suppose that we accept, for example, that a liberal society is composed of compacts between autonomous individuals. Well, what precisely is an "individual"—and (in the unlikely event that we can answer that question adequately) in what sense can an individual be understood as autonomous? Given, moreover, that autonomous individuals cannot be expected to agree on anything, how can we presume that the ground rules for society, its instrumental agreements, will be anything but contingent or provisional?

As generations of scandalized commentators have pointed out, Locke's answers to these questions can be described kindly as casual, and less charitably as vague to the point of muddled. In *Leviathan* Hobbes had gone to great lengths to ground his political philosophy in a scientific account of human nature: the opening chapters of book 1 offer a mechanistic view of the human animal, drawn from the physical science of the day, as a support for the equally mechanistic politics that follows.[50] Locke in the *Treatises* makes no such effort—nor, ultimately, do his attempts to define the "self" or the "individual" achieve much clarity in the work purportedly devoted to answering those questions, the *Essay Concerning Human Understanding*. In a notably funny bit of circular reasoning Locke states, with great confidence, that "when we . . . inquire what makes the same spirit, man, or person, we must fix the ideas of spirit, man, or person in our minds; and having resolved with ourselves what we mean by them, it will not be hard to determine, in either of them, or the like, when it is the same, and when not." *Not hard*, perhaps—but then Locke drops the topic altogether, concluding the section with a confession of ignorance:

> [We are ignorant] of that thinking thing that is within us, and which we look on as ourselves. Did we know what it was, or how it was tied to a certain system of fleeting animal spirits [i.e., the body]; or whether it could or could not perform its operations out of a body organized as ours is; and whether it has pleased God that no one such spirit shall ever be united to any but one such body [my suppositions might be criticized as absurd]. But taking, as we ordinarily now do (in the dark concerning these matters), the soul of man for an immaterial substance, independent from matter, and indifferent alike to it all, there can from the nature of things be no absurdity at all to suppose that the same soul may, at different times, be united to different bodies, and with them make up, for that time one man.[51]

Leaving aside the science-fiction elements (of which the entire section, "Of Identity and Diversity," is rife), the most striking aspect of this passage is Locke's palpable shrug of the shoulders when confronted with a question he believes beyond answering—a gesture we have seen before—and his referring of final authority to God. His treatment of the "blue problem" indeed concludes with a similar tactic: "Blue or yellow . . . can never be false ideas, these perceptions . . . answering the powers appointed by God to produce them; and so are truly what they are, and are intended to be" (II.32.16). Apparently it is not the way of the Creator to deceive His creations; He is, however, seemingly available as an all-purpose get-out-of-jail-free pass whenever Locke's philosophy reaches a point of contradiction or crisis of knowledge.

These little moments of vagueness/testaments of faith have long-term consequences for our larger topic: the history of surveillance, the tribulations of liberalism, and the development of literature over the next few centuries, can be predicted from the silences in Locke's later output. We might put it this way: while Locke lays out the pieces for a liberal, secular society (it requires autonomous individuals; it requires agreements between those individuals; toleration is a necessary substratum for those agreements to work; etc.), he never quite defines any of those terms adequately, deflecting all ambiguities to God—his own work remaining, that is to say, theistically grounded (or perhaps tethered). Several consequences follow. First, it takes a long time for the questions Locke leaves unanswered to be answered. Indeed, we have already seen Richardson wrestling with some of them, with only partial success. What is a self, and in what way might it be understood as autonomous? Richardson's apparent answer at the end of *Clarissa*—our ultimate value as discrete selves is as objects before God—is every bit as theistic (and indeterminate) as Locke's had been. But to this we might add: given the *opacity* of the self, how are we to understand other people—and to what extent can we *violate* their outer defenses to reveal whatever lies inside? This last question, as we will see shortly, was at least as practical as theoretical.

By using the deity as an ultimate point of reference, finally, Locke was guilty of a profound historical irony. The liberal-contractual tradition continues to be haunted by this tactic—or rather, has been haunted by the specter Locke's methods unleashed: no less formidable a foe than the ghost of allegory. An unlikely consequence of a career spent demolishing the last vestiges of allegorical thinking in English politics. The *First Treatise of Government*, in particular, had been a systematic dismantling of Sir Robert Filmer's argument for a patriarchal state, just as the *Second Treatise* had attempted to reconstruct the commonwealth on rational, secular grounds. This disconnection of the divine, however, from any formal presence (in the person of the king) in the body politic created an inevitable crisis of authority. This had not been the case, we note, in

Locke's 1667 *Essay*, still heavily influenced by his early authoritarian tendencies, in which toleration was finally guaranteed by a "magistrate" or "judge" ready and able to provide stability when necessary and granted broad powers of surveillance. With the diminishing of this figure, however, Locke could provide no guarantees for the durability of his system—beyond frequent recourse to God, now (as would later be the case with Swift, in a very different register) a shadowy presence with no representative in earthly politics. Thus, Locke simply had to *insist*. "The same law of nature," for example, that gives "us property, does also bound the property":

> "God has given us all things richly" (I *Timothy* 6:17) is the voice of reason confirmed by inspiration. But how far has he given it us? "To enjoy." As much as anyone can make use of to any advantage of life before it spoils. . . . Whatever is beyond this is no more than his share, and belongs to others. Nothing was made by God for man to spoil or destroy. (*Second Treatise*, par. 31)[52]

And if my idea of a fair share "to enjoy" differs from yours, indeed seems to you covetous and unwarranted? Locke has no answer. Though "the law of nature stands as an eternal rule to all men, legislators as well as others," and human laws must "be conformable to the law of nature, i.e. to the will of God," that law is finally "unwritten, and nowhere to be found but in the minds of men," who are apt to disagree about what it contains, or at very least "misapply it" (*Second Treatise*, pars. 135–36). The contours of these rules are hardly, as a Lockean of a later generation would put it, "self-evident."[53]

Of the numerous commentators who have addressed this "failure" in Locke, Ian Shapiro probably puts it best: Locke "had ultimately to rest on the leap of faith that we perceive God's intentions as rational imperatives because He has constituted us so as to perceive them, a position unavailable to the liberal establishment that subsequently appropriated his doctrine."[54] And what is this leap of faith, or rather this *insistence*, finally, but the old allegorical Will to Power reappearing in the last place one would look for it: in the articulation of liberties and the exposition of a secular, nascently democratic government? Perhaps it is the case that any assertion of a politics short of anarchy begins with such a statement of faith and assertion of power. In any case, the old allegorical Will to Power slowly reasserted itself, but with this difference: where allegorical forms of thinking and organizing reality had been an overt presence in the politics and aesthetics of Tudor-Stuart England, they now played a more covert role in a liberal-contractual dispensation purportedly hostile to allegorical premises. Or at least that's how things stood at the turn of the eighteenth century. The years that followed witnessed the unfolding of a particularly bitter and ironic dialectic: as the terms of Locke's liberalism were slowly secularized, an allegorical tendency in certain social and aesthetic structures became more and more pronounced. The loss of God as a transcendental explanation and verifier necessitated the institution of more concrete ideological measures—which inevitably, perhaps, came to resemble the energies of the old, discredited mode. Be that as it may, the success or failure of surveillance practices, through the twentieth century, could often be measured by the extent to which they were infiltrated by allegorical ways of thinking. As during the Renaissance, these ways of thinking and the forms they produced (political forms, but also aesthetic representations) received their most sophisticated development in literature—the *first* place, perhaps, that one would think to look.

III. OBSERVATION AND THE NOVEL

> The individual tends to treat others present on the basis of the impression they give now about the past and the future. It is here that communicative acts are translated into moral ones. The impressions that the others give tend to be treated as claims and promises that they implicitly made, and claims and promises tend to have a moral character.
>
> —*Goffman, The Presentation of Self in Everyday Life, 249*

Can the novel fruitfully be understood as the product of a contractual relation between an author and his or her readers? What would such an instrumental agreement look like? Adam Smith, expounding on his theory of sympathy, has perhaps already offered a clue: "As we have no immediate experience of what other men feel, . . . it is by the imagination only that we can form any conception of what are his sensations" (*Theory of Moral Sentiments*, 11). A simple enough point but no less important for being so: the novel promises its readers the truth about other people. And what do readers offer in return? Money, surely—the novel having been, unlike some of the more rarified genres, an economic enterprise from the start—but also something more elusive: credence. As instrumental agreements go, this one might seem particularly fragile or illogical, as indeed it is: the history of the novel wouldn't be half so interesting if the pact was sound. Our account of the contract, moreover, might seem painfully obvious or reductive—but that is only because at this late date it is hard to appreciate how exotic a promise *the truth about other people* must have seemed at the start of the eighteenth century. It is not, for example, a high priority in the (often didactic and conventional) literature of the period immediately preceding the rise of the novel, and for the great allegorists of a still earlier moment, the truth about other people would have meant, simply, what other people self-evidently *were:* if you spend too much time thinking about the interiority of "Duessa" or "Mrs. Inconsiderate," you're likely missing more fruitful ways to read *The Faerie Queene* and *Pilgrim's Progress.* It does not underestimate, finally, the intense inwardness of pietist writers like George Herbert or the later Donne to suggest that the ideas of selfhood explored in the novel differed markedly from the God-directed and God-justified souls exposed in their poems.

In short, we would suggest that the Lockean revolution not only unleashed new questions about the truth of other people but created a robust market for works purporting to provide this truth. While the opacity of other persons was a key problem of the day, the touchiest questions for would-be explorers of the human soul were, in a manner of speaking, procedural. As we saw, Locke's 1667 *Essay* had been frank about the need for robust surveillance in a factionalized society; by the time of the *Treatises* and the *Letter*, however, this insight had all but vanished. The reasons are not hard to perceive—toleration, as presented in the later works, carries with it certain ethical imperatives: because society relies on a citizenry of autonomous agents, autonomy is something to be respected; conversely, to paraphrase Goffman, impressions are promises or are liable to be taken that way. Autonomous citizens are (tacitly) under the obligation to live in accordance with the way they present themselves. If these formulations seem risibly naïve (and bear no resemblance to the carnival of deceptions and violations that was eighteenth-century England), we may rephrase the issue in a more practical way: in a society held together provisionally by instrumental agreements, to what extent was it possible (we'll leave aside "permissible") to infringe on the autonomy of others? For the State, the dilemma was urgent: whereas splinter groups are (relatively) easy to keep an eye on, an atomized population of millions of private persons is nearly impossible to monitor adequately. For the novel, meanwhile, it was no less a question of survival—getting to the truth about other people being the genre's reason for being. It is therefore no coincidence that the first important novel in English was an almost pure attempt—so pure as to be unrepeatable—to think through the problems of selfhood initiated by Locke.

Leaving the Island: Crusoe's "Genius"

George Herbert Mead, arch social constructionist that he was, drew a social constructionist moral from Defoe's first novel:

> The self [arises through a] social process; it has its being there. Of course, you could carry such a self as that over to a Robinson Crusoe island and leave him by himself, and he could carry that social process on by himself and extend it to his pets. He carries that on by himself, but it is only because he has grown up in society, because he can take attitudes and roles of others, that he can accomplish this. This mental process . . . is one that has evolved in the social process of which it is a part.[55]

Mead may well be correct. What seems incontestable is that it is hard to imagine someone making such a claim about the development of the self before *Robinson Crusoe* had been written. It is not uncommon, in certain kinds of criticism, to treat novelists and poets as if they were philosophers-manqué, and while it is clearly the case that Defoe was *not* this, he was, in his own register and for his own purposes, testing and exploring the kind of assertions Mead would later make. The hero, importantly, is not a contemporary of the author. Where Defoe (1661–1731) ultimately belonged to the eighteenth century (his career as a novelist began as late as 1719), Crusoe is born in 1632, ten years before the Civil War, making him four years younger than Bunyan and exactly the same age as Locke. In the terms that we have been using, Crusoe is born during the age of allegory and dies under the liberal-contractual dispensation. And in the middle? As Michael Seidel has pointed out, the years of Crusoe's exile on the island (c. 1659–87) map almost perfectly to the last years of the Stuart hegemony: Crusoe barely misses the restoration of Charles II and arrives back in England just in time for the Glorious Revolution.[56] Practically, this means that the very problems confronted by Locke in a context of political upheaval and great personal danger (followed by his own exile from England) are faced by Crusoe by himself, under something approaching laboratory conditions. We may specify further: the period of the Protectorate, the years of Crusoe's early adulthood, offered an environment friendly to speculation about the inner self (in pietistic terms, it must be added). By skipping the reigns of Charles and James, which marked the last gasps of absolutism in England, Crusoe is able to *continue* this kind of inward thinking unmolested, emerging as an older man in the nascently liberal culture of William and Mary.

His father is fully a product of the older dispensation. Although Crusoe presents his story as a prodigal son narrative, in which his key mistake in life was to ignore his father's advice to remain at home, it is also clear that staying put was never an option. His father belongs to an earlier moment of bourgeois history, in which "the middle Station had the fewest Disasters, and was not expos'd to so many Vicissitudes as the higher or lower Part of Mankind."[57] *Middle*, in this case, denotes an Aristotelian mean—or less generously, a kind of featurelessness, which allows its fortunate possessors to move from cradle to grave below the civic radar:

> Temperance, Moderation, Quietness, Health, Society, all
> agreeable Diversions, and all desirable Pleasures were the
> Blessings attending the middle Station of Life; that this Way
> Men went silently and smoothly thro' the World, and
> comfortably out of it . . . in easy Circumstances sliding gently
> thro' the World, and sensibly tasting the Sweets of living,
> without the bitter[,] feeling that they are happy, and learning by
> every Day's Experience to know it more sensibly. (6)

The language of surveillance (or of the desire to evade it) finds its way into the passage through the father's rather sinister choice of verbs and adverbs—*sliding, silently, smoothly, sensibly*—the sibilants perhaps unconsciously echoing a much older tempter and evader. His comments present an extreme—to the point of unrealistic—view of the middle class under social allegory: invisible, docile, a mass without distinctions and thus not in need of constant monitoring. In keeping with the allegory, moreover, the exterior blankness of middle class life corresponds to a blankness within: "experience" and even happiness are taken as pejoratives. From this old puritan's perspective, the soul may indeed be alone with God and thus individual—but it is individual *only* in that sense. If history teaches us anything, it is that this view of the "middle station" was passing out of existence even as Crusoe's father was trilling its praises; indeed, Crusoe's neighbors might plausibly have taken up arms in the Civil War. And needless to say, the intense speculation about selfhood, and the complex interplay of behavior and performance that would propel the middle class from the least to the most individualized and differentiated stratum of society, were well under way in Crusoe's lifetime. In short, he needn't have gone to sea or been marooned: trouble, surely, would have come to him no matter what.

But of course he *is* marooned—Defoe using the island for the same purposes as the others in our growing archipelago: as the setting for a thought experiment examining problems of society and the individual. Since at least Watt, critics have recognized that Crusoe's forced seclusion, "remov'd from all the Wickedness of the World" (101), forces him to become an autonomous person and allows him to develop something more individuated than his original, unformed persona.[58] At least as significant, however, the conditions of Defoe's experiment also restrict and otherwise determine his results. Crusoe only half outgrows his father's perspective, continuing to blame himself well into his residence on the island, for

> not being satisfied with the Station God and Nature [had placed him in]; for not [taking] the excellent Advice of my Father, the Opposition to which was, *as I may call it*, my Original Sin; my subsequent Mistakes of the same Kind had been the Means of my coming into this miserable Condition; for [had] the Providence, which so happily presented me at the Brasils, as a Planter, blessed me with confin'd desires, I [might have done well enough, etc.] (152; Defoe's italics)

Crusoe's rhetoric of minding one's "Station" goes against much of what else he has learned to this point in the narrative. Moreover, he never quite achieves clarity about the forces driving him: sometimes they seem external (as in his reference to providence here or in his frequent mentions of a "calling"); but elsewhere his language is frankly psychological ("there are some secret moving Springs in the Affections" [147]), or emotive ("confin'd desires"), or even proto-Romantic ("I was gotten into an Employment quite remote to my Genius, and directly contrary to the Life I delighted in" [30]).[59] In short, Crusoe never achieves a vocabulary of selfhood adequate to the post-Lockean age—or at least not consistently.

The limitations of Defoe's experiment become clearest, perhaps, as soon as others wash ashore—not just the aboriginal Friday, but the Europeans who turn up later. We are not the first to notice that the little society Crusoe establishes bears more than a few resemblances to a Lockean commonwealth.[60] He secures the loyalty of his companions by means of contracts, and demands that the relations with natives on the mainland should also be contractual: "This should be put in Writing, and signed with their Hands" (193). Although Crusoe is himself a Protestant, the atmosphere he establishes is broadly tolerant of other faiths, of which the island now has several. And yet, in this most Lockean gesture, Defoe also tips his hand.

> My Island was now peopled, and I thought myself very rich in
> Subjects; and it was a merry Reflection which I frequently made
> How like a King I look'd. . . . My People were perfectly
> subjected: I was absolute Lord and Lawgiver; they all owed their
> Lives to me, [though, remarkably] they were of three different
> Religions. My Man *Friday* was a Protestant, his Father was a
> *Pagan* and a *Cannibal*, and the *Spaniard* was a Papist: However,
> I allow'd Liberty of Conscience throughout my Dominions.
> (188; Defoe's italics)

To put it another way, Defoe's political thinking in *Robinson Crusoe* has not moved past the Locke of the 1667 *Essay on Toleration:* the ends Defoe imagines are fully consistent with a liberal state (covenants, liberty of conscience, toleration), but the means to secure them are still authoritarian and inspired by fear. Like the all-seeing "magistrate" of Locke's essay, Crusoe wields absolute power over his happy subjects and has them constantly under his eye, "pumping" them to "discover any of the new thoughts [he suspects are] in [them]" (175)—the island a perfect little surveillance state. That the novel, well into the eighteenth century, should fall back on despotism says little about the state of affairs in England circa 1720 but much about Defoe's insular constraints. *Robinson Crusoe* asks how a person raised under conditions of social allegory might achieve autonomous personhood in the way demanded by the new liberal dispensation; since allegorical culture is all-encompassing, the answer, it would seem, is to remove that person *entirely* from the social body and let him figure out, on his own, who he is. Yet it is also no surprise that his solution to the problem carries an allegorical taint: just as the only individual with full personhood in an allegorical state is the monarch, so Crusoe's achievement of individuality necessitates his becoming the "absolute Lord and Lawgiver" of his little kingdom; that Crusoe is a tolerant ruler and his laws resemble those urged by later liberals is little more than a personal quirk. Nor is it shocking that, once off the island, Crusoe almost immediately reverts to the thoughtless, rather empty person he had been before his exile—his period of removal having by no means prepared him for the world of post-Stuart England. And so, as with our previous islands, Crusoe's needs to be left behind. Difficult questions about personhood, the nature of autonomy, and the proper limits of surveillance were no more to be resolved at the mouth of the Orinoco than they had been in Prospero's dream-kingdom. The truth about other people could only be exposed in the hurly-burly of society. For Defoe, this meant shifting his attention to more urbanized subjects like Moll Flanders and Roxana; for us, it means a return to Richardson—and to the question of realism.

Half a century later, Watt's remains a particularly cogent account of *realism*—those canons of representation that, in his view and the views of critics from Auerbach to Lukács to Hunter, set the novel apart from all earlier literary genres.[61] In Watt's summary, literary realism begins with "the position that truth can be discovered by the individual through his senses" and, as such, is the aesthetic offspring of Locke's empiricism. It produces a picture of the world by investigating "the particulars of experience" rather than by drawing on the "body of past assumptions and traditional beliefs."[62] What this means, tangibly, is that plots eddy and flow in the manner of ordinary lives instead of hewing to established patterns (like the Aristotelian unities). Whereas a journey from Byzantium to

Britain might take a day or two in a medieval romance (like Chretién's *Cligès*), novels attempt to observe the practicalities of time and space: Henry Fielding's characters spend weeks on the road trudging from the provinces to London and back. And while allegories feature characters with names like "Archimago" and "Everyman," the protagonists of *Tom Jones, Moll Flanders*, and *Pamela* (Andrews) sound like ordinary people. Watt is careful to point out that "formal realism" (his name for the sum of these techniques) is conventional, though he somewhat smudges the issue by praising the novel's "accurate transcription of actuality."[63] In fact, *The Faerie Queene* felt no less "real" or "accurate" to a late Elizabethan than *Robinson Crusoe* felt to an early Georgian—the connotations and devices of "reality" and "accuracy" having changed in the interval.[64] Taking up a thread from earlier in the argument, we would add that the ground rules of realism were no less a product of instrumental agreements than the epistemology from which they were derived. That is to say, if the novel promised the truth about other people, it also tacitly granted that certain conventions of realism were the best way to achieve it; this meant above all an authorial voice which reported the results of his or her experience lucidly and without prejudice and according to commonly observed empirical standards.

Of course, if we stopped here, our slight shift of emphasis would be trivial. As our discussion of Richardson began to indicate, however, the novel, while certainly post-empirical, is not best understood as empirical in spirit; the novel, rather, is precisely the genre that emerges from the perceived *failure* of empiricism. If the close observation of other people, or indeed their candid testimony about their lives, actually revealed the truth about them, then the growing eighteenth-century reading public might well have remained content with memoirs, reportage, and other key genres of the time. Unfortunately, memoirs tend to be self-serving or otherwise obfuscating, and we can only tell so much about others by looking at them. A breach was opened for something new, though it cannot be said that the novel boldly stepped in to fill it; instead, the first novelists attempted, as much as possible, to conceal the new genre's differences from its parent forms.[65] As late as Hume, towards the end of the century, it was by no means clear that the novel in fact constituted a kind of writing distinct from either romance or memoir.[66] Fielding never quite found the right term for *Tom Jones* or *Joseph Andrews*, finally calling the latter, with humorous frustration, a "comic Epic-Poem in Prose."[67] It is telling that both Defoe and Richardson maintained the illusion of being merely the editors of works they presented as, respectively, first-person narratives and collections of letters. With Richardson, the pretense was fairly thin, but Defoe continued through multiple sequels to insist on Robinson Crusoe's existence.[68] The eagerness of the earliest novelists to blur the difference between fact and fiction only underscores that novels were, in fact, fiction—and thus not in any meaningful sense of the word "empirical."[69] Since Shklovsky at least, Sterne has been identified as a corrective or wake-up call to the naïveté of pioneers like Defoe, and yet from the very start, by moving quietly from fact into fiction, the novel made plain both empiricism's inability to reveal the truth about other people and the weaknesses in the author-reader contract underlying "formal realism."[70] The truth about other people would have to be arrived at by other means—and the history of the novel may be understood as a series of increasingly stark violations of the realistic contract. *Stark*, we say, but also *silent* and *smooth:* the power of the novel as a genre rested at once on its contravening the contract and the inconspicuousness with which it did so.

Towards Social Construction: Coercive Surveillance

> How often in the overflowing streets
> Have I gone forwards with the crowd, and said
> Unto myself, "The face of every one
> That passes by me is a mystery."[71]

Wordsworth's reflections, which appear in book 7 of *The Prelude*, can be taken as a late statement (c. 1805) of the problem confronting authors—and seriously complicating the efficacy of state surveillance—in the first decades of the eighteenth century. Granting the inaccessibility of others—of everyone, in fact—how, then, to get inside them and figure out what they might be up to? Although the solutions to this question were manifold, we can identify two large *classes* of approach, both of which began to gather steam in the immediate wake of the Lockean revolution. We will call the umbrella terms *empathy* and *coercion*. In short: do you watch other people in order to understand them better, or do you watch them in the hope that, *by* watching them, you will successfully influence their behavior? Each approach, it will readily be apparent, has political implications, which finally boil down to ideas about the self—as something malleable or as something ultimately existing beyond reach. It will also be clear that neither tactic, for very different reasons, could ever be entirely successful and that the subsequent history of surveillance (along both tracks) inevitably had to be dialectical—both empathetic and coercive surveillance encountering resistance and altering tactics in response. Lastly, and for reasons that may not be as readily apparent, the novel was not equally invested in empathy and coercion—though it did investigate the possibilities of both and was, in each case, a leading indicator of later developments in social theory.

Of empathy and coercion, we have had more to say (to this point in the discussion) about the latter: the social performance dynamics explored by Richardson and later theorized by Goffman clearly reflect the coercive aspects of social observation, with Pamela, Clarissa, and the rest of them always modifying their behavior in light of the "censorious" world and taking care "not [to] write what is not fit to be heard" (*Pamela* 4:110, 2:127). And yet, as we have also seen, the coercive approach does not actually bring us closer to those characters' inner lives: the more intense the communal pressures, the more elaborate the theatrics; in Goffman's terms, the "backstage" remains invisible, and Clarissa dies a mystery to those around her. It is no coincidence that the period saw a popular fascination with capturing unguarded behavior. When Mr. B. warns Pamela that, in writing her letters, she should "be wary what Tales you send out of a Family" (1:4), he is reflecting a mania at the time for tell-all memoirs by former servants and class traitors.[72] Early newspapers (including the suggestively titled *Spectator*) also capitalized on this interest, and in their attempts to expose individuals during rare moments of nonperformance were among the precursors of a subgenre that continues to this day with the various manifestations of "reality TV." On a more elevated plane, the science of anthropology, and its foundational concern with observing human behavior prior to the constraints of society, was also beginning around this time.[73]

Meanwhile, going very much in the opposite direction, it was only the shortest of steps from the sentimentalism of a Richardson to the far more radical psychology of a Hume or Smith. Smith in particular perceived that information games could all too easily be dismissed as mere hypocrisy and cautioned against dismissing a person's performative behavior as "only an assumed appearance" (28). In correcting for this error, he ended up making nearly the opposite claim: authentic selfhood could *only* emerge from social intercourse. "Man," he wrote, "can subsist only in society"—and, indeed, "were it possible that a human creature could grow up to manhood in a solitary place . . . he could no more think of his own character, . . . of the beauty or deformity of his own mind, than . . . of his own face. . . . Bring him into society, and he is immediately provided with the mirror he wanted before" (100, 129). When Mead published his work on social psychology a century and a half later, it was in the direct line of descent from Smith's *Theory of Moral Sentiments*. Mead writes:

> The human animal as an individual could never have attained control over the environment. It is a control which has arisen through social organization. . . . His own self is attained only through his taking the attitude of the social group to which he belongs. He must become socialized to become himself. . . . A self can arise only where there is a social process within which this self has had its initiation. (18, 42)

On the face of it, this line of thinking (Mead explicitly drawing on Smith, Smith on Hume) seems a natural enough outgrowth of the intense introspection we saw in Richardson and his generation. At the same time, social *construction* of this sort is contradictory to social *performance* of the kind urged by Richardson (and later Goffman). By eliminating the idea of a "backstage," a core of personality not exposed in outward behavior, Smith isn't arguing that one *becomes* one's performance or that one *turns into* whatever one is pretending to be: he is refuting entirely the distinction between self and role, inside and out. Consciousness is a product of social conditions—a plausible conclusion to draw from *Clarissa*, perhaps, but one that Richardson would find repellant.

For the liberal tradition, therefore, the social construction of Smith and Hume was at once a validation and an early challenge. Locke's conception of the individual remained, to the end, theistic, and he never adequately explained how, without divine validation, individuals might be understood as autonomous. The challenge for liberals, emerging from Locke, was to show how, with God truly out of the equation, the self might be understood as autonomous in purely secular terms—everything in a contract-based society depending on that elemental requirement. It was the dubious achievement of social construction to satisfy one part of the condition at the expense of sacrificing the other. By identifying the individual as purely a social product, Hume and (especially) Smith provided perhaps the first truly secular account of selfhood in the Christian West—certainly in the British tradition—and expunged the last bits of theistic thinking that had lingered in the likes of Richardson and Defoe. This victory came, however, at the cost of forfeiting the ideal of autonomy, with the self now indistinct from (in Mead's delightful turn of phrase) the "social process within which [it] had its initiation." Though it need not have been, this turn was, in practice, politically conservative—the emphasis on social context leading easily into a valorization of tradition and habits over singularity. As Hume put it, "The intercourse of sentiments . . . in society and conversation, makes us form some general *unalterable* standard, by which we may approve or disapprove of characters and morals. . . . [This standard serves] our purposes in company, in the pulpit, on the theatre, *and in the schools*" (our italics).[74] Comments like this, as well as Hume's numerous writings against democracy, show the coercive side of eighteenth-century surveillance theory at its most intense, the Will to Power at its most assertive, and bring us closest (though still not *that* close) to the bogeyman of internalization depicted by Foucault and his followers. The problem going forward for liberals was to preserve the constructionists' hard-won conception of the self as secular while also honoring Locke's stipulation that the self be autonomous. Secular autonomism would require, ultimately, another large, dialectical shift in thinking—and how this happened in the work of writers as diverse as Wordsworth, John Stuart Mill, and Louis Brandeis, in tandem with emerging ideas about the value of privacy, forms the backbone of our next chapter.

State politics during this period was a lagging indicator vis-à-vis the conceptual work being performed in literature, philosophy, and the burgeoning mass media—in short, the British government made little or no use of the potentially fruitful surveillance techniques implicit in constructionist theory. The potential for coercive observation was rich, but the government ultimately preferred methods that now seem almost charmingly antique. The large Catholic population in Ireland, for example, was always a potential source of subversion, and over the course of the century penal laws were introduced to restrict the spread of the faith. The first question was how to identify and codify Catholics to begin with; thus in 6 Geo. I.c.6 it is argued that children can be recognized as Catholic if they "at any time after they come to the age of eighteen years declare themselves of the communion of the church of Rome, or be present at Mattins or Vespers according to the practice of the church of Rome." A vast range of activities were labeled as indicators of popery, from burying the dead in a ruined abbey to refusing to work on a Catholic holy day; the Oath of Abjuration, designed to reveal unregistered priests, was made compulsory in 1709.[75] In short, the legislation stuck to purely external, observatory measures—all of which had been largely discredited by sentimental theory. Which is *not* to say, however, that the complex dynamics of social performance and construction hadn't permeated British society by the turn of the nineteenth century. Rather, this satura-tion occurred in the far more amorphous and nebulous precincts of "society," "the media," "public opinion," and the like. As Mill would later observe:

> Society has now fairly got the better of individuality; and the danger which threatens human nature is not the excess, but the deficiency, of personal impulses and preferences. . . . In our times . . . everyone lives as under the eye of a hostile and dreaded censorship. [People] do not ask themselves "what do I prefer?" [but]"what is usually done by persons [of my station?]" Thus the mind itself is bowed to the yoke; even in what they do for pleasure, conformity is the first thing thought of; they live in crowds, they exercise choice only among things commonly done.[76]

Mill's *On Liberty* is a major element in the next turn of the dialectic; we leave for chapter 3 what his comments implied for burgeoning ideas about the private self.

For now, however, it should be clear why surveillance-as-coercion was a nonstarter for eighteenth-century novelists and their successors—even those who abandoned Richardson's religious take on selfhood. Economically and ideologically, the novel is invested in telling the truth about other people, and while social construction *does* tell the truth about people, that truth is ultimately banal: people are products of their surroundings. It may be that the empirical demand for outward legibility and the liberal faith in personal autonomy—though clearly requiring each other—are on some level profoundly contradictory. Nevertheless, by resolving the contradiction and expunging the idea of an autonomous self, social construction also undermined the novel's reason for being. We need not look far to perceive the kind of fictional writing a social constructionist would produce; indeed, Smith himself was an elegant stylist. In the *Theory of Moral Sentiments* he deftly sketches a familiar kind of social drone:

> The man of rank and distinction, . . . whose whole glory consists in the propriety of his ordinary behavior, who is contented with the humble renown which this can afford him, and has no talents to acquire any other, is unwilling to embarrass himself with what can be attended either with difficulty or distress. To figure at a ball is his great triumph, and to succeed in an intrigue of gallantry, his highest exploit. . . . He may be willing to expose himself to some little danger, and to make a campaign when it happens to be the fashion. But he shudders with horror at the thought of any situation which demands the continual and long exertion of patience . . . and application of thought.[77]

Such characters are certainly to be found in novels—but on the peripheries, "figuring at a ball" in an Austen novel, perhaps, or "succeeding in an intrigue" somewhere in Dickens. They cannot, however, occupy the center: as the mere representations of a truth larger than themselves, they are no less allegorical than the figments of Spenser's imagination. Indeed, more *crudely* allegorical than Spenser's characters, possessing as they do an almost pure flatness and simplicity. Surveillance-as-coercion in its attempts, through unremitting observation, to make the outer and inner selves conform (or, rather, simply to eliminate the inner self) is thus explicitly a return to allegorical thinking within the parameters of the liberal-contractual dispensation. It should be no surprise that the *literary* representations that result from it are allegorical in flavor. For the novel, with its stake in the idea of autonomy, the truth about other people would have to be discovered by other means—via the path of empathy.

Against Social Construction: Empathetic Surveillance

If only it were possible. Just as surveillance-as-coercion had squeezed the inner life out of existence (or at least tried to), so surveillance-as-empathy inevitably had to rely on partial knowledge: full access to the inner core of other people always being out of reach. Far more interesting were the steps novelists took to conceal the problem, the first and most consequential being the very leap into fiction with which the novel began: the near-silent transition from autobiography and letters into their imaginary look-alikes. In the centuries to come, the novel characteristically fell into patterns of fantasy and wish fulfillment. Some of these fantasy constructions were endemic solely to the novel, but others had ramifications in the broader culture of surveillance. Of the former, we might consider the question of the narrator. The earliest works, that is, staked their truth claims on the use of first-person discourse— either through ersatz-memoir or indirectly through reproduced correspondence. Neither method quite delivered the goods. Fictional first-person narrative was ultimately as open to critique as the nonfictional variety: if real-life memoirists were self-serving (and self-concealing), who was to say that Robinson Crusoe or Moll Flanders weren't also? Even before the unreliable first-person narrator became a familiar novelistic trope (as it would with the likes of Swift and Sterne), direct discourse as a way of revealing the truth about other people had largely been discredited.[78]

The case of epistolary fiction, situated as it was within the broader and tortured history of the letter, was, if anything, even more fraught. As late as the mid-seventeenth century, the letter was still commonly valued as a means of unproblematic self-revelation. Thomas Sprat had argued that, in correspondence, "the Souls of Men should appear undress'd"— and Locke himself, an avid letter writer, encouraged the practice as part of a child's standard education:[79]

> The writing of Letters has so much to do in all the occurrences
> of Humane Life, that no Gentleman can avoid shewing himself
> in this kind of Writing. Occasions will daily force him to make
> this use of his Pen, which . . . always lays him open to a severer
> Examination of his Breeding, Sense, and Abilities, than oral
> Discourses; whose transient Faults dying for the most part with

> the Sound that gives them Life, and so not subject to a strict
> review, more easily escape Observation and Censure.[80]

With such surprisingly innocent views—which draw in part on much older theories of epistolary rhetoric—still in existence, it made sense that surveillance of letters during the Protectorate and Stuart restoration was often of the most grossly physical kind: if letters revealed "undressed" souls, then all one needed to monitor suspect persons was to intercept their correspondence and read it.[81] The single, public, state-controlled postal system, with such key developments as penny postage and mail coaches, might cynically be described as having been introduced for this very purpose.[82]

For Cromwell it had been perfectly clear that a state-controlled post "might be made the agent in discovering and preventing many wicked designs which . . . daily contrived against the peace and welfare of [the] commonwealth, the intelligence whereof [could not] well be communicated except by letters."[83] Samuel Morland, in the service of Charles II, subsequently helped establish a system of "opening, copying and resealing . . . letters that passed through the Post Office."[84] The "Secret Department" of the Secretaries of State handled much of the domestic postal surveillance, while the "Secret Office" was responsible for monitoring foreign documents.[85] In the words of a contemporary, the latter had "tricks to open letters more skillfully than anywhere in the world, some even . . . fancying that . . . it was not possible to be a great statesman without tampering with packets."[86] And so on. For the history we are tracing, it is significant that *none* of these developments was actually covert—indeed, the Post Office Act of 1711 had established the state's legal right to open private correspondence. As a result, writers adopted an array of deflecting tactics. Some authors attempted to escape surveillance through cloak-and-dagger tricks: "recipe books" containing instructions for the manufacture and use of invisible ink were all the rage,[87] and numerous authors, like Defoe during his years as a spy, wrote in elaborate codes.[88] Yet the most significant changes in letter writing, finally, were rhetorical. The letter, however naïve it might once have been as a form, was anything but naïve by the early eighteenth century. The tone correspondents took could be defiant—witness Bolingbroke's parting salvo to Swift, "if you answer me by the post, remember whilst you are writing that you write by the post"[89]—or simply jaundiced. A salvo by William King speaks volumes:

> To the Gentleman of the post-office, who intercepted my last letter
> addressed to Mrs. *Whiteway* at her house in *Abbey-Street*, together
> with a letter enclosed and addressed to the Dean of *St. Patrick's*
> [Swift]. Sir, When you have sufficiently perused this letter, I beg
> the favour of you to send it to the lady to whom it is directed.[90]

In the end, it was far more practical—and, given the elaborate tools the
government had at its disposal, more effective—simply to turn the texts
of letters into elaborate exercises in indirection, with the writer's personality carefully cloaked. As many modern critics have pointed out, "familiar
letters," as such exercises came to be called, with their set phrases and
endless conventions, were written with a public reader in mind.[91] The
term itself is double-edged: such works were designed to convey intimate
emotion—but were also formally recognizable, written in a "familiar"
style, which could be learned from popular manuals.[92] Ideally, something
of the self was revealed, but not *too* much, and always within strict formu-
laic parameters. These manuals were popular enough by the late 1730s
that two enterprising booksellers commissioned a struggling young
printer to produce a kind of introductory guide to familiar letter writing.
The result was *Familiar Letters on Important Occasions;* the author, Samuel
Richardson. It wasn't long before Richardson discovered the narrative
possibilities of his task—and *Pamela* appeared in 1740.

From our perspective, the genesis of *Pamela* makes the attitude it takes
towards her letter writing all the more surprising: for the first large section,
Pamela's communications to her parents are presented, with a minimum
of irony, as windows into her soul. Where pseudo-memoir had failed,
Richardson seems to say, epistolary novels could still be relied on to provide
the truth about other people: what need for deception in a young woman's
unmediated reports to her mother and father? That Richardson could have
taken such a position so *late* in the history of the letter is interesting—and
in the event, his experiment lasts not quite one hundred pages. As early as
the first missives, Richardson engages in mild calisthenics to fix the truth-
fulness of Pamela's testimony. At one point, perhaps anticipating readerly
suspicion at the sheer volume and detail of his heroine's confessions,
Richardson has Pamela write "I blab everything" (69). When it transpires
that Mr. B. has in fact been intercepting her correspondence and is
"charmed with [her] manner of writing" (116), Richardson faces a crisis of

plausibility—especially when the style and content of her letters do not change in response. Finally, after Pamela's departure from her initial place of employment, the house of cards collapses, and the "editor"—Richardson using the third person—is forced to step in with a few crucial plot points:

> Here it is necessary the reader should know, that when Mr. B.
> found Pamela's virtue was not to be subdued, and he had in vain
> tried to conquer his passion for her, he had ordered his
> Lincolnshire coachman to bring his traveling chariot from
> thence, in order to prosecute his base designs upon the innocent
> virgin (etc.). (123)

Clumsiness aside, this is a watershed moment in the history of the novel—a moment when the direct means of first person (memoir or epistolary) are recognized as insufficient to provide the truth about other people: inherently implausible and inevitably incomplete when it comes to necessary information. Henceforward, the novel would rely increasingly on more invasive techniques that *did* root around characters' minds: third-person omniscient, free indirect discourse, and (the natural endpoint of this logic) stream-of-consciousness narrative and interior monologue; the first few signaling a return to methods familiar from older prose fiction genres like romance (which the novel had explicitly rejected at the outset), the latter techniques newly invented.[93]

While these procedures would seem to have a direct and obvious relevance for the history of surveillance (providing, as they did, complete access to the thoughts of other people), we would suggest that their significance was more roundabout. For starters, they were pure fantasy projections: no actual surveillance method yet invented has provided anything close to the exposure we get to Dorothea Brooke's mind in *Middlemarch*, let alone Leopold Bloom's in *Ulysses*. As fantasy projections, third-person omniscient and the like might indeed be identified as signs of the novel breaking free from the practical world of surveillance: faced, in their empathetic project, with a choice between empirical standards of evidence and total access, many novelists chose the latter—the ideal of capturing autonomous souls conflicting, once again, with the basic terms of the realistic contract.

This is not to say, however, that by moving away from "formal realism" into fantasies of violation novelists were not participating in *some* form of surveillance activity: their targets in this case being not their characters but their readers. In the triangle—if we may call it that—of author, character, and reader, the last term is clearly the least stable and least guarded. The reader is enlisted in a fantasy of total surveillance, *sharing* with the author unmediated access to the thoughts and feelings of others. Alas, those people are fictional, and the participatory effect is an illusion. To the extent that the novel accomplishes its transition *silently* from "formal realism" to the more invasive techniques of the nineteenth and twentieth centuries, the reader him- or herself enters the text's sphere of influence. In fact, the reader's closest kinship is with the character in his or her abjection, the private emotions and thoughts that are laid bare anticipating and manipulating the reader's own—an effect that the reader's very sense of access and partnership with the author obscures. The instrumental agreement holds—insofar as the reader is unaware that it has been tampered with. It is not too much to say, then, that the novel is in this manner as active a player in *coercive* surveillance as any other medium.

It is perhaps to Richardson's credit that he worries about these things, admitting to his didacticism in *Pamela*'s subtitle ("Virtue Rewarded"). More to the point, as it gradually becomes evident that his original premises are unsustainable, Richardson's attentions turn from the novel's ostensible subject (the direct transcription of a young woman's thoughts and feelings) to a more sophisticated inspection of the author-reader relationship. Pamela, Mr. B., and their acquaintances are all, by necessity, close readers, parsing every detail of her letters for subtle hints about intention. By the climax of the book, a particularly tangled situation has transpired: Pamela writing letters in full knowledge that Mr. B. will be intercepting and reading them, but continuing to address her parents *as if* they were her only recipients. It is at once a demonstration and a critique of Richardson's relation with his own readership—and of the realistic contract—and Richardson goes further still:

> He was going away in Wrath; and I said, One Word, good Sir, one
> Word, before you read them, since you *will* read them: Pray make
> Allowances for all the harsh Reflections, that you will find in them,
> on your own Conduct to me: And remember only, that they were
> not written for your Sight; but were penn'd by a poor Creature
> hardly used, and who was in constant Apprehension of receiving
> from you the worst Treatment, that you could inflict on her. (1:383)

Pamela, in short, is overtly concerned with reader response, that her unintended reader read her letters in the right way—transparently Richardson's own anxiety regarding his audience.[94] Clearly, Richardson has painted himself into a corner, so long as he wishes to maintain a modicum of plausibility; as Pamela writes just a few pages later, "I have little heart to take pen in hand for the future, if he is so resolved to see all I write" (273). It is no coincidence, we would suggest, that it is at this very point that Mr. B. switches from predator to ardent suitor, thus getting Richardson out of a sticky situation—at once modeling an ideal audience response and instantaneously transforming the author-reader relation from an unlikely surveillance situation into a far more plausible economic arrangement.

> "I told you," added he, "that I would see no more of your papers;
> I meant I would not without your consent: but if you will shew
> me what you have written, since the last I saw, (and now I have
> no other motive for my curiosity, but the pleasure I take in
> reading what you write) I shall acknowledge it as a favor."
> "If, sir," returned I, "you will be pleased to let me write over
> again one sheet, I will; and yet, relying on our word, I have not
> written with the least precaution." "For that very reason," said
> he, "I am the more desirous to see what you write." (314)

One can read as much bad faith into this détente as one wishes (and Fielding read plenty); at all events, it is a supremely honest presentation of the complex and tangled end logic into which one strand of the empathetic tradition was liable to fall. In this way, the more complete withdrawal of the authorial voice from *Clarissa* was a step backwards—an evasion of the insights *Pamela* had ruthlessly explored.

We do not mean to suggest that surveillance-as-empathy led inevitably to violations of the realistic contract; indeed, an important strain of the novel continues to abide strictly by the agreements tacitly established at the start, with non-omniscient narrative voices presenting evidence of the exterior of things and no more. As we will see in the next chapter, however, even the most empirically rigorous approaches have at times been susceptible to fantasies of perfect interpretation. Pseudo-sciences (and real sciences subjected to exaggerated claims), from physiognomy and phrenology in the eighteenth and nineteenth centuries, to biometric scanning and the "smart systems" of present-day casinos, have time and again promised the truth about other people through close observation. We will see that the novel's pursuit of interiority by these means often brought it into near alliances with the developing technology of surveillance and—once again—caused disruptions in realistic representation that brought the novel closer to deterministic genres like allegory. For now, we may simply observe that realism by the end of the eighteenth century was less a formal set of conventions than a complex ideological effect, depending in equal measure on an adherence to the empirical contract, and a quiet annexation of forms and ways of thinking fundamentally hostile to empiricism.[95] And, as happened at the end of the allegorical dispensation, conflicts between power and idealism with long-lasting consequences for liberal-contractual culture were often first to be discerned on the level of the text: in Dickens's minor characters, or Poe's infallible detectives, or Clarissa's silence.

Figure 3. "Plan of the Panopticon," from *The Works of Jeremy Bentham* (1843), 4:172–73.

CODA: PANOPTIC SPACE AND SOCIAL REFORM

With Clarissa's death, we may return to Jeremy Bentham "bathed in tears" and to that icon of eighteenth-century speculation about surveillance, the panopticon. Those tears, had Bentham been able to anticipate his future career, should have been prompted not only by Clarissa's fate but also by the suicidal teleology of Richardson's experiment in social performance and the challenges it posed for reform. The arguments in his *Panopticon Letters* that have had the most lasting influence (via Foucault) are to be found in a handful of passages towards the beginning—and none more so than his promise, in the "Preface," that the prison would offer "a new mode of obtaining power of mind over mind, in a quantity hitherto without example." "The more constantly the persons to be inspected [were] under the eyes [of the inspectors]," we saw him reasoning in our introduction, "the more perfectly [would] the purpose of the establishment [be] attained." Especially in this obscure and ominous "purpose of the establishment" one seems to hear the prophet of modern authoritarianism, with the Powers That Be colonizing and rewriting the individual personality. Bentham, it has seemed plausible to conclude, is outlining a psychology of internalization, with the inmate, under the pressure of constant observation, slowly and unconsciously taking on the rules of the prison; eventually the rules become, permanently, part of his very identity.

And yet with the slightest further reading, it is all too clear how selectively Bentham has to be quoted for this conclusion to hold water. Bentham conceived of his panopticon as anything but an "indefinitely generalizable mechanism": although he imagined it might be employed in certain other institutional settings designed for "inspection" (such as workhouses and schools), he warned against its "perverse applications" and certainly did not consider it a model for society as a whole. Indeed, he surely would have resisted the coinage "panopticism" as altogether too abstract a concept. Whereas Foucault, very much a product of the twentieth century as well as an intellectual tradition given to totalizing claims, grandly pronounced that "there is no outside" (301) in a surveillance society, Bentham was convinced that the effects he hoped to achieve could only occur in a discrete and controlled— indeed, a walled—environment: as he noted at the outset, his prison must occupy "a space not too large" (40). Less a Control State, if one desires a contemporary parallel, than Caesar's Palace. Nor, while we're on this note, was Bentham sure that the psychological effects of internalization would be appropriate, let alone possible, for all classes of society. Russia, a land of "stupid people," inured to centuries of despotism, offered ready fodder for his prison houses, as did the British underclass— but one could hardly expect internalization from the better-educated, "superior ranks of life" (49, 45): the Michel Foucaults of this world would not be deceived.[96]

It is worth remembering that Bentham's panopticon writings are dauntingly extensive. After the initial series of letters, published in 1787, he composed two long postscripts, each far longer than the original series, as well as a finely detailed comparison—longer still—between his prison scheme and the convict settlement in New South Wales. These last three documents are barely known today, and most of Bentham's vast correspondence, in which he pursued his panopticon scheme for the greater part of three decades before finally admitting defeat, is only now, slowly, finding its way into print.[97] In this subsequent writing, the logic of social construction (still less internalization) is barely to be descried, but Bentham the heir to the sentimental tradition and its complex ideas about performance is evident at all points. For one thing, his intentions are explicitly philanthropic. To a modern sensibility, his plan might well seem barbaric (figure 3); compared, however, to the appalling prison conditions of the time, it was a quantum improvement.[98] Natural light, relative privacy and safety from other prisoners, indoor plumbing, no need for shackling in irons: the Newgates of popular dread could boast nothing like it.

More relevant to our point, his psychology, when examined more closely, is essentially of its age, the culmination of a century of post-empirical thinking. When Habermas remarked that "Bentham was unthinkable without Adam Smith," he was thinking primarily of economics and the immense influence *The Wealth of Nations* had on Bentham's writings about political economy.[99] But Smith's work on sympathy was no less an inspiration—and a caution: Smith's insight that, to produce "concord," a person must modify his or her behavior to win the sympathy of his or her observers would seem to find a practical echo in the panopticon, a machine designed to promote such modifications of behavior.[100] And yet Bentham had little interest in Smith's implication that the self could be remade: panoptic observation, Bentham made perfectly clear, was meant to encourage and *channel* the natural theatricality of inmates. Forty years earlier, Doctor Johnson had identified as the chief source of recidivism in jails unstructured social relations among the prisoners: "The misery of gaols is not half their evil. . . . In a prison, the awe of the publick eye is lost, and the power of the law is spent; there are few fears, there are no blushes. The lewd inflame the lewd, the audacious harden the audacious. Every one fortifies himself as he can against his own sensibility."[101] As if in answer to Johnson's insight, Bentham asserts that the prison is meant—quite literally—to *model* right conduct. Foucault, naturally, had seen the most distinctive spatial feature of the panopticon—the central position of the inspector and peripheral, sequestered aspect of the prisoners—as irredeemably oppressive, a physical embodiment of the way State power traps the individual within limiting discourses. Bentham would have found this idea utterly foreign; to take a hint from Goffman, there is an opposite way to understand the building's configuration:

> As both effect and enabling cause of [one's] commitment to the part one is currently performing, we find that "audience segregation" occurs; by audience segregation, the individual ensures that those before whom he plays one of his parts will not be the same individuals before whom he plays a different part in another setting. . . . [It is] a device for protecting fostered impressions. (49)

It is perfectly natural, in other words, for a person to act differently towards different people; different social situations require different kinds of performance, a fact likely to be lost on criminals and social outcasts. The individual, properly, is manifold—and the radiating spaces of the panopticon answer to and demonstrate this basic psychology rather than insist on centralized power. At stake is a proper structuring of the prisoners' autonomy, not their subjection to the dicta of a monolithic authority.

Thus, where Foucault makes much of Bentham's insistence on the isolation of each prisoner—the better to internalize the rules of the watchers—Bentham in fact retreats from this position almost at once. As he comments in the first postscript, "Of perfect solitude . . . I know but one use—the breaking of the spirit."[102] Isolation reduces the naturally sociable inmate to idiocy, not obedience. A few pages later, in perhaps his most startling insight, he suggests that prisoners wear masks when observed. Constant surveillance, he reasons, may well encourage sullenness and recalcitrance rather than an understanding or acceptance of the rules; so how better to encourage right behavior than dress the prisoners in costumes?

> A mask affords [remedy] at once. Guilt will be pilloried . . .
> without the exposure of the guilty. With regard to the sufferer,
> the sting of shame will be sheathed, and with regard to the
> spectators, the salutary impression, instead of being weakened,
> will be heightened by this imagery. The scene . . . will be
> decorated by—why mince the word?—by a masquerade, . . . a
> serious, affecting and instructive one.[103]

In the final reckoning, Bentham was never as sanguine as his modern readers about the process of internalization itself. For Foucault, the end result of constant watching was perfect certainty on the part of the watchers: an "omnipresent and omniscient power" (*Discipline and Punish*, 197). Bentham's concluding thoughts, in a passage that present-day commentators tend to ignore, were far more ambiguous and indeed sentimental:

> Detection is the object of [the spy]; *prevention*, that of the
> [panopticon]. . . . The object of the first was to pry into the secret
> recesses of the heart; the latter, confining its attention to *overt*
> *acts*, leaves thoughts and fancies to their proper *ordinary*, the
> court *above*.[104]

Hardly the language of an authoritarian seeking to smother individuality; rather, the phrase "secret recesses of the heart" is—perhaps consciously— a near quotation from Richardson.[105] The idea that the state could (let alone should) take over the very consciousness of its citizens could not have been further from Bentham's intentions; rather, like Richardson, he drew a sharp distinction between "overt acts," the performance that is part of everyday social behavior, and the truth of inner life, whose only possible spectator is God. With this ultimately theistic and individualized idea of personhood, Bentham's panopticon papers stake out, if anything, a residual position in the rapidly transforming culture of late eighteenth-century liberalism. Within a decade of the *Panopticon Letters*, the first strong theory of the self as both autonomous and secular would be articulated, not in a work of social theory but in poetry—and in defense of privacy.

CHAPTER THREE

Inviolate Personality

WHEN NICOLE KIDMAN MARRIED KEITH Urban in the spring of 2006, all of the usual precautions were taken. Out of fear that paper correspondence might fall into the wrong hands, the attendees were contacted solely through e-mail. Shortly before the ceremony, they were summoned by phone and told where unmarked cars would pick them up; the drivers were only then themselves paged and informed where to take their passengers. Originally scheduled for midday, the event was pushed back to nighttime, so that the proceedings might take place under the cover of darkness. Nevertheless, as an additional safeguard, a special budget was set aside to hire all of the private helicopters in that particular suburb of Sydney, so that no airborne surveillance might take place. This last measure, it is worth pointing out, failed miserably: numerous aerial photographs were obtained, and thus the remaining conventional element in such cases—endless, prurient speculation in the press over when, where, and even whether the happy event had happened—was largely silenced.[1]

At this late date, the spectacle of celebrities taking evasive measures more appropriate for double agents and drug smugglers hardly seems grotesque. Indeed, their secrecy needs no explanation whatsoever: privacy is seen by most of us not merely as a self-evident good but as a precious and fragile condition, spoiled easily by invasions from without, and thus in need of unblinking protection. Those who would violate this condition—paparazzi, telemarketers, anonymous men in well-tailored black suits—are invariably demonized in the broader culture. These attitudes are so pervasive and unquestioned, in short, that it is all too easy to forget how (relatively) recent they are. As we saw in the previous chapter, privacy is by no means an unalloyed good in a Defoe or Richardson novel: on some level, Pamela without an audience ceases to be Pamela. Certainly eighteenth-century weddings, to continue with the example at hand, were unabashedly public ceremonies, which required legal witnesses. Private nuptials were sought after only by the underprivileged and disreputable; an entire district of London (around the Fleet Prison) had become a center for "private" (that is, unlicensed and illegitimate) marriages, leading Congreve and others to make sport of the situation.[2] Before his reformation Mr. B. indeed tries to trick Pamela into a secret wedding, which he of course has no intention of honoring; she tactfully resists. To the Enlightenment mind, it was not yet obvious that the private marked a space distinguishable from the public, still less that privacy might be thought of, in the words of one critic, "as an end in itself."[3] All the same, by century's end, the groundwork for the modern conception of privacy, as a condition in need of strenuous defense, as a right enjoyed by every individual, and as a bulwark against the adverse effects of surveillance, had been laid.

To restate one of our basic contentions: the collapse of allegorical culture initiated a dialectical struggle between surveillance and privacy, as the erstwhile synonymity of inner and outer identities came asunder. Beginning at the end of the Renaissance and continuing to the present, refinements in determining character from the outside were matched (and countered) by a ripening "inner" ideology of selfhood: if one could no longer equate oneself with a social role, then what *was* one precisely—in short, what constituted personhood? Although these exterior and interior histories are closely intertwined, we spent more of chapter 2 examining the former and now turn (largely) to the latter. We chose this division partly in the interests of clarity but also in recognition of historical causality: the high value we now place on privacy is inseparable from a theory of selfhood, and of self-formation, which could only have emerged in dialectical response to the social constructionism of the eighteenth century. As we turn, later in the chapter, to nineteenth-century attitudes towards surveillance—in literature, in philosophy, in the political sphere—we will observe several continuities with Augustan ideas and practices; the salient differences, however, can only be understood in light of the truly private self, a substantially new concept. Modern surveillance responds to a modern ideology of privacy.

Our first task, then, is to examine how this concept first arose. To be sure, the Enlightenment is widely recognized as a pivotal moment, in which the modern notion of privacy came into being. We would suggest, however, that both the extent and the very nature of this change have been misconstrued because of some characteristic blind spots in the discipline of intellectual history. The first of these, which we have already addressed in other contexts, is the tendency to read literature as either a commentary on or reflection of broader social and material processes. As a result, even the most comprehensive recent treatments of privacy have largely overlooked the specific role of literature as an *agent* of change rather than merely a marker or example of it.[4] Because of a necessary rethinking of the relationship between the solitary, individual author and the solitary, individual reader, the prose and (especially) poetry of this period was the forum in which central questions about privacy were first raised and tested. A second bias is more insidious—and specific to our time period—because it is rooted in premises shared by eighteenth-century and present-day critics, without acknowledgement. A great deal of current work on privacy, that is, shares a philosophical provenance in Habermas's early study of the bourgeois public sphere, most relevantly his economic-materialist understanding of privacy as a product (or leftover) of the public. This position—that privacy cannot be considered apart from its social context—accords well with the psychology of a Hume or Smith.[5] We would argue, however, that social constructionism (whether Enlightenment or Marxist) is finally inadequate to account for the extraordinary significance most people now find in privacy. When recognizably modern claims for privacy began to be made at the very *end* of the eighteenth century, it marked a shift of dispensations; these claims, though influenced by the main lines of Enlightenment thought, were ultimately a rejection of them—not just about privacy, but also about the self, its origins, and its sources of integrity.

I. THE LITERARY ROOTS OF PRIVACY THEORY

The Right to Privacy

At stake, then, is a claim about the nature of privacy itself. To get a sense of the way in which we are using the term, consider a second wedding. A much-recounted (if, as we will see later, largely inaccurate) story about the origins of modern privacy law: when Samuel Warren's daughter was married in the spring of 1890, the cream of Boston society turned out in force; so, unfortunately, did the dregs of the yellow press. Warren's wife was the daughter of a U.S. senator and Warren himself, though trained as a lawyer, was a socially prominent paper manufacturer. His longstanding hostility towards an intrusive journalism was brought to a boil when the *Saturday Evening Gazette* went so far as to publish the wedding's guest list. By the end of that year, Warren had responded by co-authoring, with his former partner—and future associate justice of the Supreme Court—Louis Brandeis, a paper that has been called "the single most influential law review article ever published": "The Right to Privacy."[6]

In the article, which first appeared in the *Harvard Law Review*, the men begin by offering a historical argument for the establishment of a new tort: where laws once protected only freedom of the body, then freedom of mind, rapidly changing social and material conditions now necessitated a more plenary right to be let alone.[7] Observing the influence of new technologies, they wrote:

> Instantaneous photographs and newspaper enterprise have invaded the sacred precincts of private and domestic life; and numerous mechanical devices threaten to make good the prediction that "what is whispered in the closet shall be proclaimed from the housetops." . . . The press is overstepping in every direction the obvious bounds of propriety and of decency. Gossip is no longer the resource of the idle and of the vicious, but has become a trade, which is pursued with industry as well as effrontery. To satisfy a prurient taste the details of sexual relations are spread broadcast in the columns of the daily papers. To occupy the indolent, column upon column is filled with idle gossip, which can only be procured by intrusion upon the domestic circle.[8]

The first tack Warren and Brandeis take, then, is a familiar one: the lines could have been written last week (in response to data mining or *Us Weekly*, one supposes). But by the same token, they could also have been written (with minor adjustments of emphasis) five hundred years ago: the purely *material* dialectic between technology and privacy is likely as old as culture itself. At all events, something in their rhetoric—the notion of a "sacred" domestic circle, perhaps, or the quoting of the Gospel of Luke (rather than legal precedent)—suggests a fear of something deeper than physical intrusion.

Accordingly, after reviewing and rejecting several plausible existing bases for the right to privacy—property law, for example, or freedom from physical assault—Warren and Brandeis finally stake their claim on a near-mystical conviction about the human soul. They write:

> The intensity and complexity of life, attendant upon advancing
> civilization, have rendered necessary some retreat from the
> world, and man, under the refining influence of culture has
> become more sensitive to publicity, so that solitude and privacy
> have become more essential to the individual. . . . Triviality
> destroys at once robustness of thought and delicacy of feeling.
> . . . The principle which protects . . . all . . . personal
> productions, is in reality . . . that of an inviolate personality.
> (77, 82)

These are the sentiments—not to mention the stirring cadences—that one would expect not from a lawyer but from a poet; and indeed, as we will show presently, one poet in particular stands behind this passage. But first, to paraphrase: privacy is conceived of as a necessary condition for the formation of an autonomous person; integrity of soul, inversely, is the underlying justification for a new right. The various invasions of daily life are not mere annoyances but threats that might arrest the development of the self, a chrysalis-like process that, to be successful, must remain "inviolate."

It is universally acknowledged that the concept of privacy *as a legal right* emerges with Warren's and Brandeis's article.[9] It is easy, moreover, to read their piece as a triumph of common sense, which diagnosed and seamlessly filled an obvious gap in the law. Nevertheless, as the practical basis for a tort, the men are on shaky ground, and in the 120 years since publication, the debate has gone back and forth: is it legitimate to anchor such a fundamental right on so impalpable a concept as selfhood? If not, should privacy be recognized as a distinct right at all, or might it not be usefully broken down into a series of more tangible and easily graspable protections (like freedom from the presentation of one's character in a false light)?[10] For some commentators, Warren and Brandeis were inescapably men of their time and social standing, grounding their claims in an appeal to patrician sensibilities rather than logical rigor. Thus one critic could only descry "a curious nineteenth-century quaintness about the grievance, an air of injured gentility" in the essay's fear of the mass press.[11] This may represent an extreme position—yet even writers sympathetic to the conclusions Warren and Brandeis offer (and who do not find complaints about an intrusive media particularly old-fashioned or "quaint") have been oddly tone-deaf to the paper's "language" and have experienced difficulties perceiving the authors' reasoning.[12] A sticking point, not surprisingly, has been the central claim about "inviolate person-ality," a formula that has been described, variously, as "unsatisfying," "vague," a phrase "on which the authors failed to elaborate," and "too imprecise for judicial construction and principled application, let alone incorporation into public policy."[13] We would suggest these difficulties are the inevitable result of the authors importing literary *discourse* into legal *argument*—an uncomfortable fit under any circumstances.[14] For his own part, Brandeis remained consistent through his long career in claiming a spiritual rationale for solitude. In his dissent on *Olmstead v. U.S.* (a 1928 wiretapping case), he remarked, in language nearly identical to his earlier piece:

> The makers of our Constitution undertook to secure conditions favorable to the pursuit of happiness. They recognized the significance of man's spiritual nature, of his feelings and of his intellect. They knew that only a part of the pain, pleasure and satisfactions of life are to be found in material things. They sought to protect Americans in their beliefs, their thoughts, their emotions and their sensations. They conferred, as against the government, the right to be let alone—the most comprehensive of rights and the right most valued by civilized men.[15]

Even the most vociferous modern-day defenders of this position have conceded that Brandeis's claims are ontological and, finally, beyond proof.[16]

Ontological or not, these claims have a history, one that developed over the course of the eighteenth century but which cultural-materialist accounts of the period do *not* address. To recount the standard story: during the Middle Ages, "private" meant little more than "excluded from the state apparatus" (11). It was only "with the emergence of trade and finance capitalism" (i.e., with the rise of the bourgeoisie, as an economic force over against the sovereign) that "civil society" came into existence and, as a corollary, "the private" began to take shape (17).[17] The bourgeois public sphere, in Habermas's definition, was a

> sphere of private people come together as a public. They soon claimed the public sphere regulated from above against the public authorities themselves, to engage them in a debate over the general rules governing relations in the basically privatized but publicly relevant sphere of commodity exchange and social labor. (26)

For Habermas, in other words, "the private" originated in, and was never wholly separable from, "private enterprise." From these premises, certain consequences follow: during the eighteenth century "privacy" was essentially an economic category, along the lines of property, and thus could never be associated with pure solitude. "The status of private man," Habermas notes, "combined the role of owner of commodities with that of head of family" (28)—and hence the way, in Habermas and his many followers, that "privacy" and "the domestic" often come to stand for each other.[18] Still more relevant for our purposes, this line of thinking forecloses entirely on the idea of privacy as "an end in itself," a wholly autonomous state necessary for the formation of a healthy individual. In his more Adornian moments, Habermas speculates that, since autonomy is impossible (one is only "apparently set free from the constraint of society"), the "saturated and free interiority" that characterizes feelings of "privateness" may itself be an illusion.[19]

It might be argued that this is a chicken-and-egg dilemma: since *most* writers during the eighteenth century, especially during the flood stage of social construction, did not equate privacy with the formation of an autonomous personality, it is only to be expected that current theories attempting to locate the roots of modern privacy theory in the period would themselves downplay the importance of this equation. And yet that would be underestimating the intensity with which *some* eighteenth-century writers—literary writers especially—sought a more profound understanding of privacy, solitude, society, and the self.

Poetry and Solitude

Alexander Pope begins his "Epistle to Arbuthnot" with a classic demand to be let alone—"Shut, shut the door"—and describes his attempts to flee those attracted by his celebrity as a poet. Although Warren and Brandeis, in their first salvo, claimed that the invasions of privacy made possible by new technologies were a phenomenon novel to the 1890s, Pope makes it perfectly clear, almost two centuries earlier, that the pressures of public attention were nothing new:

> What walls can guard me, or what shades can hide?
> They pierce my thickets, through my grot they glide,
> By land, by water, they renew the charge,
> They stop the chariot, they board the barge.
> No place is sacred, not the church is free;
> Even Sunday shines no Sabbath day to me . . . (lines 7–12)

A familiar enough sentiment, and yet these lines also show Pope's vast distance from present-day attitudes. Pope is far from considering loss of privacy the violation of a basic right; rather, he simply vents his frustration at an inescapable—perhaps necessary—evil of literary fame. He sees poetry, ultimately, as a public practice and himself as a public authority, with no choice but to remain engaged, however "wretched" that might seem. Like most, if not all, of the great poets of the early eighteenth century, he pays lip service to the notion of solitude, but would never go so far as to shut the door entirely. To do so, to actually be "unheard," would mean ceasing to be a poet. In short, Pope represents the lingering influence of the premodern conception of privacy, in which the appeal of unshared space is always balanced by the premises of social performance or social construction. According to the latter, to recall Smith's formulation in the last chapter, man "can subsist only in society, [and] was fitted by nature for that situation."[20] As Hume puts it, "the minds of men are mirrors to one another"—and thus for all of these authors, the result of total privacy is malformation of the self (Hume, *Treatise*, 1:236).

As we also saw, however, this view of personal development produced its own set of problems—problems of authenticity and authority accelerated by the massive and rapid growth of cities like London. Richardson, confining his characters to country estates, had fretted at great length about the distinctions between performed and sincere behavior. In a city whose population had topped one million by 1800, these concerns were multiplied a million-fold.[21] Joseph Addison, writing in the *Spectator*, cheerfully witnessed London absorbing a huge variety of people and converting them to "citizens of the world."[22] Some decades later, Samuel Johnson, more closely attuned to the strong ideological pressures of the metropolis, contemptuously observes the city transforming and molding bumpkins from the countryside into a new recognizable urban type, slavishly echoing urban phrases and imitating urban mannerisms. Paradoxically, their abandonment of rural anonymity leaves them equally anonymous and, if anything, less authentic and individuated than before.[23] Johnson's most vivid description of this process comes in *London*, in which fashionable young men

> Practis'd their Master's Notions to embrace,
> Repeat his Maxims, and reflect his Face;
> With ev'ry wild Absurdity comply,
> And view each Object with another's Eye.[24]

As even Smith is able to admit, the city is apt to privilege "propriety" over "thought" and is perhaps no less dangerous for the soul, for the truly independent mind and conscience, than solitude.[25]

How, then, to preserve one's unique and authentic self amidst the commanding discourses of the metropole? As the century wore on, the answer to this question was, increasingly, "privacy." Not, we should clarify, the absolute solitude often connoted by the term today: Johnson, whatever his worries about artificiality, was never about to run off to a desert island (his response to Boswell's desire to see Tahiti: "one set of Savages is like another").[26] Even the wildly popular "retirement poems" of the mid-1700s, with their emphasis on "retreat" from city life and praise of rural solitude, were only willing to go so far. As the greatest and most sophisticated of these poems made plain, withdrawal to the country-side, "far from the madding crowd's ignoble strife," was the prerogative only of those who had the wherewithal to understand what withdrawal meant—that is to say, city dwellers. As much as Thomas Gray seeks solace in a country churchyard, he would never willingly change places with a country peasant.[27] For the writers of retirement poems, man was still a creature who lived in a polis: identity was to be forged amidst and *through* the strains and discourses of public life, but when these pressures grew too intense, rural privacy beckoned, at best, as a place for healing and recovery, and at worst, as a sort of lotos land, and rest from care.[28] It is thus with considerable ambivalence that over the eighteenth century the connotations of being alone slowly shifted from the negative to the positive, with more and more people, in the later years of the century, choosing to live private lives.[29]

Perhaps surprisingly, the paradigm shift through which social constructionist premises were finally rejected, and privacy finally embraced "as a good in itself" or, at the very least, as the necessary precondition for personal autonomy, ended up having strong generic connotations: the new arguments for privacy emerged primarily through the work of poets—its unacknowledged legislators, as it were—and were only later taken up by the broader culture. Why this should have happened at the end of eighteenth century has everything to do with the changing social status of poetry itself. In the "Epistle to Arbuthnot," Pope had assumed that poetry was a public form; in this he was simply speaking for his age, perhaps the last time that poets occupied a secure and unquestioned place in civic debate. By the time Pope concluded *The Dunciad*, his last major work, this position was slipping, as the coterie culture in which public poetry had thrived was swept away. For the poets who came after Pope—from Gray, to Young, to Cowper—this professional crisis presented itself ultimately as a problem of authority: if the poet's traditional place in public debate had vanished, what now legitimized poetic expression? Why be a poet at all if the role no longer commanded automatic respect or a broad and attentive audience?

Wordsworth's answer, in the end, would be: "to my soul I now say / 'I recognize thy glory.' . . . Our nature, and our home, / Is with infinitude—and only there" (*Prelude 6*, lines 531–32, 538–39). To translate: there are certain qualities of the poetic self, which set poets apart from other people, and authorize them to speak. The motivation to overturn social-constructionism, it bears repeating, was at heart *professional*: if poets now justified their careers by turning to something exceptional in the *self*, it was inconvenient, to say the least, to believe that the self was socially formed (and thus no different in kind from all of the other selves running around). This is not to underestimate the principled opposition many novelists offered to social construction. As we saw towards the end of the last chapter, the novel's promise to offer the truth about other people was potentially threatened by the conclusions of Smith's psychology. For economic as well as humanistic reasons, the novel had ample cause to embrace the liberal notion of individual autonomy. While novelists, however, *could* afford to entertain social-constructionist ideas, reflecting and commenting on the mores of late Augustan society, poets were forced to reconsider, radically, the nature of personhood.[30]

And, in the process, make a profoundly new argument for the importance of privacy. To readers of Warren and Brandeis, Wordsworth's Prospectus to *The Recluse* should seem uncannily familiar:

> Of the individual Mind that keeps her own
> Inviolate retirement, subject there
> To Conscience only, and the law supreme
> Of the Intelligence which governs all—
> I sing:—"fit audience let me find though few!"[31]

In a remarkable statement of indifference towards social pressures, Wordsworth identifies his own mind, a mind cultivated in "inviolate retirement," as the proper subject of poetry. Inklings of this conclusion may be found throughout the Augustan period—but where earlier authors like Gray had recognized social coercion as harmful to the self, and also understood that privacy offered relief, none had ever suggested that, in privacy, the origins and nurturing of selfhood might be at stake. To choose privacy was to be done with soul creation. It was left to Wordsworth, at the very end of the century, especially in his long autobiographical poem *The Prelude*, to connect the dots conclusively: (1) a self, to have value, must be autonomous; (2) for the process of self-generation to succeed, a person must be let alone; (3) success is far less likely to occur amidst the social and political pressures of the city, than in privacy—in his view, rural privacy; (4) privacy has lifelong benefits and continues—in pointed contrast to the experience of a Crusoe—to shore up the self after returning to civilization. In his preface to *Lyrical Ballads* (1800), we see him going through the same sequence of thoughts as Warren and Brandeis almost a century later:

> A multitude of causes, unknown to former times, are now
> acting with a combined force to blunt the discriminating powers
> of the mind, and unfitting it for all voluntary exertion to reduce
> it to a state of almost savage torpor. The most effective of these
> causes are the great national events which are daily taking place
> and the increasing accumulation of men in cities, where the
> uniformity of their occupations produces a craving for
> extraordinary incident, which the rapid communication of
> intelligence hourly gratifies. ("Preface," 1:872–73)

As in Warren and Brandeis, an initial fulmination against the crassness, invasiveness, and speed of mass industrialized culture gives way to a deeper worry about the self: "this degrading thirst after outrageous stimulation" has transformed an entire society into hypocrites and hollow men. He is not, however, without hope: "reflecting upon the magnitude of the general evil, I should be impressed with no dishonourable melancholy, had I not a deep impression of certain inherent and indestructible qualities of the human mind" ("Preface," 1:873). From these "qualities," from this "Mind that keeps her own / Inviolate retirement," it is only the shortest of steps to Warren's and Brandeis's principle of an "inviolate personality." Indeed, the line may be direct; both lawyers, well-read men, were fully exposed to Wordsworth's enormous prestige in late nineteenth-century America.[32] The fore-echoes of "The Right to Privacy" are no less striking, however, than Wordsworth's use of language left to him. Smith had only recently speculated that "society and conversation . . . are the most powerful remedies for restoring the mind to its tranquility," a tranquility that "men of retirement and speculation, who are apt to sit brooding at home" rarely enjoy (Smith, *Theory of Moral Sentiments*, 28). *Tranquility, solitude, brooding, speculation, retirement, society:* the eighteenth century had fully furnished the vocabulary for a new understanding of privacy; it only required someone to assign each term a fundamentally new value.

II. IDENTIFICATION

Solipsism and the City
Wordsworth's rewriting of eighteenth-century psychology resolved a long-standing difficulty in the liberal tradition—at the cost, it would turn out, of unleashing (or exposing) entirely new, equally intractable problems. If Locke had failed to demonstrate how a society composed of independent individuals might be conceived of non-theistically, and if the social construction of Hume and Smith, by addressing this ambiguity and explaining how human development could be understood in purely secular terms, had severely compromised the ideal of autonomy, Wordsworth now offered a true secular autonomism. In this view, privacy permitted the self to grow at a distance from the "multitude of causes" endemic to the public sphere and to achieve an integrity unmediated by social forces. Drawing explicitly on (while also modifying) the psychology of Locke, via David Hartley and the associationists, Wordsworth saw privacy as having certain crucial functions: in addition to protection, it allowed for reflection (the process by which the individual self might be developed and expanded), and it encouraged the nurturing of memory.[33] As a poet, however, interested above all in accounting for his own singularity *as* a poet, Wordsworth initially had little stake in grappling with certain questions to emerge from his psychology—questions with a wide-ranging impact, ultimately, in social philosophy and politics. Does everyone equally merit privacy? How can a society exist if its members are able to opt out of it? And—a concern at the heart of the legal debate that followed Warren and Brandeis—just what is privacy protecting, anyway?

One large class of problems follows from the essentially antisocial nature of Wordsworth's position: his psychology requires no second person—and indeed, the typical protagonists of his earliest work, from the period when he was formulating his basic theory of personhood, are radically isolated (the Old Cumberland Beggar, the Female Vagrant, the Boy of Winander, his own younger self as recounted in "Tintern Abbey"). Unfortunately for later liberal thinkers, it was by no means clear how a society might be composed of innumerable, unconnected atoms: a too-complete privacy might finally doom the liberal project. For Locke, the inability to interact empathetically with a community produced a person for whom "faces are but a gallery of pictures"—that is, someone who perceives himself to be the only substantial being in a world of simu-lacra.[34] In Wordsworth one can see the beginnings of a worrisome logical circle: liberalism depends upon autonomous identity; autonomy depends on privacy; privacy can limit empathy; lack of empathy dissolves civil cohesion and makes a liberal state functionally impossible. Indeed, the strongest push-back against liberalism over the course of the nineteenth century, from both conservatives like Fitzjames Stephen and radicals from Fourier to Engels, would be on communitarian grounds.

For his part, especially as he grew older, Wordsworth was aware of, and increasingly concerned with, the social consequences of isolation and the dangers of a mind turned entirely in on itself. As early as "Tintern Abbey" he signaled a willingness to relinquish the ecstatic and profoundly solitary experience of nature he had enjoyed by himself for the "still, sad music of humanity." By the end of his "great decade"—indeed, in the poem that essentially brought the decade to a close—he was ready to declare that "the heart that lives alone . . . 'tis surely blind."[35] Nevertheless, solipsism (and its consequences) remained an unsettling presence in the liberal discussion of individual autonomy. In a very different register, it also continued to haunt the poetic tradition: when the early Wordsworth spoke of "an eye made quiet by the power / of harmony [seeing] into the life of things," he was equating a separation of self from the public sphere with immense powers of insight and sympathy—a wishful contradiction with long-term consequences. His argument would reemerge in the Byronic hero, in Browning's connoisseurs, and in Tennyson's Lady of Shalott, for whom the merest contact with the outside world meant death. In the next chapter, we will examine more fully the political and aesthetic end logic of this thinking, in decadence.

For our present purposes, however, a second set of consequences to follow from Wordsworth's views on personhood had an immediate impact on how the nineteenth century understood surveillance. Privacy, as we have seen, was increasingly aligned with rural spaces—even as the English population relocated in greater numbers to the cities. The swelling masses of the urban proletariat, who could hardly head off to the Lake District or Mount Snowdon at will, were naturally going to lack the desirable preconditions for the formation of healthy selves.[36] For all of Wordsworth's occasional enthusiasm for the metropolis, he feared that the city might become a seedbed of disorder and revolution:

Oh, blank confusion! true epitome
Of what the mighty city is herself,
To thousands upon thousands of her sons,
Living amid the same perpetual whirl
Of trivial objects, melted and reduced
To one identity, by differences
That have no law, no meaning, and no end.[37]

Wordsworth's rhetoric seems to recall similar worries expressed fifty years earlier—and yet the fear that seeps into his tone could not be further from the easy contempt of a Johnson or the wistfulness of a Gray. For Johnson, country lads turning into fashionable urban drones were risible but harmless; similarly, when Gray speculated that his country church-yard might contain "mute inglorious Milton(s)," or Cromwells "guiltless of [their] country's blood," he was dismissing the rural population as innocuous: lacking exposure to the socializing forces of the city, his peas-ants would never reach a stage sufficient for either genius or tyranny. On social constructionist grounds, both authors could write off a majority of the population as unworthy of attention. Wordsworth's overthrow of social constructionism, however, also threw this equation out the window. On one hand, his psychology was clearly exclusionary: only a small frac-tion of the citizenry would ever enjoy the type of privacy that he thought necessary for healthy maturation. On the other hand, the vast hordes could no longer be ignored as a docile and unformed bolus: the rejection of eighteenth-century psychology meant that the anonymous "thousands upon thousands" of London, Manchester, Birmingham, and countless other towns and cities had to be recognized, too, as individuals—as indi-viduals, moreover, whose deprived circumstances rendered them danger-ously unprepared for civic life. Wordsworth, whose experience of the French Revolution was firsthand and a lasting presence in his thought, knew better than Gray or Johnson to ignore, say, the crowds at Bartholomew Fair or to underestimate their potential for violence:

What say you then
To times when half the city shall break out
Full of one passion—vengeance, rage, or fear—
To executions, to a street on fire,
Mobs, riots, or rejoicings? (*Prelude*, VII. 645–49)

In short, Wordsworth's view of personhood, though adequate perhaps to only 10 to 15 percent of the population, simultaneously exposed the *remaining* 85 or 90 percent as a problem: an invisible, unmapped amalgam of individuals, each to some degree or other a free agent. As a poet, Wordsworth could—and did—bequeath this problem to social planners and political philosophers; it is no coincidence, nonetheless, that his most redemptive vision of city life, in which his own singularity of insight is strongest, is his sonnet set on Westminster Bridge in the early morning with the mysterious 85 percent safely in bed.

> Ne'er saw I, never felt, a calm so deep!
> The river glideth at his own sweet will:
> Dear God! the very houses seem asleep;
> And all that mighty heart is lying still! ("Composed upon
> Westminster Bridge, September 3, 1802," 1:575, lines 11–14)

Privacy and the Masses

At the bridge's foot *today* lies Westminster Underground station, the most futuristic in the London Transport network—a hive of subterranean walkways and vaults that, for those of sunnier dispositions, evokes Escher's geometrical paradoxes, and for the more cynical, brings to mind one of Piranesi's imaginary prisons. Just inside the entrance is the station's CCTV office, not discretely tucked away, but a striking—indeed, unmissable—glass box, with guards watching continuous footage of "thousands upon thousands" of passengers: surveillance in action, open for all to see, taking in a teeming chaos that could not be further removed from the stillness of Wordsworth's poem. Just a few blocks away, the mirrored bulk of New Scotland Yard rises over Victoria Street. The very antithesis of the station's transparent cube, Scotland Yard is as closed off as Westminster is open, its highly polished windows reflecting people back onto themselves and permitting no scrutiny of the building's internal operations. Those working within have access to a vast network of closed-circuit cameras spread across much of London.

Two institutions, one might think, dedicated to the invasion of privacy, part of the "urban panopticon," as it has been called, of contemporary London.[38] And yet the two suggest different philosophies of surveillance and represent vastly different orders of ambition. The see-through box, to be effective, depends on our awareness of it, on the premise that passengers will modify their behaviors to fit what the operators wish to see. Scotland Yard, in contrast, its actual workings hidden, desires nothing more than that its suspects carry on as if unobserved, entirely unaware of the indicators for which the police are searching. When we look at its mirrored walls, we only see ourselves. Where one seeks to record and detect, the other aims to anticipate and thus prevent: as a senior intelligence officer at Scotland Yard put it to us, "No one is *interpreting* anything at [Westminster Station]."³⁹ The cameras are there at best to deter bad behavior and at worst to store up evidence for future prosecution. The great goal of the Yard, on the other hand, is to create an active and indeed predictive system of behavioral surveillance—to "put some science around it," in the same officer's words. Surprisingly, perhaps, the coercive psychology implicit in the less ambitious of these institutions will play a significant role in our next chapter's analysis of modern paranoia; Scotland Yard's efforts, conversely, fall within a genealogy of empathetic police work that goes back centuries, to the period we have just begun to explore.

How, then, to predict the behavior of thousands, even millions, of people—or even more pressing: how to anticipate the one in a million who might cause serious harm? By the turn of the nineteenth century, these questions could no longer be ignored. One runs the risk, in any intellectual history of this sort, of depicting state administrators as a kind of book club anxiously awaiting Locke's, or Hume's, or Wordsworth's latest pronouncements and then shifting their surveillance strategies accordingly. We do not mean to paint such a picture, but it is nonetheless important to remember the close familiarity many in government had with the pressing philosophical issues of the day: the key names did in fact pop up in more than a few parliamentary debates, and Locke's stature in particular, as an emblem of native British wisdom, was as high as it ever would be.⁴⁰ As we saw in the last chapter, the State's initial response to Locke's agnosticism about what constituted a person ("we are ignorant of that thinking thing that is within us" [etc.]) and Hume's skepticism that any such thing as a coherent person even existed had been retrenchment: the Catholic laws in Ireland relied on the crudest techniques of external observation. As others have pointed out, however, a redoubled interest in identification via state apparati had given birth, by the time of the Regency, to several of what we now think of as basic surveillance practices. Techniques that appeared to move from surface behavior to the inner self—to use data about *what* and *where* a person was to divine *who* that person *might really be* (and, ideally, to foresee his or her future actions)— naturally received the most interest.

Thus, for example, the rise of actuarial science, the tremendous surge of statistical investigation and accumulation—the word "statistics" being itself an eighteenth-century neologism. The rise of these practices has received its most familiar telling at the hands of Foucault (and Foucault-inspired critics) as a supporting element in the march to power of disciplinary institutions (often via "bureaucracy").[41] And yet the too-ready alignment of such methods with the "carceral continuum" of a nascent disciplinary State has largely missed the element of wish fulfillment and insecurity that accompanied them. Few works, perhaps, have achieved more infamy as exemplars of the attempt to fix identity via statistics than the poverty maps of late nineteenth-century London. On the face of it, they look like something designed with discourse theory in mind (and have certainly been treated that way by critics).[42] The most famous is the work of Charles Booth (figure 4), who identifies, street-by-street and block-by-block, a geographically predictable social hierarchy ranging from the squalid addresses of "semi-criminals . . . [who live] the life of savages . . . and [whose] only luxury is drink" to the more affluent streets, occupied by "a hardworking sober, energetic class." All very forbidding—but underlain, just as surely, by a certain nervousness. The idea that a man's address could predict his savagery or sobriety (particularly when "good" and "bad" blocks frequently came hard up against each other), however appealing, would not last very long in the cold, epistemic light of day. Still, the promise held out by data gathering, in the face of swelling and anonymous urban populations, was enough to inspire a series of mutually enforcing policies and publications, often implemented and supported by forward-thinking politicians.[43]

Booth's exquisitely detailed plan, designed to give the impression of complete knowledge, cheerfully lumped together thousands of individuals on the premise that "when great aggregations of population are brought together, there is . . . a tendency toward uniformity of class in each section."[44] A method ill-equipped, alas, to find a Jack the Ripper or Sweeney Todd living amidst "sober, energetic" neighbors. Our point,

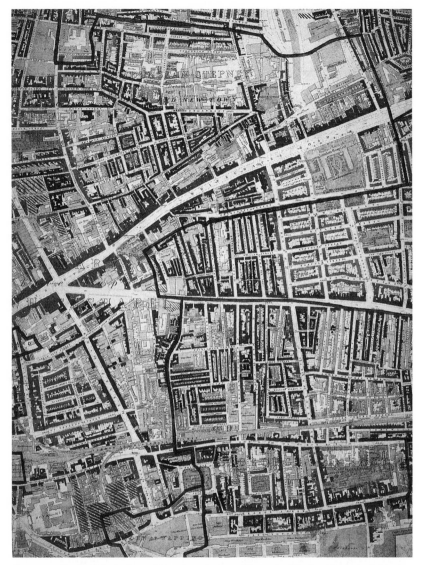

Figure 4. Charles Booth, from *Maps Descriptive of Poverty*, 1889. In the original, black outlines marked the presence of the "Vicious. Semi-criminal class"; dark blue the class of "chronic want"; light red the "fairly comfortable," red the "well-to-do"; and yellow the "upper classes." Museum of London / Bridgeman Art Library.

however, is not to mock Booth as a failed dreamer or oddball.[45] His illogical (and from some perspectives, highly attractive) leap to prediction in no way countermands a more practical (but also idealistic) starting point. Justice, understood as an egalitarian aiding of the disadvantaged, required knowing the population and its needs—and inspired a pragmatic and nuanced effort in statistical planning well in advance of the poverty maps. As late as the early eighteenth century, the most basic markers of identity remained largely unfixed: even personal names were still causing endless headaches. Far from the stable ur-identifier of modern society, names were for centuries easily and frequently changed (Defoe's regular renaming of himself was less eccentric than it now appears), to the point that Bentham, in exasperation, argued that everyone should have their names tattooed on their wrists. While declining to pursue that particular plan, the law did move to regulate naming practices and modernize the system of bureaucratic record keeping. ID cards became standard during the later eighteenth century, and John Rickman's reformed census of 1801 is rightly viewed as a watershed. "The intimate knowledge of any country," Rickman argued, "must form the rational basis of legislation and diplomacy"—a sentiment seconded by the *Times:* "It is only by learning what, as a people, we have been doing that we can learn what remains for us as a people to do."[46]

And on and on, with a long list of other governmental attempts to establish "legal identity" as an inescapable condition and requirement of modern life—all raw evidence for the familiar argument about the dream of social justice leading to the reality of a disciplinary society.[47] We do not mean to minimize the more sinister aspects of this history, all of which were perfectly evident at the time. In 1796, an authoritarian sensibility like Fichte could enthusiastically comment that

> the chief principle of a well-regulated police state is this: *that each citizen shall be at all times and places . . . recognized as this or that particular person.* No one must remain unknown to the police. This can be attained with certainty only in the following manner: Each one must always carry a pass with him, signed by his immediate government official, in which his person is accurately described. . . . No person should be received at any place who cannot thus make known by his pass his last place of residence and name.[48]

The spirit of Fichte lives on in the more dismal accounts of the bureaucratic State. What gets lost, however, is the way these developments were made possible by the steady *triumph* of autonomy and privacy over the course of the century—indeed, emerged from the internal logic of these ideologies. If Wordsworth had first thought through the problems of solitude and independence for purely personal reasons, the succeeding decades nonetheless saw a diffusion of his ideas into the educated population generally. The best-known successes of the Wordsworth cult were, for reasons we will discuss shortly, in America during the decades leading up to the Civil War—we see it in Thoreau's claim to have "never found the companion that was so companionable as solitude" or in Emerson's writings on self-reliance. But the same tone can be heard as well in Mill's ardent praise of rural privacy:

> Solitude, in the sense of being often alone, is essential to any
> depth of meditation or of character; and solitude in the presence
> of natural beauty and grandeur, is the cradle of thoughts and
> aspirations which are not only good for the individual, but
> which society could ill do without.[49]

With the ringing opening of *On Liberty*—"Over himself, over his own body and mind, the individual is sovereign"—Mill pushed the thoughts and indeed images of Wordsworth conclusively into the political sphere: every individual must be guaranteed by law the right to think, feel, and even do as he or she wishes—so long as other individuals are not harmed (alas, the expandable semantic limits of "harm" have caused no end of subsequent controversy).[50] The ultimate victory of Gladstonian liberalism—and its central policy of limiting interventionism—meant that the 1860s were a golden age for privacy in England, not just as a philosophical concept but as a practical concern.[51]

And yet, ironically, the very triumph of privacy theory almost inevitably resulted in the restriction of the privacy apparatus to a minority and a consequent expansion of official surveillance activities. Mill had articulated his call for personal liberty on impeccably Wordsworthian grounds:

> When society itself is the tyrant—society collectively over the
> individuals who compose it—its means of tyrannizing are not
> restricted to the acts which it may do by the hands of its political
> functionaries. . . . Social tyranny [is] more formidable than
> many kinds of political oppression, since, though not usually

upheld by such extreme penalties, it leaves fewer means of
escape, penetrating much more deeply into the details of life
and enslaving the soul itself. . . . There needs protection also
against the tyranny of prevailing opinion and feeling; against
the tendency of society to . . . prevent the formation of any
individuality not in harmony with its ways. (Mill, *On
Liberty*, 129–30)

Mill's greatest fear, that is to say, when he referred to the penetration and
"enslaving" of the soul—which both echoed Wordsworth's worry about
the blunting of the mind and its reduction to savage torpor and anticipated Warren's and Brandeis's dread of triviality destroying robustness of
thought and delicacy of feeling—was that the greatest injury in cases of
lost privacy would *not be felt* by the sufferers.[52] The very sign of that
"slavery"—that acquiescence to the tyranny of the majority—being an
ignorance of one's own plight. All the more reason for privacy, for those
with access to it—but what of that remaining 85 or 90 percent (a lower
number, to be sure, by mid-century)? In his own rhetoric, which declared
social pressures to be more harmful than the misdeeds of "political func-
tionaries," Mill provided an answer—if not for himself, then for many
liberals who followed him.

Such, we would suggest, is the paradoxical logic behind the poverty
maps, the 1801 census, the 1836 founding of the General Register Office,
and countless similar initiatives. If privacy was necessary for the development of an autonomous individual, but vast hordes of the poor
(especially) were not exposed to the proper conditions for healthy maturation, then it was the duty of the State to step in and bring the masses
along. Inevitably this involved a great deal of oversight and loss of
privacy—for their own good, as it were; a split within liberalism that
pertains to this day, between advocates of liberty (above all) and advocates
of welfare, was well under way. Practically, it meant that some in Victorian
society were more entitled to privacy than others, an axiom that found
ample confirmation in the built environment of nineteenth-century
London. Joseph Conrad, somewhat late in the game, wryly captured this
point in his descriptions of Belgravia, circa 1886:

With a turn to the left, Mr. Verloc pursued his way along a narrow
street by the side of a yellow wall which, for some inscrutable

reason, had No. 1 Chesham Square written on it in black letters. Chesham Square was at least sixty yards away. . . . At last . . . he reached the Square, and made diagonally for No. 10. This belonged to an imposing carriage gate in a high, clean wall between two houses, of which one rationally enough bore the number 9 and the other was numbered 37; but the fact that this last belonged to Porthill Street, a street well-known in the neighborhood, was proclaimed by an inscription [from] whatever highly efficient authority is charged with the duty of keeping track of London's strayed houses. Why powers are not asked of Parliament . . . for compelling those edifices to return to where they belong is one of the mysteries of municipal administration.[53]

But of course—Conrad's point—it was no mystery at all: the high walls, luxurious row houses, all looking more or less identical, and impossible-to-locate addresses were all aspects of an architecture of privacy (to this one might add private clubs, private squares, private hansom cabs), which the wealthy had come to expect and enjoy.

For the opposite side of the coin, one might turn to accounts by Dickens, Gissing, or Henry Mayhew—but Engels's descriptions of the working poor are perhaps paradigmatic. Over and over he returns to the central image of "masses of humanity," sleeping in piles, packed together with no privacy whatever, "robbed of all humanity, degraded, reduced morally and physically to bestiality." As with Wordsworth, the masses cannot be written off as uniform or faceless—quite the opposite, to the lasting peril of civil stability: "The brutal indifference, the unfeeling isolation of each in his private interest, becomes the more repellent and offensive, the more these individuals are crowded together, within a limited space. . . . The dissolution of mankind into monads, of which each one has a separate principle, the world of atoms, is here carried out to its utmost extreme."[54] Individualism, in this familiar analysis, is taken for granted—but under such conditions, Engels concludes, a healthy development into functioning citizens is impossible. In a curious sleight of hand—in which his reasoning is congruent with contemporary liberal thinking—*only* privacy, and the nurturing of self that it permits, can produce *socialized* adults; otherwise people fall back, as in the nightmare vision of Bartholomew Fair, on their inborn selfishness and "isolation."

The liberal State's most striking response to the literally "shameless" conditions Engels describes was the reorganization of proletarian quarters into more surveillance-friendly zones: in short, a solution that accorded with the burgeoning statistical-identity movement. Thus Mayhew's insistence upon "statistical knowledge" in his *London Labour and the London Poor;* thus Edwin Chadwick's *Report on the Sanitary Condition of the Labouring Population of Great Britain* (1842) pointed out that dwelling places "exposed to observation" could be expected to produce a better sort of worker.[55] Paradoxically, the liberal reformer's cry for psychological privacy in the poor quarters (through the limiting of physical proximity) was accompanied by a more plenary sacrifice of physical privacy and increase in surveillance (with its own psychological costs). Privacy was sacrificed, that is to say, in the name of an autonomy for which privacy had once been thought a necessary precondition. In any case, turning slums into transparent grids proved easier said than done, and in the short term the lower classes found themselves possessed of privacy's uncanny mirror image—the anonymity of mass urban poverty—and enough of that to make the State nervous.

The Police

We would suggest that it is within this matrix—widespread apprehension about the unreadability of the masses and an increasingly fraught (and class-based) valuation of privacy within the liberal consensus—that the advent of the Metropolitan Police is best understood. If anything, they arrived late: though constabularies of varying degrees of formality had long existed (notably the mid-1700s Bow Street Runners), Robert Peel's statute establishing a professional force for Greater London (excluding the City) appeared only in 1829. It begins:

> Whereas Offences against Property have of late increased in and Near the Metropolis; and the local Establishments of Nightly Watch and Nightly Police have been found inadequate to the Prevention and Detection of Crime, by reason of the frequent Unfitness of the Individuals employed, the Insufficiency of their Number, the limited Sphere of their Authority, and their Want of Connection and Co-operation with each other: And Whereas it is expedient to substitute a new and more efficient System of

Police in lieu of such Establishments. . . . and to constitute an
Office of Police, which, acting under the Immediate Authority
of One of His Majesty's Principal Secretaries of State, shall
direct and controul the whole of such new System of Police
within those limits: Be it therefore enacted (etc.)[56]

At one fell swoop, a loose and largely amateur array of local policing, of a
sort going back to the Middle Ages, was replaced by a strongly centralized
and powerful force, ready and able to defend the prerogatives of "property" and pursuing the ultimate goal—shades of modern-day Scotland
Yard—of "prevention."[57] Thus the Act allowed, indeed expected the police
to have considerable discretion penetrating the darker corners of the city:
the Act established broad "power[s] to enter" and, as an 1839 amendment
reads, "It shall be lawful for any Constable belonging to the Metropolitan
Police District . . . to take into Custody, without a Warrant, any Person . . .
whose Name and Residence shall be unknown to such Constable." This
was a move, in short, to shed light not just on shady places but on shady
people—none shadier than the undocumented. The nameless and
addressless were de facto in violation of an identity-based legal system—
and no author, perhaps, was more attuned to this particular insecurity
than Dickens. Jo, an illiterate, homeless boy, causes more panic than any
other character in *Bleak House* simply because of his uncertainty over
what "identity" means. Confronted with characters like Jo, the machinery
of the State shudders to a halt:

Name, Jo. Nothing else that he knows on. Don't know that
everybody has two names. Never heerd of sich a think. Don't
know that Jo is short for a longer name. . . . Spell it? No. HE can't
spell it. No father, no mother, no friends. Never been to school.
What's home? . . .

"This won't do, gentlemen!" says the Coroner with a
melancholy shake of the head.

"Don't you think you can receive his evidence, sir?" asks an
attentive Juryman.

"Out of the question," says the Coroner. "You have heard the
boy. 'Can't exactly say' won't do, you know. We can't take THAT
in a Court of Justice, gentlemen. It's terrible depravity. Put the
boy aside."[58]

Ignorant of any institution that might provide him a civil identity (family, school, the law), Jo simply cannot be dealt with and must be put aside—at least until he is old enough to be arrested for his inscrutability. Dickens seizes on the way the legal system struggles with the very lowest members of society, who cannot offer even their "name[s] and residence[s]" to a passing constable. "No one must remain unknown to the police," Fichte had proclaimed—but one needn't have endorsed, as Fichte did, a "well-regulated police state" to perceive the threat that Jo, and thousands like him, presented to society.

When Dickens began, several years earlier, writing about the London police, the force was barely twenty years in existence. Officers and constables are a reasonably frequent presence in his novels—most notably in *Bleak House*—but his most sustained consideration is to be found in a series of journalistic pieces he wrote towards the start of his stint editing the weekly magazine *Household Words* (1850–59); most of these items (including "The Detective Police," "Three 'Detective' Anecdotes," and "On Duty with Inspector Field") date from 1850–51, and the latest ("Down with the Tide") is from 1853. As a group they show Dickens in apparent sympathy with the aims of the police—indeed, an unstated purpose of the pieces is clearly to cast the force, still a recent phenomenon, in the best light for an unconvinced readership.[59] As they work to penetrate the anonymous underclasses, often disguising themselves as proletarian caricatures (so that one sergeant dresses up as a butcher to break up a fencing ring), privacy is always subject to a double standard. The denizens of hovels and rookeries and boardinghouses receive no consideration at all: "Ten, twenty, thirty—who can count them! Men, women, children, for the most part naked, heaped upon the floor like maggots in a cheese!"[60] Not far from the descriptions of Engels, but the graphic similes short-circuit anything like sympathy. Looking for criminals "in . . . confined, intolerable rooms, burrowed out like the holes of rats or the nests of insect-vermin," the police are merciless, unhesitating, and intrusive to a degree that still shocks. The constable "goes from bed to bed and turns their slumbering heads towards us, as a salesman might turn sheep. . . . Whenever the turning lane of light becomes stationary for a moment, some sleeper appears at the end of it, submits himself to be scrutinised, and fades away into the darkness" (228). This last passage is from "On Duty with Inspector Field," which chronicles the exploits of the real-life model for Inspector Bucket in *Bleak House*. The good public servant (much like his fictional avatar) is nearly godlike in his powers. The "intricate passages" and "conjurer's boxes" of the slums open their "secret workings" irresistibly to him and he encounters little resistance—the underclasses knowing their place: "Inspector Field's eye is the roving eye that searches every corner of the cellar as he talks. Inspector Field's hand is the well-known hand that has collared half the people here, [yet he] stands in this den, the Sultan of the place. Every thief here cowers before him, like a schoolboy before his schoolmaster" (223).

Our own "surveillance society" hardly has a figure to match the determined and all-seeing Victorian policeman, greeted with awe and deference when he walks the street. For good reason, too: it requires only a moment's consideration to see through the pretense. As Dickens establishes from the start, this tour of "Rat's Castle" and other London lowlights, is the nineteenth-century equivalent of the ride-alongs sometimes offered to celebrities or journalists by present-day police departments. Everything has been staged to within an inch of plausibility, with the goal of encouraging a comforting fantasy: that the police possess a "perfect mastery of . . . character" (227) and thus are able to locate the needles in the haystack. It is perhaps in revolt against this obvious imposture—that well-trained policemen possess a personal knowledge of *each particular* criminal in the metropolis—that Dickens veers, using the first person, into voices of the criminals: "If it's the accursed glaring eye that fixes me, go where I will, I am helpless. . . . I am no match for this individual energy and keenness, or this organized and steady system!" (228–29). The effect is at once empathetic and paranoid (the first person raises, at least for a moment, the thought that *you too*, dear reader, might finally be the object of an all-seeing gaze)—but also a bit silly and more than a bit arch: a bursting of the bubble through rhetorical overload.

In any event, the fantasy is fully congruous with the other forms of wish fulfillment we have been tracking (like the poverty maps) and stems from the same fears—a point that's clarified when Inspector Field deals with his superiors and paymasters. In their investigations of affluent suspects, the police take a gentle and discrete approach: one sergeant, for example, is praised as "a prodigious hand at pursuing private inquiries of a delicate nature." Even the less gifted officers are above all employees with a surprisingly nuanced view of privacy and surveillance as meaning different things up and down the social scale; Field himself is "submissive" to the establishment, guarding its secrets and its treasures (he is late to meet Dickens because he is finishing a shift as "the guardian genius of the British Museum")—and the detective police, it turns out, have their own "propitiating" to do as—in George Orwell's angry reduction— "bodyguards of the moneyed class."[61] While the naked and submissive masses cannot resist Field's gaze, the ruling classes certainly can—and direct it where they wish. It is perhaps in subtle protest against his own public relations work—and a restatement of his priorities as a realist author—that Dickens ends his initial sketch of "The Detective Police": "One other circumstance finally wound up the evening, after our Detective guests had left us. One of the sharpest among them, and the officer best acquainted with the Swell Mob, had his pocket picked, going home!" (206).

III. REALISM AND THE SUBGENRES

The Crisis of Representation

Within the terms we have been developing, one can see the attraction writers of realistic fiction would have had to the police: the policeman's job in obvious ways resembled the novelist's—to tell the truth about other people. Moreover, the dazzling abilities of an Inspector Field presented a distinct challenge at a time when the realistic contract was under considerable duress. The novel, in its pursuit of human interiority, had begun almost at once to violate the empirical premises of "formal realism" and to develop robustly nonempirical methods of depicting other minds: third-person omniscient narrative and free-indirect discourse, with interior monologue and stream of consciousness to follow. By the mid-nineteenth century, the bad faith underlying the first two techniques was impossible to deny, and in this atmosphere, Dickens's opening to chapter 3 of A Tale of Two Cities stands out as a singular admission of defeat:

> A wonderful fact to reflect upon, that every human creature is
> constituted to be that profound secret and mystery to every
> other. A solemn consideration, when I enter a great city by
> night, that every one of those darkly clustered houses encloses

its own secret; that every room in every one of them encloses its own secret; that every beating heart in the hundreds of thousands of breasts there, is, in some of its imaginings, a secret to the heart nearest it! Something of the awfulness, even of Death itself, is referable to this. . . . It is the inexorable consolidation and perpetuation of the secret that was always in that individuality, and which I shall carry in mine to my life's end. In any of the burial-places of this city through which I pass, is there a sleeper more inscrutable than its busy inhabitants are, in their innermost personality, to me, or than I am to them?

In the way it uses the panorama of a sleeping city to work through problems of observation and the self, this great outpouring of doubts has more than a little in common with the Westminster Bridge sonnet. Or rather, it might be the sonnet's mirror image: for Wordsworth, preserving his own singularity of poetic vision necessitates holding a teeming city of individuals at arm's length (they're safely asleep); sixty years later, Dickens acknowledges the individuality of that population as an impossible hurdle for the novelist (sleep is just a stand-in for universal inscrutability). This literary doubt has unavoidable political ramifications, with Dickens essentially throwing up his hands and admitting that inner lives can never be represented accurately: to depict the secret thoughts of another person— to be a novelist, in other words—is a peremptory assertion of authorial power contrary to the obligations of realism. So long as policemen remained mere mortals, furthermore, their treatment within realistic fiction would provide no escape from a fundamental impasse.[62]

More hope, we would argue, came from the unlikeliest of quarters. Towards the end of the last chapter, we suggested that by the late eighteenth century a segment of the scientific community was deeply invested in pursuing techniques of exterior observation designed to reveal the inner person. Although such work continues to this day (with biometric screening, facial microexpression analysis, and the like), most efforts of two centuries ago were finally revealed as, at best, overenthusiastic extensions of legitimate inquiry or, at worst, out-and-out charlatanry. Nevertheless, for a sense of the eagerness, or desperation, with which realistic prose seized on these methods, consider one final panorama of nineteenth-century London; the speaker is sitting at the window of the "D —— Coffee House," watching the crowds pass by:

> At first my observations took an abstract and generalizing turn.
> I looked at the passengers in masses, and thought of them in
> their aggregate relations. Soon, however, I descended to details,
> and regarded with minute interest the innumerable varieties of
> figure, dress, air, gait, visage, and expression of countenance.
> . . . The gamblers . . . were distinguished by a certain sodden
> swarthiness of complexion, a filmy dimness of eye, and pallor
> and compression of lip. There were two other traits, moreover,
> by which I could always detect them;—a guarded lowness of
> tone in conversation, and a more than ordinary extension of the
> thumb in a direction at right angles with the fingers . . . [63]

This excerpt is from the justly famous opening to Poe's "The Man of the Crowd." We emphasize that it is an excerpt: the narrator's exhaustive, virtuosic taxonomy of the various "types" and "visages" he spies from the window takes up nearly a third of the story. Of course, if life were like this, the job of a Scotland Yard officer would be much easier—or perhaps unnecessary. Wordsworth had once exclaimed, "The face of every one / That passes by me is a mystery"; earlier still, Iago had boasted of his ability to conceal his motives behind "forms and visages of duty." For Poe's speaker, no problem: how to distinguish an honorable clergyman from a huckster playing dress-up? Just look for the "filmy dimness of eye, and pallor and compression of lip." The "thick, sensual lips" or "fearfully pale [countenances]" of the drunkards, similarly, perfectly reflect their inner selves, their private desires and motivations.[64]

To dismiss these portraits—and similar ones that flourished in nineteenth-century fiction from Scott, to Hawthorne, to Wilde—as crude caricatures is at once to state the obvious and to miss the point. Poe, here and in much of his output, was drawing on physiognomy, one of numerous period "sciences" that promised the reading of real people as confidently *as if they were* caricatures, rendering both the willing participation of the individual and the protection of privacy unnecessary. A person's appearance, and particularly the shape of the face, revealed his or her inner self.[65] Physiognomical texts reduced character study more or less to the level of *Animal Farm* (see figure 5).[66] Thus Poe's Roderick

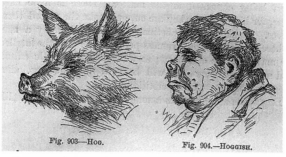

Fig. 903—Hog.   Fig. 904.—Hoggish.

Figure 5. "Hog" and "Hoggish," figures 903 and 904 in Samuel R. Wells, *New Physiognomy, or, Signs of Character* (London, 1894).

Usher has a "finely moulded chin, speaking, in its want of prominence, of a want of moral energy," and Ligeia's "love of life" is evident in "the gentle prominence of the regions above [her] temples."[67] This latter description draws on the related field of phrenology, in which the shape of the skull reflected the subject's psychology and which was, if anything, even more determinedly deterministic. The *American Phrenological Journal*, which ran from 1838 to 1911, ended each issue with their motto, a testament to phrenology's usefulness "in judging of the dispositions of those around us, by all the known external 'Signs of Character.'" Phrenology manuals read like the second coming of Renaissance character books: descriptions of head shapes are titled "the Criminal," "the Genius," etc. For the phrenology enthusiast, the world was full of stock types, instantly recognizable and classifiable by the bumps on their heads. Charlotte Brontë's early work *The Professor* features an infamous description of a schoolgirl:

> I wonder that any one, looking at that girl's head and countenance, would have received her under their roof. She had precisely the same shape of skull as Pope Alexander the Sixth; her organs of benevolence, veneration, conscientiousness, adhesiveness, were singularly small, those of self-esteem, firmness, destructiveness, combativeness, preposterously large; her head sloped up in the penthouse shape, was contracted about the forehead, and prominent behind; she had rather good, though large and marked features; her temperament was fibrous and bilious, her complexion pale and dark, hair and eyes black, form angular and rigid but proportionate, age fifteen.

Here the essential fantasy of deterministic observation is pushed to its logical extreme: every detail of a subject's personality will reveal itself—and instantly—to those who know the right way to observe.[68] There is nothing to hide behind or indeed to hide.

Ultimately, phrenology and its ilk were monuments both to a society that had become serious about privacy and to the impotence of those who would violate it—the latest of liberal culture's increasingly tortured efforts to account for a population of millions of individuals. If not for phrenology, and its supposed ability to provide that "discriminating knowledge of individual character [which] is a primary condition of much of the social improvement that the present age is panting for," what hope was there for "regulat[ing] our intercourse with our fellow-men"?[69] Taken one way, phrenology might be seen as a scientific effort to reestablish the possibility, as had existed under social allegory, of common interpretation; taken a slightly different (and we would suggest more plausible) way, it was no more than the allegorical Will to Power reasserting itself where liberal ideology was weakest (or least attentive): in the supposedly objective precincts of science. The difference in emphasis is not trivial: in the first view, the widespread enthusiasm for these interpretive modes could be read as compatible with liberalism and its goals; in the second view, the pseudo-sciences were a symptom of liberalism's vulnerability and its potential replacement by something more coercive. In either case, the symptoms of allegory and pseudo-science were the same when it came to representation: caricature and reduction. Not the most promising materials for compelling fiction—and yet it's no accident that many novelists were drawn to physiognomy and the like: as "sciences," which did not overtly violate the canons of empiricism (they were, after all, rooted in nothing more than exterior observation), they were fodder for writers still committed to realism. Spenser's Duessa was an allegorical figment; Brontë's schoolgirl, with her alarmingly small "organs of benevolence" was as "real" as Crusoe or Pamela had been.

This is not to say that it was possible to construct novels, or even short stories, entirely out of phrenological types; just as the novel, for its own survival, had had to minimize the presence of social construction, so the rise of the pseudo-sciences presented both a temptation and a threat. As with social construction, phrenology and physiognomy gave with one hand and took away with the other: the cost of a legible surface—as in the Brontë passage—being tediousness and a lack of depth. For all his enthusiastic and frequent use of phrenology, Poe, with his typical double-mindedness, also saw the other side of the equation. The title character of "The Man of the Crowd," in pointed rebuke to the narrator's initial confidence, has "a countenance which at once arrested and absorbed my whole attention, on account of the absolute idiosyncrasy of its expression. Any thing even remotely resembling that expression I had never seen before" (2:511). The remainder of the story has the narrator pursuing this figure through nighttime London and realizing, gradually and to his horror, that the man cannot be understood. The story can be read as a kind of satire on the philosophical naïveté of scientific determinism: it begins, after all, at a London coffeehouse, the symbolic locus of eighteenth-century liberalism—a hint that the narrator really should know better than to think he can read people in pre-Enlightenment ways.

For authors less philosophically invested than Poe, caricature (either drawing on physiognomy or more frankly allegorical) was a practical expedient, something to prop up the tottering house of realism; among these writers we may count Dickens—who, whatever his despair in (one paragraph of) A Tale of Two Cities, was too much of a writing animal to let theoretical consistency kill his chosen medium or end his social mission. Ultimately, caricature came to fill a crucial role within the complex realism of the nineteenth-century novel. Like the socially constructed drones "figuring at a ball" in an Austen work, these verifiable and transparent figments *made possible* empathetic, individual-centered fictions—by throwing into high relief the more conventional, three-dimensional characters. Consider, for example, the dramatis personae of a typical Dickens novel:

Noddy Boffin	Bradley Headstone
John Rokesmith	Eugene Wrayburn
Rogue Riderhood	Mr. Podsnap
Bella Wilfer	Mr. Twemlow
Lavinia Wilfer	Lady Tippins
Mrs. Veneering	Jenny Wren
Silas Wegg	Sophronia Lammle
Mr. Venus	Lizzie Hexam

Even someone coming to *Our Mutual Friend* for the first time will not need to be told that Noddy Boffin is not the romantic lead and that Bella Wilfer will likely play a deeper role in the plot than Mrs. Veneering. One might argue that the dramatis personae is finally contradictory—that John Rokesmith draws on canons of representation that go back to the "formal realism" of Defoe and Richardson, while Mr. Venus marks an obvious return of something more allegorical. It *is* contradictory: by the mid-nineteenth century, under siege from precisely the empirical doubts that Dickens elsewhere describes so eloquently, conventional realism all but *requires* allegorical support—rounded characters at the center and Podsnaps at the peripheries—to maintain its effects, ideological and otherwise. Without a Rogue Riderhood to set him off, the artificiality and constructedness of a John Rokesmith are blindingly evident. There is certainly bad faith in this: Rogue Riderhood and his ilk lack what Locke called the "perfect freedom of acting." Nevertheless, in something of a devil's bargain, Rogue's inhuman predictability helps us appreciate and indeed guarantees the changing, complex, and *believably* autonomous identities of the major characters he comes into contact with. As such, caricature is an anti-liberal tool in a larger pro-liberal strategy.

Leaving the Island: Democratic Vistas
The ends, perhaps, justified the means. All the same, there is no getting away from the elitism inherent in a caricature-filled work or from the ways that the two-dimensionality of caricature revealed a strain in the liberal worldview (with which the mainstream Victorian novel was still in broad sympathy): different kinds of people had to be dealt with differently. Fifteen percent of the population were John Rokesmiths; could the rest simply be understood as caricatures? By the mid-nineteenth century, *both* liberal politics and realistic literature, as coeval products of the contractual dispensation, had engaged in a series of increasingly extreme compromises, both to preserve the unstated agreements under which they had originally arisen and to conceal the extent to which they had strayed. The mixed form of the Victorian novel, employing radically nonempirical narrative techniques and internally contradictory forms of characterization, could claim only in the most compromised way still to be telling the truth about other people. And yet this compromise, most British writers of the time would likely have affirmed, was preferable to

the only apparent alternative: giving up on the realistic project altogether in the face of a nation composed of countless individuals, each unknowable to each, and returning to more explicitly dogmatic forms like romance and allegory. In this respect, American literature of the same period, touched by both the philosophical radicalism of Emerson and the political radicalism of Jackson, is instructive—American authors being more willing to take Lockean premises (both empirical and political) at face value, having less commitment to the preservation, at all costs, of conventional realism. It is hard to imagine a British author of the time concurring with Whitman's declaration, in his introduction to the 1855 edition of *Leaves of Grass*, that "the messages of great poets to each man and woman are, Come to us on equal terms, Only then can you understand us, We are no better than you. . . . We affirm there can be unnumbered Supremes."[70] We are well aware that Whitman represents but one position within the complex ideological situation of antebellum America and are not using him as a synecdoche for "the attitude towards the individual in the nineteenth-century United States." Nor are we ignoring the variety of aesthetic responses that reflected this spectrum, from Poe's serious engagement with British conventional realism, to purported rejections of that tradition altogether, like Hawthornian romance. Nevertheless, in obvious ways, Whitman's comments reflect a national investment in the individual (or the idea of the individual) with concrete consequences for literature, surveillance theory, and privacy. Practically, it meant that, where British writers were likely to yield on empirical principles, in the hope of preserving a core of humanistic belief, American writers engaged in a more stringent and rigorous interrogation of these problems. To bring the long history of realism we are telling to a close, therefore, the first island we must leave is Britain itself.

How, then, might a literature faithful to empiricism survive, without engaging in the typical compromises of British literature, while also acknowledging both the inviolable personality of each individual and the inevitable limitations of observation? How was a frank acknowledgment of these limitations not, finally, giving up on the initial reason for realism itself, to reach something true about the inner lives of other people? American answers to these questions were various (including the return to romance)—but two in particular command our brief attention as relevant to the histories of privacy and surveillance. Whitman's solution was the list. From the opening of "Song of Myself," section 15:

> The duck-shooter walks by silent and cautious stretches,
> The deacons are ordained with crossed hands at the altar,
> The spinning-girl retreats and advances to the hum of the big wheel,
> The farmer stops by the bars of a Sunday and looks at the oats and rye,
> The lunatic is carried off at last to the asylum a confirmed case,
> He will never sleep any more as he did in the cot of his mother's bedroom,
> The jour printer with gray head and gaunt jaws works at his case,
> He turns his quid of tobacco, his eyes get blurred with the manuscript.[71]

Whitman's catalogue bears comparison with our previous urban panoramas. He might be Wordsworth on the bridge, some four or five hours later, with the city now up and about—a Wordsworth less troubled by the crowds and ready to acknowledge each individual as such. Or he might join Poe at the coffeehouse window—though again, Poe's similarly protracted taxonomy is finally anti-democratic (the confident stereotyping of the opening and the confusion of the end both tend in that direction). Ultimately, in keeping with his own belief that "men and women and the earth and all upon it are simply to be taken as they are . . . with perfect candor," Whitman's solution to the autonomy problem is a radical parataxis: each person is observed, acknowledged, and no more.[72] Even Whitman himself (he could well be that blurry-eyed "jour printer") occupies no special position as a *character*.

And yet this solution exposes deep problems going forward, for both surveillance and literature—poetry in particular. Whitman's human inventory is pointedly noninterpretive—and although the reader is constantly tempted to perceive a structure undergirding the sequence of images (why does the lunatic follow the farmer? why is the jour printer succeeded by "malformed limbs [on an] anatomist's table"?), any larger coherence finally reflects the reader's own structures of mind. The poem is also oddly shallow: people are seen as fragments or in snippets, with only the vaguest reference to their fuller lives—that is to say, the list form at once celebrates each person's individuality and confirms each person in his or her privacy: there is no entry into the deacon or the duck-shooter beyond what Whitman *sees*. In short, by thinking through (and respecting) the limits of authorial observation, and by understanding each person as a monad, Whitman brings us all the way back to Westminster Bridge— not the sonnet, but the Underground station, with its cube of watchers desperately trying to make sense of the "thousands upon thousands" passing before them. In the twentieth century, the observer's empathetic bind, as articulated by Whitman, would be recognized as a key interpretive dilemma of modern surveillance; meanwhile, it was a problem for poetry as well. What is Whitman's subject position anyway? Has he in fact become the poetic equivalent of a CCTV camera—or, in his principle of selection (whatever that may be) and in those moments when he achieves an access seemingly beyond his capabilities (how does he know about the lunatic's mother?), has he adopted a perspective more omniscient—in other words, a fantasy? The double bind that began with Wordsworth and which seemed inescapable by century's end—a commitment on the one hand to privacy and autonomy and on the other to the artist's special ability to read the populace—will be a major theme of the remainder of this book.

Within the period, coming at these same problems from a very different angle, Melville offered an iconic figure almost perfectly complementary to Whitman's panoptic but interpretively challenged poetic eye: a central character, subject to multiple competing readings, whose identity nevertheless remains beyond access. Obviously we are referring to the title character of *Moby-Dick*. And *The Confidence-Man*. And *Pierre*, and "Bartleby the Scrivener," and *Israel Potter*. In a typical Melville narrative, we would suggest, numerous attempts to gain an interpretive foothold on this figure are entertained and then subverted, with layers of narrative peeled away, exposing finally no essential center. If Whitman's most characteristic form is the list, Melville's, for want of a better image, is the onion; both spell trouble, in the long run, for the realistic contract.[73] At issue in "Benito Cereno," Melville's most compact and programmatic critique of observation and interpretation—and, pointedly, the only one of these narratives *not* named for the central, mysterious figure—is the story of slave revolt. African captives, led by one Babo, take over a Spanish ship captained by the eponymous Cereno. When the story begins, their ship, now derelict, has drifted into the harbor of "St. Maria—a small, desert, uninhabited island toward the southern extremity of Chili"—in other words, an absolute nowhere (and not in the "utopian" sense) whose utter isolation emblematizes the interpretative chaos to follow.[74] The plot—if that's the word for it—gets going when a sealer captained by the New Englander Amasa Delano shows up, and Delano boards the Spanish ship to proffer aid. Babo and the slaves concoct an elaborate ruse to persuade Delano that Cereno is still in control, and most of the "action" takes place in Delano's head as he tries to decipher the scene before him; the truth is not revealed until near the end, and since the reader is equally in the dark up to that point, Delano serves (more or less) as the reader's surrogate. Melville throws in a third-person narrator to tell the tale, who concludes the piece with the transcript of Babo's trial, after he has been brought to justice. Further complicating matters, Melville based his story, at times to the point of plagiarism, on the memoirs of a real-life Amasa Delano, which also concluded with transcripts from real court proceedings.

At the heart of the mystery is Babo, who embodies something of a surveillance person's ultimate nightmare. Taken one way, he is perfectly documented, as identifiable and uncontroversial as a Fichte or Booth could ever wish him to be: put simply, he is property, a slave. In addition, unlike some of his co-conspirators, who were of high caste in Africa, Babo was a slave there as well. His genius, however, is to recognize that he is seen *through* his legally mandated role—and needs only to play out the expected part to dupe Delano, who, indeed, sensing that something is fishy, suspects everything *but* a slave revolt until the truth is finally disclosed. With ruthless efficiency, Melville exposes the hermeneutic codes by which a society protects itself *as* codes and thus as vulnerable to any enemy canny enough to understand and manipulate them. Delano, who is introduced as being "of singularly undistrustful good nature" (37), is Melville's great send-up of the liberal north, his disapproval of slavery balanced by a casual racism and condescension: "Like most men of a good, blithe heart, Captain Delano took to Negroes, not philanthropically, but genially, just as other men to Newfoundland dogs" (73). Blinkered by an ideology that explains (and, on the face of things, sympathizes with) Babo, he cannot truly empathize with or even recognize the individual in front of him.[75]

The effect of nearly any Melville text, but this one in particular, is a kind of radiating doubt, or dread, as the interpretive suspicions bred within the narrative slowly spread outward to infect reality itself. No source of potential authority is allowed to stand. As a reader surrogate, Delano effectively exposes the hypocrisy of Melville's liberal readership. One level up, Melville uses the third-person narrator for no other reason than to show the bad faith (as we have been tracking it since *Pamela*) of the omniscient voice: sometimes the narrator behaves himself, but at other points he peddles pure misinformation, which is not revealed as such until the end.[76] The legal deposition with which the novella closes comes as a relief with its objective tone—and yet that tone is itself a ruse, to lend credibility and a sense of neutrality to the testimony of the tale's most prejudiced characters: Cereno and his surviving crew. Finally, the epistemic toxins burst the bonds of Melville's text, to poison the source materials—the real Amasa Delano's memoir and the purportedly objective court proceedings *he* quotes—and the world in general: a world, like the world of the text, composed of interpretive conventions ripe for manipulation by an intelligent subversive. To read "Benito Cereno" is to lose faith in the customary center of narrative control, the observer.

In short, if Whitman is among the first to outline the problems faced at the underground station, Melville speaks more to the situation at Scotland Yard—security-oriented surveillance, as we noted in our introduction, being in its more sophisticated iterations a constant struggle between the watchers and the watched over control of interpretive codes. At the center of Melville's story, Babo remains a mystery, indeed inviolable: knowing that the only real way for the courts to confirm his motives and establish his mental state is for them to hear his own explanations, he simply refuses to play along. Like Iago, after whom he is explicitly modeled, he utters no word once his plot comes undone. Silent at his own trial, he also intimidates Cereno into muteness by his mere presence, to the point that he cannot even be identified to the court by his chief victim: "On the testimony of the [other] sailors alone rested the legal identity of Babo." We may, finally, take Iago and Babo as bookends to the history of realism we have been telling: the first exposing the central conceptual weakness in allegorical culture and paving the way for the conventions of realism that accompanied the liberal-contractual revolution; the second summing up more than two centuries of thinking about privacy, the nature of the self and its relation to public scrutiny, and presenting a seemingly insuperable problem for realistic fiction. When Delano leaves the island of St. Maria for the firmer turf of South America, he is also leaving behind a phase in the history of literature.

Into the Genres: The Emergence of the Detective Story

It is a moment, too, when the status of Literature as such begins to change radically. To this point, our analysis of fictional and poetic texts, from Shakespeare, to Defoe, to Melville, has dealt almost exclusively with works of a certain unquestioned aesthetic stature. Going forward, we will be moving increasingly, though by no means exclusively, into forms of writing that have often been considered subliterary—genres, for example, like the spy novel, science fiction, or works of fantasy and adventure. In a sense, this is only in keeping with some commonplaces in the field of literary studies as it is now constituted, to wit: beginning in the middle of the nine-teenth century and accelerating during the twentieth, the field of "high art" actively detached itself from less ambitious forms of cultural production to the point where, by the modern period, a "class system" of sorts pertained—one still visible, say, in most bookstores, which continue to segregate the popular genres ("Mystery," "Romance," "Espionage," and so on) from serious "Literature." Thus, the story goes, whereas a writer like Dickens, in the 1840s or 1850s could simultaneously command a large popular audi-ence and pursue serious artistic ambitions, the cultural field circa 1920 was divided into, in the upper echelons, the likes of Joyce, Eliot, and Woolf, writing for a highly exclusive, well-educated readership and disdainful of the vulgar masses, and, down below, the "culture industry," which included vastly popular writers of zero interest to the intelligentsia. During this long process of separation, some authors worked with a palpable sense of inner division; so Conrad's fiction, in Fredric Jameson's account, was

> unclassifiable, spilling out of high literature into light reading
> and romance, reclaiming great areas of diversion and
> distraction by the most demanding practice of style and *écriture*
> alike, floating somewhere in between Proust and Robert Louis
> Stevenson [etc.].[77]

In most recountings of this process, finally, the separation is agreed to have been initiated by the artists—and, depending on one's politics and preferences, the tactic was heroic (a necessary claiming of autonomy over against a mass culture debased by capitalism; thus Theodor Adorno and much of the Frankfurt School); reprehensibly elitist (Peter Bürger); or somewhere in between (Pierre Bourdieu).[78] The large number of critics taking a dim view of "high" literature's claims to aesthetic autonomy explains, among other things, why so much of Modernist studies now focuses on cultural production, broadly conceived.

Let's grant that a separation of high and lower genres indeed occurred beginning in the mid-1800s. We would argue, however, that most existing accounts, by assigning the popular genres a passive role in this history, have largely misrepresented the issue. Even critics favorable to popular literature, and who don't view the subgenres as ephemera disgorged by the culture industry to satisfy a vastly expanded but barely literate population of vulgar readers, still tend to view the elite as having forced open, in the words of one critic, "the great divide."[79] Not entertained, on the whole, is that the split between the mainstream, literary novel and the subgenres might have been initiated by writers working in the *latter*—and yet this is far closer to what happened. This is not to claim that pioneers of the various subgenres necessarily saw themselves as breaking with the mainstream, nor even that they conceived of themselves, at least at the start, as *genre* writers at all. All the same, by pursuing ideas and techniques (often with a great deal of aesthetic ambition) in opposition to conventional practices, they set in motion an inexorable process of alienation and drift. Approaching the "great divide" in these terms, most importantly, restores to the genres their historicity: the popular forms did not all arise during the same period—quite the contrary. To generalize: each genre emerged at a moment of crisis in prose fiction, as the *goals* of the novel were perceived to be in hopeless conflict with allowable *methods*. It was no coincidence, we will see in the next chapter, that modern fantasy literature began in the 1930s or that the spy novel—two very different strains of it—erupted twice, first in the era immediately preceding World War I and then again in the late 1920s. Nor, finally, was it random that the *first* popular genre of any importance—to which we will now be turning our attention—materialized during the crisis of observation, privacy, and realism we have been analyzing at length, espousing a far more fluid notion of privacy than most mainstream novelists would accept. It materialized at the hands, moreover, of a writer particularly astute, as we have already seen, about the mid-century crisis of representation.

It is probably a mistake, in fact, to see "The Murders in the Rue Morgue" as the foundational detective story. Neither are we making a counterclaim for one of the other works sometimes identified coming first: Hoffmann's "Das Fräulein von Scuderi," say, or Poe's own "The Gold-Bug," or novels by Dickens or Collins in which detectives play key roles in the plot. As has been widely recognized (and we agree with this), it is in "Rue Morgue" that the key clichés of the genre are first programmatically laid out: the genius detective (Dupin); his admiring but dim-witted sidekick, who narrates; the still more idiotic, hostile, but grudgingly admiring emissaries of the police; the seemingly insoluble crime (involving—as in so many subsequent mysteries—a murder behind locked doors); a wrongly accused suspect; a brilliant solution. As with many of his fictional successors, Dupin is an independent agent (though he cooperates with the police when he wishes), is from a good family (an impoverished aristocrat), and is obsessive about his own privacy, to the point of being a recluse—all qualities that somehow contribute to his own magical skills as a close reader (he's even an expert phrenologist).[80] It is indeed startling how many key tropes Poe puts in place; nevertheless, as with so much of his work, including "The Man of The Crowd," it is probably more accurate to read "Rue Morgue" as a thought experiment, no less ambitious than any of his other stories and likely meant as a one-off: his two subsequent Dupin tales have different fish to fry and don't much resemble it. That a vastly successful genre of popular fiction grew out of his story might be no more than a happy accident, or the result of willful misunderstanding, and should not be taken as indicative of Poe's own aims, which seem clearly to align with his ongoing and idiosyncratic critique of realism and interpretation.

The pivotal figure is Dupin himself. Despite their shared territories, the detective and the policeman occupy significantly different positions within the field of realism.[81] For all their skill when it came to "delicate matters," the police were fundamentally blunt tools—and were depicted as such, their actions teleological and finite. The suspect's arrest marked the handoff between police responsibilities and the more subtle chores of the other side of the legal system: by mid-century, jurisprudence was fully engaged with the problem of establishing *mens rea* (the guilty mind), the suspect's disposition at the moment of the criminal act.[82] It is perhaps no coincidence that the most probing and complex fictional treatments of crime were more typically told from the perspective of lawyers than policemen—and that the *mens rea* problem was, in the hardest cases, shown to be unanswerable.[83] Literary detectives starting with Dupin, however, have been *mens rea* determination machines, able not only to identify the external character but also to deduce from those outward signs an internal transcript of thought and plotting. At the start of "Rue Morgue," in a passage that has been much mocked, Dupin startles the unnamed narrator with an account of the narrator's silent thoughts for the twenty minutes previous.[84] It is exactly this distinction between the police and the detective, finally, that marks the fault line— imperceptible at first but ultimately a chasm—between the mainstream novel and genre writing. In short: Poe's solution (in this one story, remember) to the problem of surveillance and privacy is to invent a kind of superman, a patently magical figure capable of understanding the truth about other people. Whatever their ideological freighting, the police in Victorian fiction remained well within the parameters of realism—or at least, the distended and highly compromised thing realism had become. Dickens's policemen, for all their acumen, were recognizably civil servants with feet of clay, having their pockets picked on the way home from work; even Field's abilities stopped at the face, never reaching the mind. With Dupin, however, Poe, fully conversant with the British tradition constraining Dickens, shatters the realistic contract—and the subgenre asserts its independence from the literary mainstream precisely in its evasion through fantastic means of the empathetic impasse.

Given the implicit politics of this gesture, it makes sense that the detective story caught on in England rather than the United States: from the time of Conan Doyle to the present day, this particular subgenre has enjoyed a comparatively high profile in Britain—often among authors of a frankly anti-democratic cast. Again, we wish to keep the leading strands of our argument distinct. Although they began at roughly the same time and under similar intellectual conditions, the realistic tradition of the novel, with its commitment to the empirical contract, does not map in any simple way onto the liberal tradition in politics, with its similarly empirical roots and its high valuation of autonomy and privacy: not every mainline novelist espoused a liberal politics; writers of detective stories, especially in the twentieth century, worked from all points on the ideological grid. Nevertheless, the detective story throws literary-political alliances into high relief: if the genius sleuth originates as a fantasy of overcoming the mystery of other people, the figure quickly acquires a still more aggressive edge, as the resolute enemy (and eradicator) of civil protections of privacy. The detective's magical insights and talents answer to a higher law, and a more advanced sense of conscience, than the rules of a democratic society—the instrumental agreements, that is to say, that, in their compromising and compromised way, hold liberalism together. Ultimately, these talents legitimize a peremptory—and frequently, a militantly extralegal—assertion of authority.

This drift to the far right is palpable in the Holmes stories: in the first volumes, he is mainly a skilled interpreter, reading skull shapes and footprints, and the master of au courant forensic techniques like handwriting and fingerprint analysis. In his reliance on fields like statistics, he can sometimes sound like Henry Mayhew or even Charles Booth: "While the individual man is an insoluble puzzle, in the aggregate [echoes of Poe] he becomes a mathematical certainty."[85] As his powers become more preposterous and superhuman, however, Holmes's relations with the police take a sinister turn: where he was once superior but essentially allied with them, the later Holmes occasionally acts against the authorities, taking the law into his own hands, committing crimes himself, and foiling their attempts at an impartial justice for all.[86] The latter volumes of stories, in particular, are pervasively colored by claims to a higher justice:

> I had rather play tricks with the law of England than with my own conscience. (2:203)
> [After letting a murderer go]: [This] is not a case in which we are called upon to interfere. Our investigation has been independent, and our action shall be also. (2:479)

Invariably, Holmes's interventions are in the interests of the wealthy—and he seems to spend more of the latter volumes protecting the secrets of the aristocracy than bringing felons to justice.[87] This is an evolution anticipated by Poe: the last of the Dupin stories, "The Purloined Letter," requires no detective work. The culprit is known from the start, and Dupin's job is to protect, from blackmail, an "illustrious personage whose honor and peace are . . . jeopardized." Conan Doyle, however, is clearer about the stakes in this shift. In one of the later stories, a privileged adversary confronts Holmes about his profession: "So far as your efforts are directed towards the suppression of crime [I have no complaints]. Where your calling is more open to criticism is when you pry into the secrets of private individuals, when you rake up family matters which are better hidden" (2:183). In the event, the adversary needn't worry: this story, like many others, ends with Holmes's willing participation in a hush job. Whatever troubled conscience liberals might have had about the unequal valuation of privacy in contemporary England, Conan Doyle had none: in a wonderfully uncomplicated way, moral justification tends to line up perfectly with entitlement. Holmes violates and protects personal secrets along predictable lines, and, as with Dupin, we eventually hear that he, too, is descended from a good family: "My ancestors were country squires, who appear to have led much the same life as is natural to their class" (1:517).

Conan Doyle's increasing stridency suggests how conclusively the nineteenth-century battle over privacy, from his perspective, was lost. Holmes protects the privacy of the privileged while laying bare the secrets of everyone else. The evocatively titled "A Case of Identity" begins with Homes remarking to Watson,

> If we could fly out of that window hand in hand, hover over this
> great city, gently remove the roofs, and peep in at the queer
> things which are going on, the strange coincidences, [etc.] it
> would make all fiction with its conventionalities and foreseen
> conclusions most stale and unprofitable. (1:225)

It's the same scene as Dickens's opening to A Tale of Two Cities, chapter 3, but from an impossible, aerial perspective—and indeed Holmes proves just the man to remove those roofs and peer in. And he is impossible: by the end of the nineteenth century, the ideological investment in the private life had spread to all classes. The very existence of Holmes—as a notion—only underscores the extent to which privacy now belonged to everyone. For his part, Poe had foreseen the limits of the detective even as he invented the figure—and like "The Man of the Crowd," "Rue Morgue" is finally a self-consuming artifact. The strongest impression it leaves on most readers is not satisfaction at Dupin's acumen but a lingering horror at the randomness and gruesomeness of the slayings. It is typical of Poe's humor that the victims are a fortune-teller and her daughter, themselves doppelgänger for the similarly reclusive and nocturnal narrator and Dupin. In the end, no prophetic ability is adequate to a razor-wielding orangutan swinging arbitrarily through one's window—nor is Dupin able to do much beyond sort things out after the fact. It would not be too much to say that Poe is imagining the deaths of all the schemes of mind reading and pseudo-scientific prediction that obsessed his age—nor can one make much of *mens rea* when discussing an ape.[88] "Murders in the Rue Morgue" both pioneers and corrupts the detective-story form, vandalizing its own framework as a preventive measure against those who might take its thought experiment too seriously. For the form to take hold in England, Conan Doyle and others had to reject Poe as strenuously as they copied him; in the Holmes stories, without exception, crimes have motives. The deeper lesson of Poe—and Wordsworth, and Mill, and Whitman, and Melville—was learned, however, in America, as privacy was recognized not only as belonging to everyone but as a right worthy of legal protection. It is in America that the argument of this chapter concludes.

CODA: CAMBRIDGE, 1890

At roughly the same time the *Saturday Evening Gazette* was invading the social life of Samuel and Mabel Warren, a Warren family acquaintance— and, like both authors of "The Right to Privacy," a former student at Harvard Law School—published a short novel directly relevant to their predicament.[89] As Henry James explains in his preface to the New York Edition, *The Reverberator* (1888) was inspired by the appearance in an American newspaper of an article detailing the inner workings of an exclusive circle of European gentry. James describes the exposé's effects on that secretive coterie as follows: "One would so little . . . have supposed the reverberation of the bomb, its heeded reverberation, conceivable. No such consequence, clearly, had been allowed for by its innocent maker [the author of the article]."[90] James does not identify the American paper in question, but it could well have been the *Gazette*, which advertised itself as "The Society Paper of New England," or indeed any of several publications enjoying tremendous popularity, and coming under increasingly harsh criticism, during the period. The *Boston Globe* ran regular stories on the private lives of various "stars" (in their argot: "Newsy Gossip about the Stage People Who Amuse the Public")—and a running feature was called, with admirable honesty, "Table Gossip."[91] Amidst the uproar such pieces provoked, "The Right to Privacy" may be seen in many ways as a typical rather than an extraordinary response. In the words of one such polemic, the "morbid curiosity" of the public and the "audacity of newsgatherers" meant that "one might as well live with open doors and windows, or have repeating speaking tubes leading from every room into the street."[92] In Cambridge itself, at exactly the moment James was writing his novel, a speech at Harvard had decried "the silly, mean and cowardly lies that every day are found in the columns of certain newspapers, which violate every instinct of American manliness, and in ghoulish glee desecrate every sacred relation of private life." The speaker was President Cleveland—a Wordsworth fan, incidentally.[93]

Briefly: *The Reverberator* tells the tale of two families living in Paris, the Dossons and the Proberts. If the novel falls short of James's best work, it is in no small part because he presents the current debate about privacy so schematically. The Proberts, an old Carolina family, but long integrated into the French aristocracy (to the point that their first language is French), are fiercely protective of their privacy and value it in terms that, by now, should be very familiar. When their little world is "served up to the rabble" in a revealing newspaper piece, they react to the exposure as "a violation of sanctities" and as a "desecration, [a] pollution"—in short, they draw on precisely the language of the sacred deployed by President Cleveland and, a few years later, by Warren and Brandeis at the *start* of their article: "the sacred precincts of private and domestic life [etc., etc.]."[94] The contrary position, in James's narrative, is taken not by the Dossons, a widower and his two daughters recently arrived from a "clever suburb" of Boston, but by George Flack, the author of the gossip piece. A young man "professionally . . . occupied with other people's affairs," "his undertaking [is] to obtain material in Europe for an American 'society-paper'" (*The Reverberator*, naturally; 28, 15). In one of the novel's key set pieces, Flack lays out his vision for a gossip-driven press, in terms nearly identical to the charges leveled in "The Right to Privacy"—though, predictably enough, his view of things could not be further from Warren's and Brandeis's.

"It's a big proposition as it stands, but I mean to make it bigger: the most universal society-paper the world has seen. That's

where the future lies, and the man who sees it first is the man who'll make his pile. . . . The society-news of every quarter of the globe, furnished by the prominent members themselves—oh *they* can be fixed, you'll see!—from day to day and from hour to hour and served up hot at every breakfast table in the United States: that's what the American people want and that's what the American people are going to have. . . . I'm going for the inside view, the choice bits, the *chronique intime*, as they say here; what the people want's just what ain't told, and I'm going to tell it. . . . That's about played out, anyway, the idea of sticking up a sign of 'private' and 'hands off' and 'no thoroughfare' and thinking you can keep the place to yourself. You ain't going to be able any longer to monopolise any fact of general interest, and it ain't going to be right you should; it ain't going to be possible to keep out anywhere the light of the Press. Now what I'm going to do is set up the biggest lamp yet made and make it shine all over the place. We'll see who's private then, and whose hands are off, and who'll frustrate the People—the People *that wants to know*."
(62–63)

The novel reaches its climax when Flack, as good as his word, publishes some inside information about the Proberts, passed along without any consciousness of wrongdoing by the younger Dosson daughter, Francie; echoing perfectly the "newsy" patois of the *Globe* and others, the piece describes the Proberts as "rare old exclusives" (145). As a result of this indiscretion, Francie's engagement to the younger Probert son, Gaston, is put into jeopardy.

On the face of things, *The Reverberator* seems to be in general sympathy with Warren and Brandeis in "The Right to Privacy," James approximating as best he can "the style of the gutter" to convey Flack's crassness; similarly, the Proberts' grievance is recognizably akin to those made by Warren and countless others.[95] In the event, however, James takes a surprisingly tough-minded view of privacy, honing in on several of the lingering problems and hypocrisies we have been able to observe in the nineteenth-century debate. He is particularly sharp, for example, when it comes to class: though Flack is in it for the money (to "make his pile"), he is also ruthlessly clear about the leveling potential of the press.

Even as Wordsworthian arguments about personal autonomy had found broad acceptance, privacy at century's end remained mostly a privilege of the moneyed ranks. However self-serving his comments, Flack is surely correct that the exclusiveness of a Belgravia or Back Bay ("thinking you can keep the place to yourself") jars with the principles of American democracy—Whitman's nation of "unnumbered Supremes." To the extent that Warren and Brandeis adopt a tone of patrician outrage, they leave themselves open to charges of classism—"an air of injured gentility."

And yet James is not criticizing the idea of privacy, per se. Flack's vision of "the biggest lamp yet made [shining] all over the place" manages to be both absurd and horrific, and his confident prediction that, in the interests of "the People *that wants to know*," privacy itself is "about played out," neatly aligns James with the concerns of a John Stuart Mill. The language of surveillance enters this passage, as in Mill, to raise the specter of tyranny by the majority: a society in which everyone watches everyone, abetted by the mass media, with a resulting reduction to conformity and vulgarity. Where James perhaps differs from Mill is in his (American) willingness to face this outcome if it means avoiding the inequities of a society in which privacy belongs only to the restricted few. Indeed, *The Reverberator* may be read, finally, as the critique of a certain exclusionary view of privacy (which we have observed developing over the course of the century) and the mapping out of a privacy more democratic and individualist—in ways that finally anticipate and even explain the logic of Warren and Brandeis. To this end, James depicts the Proberts in a pointedly unflattering light: their secrets exposed by Flack's article, the beleaguered family receives almost no sympathy from their author but rather comes across as vindictive and hysterical.

> [Gaston's] father hadn't stirred out of the house, hadn't put his foot inside a club, for more than a week. Marguerite and Maxim [Gaston's sister and brother-in-law] were immediately to start for England on an indefinite absence. They couldn't face their life in Paris. (177)

As James depicts it, the world of the Proberts harkens back to an idea of privacy that is pre-Modern, pre-Enlightenment even: it is the exclusivity of the tribe or the in-group—in short, of "a family in which there was no individual but only a collective property" (40). Whenever James, describing the Proberts, resorts to the language of the sacred, it carries this tinge of archaic taboo—exposing, we would suggest, a similar archaism underlying all such usages (in Cleveland or Brandeis, let's say). Within its own confines, the traditionalist family is depicted as absolute, tyrannical, full of petty intrigues, ruthlessly self-policing and *without* privacy (they're "Proberts," after all), and crushing to the individual—in ways that the sternest critics of privacy law, most recently some feminist scholars, have readily identified.[96] But when the in-group is exposed to the slightest scrutiny from outside, it crumbles to dust—and rightly so, James seems to say, having nothing but secrecy to sustain it.

We began this discussion by citing a well-worn canard: that "The Right to Privacy" was inspired mainly by Warren's anger at the publication of the guest list at his daughter's 1890 wedding. Alas, the story is too good to be true: Warren and Mabel Bayard were themselves married in 1883, making a second nuptials seven years later—of their offspring, no less—highly unlikely. So far as we can tell, the fake story can be traced back to a 1960 article by William L. Prosser, who writes, "The matter came to a head when the newspapers had a field day on the occasion of the wedding of a daughter, and Mr. Warren became annoyed." Prosser cites as a source Alpheus Thomas Mason's *Brandeis: A Free Man's Life*. But Mason's account simply reads: "[The Warrens] set up housekeeping in Boston's exclusive Back Bay section and began to entertain extensively. The *Saturday Evening Gazette*, which specialized in 'blue blood items,' naturally reported their activities in lurid detail. This annoyed Warren, who took the matter up with Brandeis. The article was the result."[97] We would suggest that the canard has persisted—to the extent that it has frequently been cited verbatim in subsequent scholarship—because it speaks to the role most people now (in America, in the West) assign to marriage, as a uniquely privileged form of self-expression: an assertion of individual autonomy in the very *choice* of affinity with something larger.[98] As such, though marriage had no special place in Warren's and Brandeis's argument, it is natural that Prosser should have imagined a wedding ceremony as particularly relevant for the question of privacy protection—an idea with which most people today, from Nicole Kidman on down, would sympathize.

And so too, finally, Henry James in *The Reverberator*. In the controversy that swirls around them, the Dossons have at once the least doctrinaire and most nuanced view of privacy—a result, no doubt, of having emerged from the crucible-like environment of Boston-Cambridge. For them, like the Warrens and in obvious contrast to the Proberts, an intrusive media is simply a fact of life, and absolute privacy neither possible nor, ultimately, entirely desirable: the Warrens, after all, had sought a public profile with their "extensive" entertaining. Rather, privacy, and the integrity of character it allows, makes possible a more dexterous negotiation between the individual and his or her environment. In this relation, the individual is not necessarily a victim but can possess considerable agency over the degree and kind of exposure to which he or she is subjected. For his part, Mr. Dosson, the father, cannot understand the Proberts' fuss when Flack's article comes out: "[Weren't they] aware over here of the charges brought every day against the most prominent men in Boston?" (164). Indeed, he shares some of Flack's suspicion about secrecy as such: "Interwoven with Mr. Dosson's nature was the view that if these people had done bad things they ought to be ashamed of themselves and he couldn't pity them, and that if they hadn't done them there was no need of making such a rumpus about other people's knowing" (192). His elder daughter Delia, even more a woman of the modern era, takes a still more practical, even empowered view of the matter. If exposure is to some extent inevitable, the best thing to do is dictate the terms by which one is received:

> [Delia reflected that] in consequence of what Mr. Flack *had* published the great American community was in a position to know with what fine folks Francie and she were associated. She hoped that some of the people who used only to call when they were "off to-morrow" would take the lesson to heart. (175)

If James shares a single sentiment with Warren and Brandeis, a subtle extension of the ideology of privacy to emerge from Wordsworth, it is that autonomy is something the individual must *achieve*, over against, but also in mastery of, the countervailing forces of society; all three fin de siècle authors are characteristically American, perhaps, in their optimism that such an achievement is possible—even likely—for an individual of sufficient practical energy. In *The Reverberator*, it is the conflicted son Gaston Probert who achieves this autonomy, by choosing marriage, and the kind of privacy specific to it, over the solitude of the tribe: "I should . . . urge you to marry her," Gaston's friend tells him, "in simple self-preservation."

Gaston kept echoing. "In self-preservation?"

"To save from destruction the last scrap of your independence. [Your family] are doing their best to kill you morally—to render you incapable of individual life."

Gaston was immensely struck. "They are—they are!" he declared with enthusiasm. (205)

And thus also, wedding or not, the crucial shift of emphasis in "The Right to Privacy," as Warren and Brandeis abandon their early appeal to patrician outrage for something more individual centered and indeed applicable to *every* individual: inviolate personality. A formulation that has caused endless confusion in subsequent legal scholarship but which emblematizes a confidence perhaps unique to its place and moment in time: that a new understanding of the individual, with origins in poetic argument and nurtured through the nineteenth century, might be embodied practically as law.

CHAPTER FOUR

The Return of Allegory

A MAN WALKS INTO A small social gathering at his hotel, hoping to meet a respected playwright and novelist he has long admired from a distance. Finally introduced to the author, he is at first impressed by his idol's verbal facility—his ability to talk endlessly on any topic of current events, his impressive command of the latest gossip, and his evident social connectedness. Only after further conversation do these gifts begin to rankle: the author's views turn out to be repetitive and dismayingly conventional, showing none of the profound insights of his published material. Still more disturbing, the author seems utterly without self-reflection—unwilling, and perhaps unable, to talk about himself and apparently lacking the first requirement of a serious writer: inwardness. Asked to report on his latest work, the author claims to have completed the draft of a play—but then, as he tries to recite the piece, manages to forget every line. Later he backtracks and claims that there is no manuscript. Perplexed, and unable to square his hero's patent mediocrity with the brilliance of his writing, the man departs the soiree, leaving the author there. Heading to his room, he notices the door to the author's suite left ajar. On impulse, he enters, only to find . . . the author, in the dark, at his desk, writing.

Five years after completing *The Reverberator*, Henry James wrote a brief fable titled, simply, "The Private Life."[1] Like the 1888 novel, the tale, the first few pages of which we have summarized, examines a pressing social concern in a highly schematic and overdetermined fashion—and has thus, like its predecessor, attracted little critical attention over the years. Though it undoubtedly belongs to the vast corpus of "minor James," it nevertheless holds the attention through the sheer uncanniness of its conceit—a conceit which, by the by, deftly undercuts any triumphal conclusions about the value of privacy to have emerged from Warren and Brandeis. In the story, James presents a series of characters who embody, in very different ways, the tensions between a public existence and a cultivated interiority. Stopping for a week at a small hotel in Switzerland, the narrator ("that frivolous thing, an observer") encounters a "celebrity" author (modeled, James would later recall in his preface to the New York Edition, on Robert Browning), who has indeed split—literally—into two separate selves: on the one hand, a creature of the salons, a small-time adept of petty intrigues, fully acclimated to the life of a minor London luminary; on the other hand, a silent and hidden man who never leaves his room and who has never (until now) been seen by anyone else: the writer of genius.[2] A disturbing revelation, to be sure— yet as the week goes on, the narrator comes to recognize that each of the guests presents a different angle on the problem of private existence: there's the woman who always dresses the same and who seems trapped in her own authenticity; the famous actress whose nonstop performativity occasionally breaks to reveal a sensitive soul; the narrator himself, a typically Jamesian "searcher of hearts," standing somewhat aloof from any emotional engagement. The toughest conundrum, aside from the bifurcated author, is presented by one Lord Mellifont. A creature of perfect tact and self-presentation, he is "so conspicuously and uniformly the public character," that he has "no corresponding private life" at all: when removed from the social gaze, he literally ceases to exist. As James commented in his preface,

> Didn't there immensely flourish in those very days and exactly
> in that society . . . [the] most dazzling [men] of the world whose
> effect on the mind repeatedly invited to appraise [them] was to
> beget in it an image of representation and figuration so
> exclusive of any possible inner self that, so far from there being
> . . . a question of an *alter ego*, a double personality, there seemed
> scarce a question of a real and single one, scarce foothold or
> margin for any private and domestic *ego* at all.[3]

As the tenor of his remarks suggests, James saw the phenomenon of an *entirely* and *exclusively* public existence as endemic to his own age; indeed, his terminology—"representation," "figuration"—seems to point to a more current moment and the purported depthlessness of contemporary celebrity. It is certainly correct that his "small experiment" (as he calls it) could hardly be imagined even a few decades previous: as recently as mid-century, "the private life," in James's sense of the phrase, did not yet exist. The tale is only legible within the long history of burgeoning privacy protections we have been tracing—and *each* of his characters, Lord Mellifont included, must be read as both the product of and challenge to a now prevailing ideology.

If a single wishful misapprehension characterized the thinking of liberal privacy advocates (it's in Warren and Brandeis, as well as Mill), it was that the dialectical process generating new ideas about personal autonomy might be *arrested* at a point of ideal balance between the individual's right to privacy and the cohesive needs of society. The self protected from "instantaneous photographs and newspaper enterprise" but still a participating citizen. As we saw in the last chapter, however, "The Right to Privacy" hardly resolved the seeming incongruity between a support for personal freedoms and the implication that robust civic controls would be required to protect them: privacy could be secured only through increased government oversight. More to the point, it was by no means clear how privacy, as Warren and Brandeis defined it, could be protected *legally* at all. The view of self that began with Wordsworth arose in direct opposition to the social constructionism of the eighteenth century. The two Boston lawyers were well aware that protection from the intrusions, and the coercive pressures, of the community, was not to be found in an appeal to community values. This last paradox, it is worth noting, accounts for much of the tortured response, in the legal literature, to their paper.[4] As one commentator has observed, in the view of many contemporary writers, *law itself*

> was an invasion of privacy that must be justified on the ground
> of necessary utility. . . . Certainly, our ideas of the function and
> justification of law have changed rather drastically . . . under the
> impact of changing facts of political order. Yet so little attention
> has been given . . . to the intimate relation of law to private

> judgment and action that one must wonder, on reading our
> moral and philosophical literature, just what kind of
> amorphous, politically unattached individual [is being referred
> to in subsequent discussions of Warren and Brandeis].[5]

To put it another way: to the extent that law is an expression of community standards, it is part of the problem—just one of many social forces from which the individual requires protection in the spiritual task of developing an inviolate personality.

Most fundamentally—a difficulty evident as early as Wordsworth—the new psychology of self required no second person and seemed rather to privilege increasing isolation and ultimately solipsism (the cloistered existence of Tennyson's "Lady of Shalott"), resulting in a loss of social cohesion. There was no reason why the dialectical forces alienating self and community should not continue inexorably to their conclusion. We saw Wordsworth worrying about this as he turned more conservative, and by mid-century Mill's great antagonist Fitzjames Stephen was able to comment that,

> The whole tendency of modern civilization is to enable each
> man to stand alone and take care of his own interests, and the
> growth of liberty and equality will [only] intensify these feelings.
> They will minimize all restraints and reduce everyone to a dead
> level, offering no attractions to the imagination or to the
> affections.[6]

Stephen's (old-line conservative) remedy was a traditional communitarianism bolstered by religious faith and the firm hand of civil authority; whatever his solution, he was not wrong about the alienation to which secular autonomy led when pushed to the extreme. Along the same lines, in Clare Vawdrey—the bifurcated author in James's parable—we encounter a character whose public persona and inner nature are no longer reconcilable: each belongs in its own sphere, the relations between the two unimaginable. Similarly, the disappearing nobleman, Lord Mellifont, is no less a product of the ideology of privacy, precisely in the way that he swerves violently away from *any* notion of interiority—a thread we will take up later.

Our previous two chapters, in examining the struggle between surveillance and privacy initiated by the collapse of allegorical culture, concentrated on each side of the dialectic in sequence. That is: where chapter 2 looked mainly at the exterior history, at post-allegorical refinements in determining character and intention from the outside (in ways both empathetic and coercive), chapter 3 concerned itself primarily (though by no means exclusively) with the inner narrative and with changing ideas about solitude and the self. This sequence, to repeat, acknowledged a historical causality: the nineteenth-century argument for privacy could only have emerged in dialectical response to the social constructionism of the Augustan period. With the present chapter, our focus swings back to the exterior and to the more aggressive forms of observation most people associate with the contemporary Surveillance State. Again this is in recognition of historical causes: in the discussion that follows, we will argue that a weakened liberal consensus at the beginning of the twentieth century opened the door for punitive and pervasive forms of social watching that—inevitably—recalled the allegorical methods of the Renaissance. Indeed, one of our main contentions is that resurgent allegory has been an important mode within the literary, political, and social structures of the modern era. At the same time, it was no simple return: the allegorical mode reemerged, but transfigured, in dialectically determined ways, by the intervening centuries of liberal-contractualism. At times, it competed directly with liberalism; at other times, paradoxically, it acted as a force *within* liberalism. We will consider each appearance in turn, first looking at liberal attempts to preserve the idea of personal autonomy and privacy while also recognizing the necessity of strong governmental oversight; then we will consider the more frankly repressive, totalizing methods adopted by the enemies of liberalism. In neither case—for ease of reference, we will call the first iteration "progressive" and the second "paranoid"—did social allegory entirely *resemble* its Tudor-Stuart predecessor, least of all in its relevance to the practice and psychology of surveillance.

DECADENCE, SOCIAL PARTICIPATION, AND THE FATE OF LIBERALISM

Before turning, however, to the exterior narrative, we would follow the inner history, briefly, to its paradoxical conclusion. James's "The Private Life" derives much of its eerie impact from its presentation of a problem largely ignored by Mill, Warren, and Brandeis: how an individual, successfully protected in his or her privacy, might continue *voluntarily* to be a citizen. So concerned are these authors with shielding the inviolate self from the invasive discourses of society that they give little attention to the way a self, so shielded, might still *participate* in that community should he or she *wish* to. And yet the ramifying ideology of privacy inexorably robbed the politically inclined liberal of any way to articulate his or her citizenship—such being the plight, implicitly, of Clare Vawdrey. It is no coincidence, furthermore, that James made his twofold man a *writer*: where much of this chapter will look at the ways government officials and social planners (and the like) attempted to imagine a society consisting of innumerable (private) atoms, it makes sense that the problem would be addressed in the other direction—from the inside out, as it were—by those persons most invested in the idea of autonomy: artists. In chapter 3, we observed Wordsworth beginning to worry about how to translate solitary vision into a love of community and an attention to "the sad, still music of humanity." Nevertheless, Stephen's conclusion about "each man [standing] alone" is borne out by the drift towards solipsism in much nineteenth-century poetry. The best-known meditation on this end logic, stripped of much of its conservatism, is from Stephen's junior contemporary Walter Pater in his conclusion to *Studies in the History of the Renaissance* (1873):

> At first sight experience seems to bury us under a flood of
> external objects, pressing upon us with a sharp and importunate
> reality, calling us out of ourselves in a thousand forms of action.
> But when reflexion begins to play upon those objects they are
> dissipated under its influence; the cohesive force seems
> suspended like some trick of magic; each object is loosed into a
> group of impressions—colour, odour, texture—in the mind of
> the observer. And if we continue to dwell in thought on this
> world, not of objects in the solidity with which language invests
> them, but of impressions, unstable, flickering, inconsistent,
> which burn and are extinguished with our consciousness of
> them, it contracts still further: the whole scope of observation is
> dwarfed into the narrow chamber of the individual mind.
> Experience, already reduced to a group of impressions, is ringed
> round for each one of us by that thick wall of personality

through which no real voice has ever pierced on its way to us, or from us to that which we can only conjecture to be without. Every one of those impressions is the impression of the individual in his isolation, each mind keeping as a solitary prisoner its own dream of a world.[7]

The menace to social cohesion is clear enough, and yet Pater is simply restating a threat at the heart of empiricism that had been identified earlier by Locke and Hume. Indeed, Pater is borrowing Hume's argument that the mind is "nothing but a bundle or collection of different perceptions, which succeed each other with an inconceivable rapidity, and are in a perpetual flux and movement."[8] Lacking entirely, however, is either Locke's final guarantor of a functioning civil society (a beneficent deity) or Hume's much-diminished trust in "limited generosity" and commonsense benevolence—still less the power of habit and tradition in Stephen. Returning to Hume's epistemology in the wake of Wordsworth's secular autonomism, Pater offers no sources of cohesion—choosing instead to pursue the logic of personal privacy to the bitter end and the sacrifice of all social goals.

For Pater, the ethical consequences of solipsism and mental atomization were apparent; locked in one's own "dream of a world" and with only the most tenuous sense of self, it was pointless to engage in worldly action. In a famous series of rhetorical questions, he preached a frank epicureanism: "Not the fruit of experience, but experience itself, is the end. A counted number of pulses only is given to us of a variegated, dramatic life. How may we see in them all that is to be seen in them by the finest senses? How shall we pass most swiftly from point to point, and be present always at the focus where the greatest number of vital forces unite in their purest energy? To burn always with this hard, gemlike flame, to maintain this ecstasy, is success in life."[9] In just-so stories about the rise of British aestheticism, Pater's skeptical critique of perception turned a generation of young men (Oscar Wilde, the early Yeats, Arthur Symons, Lionel Johnson, and a host of others) into decadents. The characteristics of the art most affected by these attitudes are broadly acknowledged: high on sensual overload and private reverie, low on social engagement. We see it in the numerous personae of early Yeats (Aengus, Fergus, et al.), expressing the desire to escape from watching eyes into a world of pure beauty and "brood on hopes and fear no more," or in Symons's absinthe drinker, waving "the visible world away . . . rocked on [a] dreamy and indifferent tide."[10] And yet this account only goes so far; if the tradition we have been examining from Richardson through James suggests anything, it is that most British and American authors, in contrast to European decadents, were more likely to see themselves as fellow laborers within the liberal consensus than opposed to it.[11]

The public conversation that constituted the basis for liberal politics relied on a world apprehended the same way by everyone and, more to the point, represented in a collectively acceptable manner—a goal still cherished by authors even after the liberal consensus, and the canons of realism, began to shatter. We are not about to claim that Yeats and Symons, or indeed any of the "tragic generation," were "liberals": their stated sympathies were on the whole conservative and aristocratic.[12] Nevertheless, their concern about remaining socially relevant (a concern emphatically not shared by the French writers they emulated) is more than evident in the contradictory stances they take in their work. In his 1900 essay "The Symbolism of Poetry," for example, Yeats claims that,

> It is indeed only those things which seem useless or very feeble
> that have any power, and all those things that seem useful or
> strong, armies, moving wheels, modes of architecture, modes of
> government . . . [have their first motion] in moments of
> contemplation . . . by solitary men.[13]

On the face of it, Yeats's emphasis on the feeble and solitary would seem to bring him into line with Europeans like Stefan George or Villiers de l'Isle-Adam ("as for living, our servants will do that for us").[14] And yet this insistence goes hand in hand with an obsession over the problem of worldly action far removed from Pater's conclusion to *The Renaissance*: why would Yeats need to insist that "only those things which seem useless . . . have any *power*, and [that] all those things that seem *useful or strong*" originate in private fantasy? Or again why would Symons exclaim, at the end of a poem otherwise about escape from the "world that works," "Draw back the blinds, put out the light: / 'Tis morning, let the daylight come"?[15]

We would suggest that these writers, even as they declared their autonomy and independence from the broader culture and affirmed the primacy of private experience, were nonetheless, unlike the quietist Pater, desperate to demonstrate a residual capacity to exercise influence on the world. Stripped of any practical language to articulate their continued social participation, they were led into pure contradiction: on the one hand, the adoption of patently nonrealistic (or anti-realistic) techniques, the hermeticism and intentional vagueness of symbolism; on the other hand, exaggerated claims of power and relevance—Yeats's magical equation of withdrawal from the world and temporal authority. Not surprisingly, perhaps, the power of the solipsist was frequently figured as a kind of total surveillance: an ability to see *more*—more deeply and broadly, and with greater comprehension—than ordinary people.[16] In the most famous presentation (and probably send-up) of this paradox, Borges's Aleph, the point from which everything in the world might be seen simultaneously, just happens to be located in the basement of a Buenos Aires recluse.[17] When Symons comments that the symbolists' aims were "perhaps . . . impossible," he is recognizing the way their claims were essentially forms of wish fulfillment—or, to put it less kindly, pure fantasy.[18] Above and beyond that, however, he was indicating the way the two ends of liberalism—autonomy and social cohesion rooted in mutual agreements—had similarly reached a point of pure contradiction: from this impasse, the mainstream, committed to *both* goods, would increasingly need to reimagine the former to achieve the latter.

More ominously, whatever the politics of the decadents themselves, it is also clear how an assertion of personal authority detached from any empirical plausibility, or agreement with others, would appeal to the enemies of liberalism. If we go back, finally, to the mid-nineteenth century, we can identify a single moment in which *each* half of the dialectic of surveillance and privacy began to break into fantasy and wish fulfillment—a moment fraught with peril for the liberal consensus. We observed that Poe's invention of Dupin marked a crisis point in the exterior tradition of surveillance and observation: a moment when the subgenre of detective fiction declared independence from the empirical plausibility of conventional realism, to produce a figure with miraculous insight into the lives of other people. In hindsight, Dupin's talent seems *contingent* on his being a virtual hermit who never ventures from his house during the day—his superiority to his fellow citizens more than justifying his extralegal antics in "The Purloined Letter."[19] To reconstruct how mainstream liberalism fended off, on one hand, the threat of an atomized society, and, on the other, the rise of a politics rooted in fantasy and aggression, and to account for the fate of the surveillance/privacy dialectic in the modern era, we must now return to where the last chapter left off—to the *exact* time and place, as it happens.

I. SOCIAL ENGINEERING

Cambridge 1890 Revisited

The concluding decades of the nineteenth century may be recognized as a watershed moment, when the very triumph of its core ideals exposed contradictions latent in the liberal tradition since its inception and finally precipitated a serious breach within liberalism itself. Along with activist thinkers like Mill, Warren, and Brandeis, Pater's radical solipsism defined the choice facing the liberal tradition at the fin de siècle: either follow the dialectic of privacy to its logical conclusion (the sacrifice of all political initiatives) or finally make explicit and *admit*, as it were, what had been evident since Locke—that liberalism rests on imperfect but tactical compromises, instrumental agreements. To trace this history we go back to Massachusetts, by this point the key locus of Anglo-American social thought, turning to the other iconic, field-establishing work published there—by a friendly acquaintance of Brandeis and sporadically unfriendly brother of Henry James—in 1890.[20] *The Principles of Psychology*, at just under 1,400 pages, is a weightier work than "The Right to Privacy"—but in many ways William James is temperamentally akin to his Cambridge neighbors. The same basic tactic—using the methodologies of an adjacent discipline to shed new light on a lingering philosophical problem with relevance for liberal social planning—underpins both works; in James's case, this means bringing new developments in brain science to bear on existing questions about the nature of consciousness and to suggest new, "quantitative" strategies for the monitoring and directing of the mind.[21] Practically, this allows James to ask many of the same questions about personhood, and to undertake several of the same thought experiments, that we saw Locke carrying out in the *Essay Concerning Human Understanding*.[22] Several of James's conclusions indeed recall Locke's (identity, for example, rests on continuity of consciousness), but his best-known allegation utterly upends empiricist tradition. His philosophical predecessors erred, he observes, in reducing mental life to discrete percepts as the basic building blocks of experience—what Locke and Hume had called "simple ideas." As evidenced by the new "brain physiology," however, there are in fact no simple ideas: thought is continuous and cannot, as "in the Humian doctrine[, be] composed of separate independent parts" (*Principles* 1:234, 237). Rather, we should speak—using a metaphor already present, if unexploited, in Pater—of a "stream of consciousness":

> Consciousness, then, does not appear to itself chopped up in bits. Such words as "chain" or "train" do not describe it fitly as it presents itself in the first instance. It is nothing jointed; it flows. A "river" or a "stream" are the metaphors by which it is most naturally described. *In talking of it hereafter, let us call it the stream of thought, of consciousness, or of subjective life.* (*Principles*, 1:239; James's italics)

As James makes clear, his interest in revising the premises of Locke's epistemology is motivated to a large degree by his discomfort with their long-term practical consequences. He does not need the example of Pater to draw a connection between the mental atomization and social atomization. Hume and the Mills, he comments at the outset, have "constructed a *psychology without a soul*" (*Principles*, 1:1; James's italics).[23] By this he means that by restricting their analysis to discrete "perceptions, emotions, volitions [etc.]" and the interrelations between these sensory data, these philosophers had managed to furnish the individual mind without quite accounting for the individual: "The very Self or *ego* of the individual comes in this way to be viewed no longer as the pre-existing source of the representations [i.e., the sensory data], but rather as their last and most complicated fruit" (*Principles*, 1:2; James's italics). We might pause to observe that the definition of *soul* James is invoking, as something inborn and preexisting, is not what the term would have meant for Hume the social-constructionist: rejecting all theistic premises, he could *only* understand personhood as "the last and most complicated fruit" of experience (mainly experience among other people). Leaving aside the complicated semantic work being done here by "soul" and "self" (contrasted terms for James, synonyms for Locke and Hume), we might at least take James as evidence of the extent to which the Wordsworthian figuration of autonomy, bolstered in this case by a still-powerful theism, had replaced social construction by the late nineteenth century.[24]

James, whose work was contemporary with the flood tide of aestheticism and decadence, and whose younger brother had a professional interest in the movements, did not have to look far to perceive the social effects of mental atomization: Wilde's *The Picture of Dorian Gray*, as it happens, appeared in the July 1890 issue of *Lippincott's Magazine* just a month before the *Principles of Psychology* was published.[25] When James complains of "nerveless sentimentalists" he clearly has the decadents (and perhaps their sexual politics) in mind: "There is no more contemptible type of human character than that of the . . . dreamer, who spends his life in a weltering sea of sensibility, . . . but never does a manly concrete deed" (*Principles* 1:125).[26] It is in light of this protest that we would suggest James's insistence on the seamless *stream* of consciousness should be read. First, because it begins to restore a stable sense of self all but dissipated in Pater's (and Hume's) accounts. Second, and more important, because it makes it possible once again to talk about action and purpose— and, by extension, about productive interactions with other people. Strictly speaking, he explains, there is no such thing as the present moment; it is always "gone in the instant of becoming" (*Principles* 1:608)[27] Rather, he explains in a subsequent lecture, "the rush of our thought forward through its fringes is the everlasting peculiarity of its life. . . . In the pulse of inner life immediately present now in each of us is a little past, a little future."[28] This future directedness of consciousness, finally, which becomes a foundation of James's pragmatism, gives him a teleology and allows him to speak of life as *meaningful*. So much for burning always with a hard, gemlike flame: "The meaning [of] *a train of thought*," James counters, "*is its conclusion*" (*Principles*, 1:260; James's italics).

At the very dawn of the liberal-contractual dispensation, Hobbes had characterized human existence as a "perpetuall and restlesse desire of Power after power, that ceaseth only in Death."[29] In effect, James's view of human action is not terribly far from this; but since the onward "rush" of consciousness offers an escape from "nerveless sentimentalis[m]," he seizes on it with a distinctly un-Hobbesian enthusiasm. The future into which we are perpetually heading confronts us with a seemingly unlimited number of choices—choices that, in turn, endow our actions with moral weight: "An act has no ethical quality whatever unless it be chosen out of several all equally possible" (*Principles* 1:287). This principle of selection, furthermore, turns us into the makers of our own destinies—and ultimately into makers of the world. In a striking revision of Michelangelo's Platonist metaphor, James asserts that the mind "works on the data it receives very much as a sculptor works on his block of stone":

> We may, if we like, unwind things back to that black and
> jointless continuity of space and moving clouds of swarming
> atoms which science calls the real world. But all the while the
> world *we* feel and live in will be that which our ancestors and
> we, by slowly cumulative strokes of choice, have extricated out
> of this. . . . Other sculptors, other statues from the same stone!
> Other minds, other worlds from the same monotonous and
> inexpressive chaos! (*Principles*, 1:288–89; James's italics)

The world is not simply a product of individual endeavor but collaboration; in James's vision, the world is held in common and is thus "extricated" by, in the words of one subsequent critic, "a community of competent inquirers."[30]

As James's less forgiving readers have pointed out from the start, however, his view of meaning hardly provides a definitive answer to empirical nihilism.[31] Even as he celebrates the slow cumulative growth of culture, he acknowledges another reality—the atomistic and chaotic universe propounded by the natural sciences; when put to the test, he cannot deny that "the real world" in its most brute, physical aspect may be nothing more than a "jointless continuity of space." Nor can he quite answer the charge of solipsism: as his colleague Royce was quick to recognize, James's insistence on subjective experience slides easily into relativism, nor can it finally answer Pater's hunch that each of us is truly alone.[32] In the summary of one writer, James is vulnerable on several fronts: it is not clear "[that] he can adequately account for the concept of objective reference, [that] he can justify our belief in a common world, and [that] he can account for the personal identity of the subject in whom [a] teleology is instantiated."[33] To these doubts, James answers with a shrug: the world we feel and live in is no "inexpressive chaos." It is a gesture that establishes his pedigree beyond a doubt. In *Pragmatism*, he approvingly calls Locke, in pointed contrast to Hume, a "compromiser"— that is, a philosopher unwilling to push his speculations beyond usefulness.[34] For James, the next logical step is to turn philosophical inquiry entirely to questions of use: "*Theories thus become instruments, not answers to enigmas, in which we can rest*" (*Pragmatism*, 28; James's italics). He had given *Pragmatism* the subtitle "A New Name for Some Old Ways of Thinking." This is nearly correct: James's philosophy differs from earlier forms of empiricism less in its view of mental life than in the way it acknowledges and foregrounds its own instrumentality. We had earlier described Locke's refusal to pursue certain questions beyond usefulness (for example, the objective reference problem) as "pragmatic"—but the pragmatism was only implicit. The history of liberalism after Locke, as we have described it, is afflicted by two tendencies: first, the slow, painstaking, and ultimately unsuccessful attempt to resolve basic contradictions about the individual and about the individual and society; second, a general refusal to admit that certain key components of liberalism (realism, empiricism, a recognizable set of political beliefs) could therefore never be understood as absolutes, but instead were the products of bargains, compromises, contracts . . . instrumental agreements. And thus, perhaps, the virtue of a "New Name": a making explicit of what had been tacit for centuries. The indication, very much in the spirit of "The Right to Privacy," of a self-aware readiness to embrace the political sphere as a forum for liberalism's larger social goals—at the possible expense of *absolute* claims to privacy, individual autonomy, and the like. "The world stands really malleable, waiting to receive its final touches at our hands," James declared—"it suffers human violence willingly" (*Pragmatism*, 115). A supine and alluring world of rivers, forests, and mountains—but also men, women, and children.

Habit and Autonomy

Another signal publishing event of 1890, then, this time some 200 miles to the south of Cambridge: the appearance of Jacob Riis's *How the Other Half Lives*. That it caused such an immediate sensation is often put down to the fact that it was the first book to employ the new technology of halftone photographic reproduction—but its success owed just as much to the political atmosphere of the times.[35] It was a work that benefited greatly from the growing split in liberalism we have begun to examine, between individualist absolutists and those who would, with the best of intentions, inflict "human violence" on a "malleable" world. On the level of social policy, the last decades of the nineteenth century especially saw what had been a respectful disagreement flare up into Hobson's famous "crisis of liberalism."[36] On one side, the statist argument (the New Liberalism, echoed later in America by Roosevelt and Wilson); on the other, Herbert Spencer and the Manchester Liberals (and William Graham Sumner and the "Laissez-faire Constitutionalists" in America). The former lamented the fate of Riis's "other half"; the latter, gravitating towards social Darwinism, were content to dismiss an "undeserving poor."[37] The laissez-faireists and classical individualists decried, not without some self-interest, "state coercion" and "state morality"; the statists responded that coercion was the only way to create the preconditions for morality in the broader population.[38] Needless to say, the pragmatism of James lent itself readily to the latter argument, and many of the writers and politicians who took up the cause of reform, from Roosevelt and Wilson, to journalists like Herbert Croly and Walter Lippmann, to public intellectuals like John Dewey and Randolph Bourne, were James acolytes—and in several cases former students.[39] For these latter, Riis's shocking images of the destitute and socially excluded, and his demands for action ("What are you going to do about it? is the question of to-day"), became a rallying flag for intervention: how could citizens be equal if vast numbers were excluded from the machinery of society and crippled in their self-development? Must not a society therefore monitor and enforce equality?

The short, heady career of progressivism in America, and its intimate if sometimes strained relation to pragmatism, has been much commented on; we would argue, however, that its implications for surveillance have largely been misconstrued.[40] A common critical view is that progressivism marks the moment liberalism lost its individualist soul and was seduced by the temptations of authoritarianism—bringing with it heavy doses of surveillance by the government—one reason that, to this day, the very word "progressive" carries a sinister taint in some circles.[41] In actuality, the individual never disappeared as the central legitimizing agent of all liberal political suggestions—on either side of the statist-progressive/laissez-faire divide. Indeed, we can view the "crisis of liberalism" as first and foremost a rhetorical negotiation, a wide-ranging reconsideration of terms in the interest of opposing or justifying state control: to what extent could problematic ideas like "discipline" or "will" be made politically palatable, and to what degree might politically necessary and deeply cherished, but tactically awkward, shibboleths like "autonomy," "equality" and "freedom" be redefined?[42] That such meaning shifts were occurring was rarely acknowledged openly, for obvious reasons; and yet Hobhouse's elegant near-contradiction—"The function of State coercion is to override individual coercion"—only makes sense when considered as part of this furtive negotiation, an attempt to make acceptable to all liberals a new species of liberal power.

The science of behaviorism, with its strategies for the productive manipulation of the mind, occupies a particularly fraught place in this rhetorical struggle and quickly became a favorite target of the progressives' critics. Almost a century later, the 1920 "Little Albert" experiment and its ilk have retained a special notoriety, and yet the stated goals of "Albert's" chief tormentor merit close inspection: "Give me a dozen healthy infants, well-formed, and my own specified world to bring them up in and I'll guarantee to take any one at random and train him to become any type of specialist I might select—doctor, lawyer, artist, merchant-chief and, yes, even beggar-man and thief, regardless of his talents, penchants, tendencies, abilities, vocations, and race of his ancestors."[43] The nightmarish aspects of John B. Watson's boast can be traced back, at least, to Bentham who, towards the end of his *Panopticon Letters*, had half-seriously recommended turning his prison model to the purposes of education; as to the well-watched children, he commented, "Call them monks, call them machines: so they were but happy ones, I should not care."[44] A residue of Bentham's highly restricted view of happiness clearly remains in Watson—but Watson's idealism, specifically his belief that aggressive nurture might counteract the longstanding social iniquities of race and class was entirely in the progressive spirit. The impulse to behavioral training was not *inherently* anti-individualist in intention—or rather, its inherent coerciveness could not easily be disentangled from higher purposes. In his *Principles*, James had called "habit"—not the first word one associates with liberal politics—"the great fly-wheel of society, its most precious conservative agent":

> It alone is what keeps us all within the bounds of ordinance, and
> saves the children of fortune from the envious uprisings of the
> poor. It alone prevents the hardest and most repulsive walks of
> life from being deserted by those brought up to tread therein. It
> keeps the fisherman and deck-hand at sea through the winter; it

holds the miner in his darkness [this poetizing continues for a while]. It dooms us all to fight out the battle of life upon the lines of our nurture or our early choice [but] on the whole it is best [we] should not escape. It is well for the world that in most of us, by the age of thirty, the character has been set like plaster, and will never soften again. (*Principles*, 1:121)

From these potentially dismal premises, James concludes that it is best to make "*automatic and habitual, as early as possible, as many useful actions as we can*"—not to create a populace of happy machines, however, but to set free behaviors that *shouldn't* be automatic: "The more of the details of our daily life we can hand over to the effortless custody of automatism, the more our higher powers of mind will be set free for their own proper work" (*Principles*, 1:122; James's italics).[45]

Although the more spectacular and excessive instances of behaviorist thought have drawn the most scrutiny—Watson, Little Albert, or (the be-all and end-all of such thinking) Skinner's unintentionally dystopian proposals in *Walden Two*—we would suggest that more attention be given to the finer compromises within the liberal-progressive mainstream.[46] Behavioral training of the sort proposed by James (or even Watson), for example, might result not in the *end* of individual autonomy but rather in a certain restriction or limiting of what autonomy itself *meant*. Coercive surveillance of the type we began to observe in the eighteenth century may be said to have returned in behaviorist psychology, with new theoretical and technological shorings; the delicate balance sought by Samuel Johnson, Adam Smith, and others was sought again with new urgency— posing a special problem for a tradition rooted in personal liberties: to what extent might individuals be socially shaped while remaining individuals, and could such persons truly be considered free or equal? Might key desiderata (like "freedom") be understood as meaning categorically different things for different citizens, so long as each citizen enjoyed those goods "equally"? Behaviorism all but implied a caste system and the existence of both managerial and intellectual elites: all citizens must be free, but some must inevitably be more autonomous and individual*ized* than others. Whatever their commitment to "equality," the progressives stopped short of espousing equality of ability, which was now yoked semantically (as had been foreshadowed in Mill) to "mediocrity": while some might be trained to lead, others were qualified by nature for only the "most repulsive walks of life." How, then, to do *everyone* justice, without a return, as conservatives would recommend, to traditional hierarchies? As we have already seen, beginning with Wordsworth, a fear of popular homogeneity went hand in hand with, not counter to, a belief in personal freedom. At Bartholomew Fair, Wordsworth had worried about "thousands upon thousands" of Londoners "reduced/to one identity" by the influence of "trivial objects." Mill, similarly, had feared that "whatever homage may be professed . . . to real or supposed mental superiority, the general tendency of things . . . [was] to render mediocrity the ascendant power among mankind. At present individuals [were] lost in the crowd."[47] Given the inherently middling "general average of mankind" and "the sway of Custom" (Mill's terms), Dewey would comment, equality of ability was "false to facts and impossible of realization." The outcome of such thinking was "a mediocrity in which good [was] common only in the sense of being average and vulgar."[48] "Equality," he concluded, must not be taken too literally, not signifying "that kind of mathematical or physical equivalence in virtue of which any one element may be substituted for another. It denotes effective regard for what is distinctive and unique in each."[49]

The real-world consequence of this kind of thinking was precisely the managerial, expert-driven society with which progressivism continues to be associated and which Weber had already identified as an "iron cage."[50] James, for his part, had anticipated and argued for such a managerial turn. In his late essay "The Social Value of the College Bred," he had speculated that "democracy," like previous forms of government, might "undergo a self-poisoning" through "vulgarity enthroned and institutionalized, elbowing everything superior from the highway"—a fate that might be averted, however, by "the better kind of man." Indeed, the well-schooled comprised an aristocracy of the mind, "the only permanent presence that corresponds to the aristocracy in older countries. . . . We have continuous traditions, as they have; our motto, too, is *noblesse oblige*. . . . We ought to have our own class-consciousness. 'Les intellectuels!' "[51]

During the teens, this "aristocracy" was enthusiastically populated by the likes of Lippmann—former student of James and advisor to Woodrow Wilson—who, at the start of his very long career, espoused unabashedly elitist views that would later moderate. Taking familiar opinions to their natural conclusion, Lippman argued that the "other half" (more like

eight-ninths) was too self-interested and intellectually limited to comprehend or act upon—let alone initiate—complex public policies. Society
therefore required a "governing class" with the special ability to understand, interpret, and explain the social mechanism to the majority, now
figured as "deaf spectators."[52] Liberal elitism of this sort made for striking
rhetorical maneuvers, some of which came perilously close to Orwellian
doublespeak. "The public must be put in its place," Lippmann announced,
"so that it [might] exercise its power . . . so that each of us [might] be free
of the trampling and the roar of a bewildered herd."[53] The contemptuous-
ness of this position and Lippmann's frank embrace of authoritarian
power should not, finally, obscure his location on a spectrum of
mainstream liberal thought: with growing frequency, progressives from
T. H. Green (who introduced the idea of "positive freedom" provided by
the State) to Woodrow Wilson (whose "New Freedom," a brainchild, in
part, of Brandeis's, pushed for increased regulation of the economy)
equated freedom with both monitoring and control.[54] Even Dewey had
redefined the term as "a mental attitude rather than external unconstraint
of movements"—a mental attitude, apparently, that required considerable external shaping.[55] By the second decade of the twentieth century,
progressivism had made it possible for individualists to imagine ways
that restrictions on individual autonomy might help the individual.
Leaving itself open to attack from anarchists and the populist left, as well
as conservatives, progressivism saw the formalization and systemization
on a vast scale of the social-control and classification processes we began
to track in the last chapter. As a functioning scheme, it depended upon
(benignly intended) bureaucratized surveillance, from driver's licenses to
report cards. A decade on, what might have once seemed paradoxical
would make perfect sense: the liberal state could be both protective and
coercive, both authoritarian and liberating, both collectivist and elitist.

Leaving the Island: Progressivism and Character

On the whole, literature written in the progressive spirit has not aged
well—which is by no means to deny or diminish the immense impact it
often had at the time of publication. Richard Wright, for example,
recalling his early adulthood in the segregated South, is eloquent about
the transformative effect socially critical novelists like Sinclair Lewis and
Theodore Dreiser had on his career and life:

> My first serious novel was Sinclair Lewis's *Main Street*. It made
> me see my boss, Mr. Gerald, and identify him as an American
> type. I would smile when I saw him lugging his golf bags into
> the office. I had always felt a vast distance separating me from
> the boss and now I felt closer to him, though still distant. I felt
> now that I knew him, that I could feel the very limits of his
> narrow life. And this had happened because I had read a novel
> about a mythical man named George F. Babbitt.[56]

Both the power and shortcomings of Lewis are evident in this passage: on
the one hand, *Main Street*, with its pointed criticisms of provinciality and
its exploration of progressivism (through the career of its heroine), gave
Wright a fuller, aerial perspective on American society. At the same time,
this knowledge was highly schematic: as he notes, the experience of *Main
Street* still left him feeling "distant" from Mr. Gerald. We might refine the
claim further to say that the *quality* of the distance changed rather than
the *fact* of distance per se: where Wright had previously experienced the
profound, yet intimate separation of his subordination under Jim Crow,
Main Street allowed him the cooler perspective of clinical detachment—
that is, he could now see Mr. Gerald as a "type." The cost of Wright's new
knowledge, in short, was the "narrowing" and flattening of his boss into a
two-dimensional figure. This flattening effect at once explains Lewis's
polemical effectiveness during the teens and twenties (to the point of
"Babbitry" becoming a popular noun and Lewis being named the first
U.S. Nobel laureate in literature), and why he is rarely read with pleasure
today, at best coming off as a representative period voice. To recall Mead's
formula, George Babbitt—and, in effect, Mr. Gerald—is inseparable from
the "social process within which [he] had [his] initiation." Unfortunately,
when this attitude is adopted by novelists or artists, individual characters
are typically reduced to icons or stick figures.

H. G. Wells, surveying his own more polemical and programmatic
work, recognized the broader consequences of this view for art; in these
writings, he commented: "The blood and warmth and reality of life
is largely absent; there are no individualities, but only generalised
people. One sees . . . a multitude of people . . . but without any personal
distinction whatever. . . . This burthens us with an incurable effect of
unreality, and I do not see how it is altogether to be escaped."[57] By correctly

"identifying" Mr. Gerald as a "type," finally, "without any personal distinction whatever," Wright also identified the allegorical impulse behind the culture of expertise and classification promoted, along different vectors, by the likes of Lippmann, Lewis, and (a particular Brandeis favorite) Frederick Taylor.[58] Allegory of this variety was genetically closer to the practice of nineteenth-century phrenologists than Renaissance poets and statesmen: where older forms of allegory had located their organizing "singularity" in something transcendent—the divine gaze—the progressives looked to immanent principles of the world or society as discovered by the sciences of psychology, anthropology, sociology, history, and the like. As we saw with Brontë, Poe, and others influenced by phrenology, literature inspired by these sciences could not strictly be called anti-empirical or unrealistic—certainly not in the pre-empirical manner of Spenser and Swift, nor indeed along the lines of the revived allegory among some twentieth-century authors we will examine later in the chapter. Nevertheless, to the extent that these authors presented individuals as the products of an underlying process—the "superstructure" generated by a "base," as it were—an allegorical reduction of character was more or less inevitable.

For this reason, the civilization of the progressives' dreams could not, strictly speaking, be called a "surveillance society"; rather they harkened back to the fantasy of a perfectly transparent populace, in no need of constant watching. Taken in this light, San Francisco's Coit Tower presents a lovely mixed metaphor. Rising atop Telegraph Hill and commanding views from Oakland, to Tiburon, to the Pacific, the 210-foot building is arguably the West Coast's best-known panoptic structure; and yet the tower's equally famous WPA-era murals on the ground floor are perhaps the most eloquent visual expression of a society requiring no surveillance whatsoever. With a regularity approaching eeriness, the industrial workers of America appear in their endless numbers, with almost nothing to distinguish them as individuals. A "steelworker" in this setting is not a distinct person so much as a kind of Waldo figure, reappearing in identical form, with the same features and clothing, the same *expression*, mural after mural (often, it should be noted, at the hands of different artists, and indeed even in other WPA-style murals throughout the country)—now climbing a telephone pole, now harvesting oranges, always harmlessly absorbed in his labor (figures 6–8).

Figure 6. Coit Tower, *Steelworker*, mural (detail), 1933.

Figure 7. Coit Tower, *California Agriculture*, mural (detail), 1933.

Figure 8. Diego Rivera, *Detroit Industry*, fresco (detail), 1932–33, Detroit Institute of Arts. DIA / Bridgeman Art Library.

In crowd scenes, "deaf spectators" abound: the only alternatives to a blank expression (even on the part of a man being robbed at gunpoint!) are either the vacant, performed grin of the Hollywood celebrity on a newsstand or else the literal facelessness of the background characters. Ultimately, the figures of this genre exist only so far as they carry social relevance or occupy clear social roles (this even applies, bizarrely, to the gunman)—with the effect of total transparency (figure 9). Given

Figure 9. Coit Tower, *City Life*, mural (detail), 1933.

the limitations of this aesthetic, it is perhaps unsurprising that the most interesting and lasting literature to emerge from progressivism was not progressive in spirit, but instead took progressivism—and in particular the ironies thrown up by the progressives' rhetorical reinvention of liberalism—as a satirical target. Huxley's *Brave New World*, to which we now turn, with its intellectual and highly differentiated Alphas ("the better kind of men"), bureaucratic Betas, and faceless Epsilons (suitable for only "the most repulsive walks of life"), clearly has the elitism of a James or Lippmann in its sights—as well, it should be added, as the reductive tendencies of progressive art: those interchangeable steelworkers and orange pickers, alas, are heavy-labor Deltas through and through.

Huxley's 1931 novel—almost an exact contemporary of the Coit murals—is often grouped alongside *1984* and Yevgeny Zamyatin's *We* (1921) to form an Unholy Trinity, as it were, of twentieth-century dystopian fictions; this arrangement, however, was hardly of the authors' choosing and ignores serious differences of polemical intent.[59] Orwell himself, in his laudatory 1946 review of *We*, a piece that helped introduce Zamyatin to an English-speaking audience, was famously ungenerous towards *Brave New World*, attacking it as inadequate to twentieth-century despotism. Zamyatin, Orwell observed, possessed an "intuitive grasp of the irrational side of totalitarianism—human sacrifice, cruelty as an end in itself, the worship of a Leader who is credited with divine attributes— that [made his] book superior to Huxley's."[60] Leaving aside the more personal, Oedipal reasons for Orwell's attack (Huxley had been his teacher at Eton), one can also see that Orwell was thinking through the parameters of his own dystopia, and perhaps suffering from a certain blindness. The review appeared just as he was beginning work on *1984*, and his own novel is deeply in the Soviet author's debt: Zamyatin's semi-divine "Benefactor" is the obvious precedent for Big Brother, and Orwell's "thought police" are drawn from the earlier book's "guardians"; in both works the hero undergoes a third-act interrogation/brainwashing leading to his betrayal of the heroine (and on and on).[61] More to the point, however, Orwell largely, almost willfully, misconstrues Huxley's aims. Correctly observing that Huxley is more influenced than Zamyatin "by recent biological and psychological theories," he then fails adequately to credit Huxley for establishing these theories as the basis of his future society:

> In Huxley's book the problem of "human nature" is in a sense solved, because it assumes that by pre-natal treatment, drugs and hypnotic suggestion the human organism can be specialised in any way that is desired. A first-rate scientific worker is as easily produced as an Epsilon semi-moron, and in either case the vestiges of primitive instincts, such as maternal feeling or the desire for liberty, are easily dealt with. At the same time no clear reason is given why society should be stratified in the elaborate way that is described. The aim is not economic exploitation, but the desire to bully and dominate does not seem to be a motive either. There is no power hunger, no sadism, no hardness of any kind. Those at the top have no strong motive for staying at the top.[62]

But of course, this is to attribute intentions to Huxley that he never had. As he was writing, Orwell had before him the examples of Hitler and Stalin, and Zamyatin had written during the early years of Soviet rule: neither had to search far for "economic exploitation," "power hunger," or "sadism." By his own admission, however, Huxley took inspiration from the managerial society of the progressives—his interest being precisely in benignly intended forms of despotism of a sort Orwell believed to be impossible, but less extreme versions of which were at least implied by the hyperefficient workforce of a Taylor and advances in behaviorism after Watson. In this respect, *Brave New World* might more profitably be compared with earlier novelistic critiques—or satires, rather—of collectivism like *The Blithedale Romance*, Hawthorne's not-so-veiled account of the Fourierist settlement at Brook Farm. As a model for Orwell's endeavors, it would never measure up to *We*—hardly a failing on Huxley's part.

In a late foreword to the novel, Huxley retracted much of what he had written but remained adamant about where he thought civilization was headed: "vast government-sponsored enquiries into . . . 'the problem of happiness'—in other words, the problem of making people love their servitude. . . . I assume that the all-powerful executive and its managers will solve the problem of permanent security . . . established as the result of a deep, personal revolution in human minds and bodies."[63] To state the obvious: this is not the position of a liberal—or, at the very least, it is not the position of someone who believes in the long-term prospects of liberalism. From the perspective of twenty-sixth century London—the setting of *Brave New World*—the movement is written off as ephemeral and doomed: "There was something called liberalism. . . . [There were] speeches about liberty of the subject. Liberty to be inefficient and miserable."[64] Whatever the ironies of these passages, they reflect a consistency in Huxley that goes back to his earliest work: from *Antic Hay*, to *Point Counter Point*, through his American period, Huxley argues for the necessary existence of an elite—as in James, an aristocracy of the mind—consigning the vast majority of humanity to the "happiness" of loving a lesser existence. This frank exclusiveness is probably what Orwell found most galling about *Brave New World*, prompting his otherwise bewildering assertion that Huxley offers "no clear reason . . . why society should be stratified in the elaborate way [he describes]." But in fact Huxley could not be more explicit; as his "world controller" Mustapha Mond explains,

> [Epsilons are] the foundation on which everything else is built.
> . . . A society of Alphas couldn't fail to be unstable and
> miserable. Imagine a factory staffed by Alphas—that is to say by

separate and unrelated individuals of good heredity and
conditioned to be capable (within limits) of making a free choice
and assuming responsibilities. . . . It's an absurdity. . . . Only an
Epsilon can be expected to make Epsilon sacrifices, for the good
reason they aren't sacrifices . . . His conditioning has laid down
rails along which he's got to run . . . he's foredoomed. (222)

When Mond adds that "the optimum population . . . is modeled on the
iceberg—eight-ninths below the water line, one-ninth above" (223), one
has no sense that Huxley the sometime supporter of eugenics disagrees:
his answer to Orwell's objection would be, simply, that society *is* naturally
stratified—into the talented and untalented.[65] The London of *Brave New
World* regularizes—and ameliorates for those beneath the waterline—an
already existing condition.

The position may be compared with Lippmann's "governing class"
and "bewildered herd" and his assertion that the public must be "put in
its place"; lacking entirely, however, is the pretense that such a society
exists for *anyone's* benefit besides the ruling class, the "talented tenth"
(or one-ninth), or whatever one wishes to call it. When Mond calls the
Epsilons "the foundation on which everything is built," the "everything"
he refers to is the immensely comfortable world of the Alphas and Betas.
Huxley's futurism, his depiction of a superficial and commodity-driven
society, which has garnered most of the critical attention to his novel, is
largely a misdirect—his concern with most of the fictive population being
nil. In a nod to the tradition of Romantic individualism so important to
nineteenth-century liberalism, Huxley has one of his Alpha protagonists,
Bernard Marx, enjoy Wordsworthian "walks in the Lake District" (89).
Huxley's point is that the ideology of autonomous personhood *never*
translates to a general love of mankind or an expansion of sympathies—
quite the opposite. Wordsworth, Mill, and James, in their various ways,
had come within a hair's breadth of admitting as much, though to do so
would have meant an immense ideological sacrifice. Standing outside the
progressive tradition, Huxley was able to satirize its hypocrisy. James had
had good reason to worry that "the children of fortune" might someday
suffer reprisals from the "miners" and "deckhands." In *Brave New World*
that threat is neutralized at the expense of "submerging" eight-ninths of
the population: a motivation, Huxley seems to suggest, lying at the heart

of all utopias, as well as instrumental liberalism. Far better that the miners be held in their darkness.

As in the America depicted in the Coit murals, but again in telling contrast to the dystopias of Orwell and Zamyatin, Huxley's projected civilization cannot be called a "surveillance society" in the usual sense—and for precisely the same reason: the workers are never anything but what they appear to be and, happy in their appointed tracks, are unlikely ever to revolt. This is not to say, however, that Huxley is uninterested in the subtler, noncoercive, multidirectional forms that surveillance can take. When Bernard Marx proposes one of those Wordsworthian rambles to the beautiful and "pneumatic" Lenina Crowne, an otherwise willing Beta, it provokes a telling interchange:

> Bernard blushed and looked away. "[I'd like to be] alone for talking," he mumbled.
>
> "Talking? But what about?" Walking and talking—that seemed a very odd way of spending an afternoon.
>
> In the end she persuaded him, much against his will, to fly over to Amsterdam to see the Semi-Demi-Finals of the Women's Heavyweight Wrestling Championship.
>
> "In a crowd," he grumbled, "as usual." (89)

Largely unconcerned with the jackbooted modes of surveillance that interested Orwell, Huxley is nevertheless deeply invested in the more pleasurable and participatory forms of social watching: Lenina, like most of her fellow subjects, cannot bear to be *out* of the public eye for any length of time. Partly this is a function of training (the members of Huxley's World State are never alone from infancy onwards), and undoubtedly this training serves a commercial purpose (purchasing tickets for a wrestling match costs more than a solitary stroll); but on the deepest level, Lenina, like Henry James's Lord Mellifont in our opening example, seems to derive her very being from the social gaze—and is nothing without it. In our last chapter, we will have more to say about these commercial and largely voluntary forms of surveillance, which indeed dominate the contemporary surveillance scene. Within the constraints of Huxley's experiment, the satirical point could not be plainer: in a society where the vast majority of people are content, and actually *crave* the public gaze, disruption—on the rare occasions when it occurs—can only come from above.

And so, ultimately, Huxley brings us to the reversal of a trope we have observed appearing at key moments in the history of surveillance and representation. To this point, islands have been settings for thought experiments about observation, interpretation, and control—the subject departing, back to the everyday world, with the conclusion of the test. Huxley, of course, drew his title from one of our previous insular adventures, with John, the "savage" whom Bernard brings back to London after a brief vacation in New Mexico, standing in for Miranda. At a certain point, though, the analogy implied by the title breaks down: the advanced civilization of twenty-sixth-century London corresponds less to the "real world" of Antonio's Milan than the "experimental" one of Prospero's island. Prospero's island, it should be added, on a vast scale, utopia having finally expanded to fill the world. In a final irony, however, the civilization built by an elite for its own happiness and preservation is revealed as inadequate—for precisely the most developed and autonomous members at the very top of that elite. The London of *Brave New World* may not have been forged in the interests of the Epsilons and Gammas—but whatever one wishes to call their restricted individuality (false consciousness?), it is a source of genuine contentment—the elevator operators couldn't be happier. By way of contrast, Huxley offers Bernard's friend, the even more advanced Helmholtz Watson (named after the great behaviorist):[66]

> That which had made Helmholtz so uncomfortably aware of
> being himself and all alone was too much ability. [The fruits of
> civilization] were only, so far as he was concerned, second bests.
> Really, and at the bottom, he was interested in something else.
> But in what? . . ."Did you ever feel," he asked, "as though you
> had something inside you that was only waiting for you to give it
> a chance to come out? . . . I'm thinking of a queer feeling I
> sometimes get, a feeling that I've got something important to
> say and the power to say it—only . . . I can't make any use of the
> power." (67, 69)

Huxley draws on the language of romantic egotism with purpose—his point being that *all* attempts to account socially for the autonomous individual are bound to fail. At some point, the most talented persons will be unable to reconcile themselves with communal norms, even norms created under the most prejudicial circumstances.

At the end of *Brave New World*, therefore, Helmholtz and Bernard indeed leave the island of Britain—for much smaller islands of exile (Iceland, Samoa, the Falklands, etc.), populated by the inevitable, idiosyncratic outcasts produced by an overly managed society. In Mond's description, the residents are "the most interesting set of men and women to be found anywhere in the world. All the people who . . . got too self-consciously individual to fit into community-life" (227). With these islands of exile we reach the end of our own speculative archipelago. Pointedly, Bernard's and Helmholtz's destination is never described in any detail: it is simply the repository of the overly individuated. Any further depiction (of the population, its organization, how it runs itself) would set in motion once again the inexorable dialectics of individuality and society—and so we're left with a blank.[67] As a blank—a true utopia, a no-place—the island retains at least one of the symbolic meanings accruing to it since *The Tempest* and *Robinson Crusoe*: it is the locus of unconstrained personality. Or, to put the matter less optimistically: in a totalizing—or nearly totalizing—society, escape can only be envisioned as blankness.

II. PARANOID ALLEGORY

Utopia Redux

It is on this question of escape that *Brave New World* differs most essentially from the best-known dystopias of twentieth-century fiction. A Helmholtz or Bernard unfortunate enough to live in Zamyatin's OneState or Orwell's Oceania (or the subsequent polities of an Atwood or Philip K. Dick) would simply be brainwashed or executed. However ironic Huxley's intentions, the very existence of an alternative to Society marks him as at least influenced by liberalism. In the other two novels, the political system is imagined as ubiquitous and complete—and, of course, the same can be said of the total States on which Orwell and Zamyatin were modeling their dystopias: however "archipelagic" the gulag, the Soviet prisons were hardly islands of refuge. So long as a sanctuary could be imagined for the individual—"every one . . . who's anyone," in Mustapha Mond's précis— the individual (however conceived) could still be seen as the legitimating agent for state politics. This is no longer the case in Zamyatin or Orwell. Writing in the *Tribune* just after World War II, Orwell commented that every technological development of recent years had "favoured the State as against the Individual" and predicted "three great empires, each self-contained and cut off from contact with the outer world, and each ruled, under one disguise or another, by a self-elected oligarchy." "Looking at the world as a whole," he concluded, "the drift . . . has been . . . towards the reimposition of slavery."[68] Whatever the accuracy of these predictions (of which we will have more to say at the end of the chapter), the vision is clear: the State exists not for the individual but for itself, or for the narrow interests of an elite, or for something still more sinister like the sheer exercise of sadistic power—"cruelty as an end in itself," as he approvingly observes in his review of *We*.[69]

Under such circumstances, each individual subject (to the extent that he or she can still think of him or herself *as* an individual) can only be conceived of by the State as an obstacle to the exercise of power—if not an enemy in fact, then potentially so. Because everyone is automatically an object of suspicion, furthermore, the most overt, far-reaching, and intrusive species of surveillance—the secret police/telescreen variety that most people imagine when they first think of state surveillance—becomes necessary. One of the sharpest diagnoses of the motives behind this kind of watching and of the individual's willingness to submit to state oppression—striking, too, because it appears so early and in such an unlikely place—occurs in Rider Haggard. The hidden African kingdom Haggard's European adventurers stumble upon in *King Solomon's Mines* (1885) is an absolutist dystopia running on Stone Age technology; in the event, the crudeness of means is clarifying. Newly arrived in the kingdom, the Europeans are invited to observe a "witch hunt," a stark and unflinching vision of how power eliminates its threats—"all those who have evil in their hearts," as the king puts it.[70] In order to detect this "wickedness," the monarch employs ten "witches," whose shenanigans are little more than elaborate political theater:

> When [the witch-hunter] came within a few paces of the
> warriors, she halted and began to dance wildly, turning round
> and round with an almost incredible rapidity, and shrieking out
> sentences such as "I smell him, the evil-doer! . . . I hear the
> thoughts of him who thought evil of the king!"
>   Suddenly the end came. With a shriek she sprang in and
> touched a tall warrior with [a] forked wand. Instantly two of his

comrades, those standing immediately next to him, seized the
doomed man, each by one arm, and advanced towards the
king. He did not resist, but we saw that he dragged his limbs
as though they were paralysed, and that his fingers, from which
the spear had fallen, were limp like those of a man newly
dead. . . .

"*Kill!*" said the king. . . .

Almost before the words were uttered the horrible deed
was done. One man had driven his spear into the victim's
heart, and to make assurance double sure, the other had
dashed out his brains with a great club.[71]

It was Orwell who later adopted the term "witch hunt" (Haggard figured
largely in his boyhood reading) as a way to describe the paranoid exercise
of power by absolutist governments.[72] Haggard is at least as clear-eyed
and canny as his successor, however, about the methods of absolute power
and the motivations behind total surveillance. The usual elements are all
present and accounted for: the singling out of the individual as a threat to
the State; the ritualism of the executions; the way that comrades are
expected to turn instantly upon each other at the slightest official gesture;
the way suspicion comes to stand in for proof of guilt; the impossibility of
resistance and the inability even to protest on the part of the accused;
most of all, perhaps, the reproducibility and permanence of power (the
white observers are told by their native guide that there is no point in
overthrowing the king since an even worse one would simply spring up in
his place).

As both Haggard and Orwell grasped, absolutist States almost inevitably turn suspiciously against their own subjects—and as both also well
understood, government surveillance in the mode of the Gestapo or Stasi,
while overtly about detection, can equally be about terror as its own end.
Haggard strongly implies that the warriors identified as traitors are
perfectly loyal, and that the king is mainly interested in culling his own best
and brightest, or in pursuing still narrower aims. "No man's life is safe,"
the guide explains. "If the king covets a man's cattle, or a man's wife, or if
he fears a man that he should excite a rebellion against him, then [the
'witches' will] smell that man out as a wizard, and he will be killed." As
perilously as Haggard skirts mumbo jumbo—both the strength and

potential weakness of the subgenre, imperial adventure, in which he is working—his depiction of the exercise of surveillant power is at least as convincing as Orwell's and possibly more so. Technology—the telescreen or the Benefactor's Machine—is ultimately an aid or mediator, but Haggard presents the thing itself. We would offer, however, one proviso to Haggard's little masterpiece: just as he (here and elsewhere) warns against the excesses of State authority, he nevertheless is happy enough to see the peremptory exercise of absolute power in the service of empire—indeed, this would be the characteristic blind spot of his chosen subgenre. The white protagonists of *King Solomon's Mines* (presenting themselves as "wise men from the stars") unhesitatingly overthrow the "savage" government—leaving behind their own chosen despot (conveniently, the son of the previous king) before returning to the outside world. What neither Haggard *nor* Orwell, perhaps, adequately recognized is the way the analysis of paranoia was, insidiously, an *invitation* to paranoia, and all that comes with it, on the part of the *examiner*—a problem we will take up shortly.

We may observe first, however, that, whatever the superficial resemblances, the fictions of Orwell and Zamyatin had a genealogy far removed from that of *Brave New World;* where the latter was the satire of a certain kind of liberalism, both *We* and *1984* are better anticipated in their basic premises by a tradition of utopian socialist speculation among British and American philosophers, novelists, and even economists in the half century or so before World War I. Bellamy's *Looking Backward* (1888), Hertzka's *Freeland* (a popular English translation appeared in 1891), Howells's Altruria trilogy (1894–1907), Frankford's *The Coming Day* (1908), and especially Morris's *News from Nowhere*—yet another entry from the annus mirabilis of 1890—are among the more famous examples. Indeed, we might draw a loose analogy between the ideological climate of the mid-sixteenth century, another period of intense utopian thought, and the fin de siècle: More, we saw, had felt compelled to imagine the conditions that would make an allegorical politics possible—in stark contrast to the complex and rapidly modernizing Tudor state. In a similar way, as the compromises underpinning liberalism became more obvious and galling, it was surely tempting to imagine a politics both absolute and pure—preserving some of liberalism's key principles, like social justice, even if that meant sacrificing others, like the centrality and autonomy of the individual. In his declaration that the foundation of civil society required "unanimity" and that, under the social contract, the individual citizen must "put his person and all his power in common under the supreme direction of the general will," Rousseau had offered just such a vision of purity—or, in Berlin's condemnatory term, "positive liberty."[73] For Berlin, this expectation, that the "'positively' free self [conform to the dictates of] some super-personal entity [i.e., the State]," was inherently coercive—a point with which Rousseau would not disagree: "If anyone refuses to obey the general will he will be compelled to do so by the whole body; which means nothing less than that he will be forced to be free."[74] However ominous this prospect, by the end of the nineteenth century, utopian writers could draw on decades of practical socialist experimentation—from Owen's planned communities, to Cabet's Icarian settlements, to Fourier's phalangeries—conducted under the inspiration of Rousseau. America had been particularly fertile ground for the movement, with dozens of settlements noted by John Humphrey Noyes in his contemporary *History of American Socialisms*.[75] The very failure of these concrete efforts, finally, helps explain the proliferation of an openly speculative genre, espousing the benefits of ever more aggressive social control, the virtues of minimal privacy, a powerful state, and close surveillance—all at the expense of individual freedoms.

Earlier works in the genre, like *Looking Backward* and especially *News from Nowhere*, had strained to square the "positive" liberty of utopia with the pieties of a native audience schooled in liberal convictions (like privacy and freedom of thought and action).[76] Later entries, however—Wells's *A Modern Utopia* (1905), for example—are overt about the need for coercion. This trajectory is grimly evident in the larger span from Rousseau to Orwell: a steadily eroding view of the social animal, the historical causes of which—geopolitical, ethnic, sociological—we will have more to say about in the next section. Where Morris shares Rousseau's largely benign view of human nature (people are basically good, though we still need some order), his attitude is out of step with most late nineteenth-century utopian speculation: a half century or more of attempts at practical application had nearly eradicated the belief in mutual benevolence. In Fourier's phalangeries the different, "natural" classes of workers had been sorted out and trained, issued their own uniforms, and expected to submit to higher authorities (up to the "omniarch" planned for the Constantinople phalanx). Fourier had been clear about the failings of earlier planned communities: a misguided belief in "equality," above all, along with a nervousness about collectivism—and a tendency to admit too many of the wrong sort: "Every government having regard to good morals ought to repress the Jews, compel them to engage in productive labor, admit them only in the proportion of one to a hundred."[77] With real-world efforts having turned to authoritarianism, it is no surprise that most later nineteenth-century utopian writers, and practically all of their twentieth-century dystopian successors, should have followed suit; with a darkening view of human character, utopia had darkened as well.

We have already, at all events, observed a similar trajectory in the liberal-progressive tradition—and indeed, in his late (and surprisingly dour) essay "The Moral Equivalent of War," James attacks Morris, and his vision of a violence-free agrarian paradise, as unrealistic. However much we wish to credit the better angels of our nature, James argues, the vast majority of people continue to subsist on a "pain-and-fear . . . economy."[78] That is to say: under conditions of war and privation, a society will naturally cohere through the passionate involvement of the citizenry; these passions also ensure the discipline and effectiveness of military forces. Although bonds of this sort are, necessarily, weaker in civilian life, they continue to govern the way most people behave—and thus "the duties, penalties, and sanctions pictured in the utopias [of Morris and others are] too weak and tame to touch [the ordinary citizen]." Such people would never be swayed by the "mawkish and dishwatery" feel of "present-day utopian literature"; rather, a functioning society must be united by a collective—and relentlessly enforced—sense of purpose: "What the whole community comes to believe in grasps the individual as in a vise. The war-function has grasped us so far; but the constructive interests may some day seem no less imperative, and impose on the individual a hardly lighter burden." In place of idealized visions, then, a resolution to control the populace by taking advantage of essential (and in other contexts undesirable) impulses.

James himself was no builder of castles in the sky; it may be argued that the final flowering of his vision in "The Moral Equivalent of War" was not to be found in any ideal society, but rather in the late progressive initiatives of the New Deal—programs like the Civilian Conservation

Corps, which harnessed the energies of the unemployed in quasi-military social projects. Nevertheless, a suspicion of the lower "eight-ninths" akin to James's underpins much utopian writing of the period: with the exception of *News from Nowhere*, the "pain and fear" economy continues to motivate these works, and most resemble the first *Utopia* in their methods and conclusions. Even the relatively benign twenty-first-century Boston of *Looking Backward* is highly regimented.[79] In Wells, more plainly, "the compromise of Liberty" is recognized as a necessary precondition for economic equality and social order. "The modern view," he comments, "with its deepening insistence upon individuality [begins] to see liberty as the very substance of life, [to think] that indeed it is life, and that only the dead things, the choiceless things, live in absolute obedience to law." In fact, Wells continues, justice requires an attenuation of freedom and a limiting of individual desires for the larger good of the community.[80] More's strictures thus return, bolstered now by a more efficient technology. Concurring with his sixteenth-century predecessor, Wells asserts that the "almost universal claim to privacy amongst modern people" makes efficient surveillance nearly impossible.[81]

> In the typical modern State of our own world, with its population of many millions, and its extreme facility of movement, undistinguished men who adopt an alias can make themselves untraceable with the utmost ease. The temptation of the opportunities thus offered has developed a new type of criminality. . . . This is a large, a growing, and, what is gravest, a prolific class, fostered by the practical anonymity of the common man. . . . It is one of the bye products of State Liberalism, and at present it is very probably drawing ahead in the race against the development of police organisation. (166)

Wells's solution, a "scheme by which every person in the world can be promptly and certainly recognized," again recalls More's, but with an excited sense of new technological possibilities, some real, some remarkably prescient. Movements are strictly limited, the citizenry is issued identification cards (the passport was just coming into widespread use at this time) and then entered into what is essentially a massive database overseen by a worldwide "brain": "I have compared the indexing of humanity . . . to an eye, an eye so sensitive and alert that two strangers cannot appear anywhere upon the planet without discovery."[82] The all-seeing "World-state" of *A Modern Utopia*—an obvious precedent for Orwell's Big Brother—takes upon itself such tasks as the regulation of breeding, and ensuring "certain minimum[s]" (of "personal efficiency," of "physical development," and so on). Those "incompetent persons" and "people of weak character" who cannot carry their weight or comply with the general will—who, in short, "spoil the world for others"—must be subjected to "social surgery" and forcibly excluded from the body politic: no islands of refuge here.[83]

Paranoia and the Surveillance State

> No-one would have believed in the last years of the nineteenth
> century that this world was being watched keenly and closely by intel-
> ligences greater than man's and yet as mortal as his own; that as men
> busied themselves about their various concerns they were scruti-
> nized and studied, perhaps almost as narrowly as a man with a
> microscope might scrutinize the transient creatures that swarm and
> multiply in a drop of water. . . . Yet . . . intellects vast and cool and
> unsympathetic regarded this earth with envious eyes and slowly and
> surely drew their plans against us. And early in the twentieth century
> came the great disillusionment.
>
> —H. G. Wells, *The War of the Worlds*[84]

To refine a suggestion that we made at the beginning of this chapter: the primary modal opponent in the modern era to a weakened liberal consensus, was a resurgent form of allegory colored by three centuries of liberal-contractual hegemony. This revived allegory, operating within the politics, the social structures, and—as we have begun to see—the literature of the period, was intrinsically paranoid in temperament. Indeed, this char- acteristic paranoia, beginning in the late nineteenth century (and continuing to the present day), is what most clearly distinguishes the modern iteration from the Renaissance forms of social allegory we exam- ined in chapter 1, paranoia being the toll exacted on allegory for passing though the liberal dispensation. As with our earlier inquiry, we are not interested in the *genre* per se, but rather in the ways that allegory, as a *mode*, involves ways of organizing reality that are as operative in everyday life as in the aesthetic structures of a novel or poem. When we claim, finally, that twentieth-century allegorical culture was "paranoid," we echo Richard Hofstadter's well-known account of the way paranoia can infect large segments of a populace or, in extreme cases like Fascism, take over the body politic entirely.[85] In Hofstadter's account, subsequently refined by his numerous followers, the paranoid "style" in politics is characterized by "the feeling of persecution . . . systematized into grand theories of conspiracy."[86] The existing order is revealed to be a "sham"; as Hofstadter observes,

> A gigantic yet subtle machinery of influence [is perceived to have been] set in motion to undermine and destroy a way of life.
> . . . The distinguishing thing about the paranoid style is not that its exponents see conspiracies or plots here or there in history, but that they regard a "vast" or "gigantic" conspiracy as the *motive force* in historical events. History *is* a conspiracy, set in motion by demonic forces of almost transcendent power, and what is felt to be needed to defeat it is not the usual methods of political give-and-take, but an all-out crusade. The paranoid spokesman [thus] sees the fate of this conspiracy in apocalyptic terms. (Hofstadter's italics)[87]

Just as the individual paranoid sufferer understands each obstacle in his or her life as emanating from a single malevolent source, so the political paranoiac reads every random detail of civic life as having been *intended;* he or she detects, in Hannah Arendt's resonant summary, "an all-embracing omnipotence . . . at the root of every accident."[88] In chapter 1, we borrowed the term "singularity"—the organizing point of any allegorical system—to describe this kind of "all-embracing omnipotence"; as should already be clear, however, the distance between a paranoid singularity and the transcendent verifiers of Renaissance allegory is profound.

With typical prescience, Jonathan Swift had identified and critiqued many key elements of modern political paranoia nearly two centuries before the fact. The society on his flying island of Laputa, we recall, is riven by "Apprehensions . . . of impending dangers," with which it deals in the most repressive ways imaginable—unremitting and brutal surveillance of the populace who live on the earth below. Massive oversight, however, does not translate into confidence or stability: the Laputans are addicted to meaning-generating systems, like astrology, that, far from clarifying or predicting anything, merely reinforce and worsen their terror. For Swift, this chronic insecurity was the inevitable consequence of secularization: where the divine right monarchies of the late Renaissance had been underwritten by God, God's eye had now vanished from the commonwealth. Citizens, left to their own devices, had created their own political structures, which had inevitably failed to achieve the coherence and stability of the previous dispensation—quite the opposite. On this view, it is worth pointing out, *all* post-theistic societies—including (or *especially*) liberalism—could be seen as inherently paranoid: doomed to fail in their highest aspirations and then turn suspiciously inward. This was certainly Swift's view of secularism, a position offered more recently by religiously oriented scholars of paranoia.[89] We would suggest that this interpretation is half correct: far from being a disease of secularism generally, still less a disease of liberalism, paranoia is the mark left by liberalism and secularization *on the allegorical sensibility specifically*. Paranoia is what happens to allegory in a secular age. The impulse towards totalization is in polar contrast to the liberal notion of compromise, the "give and take" of instrumental agreements. When the "singularity" organizing each element of the social order is understood to be *human*, rather than divine, history and society begin to feel like conspiracies. The place of God is commandeered by something demiurgic—"demonic forces of almost transcendent power"—the "almost" in Hofstadter's formula acknowledging their human origin: in freemasonry, world Jewry, men in sleek black suits, or whatever nexus of iniquity one cares to nominate.[90]

Liberalism itself, as one might expect, figures high among these "demonic forces"—and invariably paranoid allegory involves a violent rejection of the key liberal-contractual tenets.[91] Over against empiricism, for example, and the instrumental agreement that all knowledge derives ultimately from sense impressions, paranoia offers, in the words of one critic, the "construction, from false premises, of a logically developed and in its various parts logically connected, unshakeable delusional system."[92] In Arendt's mordant observation, discussing the rise of Fascism in Europe, paranoid propaganda appeals to the masses on specifically nonempirical grounds:

> They do not believe in anything visible, in the reality of their
> own experience; they do not trust their eyes and ears, but only

their imaginations, which may be caught by anything that is at once universal and consistent in itself. What convinces the masses are not facts, and not even invented facts, but only the consistency of the system of which they are presumably part.[93]

Facts, to clarify, are not out of place in the paranoid worldview—indeed, clinical paranoiacs can often be identified by the assiduousness with which they collect facts as evidence of their chosen reality—but rather the relation of those facts to a larger system of meaning.[94] Almost inevitably, the data amassed by the paranoiac run afoul of common sense or fall into sheer contradiction: the government is all-powerful but is nevertheless threatened by the mere existence of a single free-thinking individual; Bolshevism is naturally repulsive to red-blooded Americans, but is so dangerously appealing to these same people that it must be censored. As Adorno points out, the demonic enemy is usually understood to suffer from "relative social weakness" while also somehow enjoying a "sinister omnipotence" (the classic example of this, for Adorno, would be the Jews).[95] To these apparent difficulties paranoid allegorists respond either with blanket assertions of faith or an infinite regress of explanatory master narratives—which is ultimately the same response.[96]

The perceived "omnipotence" and utter corruption of the enemy, in turn, puts an end to any notion of toleration: competition between rivals necessitates tactical, instrumental agreements—but with an "amoral superman" (Hofstadter's term) or "Axis of Evil" (a more recent coinage), the very idea of negotiation suggests both ethical and political weakness. "Since what is at stake," Hofstadter notes, "is always a conflict between absolute good and absolute evil, the quality needed [in a leader] is not a willingness to compromise but the will to fight things out to a finish. . . . Since the enemy is thought of as being totally evil and totally unappeasable, he must be eliminated."[97] The notional power of the enemy not only justifies but necessitates the peremptory seizure of power by the elect; paranoid individuals (or movements) respond to perceived threats with acts of preemptive revenge, which can go as far as extermination. Conspiracies are repaid with conspiracies (and political structures that end up taking the shape of conspiracies), the threat of absolute power countered by the exercise of absolute power by the absolutely good.[98] With this seizure of control, finally, the dialectic of privacy and surveillance rewinds all the way back to its beginnings. Though the para-noiac greatly desires privacy, he or she cannot believe in its existence: understanding him or herself to be the object of an unwavering, malevo-lent attention, he or she must, in response, keep all potential enemies under constant watch.[99] Writ large, this attitude stands behind the massive surveillance organizations paranoid States muster against their own populations, the individual members of which, as we have discussed, are regarded as potential opponents. *As* potential opponents of the State, the targets of surveillance have no title to privacy themselves—and the autonomy that privacy might nourish is, naturally, a further threat to be eradicated. The peremptory elimination of (imagined) opponents becomes more of a tiresome chore than a moral and humanistic outrage. On the deepest level, then, the very distinction between private and public life breaks down—or returns to a primordial synonymity: the subject of a paranoid State has no more title to an interior life (no more than one can conceive the black-suited agents of the State having interior lives) than the subject of a Renaissance allegory—though the equation of inner and outer selves is the effect of human attention, not the divine gaze.[100]

The utopian speculations of Morris, Bellamy, and Wells are best understood, we have argued, as stemming from a discontent *within* liber-alism, an anger on the part of erstwhile liberals at the necessary compro-mises of a consensus-driven society and a determination to achieve some goods—a certain vision of social justice, for instance—by other means. We would suggest, however, that liberals themselves ultimately contrib-uted little to the resurgence of social allegory; a far more fertile source would be the large population disenfranchised by—or alienated from—liberalism and thereby susceptible to paranoia. Among these one might number conservatives hostile to either the leveling or the relativist tenden-cies of liberalism, or members of traditional communities, or communi-ties of faith threatened by liberalism's modernizing (indeed, progressive) impulses.[101] Most tellingly, one might point to an entire professional class—an analysis associated most closely with Harold Perkin and inspired by Max Weber's classic examination of bureaucracy—generated, at least in part, *by* liberal governments but with no firm commitment to liberal ideals and bound to feel threatened by the workings of a meritocracy.[102] In an ugly irony, the very organizational successes of liberalism in its progressive phase had absorbed and given voice to a population previously without political efficacy—had provided, in short, both a political structure and a cohort capable of driving liberalism to extinction.

Well before the culmination of this dismal history in the 1930s and 1940s, a combination of social and geopolitical trends had already provided ample kindling for paranoid conjecture. Restricting ourselves to Britain for the moment, we need only list the most familiar of these trends, all of which pointed to a diminishment of national prestige abroad and to instability at home: (1) imperial competition, especially with Russia in central Asia, and with Germany/Prussia as a seemingly new kind of aggressive military power; (2) the development of labor unions and an increasingly organized proletariat in large cities like London and Manchester; (3) the large influx of foreign populations (to London and elsewhere), often political refugees of dubious loyalty to Great Britain and possibly inclined to anarchism, radical socialism, etc.; (4) instability in the colonies, breaking into open rebellion (India, 1857 and after) or all-out war (South Africa, 1880, and then more intensely at the turn of the century); (5) relatedly, Irish Nationalism. As one would expect, these numerous irritants figure prominently in mainstream novels of the period—most notably Conrad's analysis of anarchist refugees in both *The Secret Agent* and *Under Western Eyes*, and Kipling's several works dealing with the "Great Game" waged between England and Russia in Afghanistan and Northern India (*Kim*, "The Man Who Would be King"). It is telling, however, that the sharpest response, and the response most inclined to paranoia, should have occurred in the subgenres—for the same reasons we began to discuss last chapter: with their strategic departures from conventional realism into fantasy, these fictions could better represent (or express) the extremes of national anxiety than works constrained by plausibility. Patrick Brantlinger has written at length on the relation of the gothic—the quintessential genre of dirty and dangerous unspoken secrets—to imperial insecurities and a distrust of foreign groups at home.[103] Meanwhile, in a very different register, Sir George Chesney's *The Battle of Dorking* (1871) was perhaps the first in a line of "invasion fictions"—that is, narratives imagining England under attack from its European enemies. In *Dorking* the opponent is Germany, and the invasion is successful—the novella imagines England as a German colony. In later works, the threat is repelled through counterespionage, as in Erskine Childers's *The Riddle of the Sands* (1903), or dumb luck; despite (seemingly) belonging to a different genre—science fiction—the key instance of the latter is *The War of the Worlds*, with Martians, their "intellects vast and cool and unsympathetic," ably filling in for the Prussians.[104]

As we retrain our focus on the subgenres, it is worth restating a basic premise: that the subgenres erupted out of the literary mainstream in response to historically specific anxieties; thus Poe's invention of the detective story occurred at a moment when both sides of the surveillance/privacy dialectic were severely strained and thereby susceptible to the fantasy of a Dupin, a recluse with unrealistic insight into the lives of other people. By the same token, it follows that genres should occasionally expire or go dead. We do not mean by this "stop getting written"; rather, as the particular anxieties that have given rise to the genre recede or change, works within that genre may change in response or—more likely—*not* change at all. When the latter happens, the genre ossifies into its conventions—and may persist as such, as a relic of its foundational moment, in perpetuity. In this light, the course of the detective story is indeed instructive: whereas most detective writing settled comfortably into a set of tropes and clichés—the butler did it!—the first British detective writer radically reversed himself over the course of his career. Sherlock Holmes's slow drift, which we examined in chapter 3, from an ally of the police to their frequent opponent, from a solver of mysteries to a keeper of secrets (usually of the privileged), goes hand-in-hand with Conan Doyle's embrace of a paranoid rightist politics. In the earliest stories, civil society is still seen as relatively wholesome: London may be infested with criminals, but the police are still to be supported in their upholding the rule of law. In the later Holmes, however, society itself is underlain with conspiracies, the body politic unhealthy and sinister—and this, in turn, justifies the detective's extralegal seizure of authority, often with the police as his dupes.

Conan Doyle had, from the start, a weakness for conspiracies— "secret agencies at work all round us," as he had put it in *The Sign of the Four* (1890, naturally)—but in the first stories, they menace England from without. Thus the Mormons, mafia, and Ku Klux Klan make early appearances. By contrast, at the end of the first Holmes cycle, Conan

Doyle invents—to recall Arendt's formula—"an all embracing omnipo-tence which is supposed to be at the root of every accident": Professor Moriarty. The first "super-villain" in literature, Moriarty is described as simultaneously ubiquitous and invisible: "the man pervades London, and no one has heard of him."[105] Behind each local crime, Holmes has "been conscious of some power behind the malefactor, some deep organizing power which forever stands in the way of the law. . . . He is the organizer of half that is evil and of nearly all that is undetected in this great city."[106] Holmes's separating individual transgressions from the "deep organizing power" behind them is significant: the former require a detective—but against "a gigantic yet subtle machinery of influence," one can only respond with like violence. "The paranoid spokesman," as Hofstadter observes, can only see "the fate of this conspiracy in apocalyptic terms"— and so the first Holmes cycle concludes with Holmes destroying Moriarty and (Conan Doyle's original intention) himself as well. W. H. Auden's classic distinction between detective fiction and the literature of espio-nage is still apropos: where the former is concerned with the "dialectic of innocence and guilt," the latter deals with "the ethical and eristic conflict between good and evil, between Us and Them."[107] In these terms, Holmes has largely ceased to be a detective long before the final Holmes story; in that tale, moreover, written during World War I, he subverts a German plot to gather intelligence, not through the piecing together of clues but through deception, betrayal of confidences, and brutal force. Holmes ends his career as a spy.[108]

The Morphology of Paranoid Fiction (The Rise of the Spy Novel)

"By God!" he whispered, drawing his breath in sharply, "it is all pure Rider Haggard and Conan Doyle.

"You believe me," I said gratefully.

"Of course I do," and he held out his hand. "I believe everything out of the common. The only thing to distrust is the normal."

—John Buchan, The Thirty-Nine Steps[109]

Needless to say, detective fiction continued to be written in great quantities after the turn of the twentieth century. As a challenger to the realistic contract, however, its job was complete: as genius sleuths with implausible access to the minds of other people, Poirot, Peter Wimsey, and Philo Vance do not advance significantly on Dupin. Especially in its familiar country-house variety, the genre expressed a comfortable conservatism that stopped well short of paranoia—though other strains, like the American gumshoe narrative, ventured into darker territory. Far more assaultive on conventional realism—in identifiably paranoid ways—than any species of detective literature was the spy novel. As the trajectory of Holmes's career suggests, the spy novel was at once a successor genre to the detective story and an attack on some of its most cherished shibboleths. Like the detective story, the spy novel had an identifiable moment of origin—or rather, we should say, two such moments. It is generally agreed that espionage writing falls into two distinct traditions, which arise semi-independently and at significantly different historical points. We might call these traditions "naïve" and "skeptical": in the former, the nation is inevitably under threat from shadowy conspirators (acting usually on the behalf of enemy governments), and the protagonist is uncomplicatedly heroic. In the latter, the central spy figure is morally ambiguous: by committing ethically questionable acts on behalf of the State, he in turn calls the greater national ideology into question.[110] Although both lines engage with paranoia, only the first *suffers* from the condition, as it were—and it is this tradition that we will look at first.

When we claim that the spy novel arises at a specific historical moment (or two), we should clarify: we are not denying the copious literature about espionage produced before the early twentieth century, from the book of Numbers, to the tenth book of the *Iliad*, to "The Friar's Tale," to James Fenimore Cooper's *The Spy*. There is, nonetheless, an important distinction to be drawn between, on the one hand, works that include spies as characters or which take up espionage as a theme, and, on the other hand, the spy novel proper, with its characteristic tropes and attitudes. In this respect, the contrast with slightly earlier mainline novels like *Kim* and *The Secret Agent* is telling—with espionage authors simultaneously acknowledging the influence of Kipling and Conrad and firmly setting their own work apart. The epigram with which we began this section, drawn from chapter 3 of *The Thirty-Nine Steps*, John Buchan's 1915 classic of the genre, could not better illustrate this ambivalence. In the north of England, and on the run from deadly German agents, the hero, Richard Hannay, comes upon a rural innkeeper with literary aspirations.

"Nothing comes here but motor-cars full of fat women, who
stop for lunch, and a fisherman or two in the spring, and
the shooting tenants in August. There is not much material to
be got out of that. I want to see life, to travel the world, and
write things like Kipling and Conrad. But the most I've done
yet is to get some verses printed in 'Chambers's Journal.'"
(22–23)

In order to enlist the innkeeper's aid, Hannay spins an exciting and
completely fictitious account of his perils, which his auditor first
compares to Conan Doyle and Rider Haggard—and then swallows
entirely: "the only thing to distrust is the normal." It is a tricky balance
for Buchan to strike. *The Secret Agent* is obviously a model for Buchan's
own work,[111] yet at the same time Buchan clearly wants to keep his
distance: the innkeeper's aesthetic pretensions are vaguely risible, and
Hannay's own tale is ultimately far closer in spirit to the subgeneric tradition of adventure fiction. Buchan's successor Eric Ambler puts it still
more bluntly: "You could say Conrad's *Under Western Eyes* is a spy story,
but no-one ever calls it a spy story. It's respectable."[112] The terms of his
quip are worth pausing over: most evidently, Ambler is acknowledging
the quasi-literary status of his own (less respectable) novels; less directly,
however, he is recognizing the ways that Conrad treats the plotting of
Russian revolutionaries in Switzerland (or expatriate anarchists in
London) as an entry into, or metaphor for, his larger ethical or aesthetic
(or even ontological) concerns. In the "spy story," by contrast, the *plot*—
the paranoid dynamics of the conspiracy and the equally paranoid logic of
its ultimate defeat—is central and self-sufficient.

In its earlier, "naïve" iteration, the spy novel arose in the years just
before World War I, in an atmosphere of nativist bigotry, fear of invasion,
and a profound distrust of the freedoms inherent to an open, liberal
society. It was a brew that left ugly traces in many of the works emerging
from it, as in the extreme xenophobia of a William Le Queux, or the blood
lust and violence worship of a "Sapper" McNeile—attitudes more than
honored by their successor Ian Fleming.[113] As a genre, the espionage
thriller is most interesting to us for the way it typifies the *morphology* of
paranoid allegory; paranoid allegory, that is to say, manifests itself through
certain aesthetic structures, which do not, ultimately, much resemble

their Renaissance predecessors. We may take *The Thirty-Nine Steps*, which lays a fair claim to being the first significant work in the genre, as paradigmatic. A quick summary: Hannay, a mining engineer from the colonies, has returned to London. Just as he's beginning to feel fed up with the place ("the talk of the ordinary Englishman made me sick . . . and the amusements of London seemed as flat as soda-water that has been sitting in the sun" [1]), he is accosted outside his apartment by an American who has discovered a conspiracy:

> Away behind all the Governments and the armies there was a
> big subterranean movement going on, engineered by very
> dangerous people. He had come upon it by accident; it
> fascinated him; he went further, and then he got caught. I
> gathered that most of the people in it were the sort of educated
> anarchists that make revolutions, but behind them there were
> financiers who were playing for money. (33–34)

Buchan is hardly less xenophobic than Le Queux or Sax Rohmer (the inventor of Fu Manchu)—and if the coded "financiers . . . playing for money" was not sufficiently clear, the American spells it out more clearly: behind "the biggest job [you were] bound to get to the real boss, ten to one . . . a little white-faced Jew in a bath chair with an eye like a rattlesnake" (3–4). In short order, as has since become an unavoidable cliché, the American is murdered, Hannay implicated, and the chase is on—both by the police and (far more seriously) by the bad guys, who think that Hannay now knows their secrets. In the event, the "real boss" pursuing Hannay turns out to be German, and the conspiracy hinges on Prussian attempts to steal British and French military plans in advance of the coming war.

Once he's on the run, Hannay is converted to a paranoiac—seeking (and finding) evidence of the conspiracy everywhere he turns. And yet—crucially—the world in which he newly finds himself *looks exactly like the world he has left behind*. To be precise: we earlier described paranoia as "anti-empirical," citing Arendt's observation that paranoiacs "do not believe in anything visible, in the reality of their own experience; they do not trust their eyes and ears." The world of the senses having been revealed as a sham, a mere veil for "subterranean" plots, this is certainly true. The very *ubiquity*, however, of the master plot makes it impossible for one to distinguish between the normal and the abnormal—or, rather, everything is subsumed by the latter. As John Farrell puts it, paranoia undermines "our ability to distinguish our thought from coherent delusion or manipulative contrivance."[114] Accordingly the world of the paranoiac is *perceived* exactly like the world of empirical reality—it sounds, smells, feels (etc.) precisely the same—but is understood to be entirely depraved, the demonic "singularity" having potentially corrupted everything. In the words of Buchan's literary innkeeper, "the only thing to distrust is the normal," a comment that echoes Holmes's earlier remark that "there is nothing so unnatural as the commonplace."[115] Like the empirical realist, then, the paranoiac relentlessly gathers the evidence of the senses—not as the building blocks of knowledge but as confirmation of what he or she already knows. By the same token, the paranoid hero's actions are directly *opposite* to those of the detective, who is a kind of super-empiricist: where the detective's implausible skill leads him to the *one* clue exposing another's hidden guilt (the hair of an orangutan, say—always the needle in the haystack), the paranoid hero receives *everything* as a token of societal corruption. And so it happens, in paranoid plots, that the world proves to be ubiquitously and indiscriminately evil, the demonic force *possessing*, as it were, the everyday in free-floating ways: the best friend a betrayer, the gentle neighbor a Bolshevik, the stranger accidentally encountered on the street no less than the Adversary himself. Such contrivances are the common cloth of countless paranoid thrillers (the television show *24* took this to unintentionally self-parodying excesses), and in much the same spirit, Hannay seeks refuge in a random Scottish manor house—one of countless houses he might have stumbled into: "I had walked straight into the enemy's headquarters!" (47).

Because, finally, everything in the world has been corrupted (or potentially corrupted) by the evil singularity, it also follows that *correct* interpretation can only happen via a sort of miracle: when any random house might be the enemy's headquarters, how can one rationally determine which house is the right one?[116] This is a difficulty that Buchan seems to recognize in a sequence that far surpasses anything else in the book in suspense, complexity, and sheer literary quality (oddly enough, Alfred Hitchcock chose not to include this scene in his film). Having tracked his trio of German opponents to a seaside town, Hannay comes upon their hideout; it is not, to put it mildly, what he has been expecting:

> I saw Trafalgar Lodge very plainly, a red-brick villa with a
> verandah, a tennis court behind, and in front an ordinary
> seaside flower-garden full of marguerites and scraggy
> geraniums. There was a flagstaff from which an enormous
> Union Jack hung limply in the still air. . . . I wasn't feeling very
> confident. (78)

Although certain details of the scene suggest peril (the limp flag and, of course, the name of the house), the total effect is of utter normalcy. Strange, therefore, that for both Hannay and the reader, this very banality is both uncanny and unbearably ominous: for the first time in the book, Hannay does not know what to think—a confusion that only increases when he enters the lodge with the idea of confronting his enemies face to face. Though he has encountered them several times previously, the trio now seem, to all appearances, "three ordinary, game-playing, suburban Englishmen, wearisome, if you like, but sordidly innocent." His mind reels: "The whole business had mesmerized me. . . . I took my place at the table in a kind of dream" (86). The scene depicts a moment of pure, vertiginous crisis: Hannay cannot, as it were, "believe in the reality of his own experience"—normality and pure evil having become indistinguishable. For Buchan, as paranoid as his hero, Hannay's plight can only be resolved miraculously—not, as in the detective novel, through super-human empathetic or intellectual skills, but simply because he is the hero. In Hofstadter's sense of the word—and also in the etymological sense of an "uncovering"—it is an apocalypse; after an extended period of confusion, for an almost arbitrary reason (a minor gesture by one of the German spies), Hannay's mind suddenly clears:

> In a flash, the air seemed to clear. Some shadow lifted from my
> brain, and I was looking at the three men with full and absolute
> recognition. . . . The three faces seemed to change before my
> eyes and reveal their secrets. The young one was the murderer.
> Now I saw cruelty and ruthlessness, where before I had only
> seen good-humour. . . . Now that my eyes were opened, I
> wondered where I had seen . . . benevolence. (87)

"The normal" has indeed proven untrustworthy.

It might well be argued that an allegory in which *everything* is a token, in which everything is a "vehicle" for one terrible truth, is no allegory at all—it certainly would not be recognized as such by Chrétien or Spenser. In the late sixteenth century, we recall, the difficulty of representing a complex ideology, viewed as entirely good and underwritten by the godhead, resulted *formally* in allegory of great complexity—whether the literary intricacy of *The Faerie Queene* or the elaborate statecraft of the Tudor-Stuart court. Paranoid allegory, in contrast, tends towards radical simplification: once the demonic singularity has been identified (the Jews, the Illuminati, whoever), everything in the world reduces (at least potentially) to a demonic manifestation, justifying the chosen hero's violent, redemptive actions. As a number of critics have pointed out, paranoia and narrative building are closely related activities, and paranoia is strongest when scattered observations can be connected into a plot.[117] Father Coughlin, to give a famous example, moved from broadly held observations about civil decline to a far simpler and more personally derived narrative of heroes (everyday Americans) fighting an all-powerful enemy (Wall Street). Once the faceless scapegoat was replaced by an identifiable villain (the Jews), this worldview could assume its final form, as a story clarifying the "motive force in historical events": Jews were responsible for the French Revolution, the League of Nations, and so on. Of course this particular form of narration isn't exactly elegant: metaphor, nuance, and irony might lead to misinterpretation or complicate the picture.[118] Far from aestheticizing politics, as Benjamin and Bürger would have it, Fascism—of a Coughlin or a Hitler—tends towards the stark black and white of Us and Them, with aesthetic crudeness the tradeoff for effectiveness at swaying (often poorly educated) audiences. Morphologically, one might say, paranoia divorces the allegorical Will to Power, which it possesses in abundance, from allegorical *aesthetics*, which it barely possesses at all (beyond the glorification of the hero and the vilification of the Enemy). As *represented*, the world of paranoid allegory is no way remarkable—except, perhaps, for a certain coarseness. Everything must be viewed with distrust—or rather, as already guilty; for this reason, however pervasive and unremitting, paranoid surveillance leaves itself at a loss to distinguish actual culpability.

III. SURVEILLANCE AND THE SUBGENRES

Two Panopticons

Because of this representational similarity, one might suppose the mainstream literary novel to be perfectly adept at depicting the paranoid condition; this does not prove entirely to be the case. Still operating within the terms of formal realism, the mainstream novel struggles to recreate reality as it appears to a paranoid mind. Under such circumstances, although the world *looks* normal enough and can be represented "realistically," it nevertheless *feels* untrustworthy—a Potemkin existence, as it were, in which one's surroundings may always be a stage set or series of props manipulated by the Enemy. We might call this sensation the "paranoid uncanny," which manifests itself, as in the Trafalgar Lodge sequence, as a pervasive dread utterly lacking in works with a greater sense of empirical certainty. For reasons we will explore shortly, subgenres like speculative fiction and fantasy writing, because of their looser commitment to (or utter rejection of) conventional realism, are better equipped both to entertain the paranoid worldview and—more interesting for our purposes—to critique it. The best that realistic works of fiction can do—which is not negligible—is to depict the conditions of a paranoid society and to tally the emotional cost of living under those conditions. In this respect, the contrast between Buchan and Conrad is emblematic; as we have earlier hinted, Buchan drew freely from Conrad when populating *The Thirty-Nine Steps:* Hannay, the director of the Foreign Office, and several other characters have obvious precedents in *The Secret Agent;* even the Trafalgar Lodge sequence can be traced back, in some respects, to Conrad's techniques.[119] Where Buchan does *not* follow Conrad, predictably, is in the great Polish modernist's sense of irony: in stark contrast to the fiendishness of Buchan's German villains, Conrad offers an anarchist underworld notable for its lethargy and incompetence. When the time comes for the central action (a terrorist bombing), no one can be bothered, and the job goes to a mentally disabled man who botches it. The arch-provocateur, a Russian embassy officer, falls somewhat short of Fu Manchu as a criminal mastermind: his plot to blow up the Greenwich observatory is both ridiculous and doomed from the start. More to the point, Conrad offers a vision of English society as a closed system, in which both the criminal and constabulary classes enjoy a symbiotic and, for all intents and purposes, morally equivalent arrangement. The police and most of the anarchists view each other less as deadly enemies than as fellow players in a mutually beneficial game with few lasting consequences. More than one critic, in short, has deemed *The Secret Agent* an attack on "the whole value system" of British society—a good distance, in short, from the Us (the few true-hearted British) vs. Them (conspirators of all stripes) mentality of Buchan and his cohort.[120]

Conrad's pervasive ironies, however, should not blind one to the line he is unwilling to cross: society may be corrupt, but it falls far short (in competence, among other things) of conspiracy; the *authorial* stance, in stark contrast to Buchan, is by no means paranoid. In *The Secret Agent* only one character earns that descriptive: the bomb-making, unnamed "Professor," who stands ever ready to destroy himself if approached by the police; a case of thwarted ambition, he fits the classical clinical picture (before Freud and others had developed it) of the paranoiac: "The Professor's indignation [at being ignored] found in itself a final cause that absolved him from the sin of turning to destruction as the agent of his ambition" (102). In the concluding lines of the novel, Conrad acknowledges the Professor's capacity for violence while dismissing his ability to affect society in any way: "He passed on, unsuspected and deadly, like a pest in the street full of men" (268). The nearest analogue would be a latter-day incendiary—who, as it happens, modeled himself on the Professor: Ted Kaczynski.[121] Like Conrad's character, the Unabomber was capable of catastrophic actions but delusional and ultimately pathetic in his larger political ambitions. By way of contrast, Conrad's other great novel about espionage, *Under Western Eyes*, is possibly the least delusional and most profound *study* of paranoia in modern literature—entirely justifiable paranoia, given the paranoid structures endemic to czarist Russia. Centering, like *The Secret Agent*, on a terrorist act and its ramifications, the novel is set first in Russia itself, and then among a community of Russian revolutionaries in Switzerland. From personal history—which included the brutalization of both parents at the hands of the Empire—Conrad had no illusions about despotism, acutely depicting both the paranoia of an autocratic State, "the merciless suspicion of despotism," and the paranoia of anyone living under its shadow:

> Before his eyes everything appeared confused and evanescent.
> He dared not [talk with his companion]. "He may be affiliated to

the police," was the thought that passed through his mind. "Who could tell?"[122]

In passages which Orwell echoed in 1984, Conrad analyzes the psychological impact of state surveillance on his protagonist, whose mania leads him first to betray an acquaintance to the authorities and ultimately, as a "conspirator everlastingly on his guard against self-betrayal in a world of secret spies," to betray himself.[123] In *both* novels, as Thomas Mann and others have recognized, Russian despotism stands in stark contrast to the British rule of law—in which Conrad, however mordantly, believed.[124] As long as Conrad remained a realist, his work lingered—whatever the local conservatism of his views—within the liberal tradition of the novel: often *about* paranoia, but not paranoid in structure or sensibility.[125] A truly effective critique of paranoia *from within* would have to meet the condition at least halfway—not a compromise Conrad, or anyone still working within realism, could readily make. For such a critique something more *fantastic*, in a manner of speaking, was necessary.

The two best-known images of total, panoptic surveillance in twentieth-century prose indeed come to us from the subgenres of speculative fiction and fantasy: Big Brother's telescreen and the Eye of Sauron in *The Lord of the Rings*. Of the two authors, Orwell is without doubt the more influential and seen as more serious-minded, with an army of critics, academics, and politicians insisting ad infinitum (for any number of reasons) that "Orwell was right" and that 1984 was "prophetic."[126] This is as Orwell would have it: where Zamyatin had hedged his bets with long passages of surrealistic and mercurially comic writing, Orwell insists on the plausibility of his dystopian scenario.[127] Tolkien, on the other hand, makes no attempts at plausibility and has usually been viewed by serious critics as "juvenile trash," escapist "balderdash," "boy's own" stuff, etc.[128] Edmund Wilson, reacting to the trilogy's "Us and Them" ethics, considered it "a children's book [that had] somehow got out of hand," which "present[ed] the drama of life as a showdown between Good People and Goblins."[129] Hardly a work of "prophecy"—and yet there's the basic scenario: a small band of dedicated fighters, willing to sacrifice their lives, slip in under the surveillance system of a great power, blend in with an alien population, and deliver a devastating blow to the heart of its empire, leaving armies bewildered and a populace terrified. Even a tower or two crumbles to dust. As an examination of how surveillance works—and under what circumstances it fails—Tolkien is offering an argument opposite to Orwell's. In *The Lord of the Rings*, a determined enough individual, with an adequate understanding of the Enemy's (literal) blind spots, is able to rebel in plain sight. On a basic level, this denies Orwell's first premise: that an effective and all-perceiving surveillance mechanism is even *possible*. Having assumed this, Orwell further argues that such a mechanism will eventually drain all desire to escape it, or even deride it, and that this state of affairs, once achieved, will persist "forever." We would not deny Orwell his laurels: he remains unmatched in his imagining of the mechanics of surveillance and the political structures that make surveillance possible. We would suggest, simply, that Tolkien is more convincing about why total surveillance finally fails than Orwell is in imagining its success.

Perhaps surprisingly, the difference between the two authors is largely religious in character: where Orwell the atheist is in awe of the absolute State, Tolkien the Catholic is able to dismiss any earthly, coercive attempts at total surveillance. Imperturbably convinced that the only true and infallible observer is God, he has no trouble diagnosing the fallibility of any mortal hand or eye. To recall an example from our introduction: one may put a CCTV camera on every street corner in Hull, but it won't stop the operators from ogling prostitutes instead of preventing crimes. In *The Lord of the Rings*, the imagery of repressive observation is entirely on the side of Mordor and Sauron, from the palantiri (seeing-stones whose name means "that which looks far away") to the towers of Orthanc and Minas Morgul: "The topmost course of the tower revolved slowly, first one way and then another, a huge ghostly head leering into the night."[130] The key panoptic image is of course Sauron himself—little more than an Eye atop Barad-dur:

> In the black abyss there appeared a single Eye that slowly grew.
> . . . [It] was rimmed with fire, but was itself glazed, yellow as a
> cat's, watchful and intent, and the black slit of its pupil opened
> on a pit, a window into nothing. Then the Eye began to rove,
> searching this way and that; and Frodo knew with certainty and
> horror that among the many things that it sought he himself
> was one. (355)

An effectively scary image—an image of justified paranoia—yet despite the formidable machinery at his disposal, Sauron ultimately ignores Frodo walking, in the very middle of his kingdom, towards Orodruin with the One Ring around his neck: the Dark Lord comes out roughly even with the average CCTV operator.

In Wilson's snarling review ("Goblins"!), one detects a familiar impatience with the substance of fantasy literature; indeed, of the subgenres we have been examining, fantasy writing remains the most déclassé—suitable perhaps for children but thereafter best left to eczematous adolescents (of any age) unable to line up a date on a Saturday night. We would suggest that this irritation has something to do with the genre's peculiar relation to conventional realism: whereas the detective story and spy novel erupt *out of* the realistic tradition, fantasy seems to dismiss or ignore the fact that realism ever happened and instead reaches back to a moment *before* realism, when representational conventions permitted (as in Spenser, say) the occasional monster. Similarly, whereas the politics of the detective story and spy novel are *anti*-liberal, fantasy writing emerges from lingering *pre*-liberal attitudes—religious ones in particular. Tolkien's many and vigorous denials of specific allegorical significance do not change the fact that his novel is of an allegorical *nature:* his canons of representation, especially the more fantastic ones, comply with the requirement to depict the world as divinely ordered, in which true Kings are Kingly, and false ones are not; a world where the enemy goes by the name of the "Dark Lord" or, even more handily, the "Enemy." The sensibility can come across as childish or unsophisticated—and yet, for this very reason, fantasy is particularly well equipped to *critique* modern paranoia: with its eyes firmly set on the transcendent singularity of God, it can easily dismiss the demonic singularities of paranoia in a way that realistic or liberal writing, confined to nonfantastic means of representation, finds difficult. To find a literary precedent for Sauron one cannot look much later than Milton; in *Paradise Lost*, for example, Satan sits "like a Cormorant" on the Tree of Life:

> nor on the virtue thought
> Of that life-giving Plant, but only us'd
> For prospect, what well us'd had been the pledge
> Of immortality. So little knows

> Any, but God alone, to value right
> The good before him.[131]

In a brilliant visual irony, evoking Argus Panoptes atop his "hilly height," Satan takes up a commanding vantage point (the garden is laid out below him) without understanding the deeper significance of the vantage point itself: an emblem of all-seeing control turns instantly into a sign of ignorance. God, of course, "from his prospect high, / Wherein past, present, future he beholds" (3.77–78), sees and comprehends all. Without such an understanding—even if one sees everything—surveillance is fruitless; this is the condition not only of Satan atop the Tree, but of everyone (who isn't God) in Milton's fictive universe—and it is also Sauron's plight. Pointedly, he is always represented as a single eye: lacking depth perception, the necessary empathetic mind, he is hopelessly bad at fathoming motives, or at anticipating an irregular narrative. As Gandalf puts it, "The only measure that he knows is desire, desire for power; and so he judges all hearts. Into his heart the thought will not enter that any will refuse it, that having the Ring we may seek to destroy it" (282–83). Sauron, in a larger sense, cannot see beyond his own personality—and egoism, as a basic mortal condition, is hardly limited to the "Dark Lords" amongst us.

Ultimately Tolkien is less *worried* about Sauron than Orwell is by Big Brother. Set beside Tolkien's professorial calm (even when describing elves and mastodons), Orwell in *1984* can sometimes seem overwrought, his language saturated with the physical symptoms of terror: "his heart was thumping," "his heart bumped," "his heart quailed," "his heart galloped," "his heart sank," "his heart . . . leap't," "his heart bounded," "his heart seemed to turn to ice," and various other feats of cardiac gymnastics.[132] Like Conrad, however, Orwell came honestly by his knowledge of paranoid statecraft—and of the psychological toll it can exact—having experienced it firsthand:

> The worst thing of being wanted by the police in a town like
> Barcelona is that everything opens so late. When you sleep out
> of doors you always wake about dawn, and none of the
> Barcelona cafés opens much before nine. . . . It was a queer
> situation that we were in. At night one was a hunted fugitive,
> but in the daytime one could live an almost normal life. . . . The
> streets were thronged by local and Valencian Assault Guards,

> Carabineros and ordinary police, besides God knows how many
> spies in plain clothes; still, they could not stop everyone who
> passed, and if you looked normal you might escape notice.[133]

The passage is from *Homage to Catalonia*, Orwell's account of his participation in the Spanish Civil War, which provided his schooling in the ways
of both Communist and Fascist authoritarianism. Having signed up with
a Trotskyist militia, he barely escaped Spain with his life, as the republican cause, under the sway of Stalinist Russia, subjected itself to catastrophic internal purges. His descriptions of Winston Smith's erratic
heart no doubt originate, therefore, in authentic feeling; nevertheless, as
one turns to *1984*, it is striking how *little* of the Spanish adventure translates to his depiction of Oceania. In contrast to Orwell's experience in
daytime Barcelona, Oceania offers a secret police incapable of either
distraction or misreading, and no place to hide: the genteel old man in the
shop is an agent of the Thought Police; the trusted confidant is a torturer;
the very trees of the countryside may contain microphones. At the end of
his time in Spain, Orwell and his wife caught a train to France and made
it over the border with bogus papers. The thought that Winston or Julia
might similarly flee, let alone carry out a *Lord of the Rings*–style operation
against the Inner Party, is laughable: according to the logic of the novel—
which is no less paranoid than the work of Buchan or Rider Haggard—
there is neither resistance nor escape.

One of the more persistent canards to have clung to *1984*—a reading
particularly beloved by neoconservatives—is that the novel is primarily
anti-Soviet and Big Brother largely drawn from Stalin.[134] While this is
certainly true of *Animal Farm*, however, as well as *Homage to Catalonia*
and (to a lesser degree) *The Road to Wigan Pier*, *1984* takes its coloration
from Orwell's disillusioning experience of World War II. As had happened
before in Spain, Orwell began the conflict with high—even utopian—
expectations; writing in the *Partisan Review*, he commented that England
could defeat Germany only in tandem with an overthrow of capitalism.
Citing a "widespread readiness for sweeping economic and social
changes, combined with absolute determination to prevent invasion,"
and popular support for "a policy in which resistance to Hitler and
destruction of class-privilege were combined," he concluded that England
could not "win the war without passing through revolution."[135] By 1943,

he had to eat his words: the leadership of Churchill and the conservatives had proven effective, and the proletariat, far from rebelling, had been galvanized by the Blitz into enthusiastic support for the government. "The real moral of the last three years," Orwell commented, was "that the Right has more guts and ability than the Left—[and] no-one will face up to it."[136] In an astonishing 1944 follow-up letter, he excoriated himself for his faulty predictions and essentially bade farewell to his long-held socialist-democratic ideals:

> Now that we have seemingly won the war and lost the peace, it is possible to see earlier events in a certain perspective, and the first thing I have to admit is that up to at any rate the end of 1942 I was grossly wrong in my analysis of the situation. . . . I had not only assumed (what is probably true) that the drift of popular feeling was towards the Left, but that it would be quite impossible to win the war without democratizing it. In 1940 I had written, "Either we turn this into a revolutionary war or we lose it," and I find myself repeating this word for word as late as the middle of 1942. . . . There were excuses for this belief, but still it was a very great error. . . . The same people [as before] own all the property and usurp all the best jobs. . . . The United States is indeed the most powerful country in the world, and the most capitalistic.[137]

Most interesting for us is the short duration of this contrite mood; by 1945 Orwell had rebounded into something far more aggressive and edgy: a withering contempt, unprecedented in his earlier work, for the English working class ("enormous crimes and disasters . . . not only fail to excite the big public, but can actually escape notice altogether"), and a tendency to view the United States and Soviet Union as morally equivalent— witness his prediction that the world was headed towards "the re-imposition of slavery" and the establishment of "three great empires, each self-contained and cut off from contact with the outer world, and each ruled, under one disguise or another, by a self-elected oligarchy." The world, in other words, of *1984*.[138]

It is not too much to call the attitude of the late Orwell "paranoid"— with the same aggression and the same defense mechanisms (the same "means of coping with the inevitable discrepancy between the way . . .

things ought to be and the way they are") that one sees in all paranoid productions. The same flights into implausibility and wish fulfillment as well: however powerful the vision of Oceania, it fails to convince in most respects, not least in its account of total surveillance. The anger, it bears repeating, is not turned outwards towards the Soviet Union but inwards, at England. Orwell's contempt for the workers provides a baseline for his analysis of how Oceania works: the Thought Police essentially write off 85 percent of the population. Whereas Wordsworth had found roughly the same percentage—the crowds at Bartholomew Fair—terrifying, the "prole" quarters are so abject that they do not require watching or the expense of manpower. In his critical writings, Orwell had marveled at a nation of somnambulists: "people just keep on keeping on, in a sort of twilight sleep in which they are conscious of nothing except the daily round of work, family life, darts at the pub, . . . bringing home the supper beer, etc., etc."[139] This observation comes back nearly verbatim in 1984, when Winston, hanging out in a Cockney pub, finds his interlocutors unable to focus on anything political. Nevertheless, O'Brien's assurances that the proles will never attain political consciousness, and thus never pose any serious threat, ring hollow. Unlike Huxley, who provides a plausible explanation for how eight-ninths of the population might be happily submerged (forever), Orwell can only rely on proof by assertion: for Oceania to function, its inhabitants (as well as the readers of 1984) must overlook the fact that the slum districts, where "people swarmed in astonishing numbers," can never be properly and entirely watched—a living, breathing monument to the limits of Big Brother's power and ability to see. In much the same way, the sheer amount of time lavished on Winston's destruction—the long interrogation that occupies most of part 3—can only remind us of the teeming millions outside, who can never be afforded the merest fraction of such attention. Can a mind, anyway, truly be controlled completely and a dissident purged of even the slightest disloyal thoughts? Orwell acknowledges the shakiness of this notion (unintentionally) when O'Brien suddenly develops the miraculous ability to read Winston's consciousness ("you are thinking. . ." "the word you are trying to think of is . . . ,"etc.).[140] Orwell indeed ends up sounding like the mirror image of Conan Doyle or Poe—and for genetically analogous reasons: faced with a disconnect between his vision of reality and the constraints of conventional realism, the author invents a character with magical insight into the minds of others—the magician here as antagonist (O'Brien), rather than protagonist (Holmes, Dupin).

Like Moriarty, or the villains of Buchan and Childers, O'Brien and the Inner Party that stands behind him have the character of a demiurgic projection, a "demonic [force] of almost transcendent power." Far more explicitly, however, than other authors of a paranoid bent, Orwell presents his conspiracy as the antitype of a religious order—the Catholic order, to be more precise. Always suspicious of the Church, Orwell's simmering anti-Catholicism was set to boiling by his experience of the war in Spain, in which priests colluded with the Fascists.[141] Commenting that "very few people, apart from the Catholics themselves, seem to have grasped that the Church is to be taken seriously," Orwell came to view the organization as a signally efficient despotism.[142] Accordingly, in *1984*, the State derives its shape from the Roman See:

> Hereditary aristocracies have always been short-lived, whereas adoptive organizations such as the Catholic Church have sometimes lasted hundreds or thousands of years. . . . A ruling group is a ruling group so long as it can nominate its successors. The Party is [concerned only with] perpetuating itself. *Who* wields power is not important, provided that the hierarchical structure remains always the same.[143]

O'Brien, in turn, is repeatedly described either as "priestly" or as "a priest of power"; when Julia and Winston visit him at his apartment, he offers them both wine and wafers; his very name suggests the local Irish cleric, and Winston's long torture is an extended parody of the confessional, in which "all the confessions that are uttered . . . are true. We make them true."[144]

The most telling exchange between O'Brien and Winston during part 3 is, not surprisingly, about God. When Winston restates his frequently expressed faith in the proles, O'Brien is incredulous:

> "Do you see any evidence that this is happening? Or any reason
>   why it should?"
> "No. I believe it, I *know* that you will fail. There is something in
>   the universe—I don't know, some spirit, some principle—
>   that you will never overcome."

"Do you believe in God, Winston?"

"No."

"Then what is it, this principle that will defeat us?"

"I don't know."[145]

A positive answer would have produced a very different book. Just as Tolkien's faith offered a hedge against paranoia, and a position from which to critique its political manifestations, so Orwell, having lost his faith in liberal democracy and never having had religious faith, was left with no bulwark against the paranoid logic of the right; with either of those faiths, he might have achieved a more nuanced and believable view of state surveillance or at least escaped a spectacular plunge into the worldview of his erstwhile opponents:[146]

> The Gestapo is said to have teams of literary critics whose job is
> to determine, by means of stylistic comparison, the authorship
> of anonymous pamphlets. I have always thought that, if only it
> were in a better cause, this is exactly the job I would like to have.
> To any of our readers whose tastes lie in the same direction I
> present this problem: Who is now writing "Beachcomber's"
> column in the *Daily Express?* . . . I would bet five shillings that
> the present "Beachcomber," unlike [the previous one,] Mr.
> Morton, is not a Catholic.[147]

In contrast to the naïve tradition of the spy novel (and other forms of right-wing fantasy), Orwell illustrates the extent to which paranoid ways of thinking had infiltrated the precincts of an erstwhile *liberalism*—a loss of faith in equality, and in the possibility of achieving social justice, going hand in hand with an acceptance of paranoid logic: that society and history were conspiracies. The surrender of liberalism's key motives almost necessitated an acceptance of the enemy's viewpoint—not, however, as an expression of the Will to Power but as a gesture of despair. In contrast, moreover, to the often pulpish, pseudo-literate quality of right-wing paranoid production (Buchan and Rider Haggard stand at the *more* respectable end of a continuum that extends all the way to *The Turner Diaries* and *The Overton Window*), Orwell helped make paranoid writing a respectable mode for the serious author of disillusioned, liberal sensibilities. The path he opened up has since included the likes of Heller,

Pynchon, Vonnegut, and Gaddis—explorers all of the "paranoid uncanny," conventional realism having come to seem, for some writers at least, as untenable as out-and-out fantasy.

Latter-Day Realism and the Better Sort of Spy Novel

> [Our best man] found out something, but his enemies knew and he
> was pursued. . . . He staggered into [camp] with ten bullet holes in
> him. . . . He mumbled [that] Something [was] coming from the West
> . . . [and] died in ten minutes.
> —*John Buchan, Greenmantle*

In 1965, as John le Carré was enjoying his first international success with *The Spy Who Came in from the Cold*, Jacques Barzun wrote an essay in *The American Scholar* titled "Meditations on the Literature of Spying." The piece was noteworthy as one of the first attempts by an academic critic to discuss the genre—even though, as quickly became clear, Barzun came not to praise, but to bury. About spy novels, he commented:

> The great illusion is to believe that [the agent's experience
> betokens] maturity, worldliness, being "realistic." The truth is
> that . . . the . . . spy [is essentially a] bright boy . . . of nine years.
> Nine is the age of seeking omniscience on a low level. The spy's
> ingenuity. . . , his shifting partisanship without a cause, like his
> double bluffs, his vagrant attachments, and his love of torturing
> and of being tortured are the mores of the preadolescent gang.
> . . . For adult readers to divert themselves with tales of childish
> fantasy is nothing new and not in itself reprehensible. What is
> new is for readers to accept the fantasy as wiser than civil
> government, and what is reprehensible is for the modern world
> to have made official the dreams and actions of little boys.[148]

As a late liberal response to the literature of paranoia, this is not half bad, with Barzun identifying danger on both aesthetic and civil grounds. Aesthetically, the work of Buchan, Childers, and the writers of their faction can masquerade as realism—precisely because, as we have discussed, the projections of the paranoid uncanny are often indistinguishable from empirical reality; Barzun is quite correct to insist on the origins of these works in "coherent delusion." He is also, furthermore, alert to the links between aesthetic representation and politics: writing only fifteen years after the end of World War II, he has a liberal's (rational) fear of what happens when the instrumental agreements of "civil government" are supplanted by the violent and absolutist structures of paranoia. Where his analysis fails utterly, however, is in its application to le Carré. As we mentioned earlier, the "spy novel," far from being a unitary genre, instead describes two very different schools of writing: first, the outpourings of Buchan and company; second—and later, after the disheartening experience of World War I—a skeptical and reflective tradition more inclined to question the value of a spy's actions and, by extension, the value of the system he or she defends. Most likely Barzun was unable (or disinclined) to distinguish between the two strands of writing before him, when he lumped le Carré, emphatically of the skeptical tradition, with the purveyors of "childish fantasy." When he describes the spy's "love of torturing and being tortured" as "preadolescent," he well could be describing Sapper McNeile, or Buchan, or Ian Fleming—but, if anything, le Carré is hidebound in his aesthetic and moral ambitions rather than infantile.

A peculiarity over the course of Le Carré's career has been the sheer frequency of attacks more or less in the spirit of Barzun's essay: distinguished authors (John Updike and Salman Rushdie in recent years), or guardians of the high literary, using the publication of a le Carré novel as the occasion to explain why espionage fiction does not meet the standard of "serious literature."[149] It is hard to think of another sector of the high/low border being policed quite so vigorously—and the obvious implication is that the intensity of invective is proportional to a perceived threat: where detective fiction, or horror fiction, or bodice-rippers, or the naïve, pulpish tradition of the spy novel are seen as safely belonging to the subgenres, the status of le Carré's work, or Somerset Maugham's, or Graham Greene's in cloak-and-dagger mode, is more ambiguous.[150] We would suggest that this ambiguity has much to do with the fortunes of conventional realism in the twentieth century—that the spy novel in its later, more skeptical, iteration is indeed an effective barometer of these fortunes; as such, it is also a logical study with which to end the present discussion.

As it has partly been the purpose of this chapter to examine, the field of literature by the middle of the twentieth century had effectively moved away from conventional realism. High Modern experimentation, which we will inspect further in chapter 5 when considering the temporal structures of contemporary surveillance, tended to position itself explicitly against the well-made, realistic novel.[151] Beyond that, we have observed the way the structures of allegorical thinking slowly migrated into serious writing—whether in the parables of socially conscious authors affected by progressivism or in later, post-Orwellian explorations of the paranoid uncanny. Moving in the other direction, the reflective tradition of the spy novel planted its flag firmly on the grounds of conventional realism; indeed, espionage is one of the few subjects that continued to inspire fiction of an identifiably nineteenth-century variety. As Maugham, whose *Ashenden* (1928) stories are commonly considered the first important work in this line, made clear, the choice of means was, as much as anything, a moral one. In contrast to the daydreams of a Buchan or Childers, the *Ashenden* stories deal with the day-to-day activities of a professional—are in fact derived from Maugham's own work as a spy in Switzerland during the war. Quite unlike the derring-do of a Richard Hannay or Bulldog Drummond, Ashenden spends much of his time doing nothing at all. In his preface, Maugham assures his readers that, in fact, espionage is mostly tedium: "The work of an agent in the Intelligence Department is on the whole extremely monotonous. A lot of it is uncommonly useless."[152] The effective spy, still more frustratingly, usually has little comprehension of his role within the larger world of espionage:

> Ashenden was well aware that he would never know [the consequences of his actions]. Being no more than a tiny rivet in a vast and complicated machine, he never had the advantage of seeing a completed action. He was concerned with the beginning or the end of it, perhaps, or with some incident in the middle, but what his own doings led to he seldom had a chance of discovering. It was as unsatisfactory as those modern novels that give you a number of unrelated episodes and expect you by piecing them together to construct in your mind a connected narrative.

The swipe at High Modernism is tactical: *because* "the material [spying] offers for stories is scrappy and pointless," it is the author's imperative to "make it coherent, dramatic and probable." Thus, if the first half of the passage suggests that the best way to represent the experience of spying might well be through recourse to the techniques of a Woolf or Joyce, the second half shows Maugham's conservative refusal to follow this suggestion: the consciousness of the spy, for Maugham, offers literary narrative new fodder for what it has always done. His ambition is to bring the traditional resources and priorities of fiction to bear on the new ethical material of contemporary espionage. That means coherent plots with rounded characters and climaxes where they should be, a lucid prose that doesn't draw attention to itself, and above all, an unobtrusive realism whose unobtrusiveness is in fact the result of centuries of accumulated convention.

And yet Maugham's fidelity to inherited forms—which he passes on to le Carré (and Greene, and Deighton, etc.)—only half explains the hostility towards the "reflective" spy novel in the literary mainstream. The choice of conventional realism, though unfashionable, would not be sufficiently disturbing for an Updike (or any serious author similarly committed to the realist novel); rather, the spy novel's use of realism is largely an assault on the traditional liberal associations of the mode. Barzun, elsewhere in the essay that we have quoted, is certainly on to something when he comments that "the great democratic virtue is to be 'interested in people,' which undoubtedly fosters sympathy and helpfulness. But it also fosters mutual surveillance and social tyranny."[153] The dissonance between these outcomes presents the more skeptical and serious branch of the spy novel with its great theme: that the sympathetic interest in other people—as we have seen, one of the core values of Western liberalism—can easily turn into a weapon, a means of personal violation. The spy, as presented by Maugham, Greene, and le Carré, is— like Iago, at the very start of the realist tradition—a monster of empathy; again and again, these authors offer plots in which the innocent die *because* of the protagonist's capacity for fellow feeling. Inevitably, the psychological and surveillance activities of the spy raise a perhaps insurmountable contradiction between the values of the societies they are pledged to uphold and their professional means of upholding them.

Thus in the best of the *Ashenden* tales, called simply "The Traitor" and drawn directly from Maugham's first assignment in Switzerland, Ashenden persuades an Englishman living in Lucerne, who's gone over to the German side, to make a risky journey to gather intelligence. While the man thinks that he will be aiding the German cause, Ashenden knows he is sending the traitor to his death: English agents are waiting to apprehend him, and a firing squad is inevitable. The first part of the story involves Ashenden's gaining the trust and friendship of the traitor and his German wife; the last and more emotionally uncomfortable phase takes place after the traitor has gone off on his death mission. All that's left for Ashenden to do is to watch the wife go to pieces after her husband does not return. Here's how the story ends:

> "Oh, God, oh, God," she moaned.
> She turned away, the tears streaming from her weary eyes, and for a moment she stood there like a blind man groping and not knowing which way to go. . . . The doubt, the gnawing doubt that had tortured her during those dreadful days of suspense, was a doubt no longer. She knew. She staggered blindly down the street.

Given the deep, historical investment of the novel as a genre in the value of empathy—an investment sustained by more radical forms of serious literature during this period—what reason for being is left *to the novel itself* when this value has been subverted? Typically, the Maugham, Greene, or le Carré hero redeems himself through an exercise of sympathetic understanding that *transcends* the corruption of his milieu; it is not clear, however, that this sympathetic catharsis is sufficient to redeem the novel as a genre. In either case, Maugham's "The Traitor" fails without its conclusion—without, that is to say, Ashenden witnessing the consequences of his actions and feeling sympathy for even the most unsympathetic of characters, the viciously xenophobic wife of a traitor. Not surprisingly, in subsequent espionage fiction, the spy's actions are often ultimately self-sacrificial—and we may take Alec Leamas's death at the Berlin Wall, at the end of *The Spy Who Came in from the Cold*, as paradigmatic.

In our next and final chapter, we will turn our attention briefly to the High Modernists, as a way of examining the *temporal* significance of surveillance. Curiously, one subset of modernist authors wrote about espionage prolifically—specifically, the second generation of British Modernists who clustered around W. H. Auden (Cyril Connolly, Christopher Isherwood, Edward Upward, Cecil Day-Lewis—but Auden himself above all). Richard Hoggart marvels that these authors were "all so interested in the apparatus of the spy story."[154] For them, the spy was a potent figure for—recalling Barzun again—"omniscience on a low level" and the attraction to childish fantasy over the untempting, if "wise," prospects of "civil government." On these terms, ironically, the subject matter of espionage—of the Buchan variety, rather than Maugham's—was perhaps made safe for Modernism, not as the object of realistic, novelistic treatment but as an emblem, a metaphor for their characteristic outlook. Samuel Hynes, Edward Mendelson, and others have described it well: fatalistic, precocious, committed to the coterie (or the isolated individual) over against a bourgeois society and prone to read the world as full of signs and codes portending future disaster—an outlook we will have occasion to discuss further.[155] Ultimately, however, Auden would make his best use of the spy, not as a sincere metaphor for modern alienation but in heavy scare quotes—that is to say, as a figure of camp. In *The Orators*, Auden gleefully name-drops Bulldog Drummond and relocates the entire world of espionage back into the schoolroom. At almost the very moment Maugham sets out to rescue spy fiction from its louche parentage, Auden imports it whole. Fully aware of the present and future distaste for its "boy's-own" associations, a distaste that his own later criticism will come to reflect, he anticipates and circumvents the sneers of the high literary guardians by embracing the pulpish side of the genre. Presenting the material of an older spy fiction in a new, experimental framework effectively presages a more distant age of irony.

> [We know], but not from the records
> Not from the unshaven agent who returned to the camp; . . .
> The agent clutching his side collapsed at our feet,
> "Sorry! They got me!"
> *The Orators*, Ode V

CHAPTER FIVE

Towards a Theory of Liberal Reading

A COLLEAGUE RELATES THE FOLLOWING anecdote about teaching *The Waste Land* to first-year students: *they were all gifted, but none had previously read the work. We got through the first two sections without incident, but when we hit part 3 there was trouble; it involved, specifically, Eliot's depiction of the typist's late afternoon tryst with the young man carbuncular, one of the less pleasant passages in the poem. As she "lights / her stove, and lays out food in tins" in preparation for the assignation, it transpires that she already has company:*

> I Tiresias, old man with wrinkled dugs
> Perceived the scene, and foretold the rest—
> I too awaited the expected guest.
> He, the young man carbuncular, arrives,
> A small house agent's clerk, with one bold stare. . . .
> The time is now propitious, as he guesses,
> The meal is ended, she is bored and tired,
> Endeavours to engage her in caresses
> Which still are unreproved, if undesired.
> Flushed and decided, he assaults at once;
> Exploring hands encounter no defence;
> His vanity requires no response,
> And makes a welcome of indifference.

(And I Tiresias have foresuffered all
Enacted on this same divan or bed;
I who have sat by Thebes below the wall
And walked among the lowest of the dead.)[1]

As our colleague read, he could see one young woman growing more and more restless, *and I had hardly finished when she exclaimed, "Oh come on—why doesn't Tiresias just do something?" Some of the more polished students smiled, but I was taken aback. I stumbled through the standard answers—for example: Tiresias is a prophet, and everything he sees is fated to happen—before turning to Eliot's own notoriously arcane notes in the back. There, of course, we are informed that "Tiresias, although a mere spectator and not indeed a 'character,' is yet the most important personage in the poem. . . . What Tiresias sees, in fact, is the substance of the poem."[2] My student looked unhappy—and far from convinced—and class moved on.*

The student's reaction is an interesting example of the way naïve or emotive readings can disrupt decades of accumulated critical cliché. That is, if we are accustomed to thinking of Tiresias as only a virtual presence in the text, we hardly worry about his inaction; and yet, he seems to be *right there*—a spectator, as Eliot says. The discomfort one feels while reading the poem must stem from three aspects of Tiresias's behavior in particular. First, the simple fact of his watching, which presents a species of surveillance we have not yet encountered in this study. His position is weirdly unlocalized: simultaneously intrusive—far more intrusive than even the most alarming scenarios of an Orwell or Zamyatin—and not there at all. Is Eliot's depiction of a monitoring perspective at once absent and all-seeing to be taken as plausible? If so, it presents disturbing and to this point unaddressed ramifications for privacy theory. Or is the scene, on the contrary, the product of some panic about personal space and thus most interesting as an hysterical or paranoid symptom? Second, to echo the dismayed undergraduate, and to set aside the question of realism for a moment, Tiresias does nothing: both present and fully aware of what's about to happen (and seemingly more disturbed by the "assault" than either of the jaded participants), he takes no steps to stop it. If the student's gut reaction is to be trusted, then perhaps the causality Eliot suggests in his notes is backwards (and intentionally misleading): instead of answering that Tiresias fails to act because he is virtual, it might have been more accurate to say that Eliot, confronting—or failing to confront—a problem in the relation between knowledge and action, had to depict Tiresias *as* virtual. As cans of worms go, this one is ancient—a problem going back, at least, to Socrates's assertion that knowledge of the Good necessitates right action and Aristotle's commonsense rejoinder to the contrary.[3] More recently the same debate has underpinned arguments about the nature and limitations of the public sphere as, in Thomas Keenan's useful paraphrase, "the site where knowledge and action are articulated."[4] *Should* Tiresias step in and do something? If so, why doesn't he? And if not, what is he doing there in the first place? We cannot help but notice that the *pathos* of the scene—our third source of unease—resides almost entirely with the *watcher*, not the watched. The typist and clerk are presented with forthright contempt, while Tiresias is a figure of agony. But what is the *source* of this pathos, and what about Tiresias's position *as* a surveiller entitles him to our sympathy? What, in short, is the nature of his foreknowledge (or, as Eliot specifies, "foresuffering")?

Strictly speaking, Eliot is raising these issues only because he has other fish to fry, concerns about authority which we will discuss much later in the chapter. Nevertheless, it should also go without saying that his brief domestic drama confronts us with problems our analysis to this point cannot adequately explain. As we have seen, the principal motives for surveillance in the centuries following Locke generally fall under two categories: empathy and coercion—that is, surveillance for the purposes of understanding and anticipation, and surveillance as an attempt to change behavior through applied pressure. In pursuit of the former, the nineteenth century dreamed up characters like Inspector Field (and Sherlock Holmes), able to penetrate the darker regions of the metropolis and the mind and unerring in their interpretations of the evidence before them; these heroic figures were subsequently transposed into the equally perceptive, demonic persecutors of twentieth-century paranoia. Meanwhile, the coercive aspects of surveillance found expression in constructionist psychologies from Hume and Smith to Mead, and in practical measures from the panopticon, at the end of the eighteenth century, to ambitious experiments in social engineering by twentieth-century progressives. In *both* cases, the path from knowledge to intervention was assumed to be clear: understanding the surveilled individual was a challenge—i.e., the main thrust of critiques from Melville to

Tolkien—but once understanding was achieved, one would presumably know how to act towards that person. With Tiresias, however, we witness a radical decoupling of the bond between knowledge and action hitherto foundational to surveillance theory: he has full access, as it were, to the typist's meager flat (e.g., "On the divan are piled (at night her bed) / Stockings, slippers, camisoles and stays"), but his complete understanding of the scene before him—and, most important, of future events (the goal of all surveillance activity)—translates into an unwillingness, or an inability, to *do* anything. In his ambivalent and confusing position, Eliot's Tiresias seems almost as much a creature of our own moment as the era that produced him; indeed, in the argument that follows, we will treat him as an early indicator of several key problematics in surveillance today.

I. TWO KINDS OF AUTONOMY

Chicken Littleism
Of course, distinguishing those key problematics from oversimplification and hysteria can be a challenge.

> Now more than ever, we are under surveillance. When we use a credit card or an ATM, when we call on our cell phones or use EZ pass, when we surf the web or simply walk down the street, we leave traces.[5] As the demand for identification is made in the spaces of shopping precincts, underground or city plaza, a demand to render ourselves visible to security authorities of many kinds, our ability to simply walk around, to see and be seen in public space diminishes.[6] We may not be heading backwards to the death squads of the Cold War, . . . but we may be heading for a global tyranny of security.[7] The intelligence agencies, the law enforcers and big business will press on. . . . If we continue to accept the demands of the law enforcers and the businesses without question or challenge, "they" are gradually gaining control. Society has already lost the battle for personal privacy.[8]

We present this chorus of Cassandras not in mockery, but precisely to illustrate the way, in current debates, that legitimate concerns about surveillance and privacy, like the spread of "dataveillance," are typically entangled with alarmism ("global tyranny of security"), exaggeration ("simply walk[ing] down the street"), and imprecision (the ever-implacable "they," who are gradually gaining control). In our introduction, we began to discuss the intellectual premises underlying much of this conversation: the still-potent vision of a disciplinary society, with few, if any, opportunities for resistance, presented by Foucault (a vision revised, but not fundamentally challenged, by subsequent theorists like Deleuze and Bauman); and a certain technological determinism combined with post-modern accounts of the death of privacy. In recent years, however, this (largely) dismal theoretical picture has been complicated by a growing practical recognition of the benefits that can come with responsible monitoring. As has been widely reported, for example, the key-card systems that permit access to offices and dormitories on many American campuses, while a conspicuous instance of data gathering and potential privacy invasion, are often welcomed by undergraduate coeds as a source of security.[9] It has even been suggested that, given the proliferation of such identity systems, something more centralized and totalizing might ultimately be in everyone's interest.[10] On the whole, however, these pragmatic considerations (whatever their merits) have had little impact on the ongoing speculative discussion. Few attempts have been made to square the apparent, or potential, virtues of surveillance with the generally apocalyptic rhetoric of the field, which has tended consequently to default to one of two positions: on the one hand, a vague appeal to "resistance," occasionally going so far as to legitimize terrorist activities against the state; on the other hand, a bowing to the logic of total and indiscriminate surveillance while recommending that it be deployed on behalf of forward-thinking causes.[11] Thus Peter Singer's recent advocacy of panoptic control:

> In the Panopticon, of course, transparency would not be limited
> to governments. Animal rights advocates have long said that if
> slaughterhouses had glass walls, more people would become
> vegetarian. . . . Bentham may have been right when he said that if
> we all knew that we were, at any time, liable to be observed, our
> morals would be reformed. . . . The mere suggestion that
> someone is watching encourage[s] greater honesty.[12]

One may love Big Brother, apparently, so long as that also includes hating Big Macs. As we saw in chapter 4, progressive aims can slip into coercion with ease—especially when progressives are willfully blind to their own coercive tactics and desires.

Beyond (or beneath) the numerous perplexities and hypocrisies of current debate lies a more plenary source of mystification—evident in several of the passages we have already cited but which one last entry should throw into stark relief: "Surveillance studies is in part a concerted attempt to trace some of the extraterritorial power relations of the present, visible in all manner of devices and systems, from cell phones, to Web 2.0, from security cameras to biometric passports, and from credit cards to national ID cards."[13] A daunting list indeed, not least because the elements listed belong to fundamentally different species of surveillance—and thus the extent and consequences of their interactions cannot simply be implied or assumed. Security cameras might be mounted by individuals, or corporations, or the State—with sharing of the recordings and cooperation between those groups far less common than one might think—and in each case producing very different effects.[14] Credit cards belong to the commercial world, whereas national ID cards and passports (biometric or otherwise) are issued by governments (and thus not "extraterritorial"). The *type* of surveillance made possible by a security camera, and the motives for that type of surveillance, belongs to a different order of power from data mining—and while tapping a person's conversations involves, almost certainly, a hostile breach of privacy, one's use of a credit card, or the Web (or to a lesser degree, which is also different in kind, a passport) is voluntary. In much the same way, the first commentator throws together the tracking of one's ATM use, one's driving with an EZ pass, one's talking on a cell phone, and one's "simply [walking] down the street" as if they were all the same thing: surveillance. If this study has suggested anything, however, it is that surveillance is *not* one thing, but an order of genetically related activities—and that, moreover, this rampant blurring of distinctions between different kinds of activity has been costly, not least because actual infiltrations and harmful overlaps have thereby been obscured. We must dismiss the tendency to call *everything* surveillance, a point reached, for reasons we will discuss later, by Jean Beaudrillard:

> [Although] huge billboards [invite] you to relax and to choose in
> complete serenity . . . [t]hese billboards, in fact, observe and
> surveil you as well, or as badly, as the "policing" television.[15]

To call a billboard (or a television, for that matter)—an object without voli-
tion, cognition, or the ability to *see*—a form of "surveillance" is to have
pushed the term beyond any usefulness or theoretical coherence. Far
more damaging, however, has been the extension of conclusions and
recommendations legitimate to one species of surveillance indiscriminately to others. The restrictions that come with passports or with the
sharing of credit card information may indeed be a source of concern and
may indeed spur concrete courses of action. But to apply those analyses,
and those recommendations, to the problems of cell-phone monitoring
or "simply [walking] down the street" patently makes no sense. The lack
of even a basic taxonomy of surveillance activities has all but ensured the
rampant confusion and misapplication of policies.

As we move towards such a taxonomy, we would begin by reaffirming the
reality of privacy in the contemporary world. In contrast to the frequent
assertions one encounters that privacy has "vanished" under the eye of
surveillance or, as David Lyon has put it, that the "notion" of privacy "is
not sufficient for understanding and responding to the challenges
of surveillance today," we would suggest that privacy in fact forms a
necessary substrate for all considerations.[16] The dialectical struggle we
have traced between privacy and observation, having begun in the late
seventeenth century, had by the beginning of the twentieth produced an
ascendant vision of personal autonomy rooted in the solitary self. As
simple introspection indicates, this ideology remains, in all crucial
respects, unchallenged in our society: most of us, to a degree unprecedented in history, are alone in our thoughts and actions most of the
time—and derive our sense of personhood, for better or worse, from this
solitude. We may, certainly, be filmed "simply [walking] down the street,"
but the access this allows to our inner lives is negligible. Part of the pathos
that clings to Eliot's Tiresias, surely, is the way his watching of behavior,
and indeed knowledge of future actions, does *not* translate into empathetic understanding: in a way that most readers can recognize all too
readily, the typist and clerk remain solitary and mysterious, indicating

little of their interiority to Tiresias or to one another (or, for that matter, the reader) throughout their little scene. At the height of the previous, allegorical, dispensation, Elizabeth I had characterized herself, in a trope made much of by Kantorowicz and Foucault, as possessing "two bodies"—her way of indicating how, under the conditions of divine right monarchy, the sovereign was at once a discrete individual and synonymous with the body politic.[17] In the contemporary world, we may similarly speak, in essentially anti-Foucauldian terms and in a historically contingent reversal of Elizabeth's trope, of each individual as similarly divided: as a private citizen, and as a participant in the social.

This split, to clarify, is a direct legacy of the division within liberalism that we discussed at the end of chapter 3 and the beginning of chapter 4: on the one hand, an ideology of privacy allowing little room for communal life, with each individual alone in his or her autonomy, an atom among atoms; on the other hand, a communal, progressive ethos, requiring social cohesion and cooperation for the achievement of certain goods (like justice, mutual security, education, and so on). As we saw, by the early twentieth century it was clear that such cohesion could be achieved only through a great deal of management, through the creation of controlled systems in which the participating individual would be expected to surrender some degree of his or her absolute, private autonomy in order to enjoy common benefits. *Systems*, we would emphasize. Though we can only glancingly engage with the field of systems theory, we would insist on the plurality of these controlled environments, not following Parsons (or, in a different way, Niklas Luhmann) into a vision of society itself as an all-encompassing master system.[18] We make this claim for two main reasons. First, as will become clear, most systems can function only through the operations of surveillance—but the "laws of physics," as it were, can vary widely from environment to environment (and differ considerably depending on whether the environment is governmental [for example a school] or commercial). A necessary step in clarifying the current conversation therefore requires keeping different systems distinct: surveillance activities, and the concerns they raise, will often be categorically different as one moves from one to another. Second, the vision of society as an all-encompassing system slides perhaps too easily into the anti-humanism of seeing people as secondary to the functioning of the machine—a charge leveled at Luhmann by both Habermas and

Jean-François Lyotard.[19] From our perspective, the chief problem with this view is that it ignores the other legacy of liberalism: the real, private autonomy of each person. Indeed, even if modern liberal society *could* be envisioned as one thing, the individual would remain autonomous—*both* in his or her privacy *and*, in a different way, we will claim, as a social participant. *Two kinds of autonomy*, then, if not "two bodies," with the second kind (at least notionally) infinitely multipliable, to include each participatory environment in which a single person is active.

Contemporary Lockeanism

Before we pursue the implications of this stance any further, we should distinguish our contentions from other theories of contemporary politics, which they might superficially resemble. Reconciling the conflicting claims of "private and public right," for example, has been a central part of Habermas's project for the last half century—and we are by no means the first to point out the political ramifications of the separation of the two domains.[20] In contrast, however, to many liberal interpretations of modernity, including Habermas's, and nearly all anti-liberal accounts (in the last two decades, Giorgio Agamben's has been perhaps the most influential), we do not see the relation between private autonomy and social participation as oppositional.[21] To do so would mean aligning ourselves, as these scholars have, with the tradition of "positive liberty" (as Berlin puts it) descending from Rousseau: the individual's autonomy understandable only within the context of society; the individual indeed liberated from the state of nature by equating his or her individual will with something larger—a general will. A political master narrative well described by Lyotard as "emancipatory": "It is assumed that the laws [society] makes for itself are just, not because they conform to some outside nature, but because the legislators are, constitutionally, the very citizens who are subject to the laws. As a result the legislator's will—the desire that the laws be just—will always coincide with the will of the citizen, who desires the law and will therefore obey it."[22] In chapter 4, we discussed the coercive, totalizing ends to which socialist, utopian writers like Bellamy and Wells took these premises—and then also analyzed the ease with which these habits of thought were absorbed into a paranoid politics.[23] By the end of World War II, with Nazism viewed by most contemporary writers as the culminating disaster of the "emancipatory" tradition, the master narrative had, in Lyotard's blunt assessment, "lost its credibility."[24] The result of this disaster has been an exploded Rousseauvianism: a distrust, that is to say, of any and all state attempts to create the conditions of liberty and a tendency to see all state actions (and the initiatives of the State's partners [in global capitalism, etc.]) as inherently subjugating—*coupled with* an inability to account for human dignity and freedom in any other way. A clinging to Rousseau's monist assumptions long after any faith in the social benefits of those assumptions has vanished, leaving the author with a choice of quietism or a vaguely anarchistic rhetoric of revolution— which, practically, comes to the same thing.[25]

In this book we have proposed a version of Lockeanism to counter this view of society. As we saw in chapter 2, Lockean liberalism is not, in Lyotard's sense of the word, "emancipatory"; rather, confronting the twin evils of divine right authoritarianism (the true precedent for Rousseau) and the anarchy of factionalism, Locke had envisioned society as composed of instrumental agreements between real or potential rivals. The individual was "emancipated" only in the sense that, free from the dangers of oppression or violence, he or she might then pursue his or her own goods. Most important for our purposes, this argument, in addition to producing a relatively modest view of state power (modest relative both to Rousseau and to the theorists of divine right), also preserved, as its principal assumption, the native dignity of the individual: as Locke makes clear, individual dignity and autonomy precedes the social—is indeed the *reason* for the social, not its product.[26] It is perhaps unsurprising there-fore that Locke should play such a slight role in the calculations of the theorists we have mentioned. In Agamben's *The Coming Community, The State of Exception*, and *Homo Sacer*, for instance, the name "Locke" appears precisely once, and his work is never dealt with substantially.[27] By contrast, both Hobbes and Rousseau, who preserved the monism of divine-right monarchy on quasi-secular terms, are engaged with at length. For Hobbes, as the much-quoted phrase goes, life outside of society could only be seen as solitary, poor, nasty, brutish, and short—a view according well with Agamben's distinction (which he traces back to Aristotle) between man as *zoë* ("the simple fact of living in common with all living beings") and man as *bios* ("which indicated the form or way of living proper to an individual or group").[28] This distinction allows Agamben then to claim that the individual outside of society is placed in a "state of exemption," without rights or dignity, the condition of "bare life, that is to say, the life of *homo sacer*."[29] In Locke, by way of contrast, there is no such thing as *homo sacer*—his calculations beginning not with "bare life" but with an assumption about intrinsic human value. In the centuries after Locke, this overtly theistic idea was gradually secularized; it might well be argued that even in the secular language of personal autonomy it retains a theistic tinge. As we noted in chapter 2, however, *any* politics short of anarchism involves both a choice of beliefs and an assertion of power—and this, in any case, is where liberalism has staked its claim— authoritarianism and chaos being unacceptable alternatives.

When we describe the individual, then, as possessing two kinds of autonomy, we are preserving this streak of Lockeanism; where Foucauldians like Agamben would have difficulty describing the modern state citizen as autonomous in *any* sense, we would view the individual as autonomous *both* within the sphere of privacy (the domain of isolated selfhood) and within each of the systems (including, quite possibly, "the State") in which he or she is a participant. Indeed, the former kind of autonomy, which goes back, via several transformations, to Locke's native human dignity, is ontologically prior to the second kind and underwrites it. We recognize that autonomy of the second, systemic variety might be a bone of contention; as we saw in the last chapter, the progressives, while preserving the free individual as a core desideratum, nonetheless played fast and loose semantically with key liberal terms—thus Hobhouse's comment that "the function of State coercion is to override individual coercion" or Dewey's careful defining of "freedom" as "a mental attitude rather than external unconstraint of movements." In much the same way, the individual's autonomy within the participatory systems will always be to some degree under coercive pressure, the degree varying as one moves from system to system. We would suggest, however, that as long as the person's participation is grounded in his or her status as a private individual *outside* the system, and thus subject to a tacit or explicit instrumental agreement between him or herself and the system, his or her actions and choices within will, in a significant way, be autonomous. To an extent not widely recognized, this systemic autonomy is not only not contradictory with the presence of surveillance but in fact is often made possible by it: a necessary final consideration, as we turn to our own taxonomy, is the possibility that in the contemporary world many traditional liberal values persist *only* by virtue of careful and regulated monitoring.

II. A TAXONOMY OF CONTEMPORARY SURVEILLANCE

Systemic Surveillance

We may begin our analysis of surveillance types with this basic distinction between private existence and the participatory systems that constitute social life; if surveillance practices and concerns differ widely as one moves from system to system, an even wider gap exists between those kinds of surveillance and the surveillance one encounters in the private world of isolated selfhood. We may start, then, with the participatory systems: briefly, these are where one finds most of what we have been calling "surveillance as coercion"—watching people, that is, not primarily to understand them (i.e., empathize with them) and thus anticipate their actions, but rather in order to influence or control those actions through applied pressure. Governments, whether democratic or autocratic, make full use of this kind of surveillance—but it belongs equally, if not more so, to the commercial sector: the tracking software, the loyalty card programs that register one's every purchase, and the algorithms that aggregate one's spending habits (and subsequently stuff one's inbox with personalized advertisements each morning) all belong to this kind of monitoring activity.[30] When Deleuze refers, somewhat apocalyptically, to "ultrarapid forms of apparently free floating control that are taking over from the old disciplines," he is largely thinking of this commercial endeavor:

> Marketing is now the instrument of social control and produces the arrogant breed who are our masters. . . . In the business system [we see] new ways of manipulating money, products and men. This is a fairly limited range of examples, but enough to convey what it means to talk of institutions breaking down: the widespread progressive introduction of a new system of domination.[31]

In much the same spirit, another commentator observes that "panoptic" observation has given way to "information-gathering systems [and] databases," resulting in a "system of social regulation in which data collection . . . is mined for profiles. . . . Identity itself becomes an interface [in] an environment that is bleakly Orwellian, grimly Kafkaesque, [functioning through] insidious invisibility [and] menacing covert procedures."[32]

Before we surrender, however, to "the arrogant breed who are our masters," we should pause to observe the sheer diversity of systemic environments in which a person can find him or herself: some, as we shall see, are relatively contained (entertainment venues, for example), while others are open and vast—with significantly different pressures. One's experience of the Social Security system may indeed, at times, be "grimly Kafkaesque"—but one's submitting to commercial data collection and information gathering will *likely* stop short of *Animal Farm, 1984*, or *The Trial*. We may (selectively) generalize. To cut through the doom-saying: in the terms that *we* have developed, we may say that the tendency of any systemic, participatory environment will be allegorical. As both Lyotard and Parsons observe—with different degrees of approval—it is in the interest of any system to turn participating individuals in it into better, more efficient participants.[33] Outside the system, that is to say, one may be a complex, three-dimensional being—but any one system will inevitably be interested in only *some* aspects of a person's individuality: the part that purchases MP3s, let's say, or the part that occasionally runs red lights, or the part that wishes to travel to Kyrgyzstan next Tuesday. Since a system measures success according to the efficiency of its input-output operations, it will necessarily privilege those behaviors or aspects of personality that allow it to run more smoothly, productively, quickly; other behaviors—complex, irregular, or unpredictable—will be a matter of indifference or outright hostility. The individual participating in the system therefore risks a selective (and often temporary) narrowing to something less than a three-dimensional person: a High Roller, a Lawful Permanent Resident, an Alien Person of Exceptional Ability—a token or figment, in any case, within the stable allegory. For reasons that should be apparent, finally, systemic *aesthetics* will also tend towards the allegorical; thus the vision of a harmonious industrial society offered by the Coit Tower murals requires happy workers, not differentiated ones—and so many of the farm laborers and factory hands look eerily alike. A situation deftly parodied by Huxley, with his Deltas and Epsilons.

It is simply incorrect, however, to view the surveillance situation within these systems as *purely* coercive or evil (Deleuze calls "control" "the new monster") and equally lazy to assume that the individual is always supine or "foredoomed"—like Joseph K. or Winston Smith.[34] To identify the *intentions* of a system—even if we grant, for the sake of argument, that the most dystopian authors are correct about those intentions—often has little or nothing to do with how the system really functions. When the Coit Tower's workers go home after a day of blissful orange picking or hydroelectric dam building, can we be certain that they will remain undifferentiated zombies? As numerous sociological studies focusing on local practices—that is, on how individuals actually use the systems in which they find themselves—have suggested, systems are often at the mercy of individual initiative. Michel de Certeau begins a chapter in *The Practice of Everyday Life*, by far the most influential such study, with a fantasy of systemic surveillance, precisely to demolish it:

> Seeing Manhattan from the 110th floor of the World Trade Center. . . . The gigantic mass is immobilized before the eyes. . . . An Icarus flying above these waters, [one] can ignore the devices of Daedalus in mobile and endless labyrinths below. His levitation transfigures him into a voyeur. It . . . transforms the bewitching world into a text that lies before one's eyes. It allows one to read it, to be a solar Eye, looking down like a god. . . . The 1370 foot high tower that serves as a prow for Manhattan continues to construct the fiction that creates readers, makes the complexity of the city readable, and immobilizes its opaque mobility in a transparent text.[35]

The passage cannot help but evoke previous panoptic fantasies: if not Sherlock Holmes's Icarian daydream of flying over nighttime London and peering into each house, then Satan atop the Tree of Knowledge, enjoying his sweeping perspective without grasping the crucial role in history his own perch will later play (de Certeau was writing in 1974, when the Trade Center must have seemed invulnerable). Unlike Milton's Satan, however, or Foucault, to whom he is directly referring, de Certeau has no illusions about "transparency": concentrating, like Deleuze and Bauman, though to a very different end, on ordinary individuals—the targets of power—de Certeau spends most of his time on street level, observing, "beneath the discourses that ideologize the city, the ruses, and combinations of powers that have no readable identity, [and which are] impossible to administer."[36] Even the most rigidly rectilinear grid of a street plan cannot prevent jaywalking or cutting through an alleyway—is indeed a constant temptation to such behavior.

Crucially, de Certeau's focus on the everyday lives of "an innumerable collection of singularities" (i.e., individual people) does not deny the power or functioning of systems or the presence of panoptic surveillance. Rather,

> one can follow the swarming activity of [everyday actions] that, far from being regulated or eliminated by panoptic administration, have reinforced themselves in a proliferating illegitimacy, developed or insinuated themselves into the networks of surveillance, and combined in accord with unreadable but stable tactics to the point of constituting everyday regulations and surreptitious creativities that are merely concealed by the frantic mechanisms and discourses of the observational organization.[37]

As de Certeau recognizes, the presence of autonomous agents within a system necessarily changes the way the system functions—sometimes by means of resistance but just as often through "surreptitious creativity," as individuals rewrite the panopticon's rules to their own advantage.[38] In his study of this phenomenon on the State level, James Scott observes that "designed or planned social order," because it is schematic, "always ignores essential features of any real, functioning social order": "To the degree that the formal scheme [makes] no allowances for these processes or actually [suppresses] them, it [fails] both its intended beneficiaries and ultimately its designers as well."[39] Like de Certeau, however, Scott is not making a case against systemic power or for a kind of happy anarchism; as he comments, the State "is the ground of both our freedoms and unfreedoms."[40] The world of pure privacy and pure freedom, the world of "innumerable singularities," is chaotic and dangerous—and systemic control, for better or worse, has become the guarantor of a civil society. *Surveillance*, by means of which participatory systems function, and by means of which the instrumental agreements that hold society together are monitored, has become such a guarantor. An adequate taxonomy, then, must take into account the necessity of surveillance, even as it explores possibilities of resistance, escape, or redefinition.

A Notional Graph

Practically speaking, such a taxonomy must identify the handful of variables that produce the vast panoply of systemic surveillance situations. In the event, we would suggest that the key variables are only two in number: the degree of (allegorical) coercion exerted by the system on the individual, and the degree to which the individual's participation in the system is voluntary. The former: to what extent does the system attempt to narrow or convert the individual into a figment? Some demand more than others, but all, aiming for what Lyotard calls "optimal performativity," hope to create predictable and efficient (and therefore, to some extent, allegorical) behavior within their confines.[41] By voluntariness we simply mean that some systems allow or even depend upon voluntary entry, whereas others imagine themselves as mandatory; nonparticipants will often be marked as outlaws or, in the worst cases, as inhuman. One might picture these two variables as the axes of a notional graph: as allegorical coercion and voluntariness increase or decrease, different conditions are created which affect the stakes, techniques, and consequences of surveillance. It should be clear enough that certain systems are strongly coercive and largely involuntary, for example, while others are objects of choice and hardly coercive at all: no monolithic practice or set of practices can function well under all conditions. While it would require a longer (and different kind of) book to analyze the full array of points on this grid, a few paradigmatic cases should suffice to show how different the tensions in surveillance can be as one moves from system to system. Paradigmatic and, we hope, somewhat familiar by now:

1. A man walks into a casino . . .

In the *Panopticon Letters*, Bentham had specified that the psychological effects he hoped to achieve could only be produced in a "space not too large." As a surveillance environment expands, the forces of observation necessarily disperse and the variety of possible behaviors by individuals similarly grows. Accordingly, when this logic is applied to strictly delimited commercial environments, and especially to entertainment-oriented venues, one tends to encounter a high degree of both allegorical coercion *and* voluntariness. As we saw at the outset of chapter 2, the pressure of surveillance at a casino is unremitting and obviously serves the commercial interests of the institution—not just as a defense against theft but as a signal to the patron that he or she is expected to behave in a certain way (a reckless, thrill-seeking, carefree way). The purpose of the establishment is to convert the responsible citizen into an irresponsible patron and the irresponsible patron into a regular. We are thus in no way sidestepping questions of addiction and compulsive behavior: anyone who has observed a row of septuagenarian pensioners hooked up to slot machines by their frequent-player-card necklaces and frittering away their monthly checks will understand the sinister side of this psychology; certainly there are gambling addicts in every casino who perhaps do not imagine their presence as voluntary (and in any case, their families would not likely see it that way). Nevertheless, we would argue, the *degree of concern* one should have about casino surveillance (and its equivalents in similar situations—amusement parks, cruise ships, etc.) is relatively small: most people participate occasionally and voluntarily, and the effect of surveillance is largely *pleasurable.* In contrast, say, to the conditions of a KGB interrogation room (high coercion, low voluntariness), the dynamics of the casino create a desire to return frequently.

Controlled environments of this sort are, in a sense, reassuring: in marked contrast to the complexities and stresses of everyday life, it can come as a relief to know that one is understood, that one's desires matter and can be anticipated. Over against the usual anonymity, one merits watching and one's actions have predictable consequences. If the price of this attention is a selective, *temporary* narrowing of one's three-dimensional personhood—a narrowing that, itself, can be pleasurable—then so be it: this is an instrumental agreement into which millions of customers (not just of casinos) enter willingly each day. The fresh towel waiting on your deck chair when you get back from a dip in the cruise liner pool means that you are being looked after and that any misfortune will be rectified or prevented. Surveillance of this sort is not experienced as hostile, suspicious, or uncomfortable, but rather is welcomed by its objects as a hedge against a world often perceived as chaotic and indifferent. On the deepest level, it is entirely likely that individuals who seek this kind of attention are the spiritual descendants of Lord Mellifont—Henry James's odd nobleman, who, when removed from social interaction, simply vanished from the face of the earth. Lord Mellifont, we implied, offered an ironic codicil to our long history of privacy rights: for some people, at least, the withdrawal of the divine gaze, which had underwritten personal identity during the allegorical dispensation, would have been perceived entirely as a loss. With the secularization of personal identity, such people would have naturally sought an underwriting gaze elsewhere. And just as the Wordsworthian ideology of privacy had marked an attempt to draw the justifying eye inward, so a commitment to life as spectacle, or exhibitionism, would locate (or at least seek) justification in the collective. Almost at the start of this history, Adam Smith had been perfectly aware of the theistic tinge his own, ruthlessly secular psychology could potentially acquire. As he commented, in archly sacramental language, "We scarce dare to absolve ourselves, when all our brethren appear loudly to condemn us." The collective gaze causes us to posit the existence of an "impartial spectator of our conduct"—essentially an internalization of social norms—to the extent that our "judgments are steadily and firmly directed by the sense of praise-worthiness and blame-worthiness."[42] When Žižek refers, some two centuries later, to the "Other's Gaze serving as the guarantee of the subject's being[:] 'I exist only insofar as I am looked at all the time,' " he comes surprisingly close to Smith's position.[43] An eighteenth-century pleasure garden, a twenty-first-century casino, or, to extend the analysis, the cathartic nature of self-presentation and avatarism associated with digital social networking: in each case, the experience of entering (voluntarily) an environment in which one's every action will be closely watched and in which one is pressured into certain behaviors, with a commensurate reduction of one's complex selfhood, can go far beyond mere pleasure.

2. A man walks into a small social gathering . . .

. . . bearing a gift he has purchased using his Target rewards card. When commercial surveillance operates on a broader field and is not confined to restricted environments (like casinos or cruise ships), the level of allegorical pressure it can exert on individuals is inevitably less intense (though it can still be considerable); by the same token, the degree of voluntariness, depending on the nature of the business, is often proportionally lessened as well. Large retailers like Target or Wal-Mart employ tracking software, data mining, filtering, (etc.) in the interests of turning the individual into a better, more loyal, free-spending customer. Again, since the person's participation is largely by choice, one cannot leap to the most dire conclusions (Deleuze's "new system of domination" and "arrogant breed who are our masters"): one is under no obligation to use Amazon; one *needn't* sign up for a rewards program; even Wal-Mart, grudgingly, accepts cash transactions that don't register the purchaser's identity in the company's massive Bentonville mainframes. One can, indeed, grow one's own food and sew one's own clothing. Nevertheless, the sheer convenience and efficiency (and often the substantial cost savings) of purchasing the necessities of life in a regular, recordable way means that few individuals, in practice, opt out entirely. To generalize, the degree of concern with these forms of surveillance should rise in proportion to the degree that the services offered are *necessary*—with the individual, potentially, forced to conform against his or her will. Not infrequently these services will involve areas where commercial activity overlaps with, or replaces, government oversight. It is foreseeable that the increasing power of corporations, not just to collect information about consumers' behaviors and predilections but over the political system in general (through lobbying and think-tank pressure most obviously, but also through the unacknowledged privatization of government activities, including intelligence gathering), will make the worst excesses of this kind of surveillance increasingly difficult both to detect and to check.

An equally insidious danger from this kind of surveillance, finally, is not to be located in the consciousnesses or even the actions of individual participants, but rather in the techniques of social sorting, in which companies engage to optimize sales and performance.[44] Even though it is the goal of any system to turn all participants (to some degree) into allegorical tokens, it does *not* follow that each individual will be turned into the same *kind* of token: the stability of any working allegory derives, in no small part, from an internal division of labor. As recent studies have come to recognize, systems typically select and categorize their members, controlling access to attention, rewards, and—most important—information, with certain content selectively doled out to some and not to others. Google, for example, tailors search results in light of each user's previous history and also tracks the "type" of each person searching (as determined by fifty-seven "signals"—for example "location of IP address" or "font being used.")[45] If a professor of Hellenistic archaeology and a journalist working on Northern African uprisings were both to search for "Libya," they would receive different sets of results. A worrisome enough case—but the situation turns far more serious when necessary social resources are at stake: who receives benefits (medical attention, welfare assistance, etc.), and who is denied them, and who can tell when the process of disbursement is effectively cloaked? In a poorly regulated system, or when the interests of one system (corporate) have infiltrated or replaced those of another (governmental), the opportunities for bias (of both the traditional kind [race and gender], as well as far more subtle varieties) are vast—and largely unpoliced. When access to crucial information is withheld or otherwise manipulated, key liberal require-ments, like individual autonomy and freedom of action, begin to suffer: if one only receives news (about Libya, let's say) fitting one's "profile," that profile, sooner or later, begins to influence one's habits of mind. In short, the instrumental agreements underpinning this kind of surveillance are particularly susceptible to abuse—and abuse comes at a particularly high cost. In recent years, it is worth noting, the problem of information sorting has received increased popular attention—even if policy, in legis-latures and courts, has lagged far behind public concern.

3. Nicole Kidman and Keith Urban get married . . .
. . . but before they can do so, information regarding their age, gender, nationality, family ancestry, residency status, mental state, marital and sexual history must be processed by the government. They must also present government-issued identification cards at the ceremony itself, which is presided over by a government-authorized and licensed minister. As anyone who has tried to get married (or learn how to drive, or start a business) can attest, governmental systems usually *demand* the participa-tion of all individuals—the degree of voluntariness in most cases being negligible. Without official identification, it can be difficult to live what we think of as a modern, comfortable life; without the use of State infrastruc-ture, and a submission to the monitoring that entails, it can be difficult to accomplish much of anything. Even the Unabomber, who had otherwise opted out of civil society, had to use the postal service from time to time. This very necessity, however, has led to the near-ubiquitous critical habit of assuming that the largely mandatory nature of State-participation leads automatically to extreme *coercive* pressure. In fact, if we differentiate adequately between our two key variables, we frequently find the reverse to be true—the government lacking the motivation (and just as often the ability) to *shape* its citizenry in particular, allegorical ways. In part, this is

simply a question of scale: as Scott puts it, in terms de Certeau would agree with, "a human community is . . . far too complicated and variable to easily yield its secrets to bureaucratic formulae"; as a result, any "formal scheme" of monitoring is "parasitic on informal processes [it can neither] create [nor] maintain."[46] Even in Orwell's Oceania, the State's blindness to 85 percent of the population—the proles—somewhat undercuts, despite the author's loudest insistence, the purported dominance of the Thought Police: the State, like all States fictional or otherwise, simply lacks the time and manpower to micromanage each participant. Our happy couple, simply because they exist among millions of happy couples, can wed in St. Patrick's Cathedral or Caesar's Palace and is unlikely to face ideological, racial, or, increasingly, gender restrictions from the government.

On a more fundamental level, the assumption that, were the economies of scale less daunting, any State *would* necessarily exert a maximum of allegorical pressure on its citizens is highly dubious. For critics of a paranoid stripe, *any* State surveillance is oppressive and—more dubious still—indicative of broader, coercive objectives. The presence of automatic cameras, for example, photographing the license plates of drivers running red lights becomes proof positive of a more pervasive State control—thus Thomas Levin:

> [In] Michel Foucault's analysis [of] what he called a "disciplinary society," the controlled space of the panopticon has since become synonymous with the vast repertoire of surveillant practices that have so profoundly marked the modern world. When we hesitate to race through a red light at an intersection where we see a black box, not knowing whether it contains a working camera but having to suppose that it might, we are acting today according to the very same panoptic logic.[47]

A singularly unfortunate example, given (a) the demonstrated value such "black boxes" have had in reducing traffic fatalities; (b) the (resulting) widespread support these devices have enjoyed from most citizens; and (c) the fact that we probably *should* "hesitate to race through a red light at an intersection." Most problematic, however, is the logical slippage that allows Levin to move from his rather weak example to the "panoptic logic" of a "disciplinary society." In the case of the "black boxes," a minimum of voluntariness (it is against the law to run red lights) does *not* translate into powerful allegorical coercion: aside from (occasionally) turning drivers into "people who do not run red lights," their shaping power is minimal. Indeed, in entire sectors of society, it is patently not in the interest of a democratic government to exert strong allegorical coercion: to the extent that a liberal society requires a population of autonomous and *varied* individuals to flourish, it cannot, for its own continued health, turn that population into drones. For this reason, in those sectors where theorists of a "disciplinary society" are most likely to detect discursive power (even of the most individuating kind—the discourse of education above all), we are inclined to see something rather different: particularly intense negotiations over the instrumental agreements (including those pertaining to surveillance) that hold the social system together.[48] Negotiations—even battles, so long as they are rooted in the respect for the life and dignity of others that leads one *not* to "race through a red light at intersections"— that can never be resolved so long as liberalism survives.

Lastly, and to reset the argument on a more practical level: it is also the case that most citizens welcome some monitoring in order to forestall violence and are glad to have someone watching over (to pick some obvious examples) the air transportation network, the environment, the financial system (the events of 2008 hardly made us long for *less* financial monitoring). Citizens of developing nations are often surprised at the Western (and specifically American) hostility to government surveillance: a middle-class Mexican citizen, for example, is far more likely to equate "surveillance" with "security" than "intrusion"; an Indian villager may welcome government data records as proof to the world that he or she exists.[49] Certainly we would agree that state surveillance can be a threat to our freedoms; we would also insist, to repeat, that it is one of their guarantors: liberalism as social consensus can survive only within controlled and vigilant environments.[50] To point out that the misuse of surveillance is one of the main ways that contracts get violated is not to void the equally important truth that surveillance is the main way violations are identified and policed.

Surveillance in the State of Nature

We have already discussed at length, notably in the last chapter, the problem of surveillance in the domain of private existence. Just as surveillance in the participatory systems is where one mostly finds what we have been calling "surveillance as coercion," so surveillance in the private world—the world of innumerable, atomized, autonomous agents—is devoted mostly to empathy: the monitoring of others for the purposes of understanding them and anticipating their behaviors. Coercive surveillance, as practiced in the participatory systems, looks inward in an attempt to control and refine; empathetic surveillance is turned outward in an attempt to defend against possible external threats. To repeat: we may think of the private domain, which encompasses all possible participatory systems, not as a gigantic master system in the manner of Parsons, but rather as the territory shared by all individuals. In short, to go back a little, a situation not so different from the "State of Nature"—at least as Locke understood the term. Throughout this book we have pointed out the weaknesses of empathetic, preemptive monitoring and have critiqued the paranoid overestimation of its reach and accuracy. This is not to underestimate, however, the advances made in recent years, particularly in certain sectors of high technology. Facial recognition software, long an object of jaundiced contempt in the intelligence community (if not the minds of screenwriters), has at last begun to achieve a measure of accuracy; data mining, once a crude sorting device, has outgrown its simple "pattern-matching" roots and can now recognize "fuzzy" correlations and associations.[51] It is also undeniable that "algorithmic" approaches represent a potential revolution in the operation of dataveillance, not least in their ability to "oscillate back and forth across different domains"—that is, to make use of links between disparate systems.[52] Just as commercially developed "algorithmic calculations" have been adopted for military use, so the resulting "war-like architecture" of algorithmic surveillance has moved back into everyday public security: methods of payment for an airline ticket, for example, can be compared to luggage weight and in-flight meal selections to determine potentially risky passengers.[53]

The rhetoric of triumphant technology is all but overwhelming—and yet, as always, the most advanced interpretive systems necessarily rely upon a human element: algorithms, biometrics, risk-profiling programs, (etc.) are an advance on, but not different *in kind*, from phrenology, physiognomy, and all of the various detective sciences that came and went, starting in the eighteenth century. It is the human programmer or director who decides what "looks" suspicious and who instructs the device what to flag: all results—even correct ones—are inevitably the product of subjective intuition at one remove, not objective processes. We might mention the casino surveillance manager who suggested to us that, at bottom, his work was summed up by the police acronym "JDLR"—digital predictive surveillance, however advanced, being an attempt to codify that gut feeling, to objectify the sense that something "just don't look right."[54] If the original program designer's feelings are off, then so too the program. In our introduction, we alluded to a character in the film *Enemy of the State*, a former NSA spook played by Gene Hackman. That character is something of an homage to Hackman's earlier portrayal of Harry Caul in Francis Ford Coppola's *The Conversation*. In the earlier movie, probably the best-known (and best) cinematic examination of the "JDLR" mentality, Caul, a private surveillance man, is hired by a jealous, glowering husband to watch his pretty young wife and her lover. With malice aforethought, the movie fetishizes the elaborate and intimidating technology (state of the art, circa 1974) that Caul uses to record the unsuspecting couple's discussions. Reviewing his tapes, Caul comes to believe that they are in danger (the key line he listens to repeatedly: "he'd *kill* us if he had the chance"). As it turns out, the two are plotting the husband's murder—and after they have successfully carried out their scheme, Caul, listening to the conversation again, realizes that while he had heard the words correctly, he had missed the intonation ("he'd kill *us* if he had the chance").[55] In his first postscript to the *Panopticon Letters* Bentham dropped a suggestion subsequently ignored by his most admiring followers: that the ideological force of the panopticon is ultimately directed not at the prisoner in his cell but at the watcher in his tower. The vision panoptic surveillance presents, of dangerous criminals perfectly recognized and safely in their places (as we recall, Bentham even suggests that the prisoners wear identifying masks when observed—"a serious, affecting, and instructive . . . masquerade") is dangerous when believed in—especially when that vision is applied to society: a society with no identifying masks, in which the most powerful threats are mobile, and in which even the smartest watchers are apt to mistake the most basic sensory evidence. In *The Conversation*, all of the technology in the world does not save Caul from misinterpreting the simplest data: no surveillance agent or programmer approaches his or her task without bias or (potentially fatal) preconceptions.

Ultimately, the workings of surveillance in the State of Nature can be reduced to a limited set of problems; far more complex and difficult, to our way of thinking, is the interplay between participatory systems and private individuals (that is, individuals *not* participating within systems yet nevertheless drawn into engagement with them). Not coincidentally, this is where some of the shakiest thinking in surveillance studies today is to be found. All encounters between the private and the participatory are inevitably fraught—but however obvious the risks to the individual, the worst dangers are not only, or even predominantly, on that side. Systems try to draw people in, to make them relinquish as much of their absolute, private autonomy as possible; this is often accomplished by laying themselves open ("you're always welcome at the casino/ amusement park/airport"). By the same token, however, individual agents are always trying to game systems (through criminality) or destroy them (through terrorism). The surveillance budget of any system is therefore confronted with an inevitable conflict between inward-turning coercion, aiming at efficiency and improvement, and defensive attempts at empathy. Few surveillance mechanisms—one might again imagine the situation at a casino—are equally adept at both tasks; indeed, the very efficacy of a system's empathetic tactics may subvert its attempts at coercion, or the reverse. As we observed in our introduction, the interaction between a system and the individual comes down finally to a war of narratives—and on the whole, the advantage lies with the latter, who is able to create his or her own story line, which the system must try to anticipate. Or rather, we should again clarify, "systems": the sheer number of participatory systems, often in competition with each other (Wal-Mart and the casino don't willingly share our money, still less Wal-Mart and Target), means that the systems themselves exist, as it were, in the State of Nature with the individual, not the other way around: in our schema, a casino and a casino robber are for all intents simply two interacting "individuals."[56] The watchman lies in pieces. Though the *sharing* of personal information between systems is, and will likely continue to be, a source of concern for lawmakers, the natural *competition* between systems is inescapable—and will often, again, be to the individual's benefit.

Nevertheless, the most typical error in analyzing system-individual interactions is to claim that the latter is simply dominated by the former. One critic, for example, points to the Oyster Card, the travel pass used on the London Underground, as a demonstration of the inescapable reach of the Watchers.

> One . . . experiences . . . a multitude of nebulous demands for identification. . . . Moving quickly through the crowds of the ticket hall . . . a young woman stops to top up her Oyster payment card at a nearby machine. . . . From behind the glass, the *Transport for London* worker taps at the computer keyboard, . . . "I can tell you that you began your journey at Russell Square at 15:20 pm . . . we just need the exit data to complete the transaction."[57]

The fact that our "young woman" could have chosen not to use the Oyster Card and could instead have purchased a single ticket in cash matters little to this sort of argument, which is readily identifiable as paranoid in structure.[58] In fact, as difficult as it is to live outside of the system on a *permanent* basis, it is far easier to escape it in a selective and temporary way than we often suppose. Thus, to conclude our taxonomy with something of a reductio: in 2009, Evan Ratliff, a writer for *Wired* magazine, attempted the impossible—to drop off the grid for a month and remain hidden while thousands of tech-savvy readers tried to track him down. "Disappearing," it turned out, proved less difficult than he had imagined—enough so that he eventually began intentionally letting clues to his location slip in order to level the playing field.[59] In the meantime, his vanishing act involved some resolutely low-tech and commonsense strategies: he used prepaid cell phones; he rode the bus from city to city instead of traveling by air; he disguised his identity (by growing a beard and wearing a Georgia Tech hat). As it happened, the minimizing of one's digital footprint was not just manageable, but instinctive, particularly in socially risky situations. If you want a copy of *Paris, Texas*, you buy it online, with a credit card, and use your loyalty number; if you want a copy of *Debbie Does Dallas*, you use cash—and maybe wear a Georgia Tech hat.

III. TIMELY AESTHETICS

A Smaller Account of Postmodernism
To the extent that aesthetic and cultural theorists share the Oyster Card critic's assumption—that the individual is subsumed or overwritten

entirely by a system understood to be totalizing and omnipresent—we would identify them as similarly paranoid: not *depicting* paranoia, but paranoid in sensibility. Such arguments have a long history predating the experience of contemporary surveillance, most notably in the Marxist tradition—in Gramsci's extension of the notion of false consciousness, in Adorno's and Horkheimer's account of the culture industry and, less formally, in some of Orwell's writings that we discussed last chapter. In our introduction, however, we began to examine how (mainly Foucauldian) ideas about panoptic surveillance, in combination with this older critical tradition, have been deployed to explain formal practices and modes of representation typically thought of as "postmodern." To review: under the conditions of panopticism, it does not ultimately matter whether the inspector (or any of his surrogates in a "surveillance society") is present in the central tower: internalization, which is understood to be universal in such a society, happens anyway. Indoctrination occurs, gaze or no. With the dropping away of a central, legitimating eye (which Baudrillard finally identifies with the eye of God), one is left with only a play of representations and appearances, with nothing to guarantee their actual existence. Thus Peter Weibel: "Representation [enjoys primacy] over reality, the copy over the original, illusion over truth." The spectacular, transient, yet flat and empty aesthetics commonly associated with postmodernism—as Jameson puts it, "a new depthlessness, which finds its prolongation . . . in a whole new culture of the image or simulacrum; [and] a consequent weakening of historicity"—is a direct effect of this loss.[60]

In principle we would disavow any theory that to be true requires the vast majority of people to be stupid. Baudrillard's declaration, in "The Precession of Simulacra," that the "sovereign difference" between the real and the simulation "has disappeared" has identifiable origins in Debord's work on spectacle, as well as—going further back—Adorno's and Horkheimer's famous suggestion (but note the crucial distinction in tense, which makes all the difference) that "real life is becoming indistinguishable from the movies."[61] The line has subsequently been taken up by smart people who should know better; thus Agamben ("In the society of the spectacle [language] reveals the nothingness of all things") or Jameson (postmodernism entails "the transformation of reality into images, the fragmentation of time into a series of perpetual presents").[62]

With numbing regularity, the same examples—usually from pop culture, usually American—are hauled out as evidence of the "hyperreal": the city of Las Vegas, the city of Los Angeles, and, preeminently, anything associated with the Disney corporation. The work of Umberto Eco, itself written in an informal pop style, probably marks the nadir of this tendency. Comparing the animatronic wonders of Disneyland to the outside world, he comments:

> When, in the space of twenty-four hours, you go (as I did
> deliberately) from the fake New Orleans of Disneyland to the
> real one, or from the wild river of Adventureland to a trip on the
> Mississippi, where the captain of a paddlewheel steamer says it
> is possible to see alligators on the banks of the river, and then
> you don't see any, you risk feeling homesick for Disneyland,
> where the wild animals [animatronic alligators] don't have to be
> coaxed. Disneyland tells us that technology can give us more
> reality than nature can.[63]

Not content to shoot fish in a barrel, Eco rakes them with machine-gun fire. In fact, it is probably fair to say that no one has ever (yet) mistaken a Disney robot for the "real thing," let alone Disneyland for the real world—least of all Eco, despite his disingenuous and vague use of the pronouns "us" and "you." The same might be said about the original cave paintings at Lascaux vis-à-vis their reproductions in a nearby museum (Baudrillard's example) or the phenomenon of "'pastness' and pseudohistorical depth, in which the history of aesthetic styles" has purportedly replaced "'real' history" (Jameson's example and scare quotes).[64] Or, finally, the phenomenon of reality TV—the significance of which has entirely, and predictably, been exaggerated—as against real life. (TV "reigns so absolutely that it thereby makes the reality of the home . . . phantomlike and invalid.")[65] Indeed, despite their proclamations about the new reality (or unreality) of simulacra, none of these theorists is able to account, within the theoretical terms he has laid out, for his own undiminished intelligence, his own ability to pierce the veil.

Structurally speaking, this strain of postmodern theory is analogous to anti-liberal political writers' inability to conceive of individual autonomy or dignity apart from the absolute State; it proceeds from the same collapsed monism, turning—in de Certeau's priceless phrase—"the misfortune of their theories into theories of misfortune."[66] In Baudrillard's account, the history of the image passes through four successive phases:

> it is the reflection of a profound reality;
> it masks and denatures a profound reality;
> it masks the *absence* of a profound reality;
> it has no relation to any reality whatsoever: it is its own pure simulacrum. . . .
> . . . The first reflects a theology of truth and secrecy (to which the notion of ideology still belongs). The second inaugurates the era of simulacra and of simulation, in which there is no longer a God to recognize his own, no longer a Last Judgment to separate the false from the true.[67]

To draw such a conclusion is to throw the ontic baby (reality) out with the epistemic bathwater—such nihilism typically being the fate, and mirror image, of a frustrated Platonism. With the loss of the transcendent verifier (ultimately God, but in the past any established state ideology would suffice), *nothing* can be believed in, and the image slides automatically into its demonic anti-type: the normal world looks exactly as it always has, but is understood to be a simulacrum, a sham, under the control of malicious forces. For Baudrillard, a somewhat under-described "capital" usually serves as the all-purpose bogey: "a monstrous, unprincipled enterprise, nothing more. . . . A sorcery of social relations."[68] The individual, exiled from a stable symbolic order, is left powerless, at the mercy of appearances—and, in the inevitable anti-humanist turn, is finally reduced to little more than a simulacrum him-or-herself.[69]

In short, sticking with the terms that we have developed, Baudrillard, Eco, and like-minded theorists of the postmodern are operating within the paranoid uncanny. To the extent that novels, poems, and other forms of aesthetic production exhibit the tendencies these theorists identify as typical of postmodernism (flatness, depthlessness, ahistoricity, a banality that also manages to seem unreal, all with a sense of lurking malice), they too are operating within that mode. Ultimately, we are not concerned to replace one term with another: far more interesting for us is what this paranoid sensibility suggests about postmodern (or whatever one wishes to call it) theory and art. The paranoid uncanny, when it first arose early in the twentieth century (well before the purported advent of postmodernism), had clear political and ethical connotations: as we saw, when analyzing Buchan and the first tradition of the spy novel, it was the expression of far-right sensibility. To see the apparently ordinary world as actually corrupt, illusory, and under the sway of demonic forces—and thus in need of violent and heroic purgation—was the mark of an anti-liberalism that turned easily into outright fascism. This is not to say that Buchan, Conan Doyle, and the like were "postmodernists"; rather, postmodern art and theory were the product of a postwar intellectual elite, most of whom likely nursed lingering leftist (or liberal) feelings but who had nonetheless, in a spirit of disillusionment, acceded to the paranoid structures of thought and feeling native to the right. It is a trail we saw blazed by Orwell at the very end of his career—and one needn't look far to see similar disillusion amidst the leftist elites in 1950s Europe and America, during the general conservative retrenchment of Churchill and Eisenhower, Adenauer and de Gaulle.

It is perhaps telling, though, that literature in this mode has suffered diminishing fortunes—in the United States, at least—during the last decade. The paranoid style will always find an audience: the demographic that made best sellers of *Fu Manchu, Greenmantle,* and *Bulldog Drummond* survives today as fans of *24,* or Tom Clancy's novels, or *Enemy of the State.* So long as there's a large population susceptible to the suspicions and hatreds of paranoia, a paranoid art—generally a pulpish one—will continue to be produced. *Postmodernism,* however—at least postmodernism of the variety that we have been discussing—identifies that period (from war's end to, perhaps, the turn of the twenty-first century) when the adoption of paranoid thinking by the artistic elite—and, it should be added, an erstwhile liberal elite—was intellectually respectable. For the moment at least, this no longer seems to be the case. While "serious" literature in this mode, from Pynchon to Gaddis to Vonnegut, did not follow right-wing pulp into a valorization of violence—and, in contrast to much postmodern theory, often had a sense of humor about its own cynicism—it did, by giving in to the logic of hidden control and total surveillance, tend towards quietism and a sense that human effort (and even human intelligence) ultimately did not matter. "Offhand," the antihero of Pynchon's first novel comments after nearly five hundred pages of dense narrative, "I'd say I haven't learned a goddamned thing."[70] We would not identify a single moment when things changed, or insist on a simple causality, with September 11, 2001, as an axis point in the Zeitgeist; David Foster Wallace's essay "E Unibus Pluram: Television and U.S. Fiction," for example, which is now widely viewed as an early (and itself highly ironic) salvo in the revolt against "postmodern irony," came out in 1993.[71] Nevertheless, it is striking how quickly after the Trade Center attack works in that mode came to seem naïve or *dated*—the attack dealing at least a temporary rebuke both to the quietists and to the believers in an all-pervasive and all-knowing government/corporate surveillance, capable of neutralizing in advance any potential threat.

Whatever the future fortunes of an art of simulacra, self-reflexivity, ahistoricity (and so on), it accords with our larger argument that these forms of representation should, over the long haul, phase in and out of prominence—and that, far from being exclusive to the decades after World War II, they should have a history going back to the paranoid sensibility of the early twentieth century or, even further, to the Renaissance forms of allegory they inevitably evoke. Even Lyotard's work on the postmodern (which still seems to us the most intelligent and humane, and which steers away from specific aesthetic effects to address larger trends in intellectual history), while purporting to be the identification of something new, is, rather, an elaborate exercise in reinvention. The crux of his argument, that the most powerful "Grand Narratives" of European history since the Enlightenment "lost [their] credibility" amidst the disasters of the twentieth century, is surely correct—but only within a Continental European context.[72] The most important of these "metadiscourses"—"the emancipation of the rational or working subject"—is, as we have seen, Rousseauvian in origin. When Lyotard accuses the Habermasian theory of communicative rationality, in which "the rule of consensus [between citizens] is deemed acceptable if it is cast in terms of possible unanimity between rational minds," of rehashing this "narrative," he is identifying Habermas as a latter-day Rousseauvian monist.[73] Fairly or not, that is to say, he is associating "consensus," as Habermas uses the word, with a unanimous general will. Within the Anglo-American tradition, however, this history is largely irrelevant; for Locke, divine right monarchy was a "master narrative" eminently in need of smashing, and the model of consensus he offered in response (which Habermas may be closer to than Lyotard is giving him credit for)—tactical, instrumental, pragmatic, and in no way "emancipatory" or premised on unanimity—did not offer a counter-allegory in replacement.

For this reason, perhaps the most striking aspect of Lyotard's own prescriptions in *The Postmodern Condition* is the way they reinvent Locke—albeit with a French vocabulary and under the influence of the linguistic turn. In place of the grand narratives, Lyotard takes "agonistics [to be] a founding principle [of] social relations"; in other words, people are naturally competitive and pursue different goods.[74] In the "games" people play against each other, therefore, (he acknowledges Goffman as an inspiration) consensus of a Rousseauvian or Habermasian sort is far less important than toleration: "Postmodern knowledge is not simply a tool of the authorities; it refines our sensitivity to differences and reinforces our ability to tolerate the incommensurable."[75] Disavowing the top-down logic of a general will, Lyotard insists, in much the same spirit as de Certeau or Scott, on a "local determinism," in which interactions between individuals are inevitably "the object of a contract, explicit or not, between players (which is not to say that the players invent the rules)"; it is finally this "set of pragmatic rules that constitutes the social bond."[76] The post-structuralist vocabulary does not sound much like Locke in the *Essay on Toleration* or *Second Treatise*—but the sequence of thoughts is similar enough and can similarly be traced to the recent experience of social upheaval and violence. It also perhaps explains the enthusiasm with which Lyotard has been received in an Anglo-American context. An allegorical order is replaced with something tactical, instrumental, pragmatic, and (in contrast to the Hobbesian or Rousseavian social contract) local. That Lyotard (like de Certeau) does not follow Locke into an assertion of natural rights or the autonomy of the individual subject—or, it should be added, into a plausible politics of any kind— means, simply, that he finally is no liberal: the Anglo-American *liberal* tradition, at least, has no place in a political outlook still shaped by the linguistic turn.[77] Nevertheless, the convergent evolution, if we may call it that, is telling: *The Postmodern Condition* and *Second Treatise* may both be seen as responses to a collapsed monism—the Continental collapse occurring more than two centuries after the analogous event in England.

Present-Day Surveillance and the Image

This is not to call Locke a "postmodernist" before the fact, or to identify the liberal tradition in England and America as nascently postmodern. While we challenge the *ways* that most scholars of the postmodern identify aesthetics—or, indeed, the basic conditions of being in the world—as having changed in contemporary life, we do not deny that these conditions have in fact changed. Although we question the role that Baudrillard and his school see surveillance playing in the development of a distinctively postmodern sensibility, we would argue that contemporary surveillance, or the experience of it, *has* brought about the most profound change in the perception of reality since the turn of the nineteenth century—a change affecting nearly every category interesting to modern theory, most notably ontology, aesthetics, and ethics. To state it in the plainest terms: where most attempts to theorize the aesthetic consequences of surveillance concern themselves primarily with its effect on the perception of space—a concern recognizable in theories of the simulacrum, the "hyperreal," and our own delineation of the paranoid uncanny—we would suggest that an equal, if not larger, impact has occurred in the perception of time.

That this impact has largely gone unnoticed is due in no small measure to a blurring of the categories that we have been careful to keep distinct in our own taxonomy of contemporary surveillance. The *spatial* impact of surveillance, that is to say, has largely occurred within closed participatory systems; valuing stability and predictability, they inevitably tend towards allegory, privileging the spatial and the static over the temporal—thus the uncanny effects on everyday perception caused by systemic coercion. In contrast, the *temporal* impact has mostly resulted from what we have been calling surveillance in the State of Nature—a practice that is fundamentally defensive, anticipatory, and preemptive. To get a sense of what we mean by this, consider the following thought experiment. We reproduce, in duplicate, perhaps the single most notorious surveillance-generated image of the last several decades—notorious mainly as an emblem of surveillance that has *failed* catastrophically. Mohamed Atta and Abdulaziz Al-Omari breeze through the security gate at Portland International Jetport (figure 10).

Imagine a situation in which these two images, though physically identical, had radically different origins: that the first was—what in fact it

Figure 10. AP Photo/Portland Police Department.

is—a freeze-frame still, isolated and selected (long after the moment of recording) from a continuous tape loop; while the second was a photograph, the product of a conventional camera poised at exactly the same angle as the closed-circuit device, and snapped by an individual at precisely that moment. If such a situation could be envisioned, the question would naturally present itself: *are the two images the same?* Despite the resemblance, clearly, they would in some ways be profoundly unlike each other—and at least four distinctions present themselves immediately.

First, one might refer to the *temporal structure* of the image. While a photograph clearly belongs to the present—the basic photographic gesture being *pause, moment*—the video still, in Winfried Pauleit's elegant phrase, looks towards a "future perfect."[78] The power of the image comes from an event that has already taken place but which within the still's own time frame is yet to happen; indeed, the motive for isolating this particular moment in the video loop depends on the narrative having already been brought to completion. In this manner, Pauleit's idea of a "future perfect" can be fruitfully contrasted with Barthes's similar-sounding concept of an "anterior future." The experience of looking at any photograph, Barthes concludes towards the end of *Camera Lucida* (1980), is to perceive the inevitable calamity of death. Considering a picture from 1865 of a young man condemned to be hanged, Barthes comments:

> I read at the same time: *This will be* and *this has been;* I observe
> with horror an anterior future of which death is the stake. By
> giving me the absolute past of the pose (aorist), the photograph
> tells me death in the future. What *pricks* me is the discovery of
> this equivalence. In front of the photograph of my mother
> as a child, I tell myself: she is going to die: I shudder . . . *over*
> *a catastrophe which has already occurred.* Whether or not
> the subject is already dead, every photograph is this
> catastrophe.[79]

Despite some superficial similarities between the ways a photograph and a video still look towards the future, the contrasts could not be more striking, the video still—a *surveillant image*, to introduce the term—lacking both the universality and (often) the pathos of the photograph, and deriving its specificity from a completely different source. *Every photograph of a person looks towards a single disaster: death.* The meaning of a video still, on the other hand, originates in a specific event and can only be understood retroactively. Where the photograph is powerful because of what must unavoidably happen, perhaps far in the future, the video still requires the signifying narrative to be *complete*. Indeed, in these terms most video footage has no meaning at all. While the specifying event (if there is one), moreover, might be awful (a terrorist act, for example), it could just as easily be prosaic (a man stealing a can of beer from a bodega): pathos and terror are not necessarily the concomitants of video footage. While the surveillant image, finally, circumscribed and precise, is embedded in a particular narrative structure, the photograph belongs to an earlier, Romantic, aesthetic of the frozen moment: it derives all of its force from the *now* of the apprehensive act and the "anterior future of which death is the stake."

We might pause to review the ways this *narrative structure of the image*—the second distinction we would draw—upends much of the postmodern theory we have been discussing. Recall our parable from the introduction, of Atta and Al-Omari driving to the airport: *filling up their rental car at the Jetport Gas station, taking out money from a local ATM, spending more than twenty minutes wandering the aisles of the local Wal-Mart,* and so on—always anonymous and invisible amidst their enemies and future victims. As we observed in that discussion, though they left behind innumerable traces, a coherent, sequential narrative could be made of those traces only in hindsight—control in a surveillance situation effectively boiling down to control of narrative. To see the miscellanea of everyday life as possessing this temporal structure is to arrive at a view of the image nearly the opposite of Baudrillard's ("history is our lost referential, [having] retreated, leaving behind it an indifferent nebula . . . emptied of references") or Jameson's ("the transformation of reality into images, the fragmentation of time into a series of perpetual presents").[80] To draw a conclusion as they have is, as we have suggested, to apply the essentially spatial, undifferentiating logic of paranoia to the perception of time. If the present is a "hyperreal," characterized by "models of the real without origin or reality," then surely the same may be said of how history is now perceived: all of the past drawn into an eternal Now, and reduced to depthless equivalence.[81] The bombing of Hiroshima, the defenestration of Prague, Nicole and Keith tying the knot: simulacra. If, on the other hand, the images of present life are understood to possess a narrative structure, history reenters the picture with a vengeance: each object shot through with implications about an all too real past and future.

Who, however, is *responsible* for those narratives? To return to our thought experiment: in the case of the photograph, it is (with some necessary provisos) the photographer, who perceives a significance in the moment and, in an aesthetic gesture, arrests it. In the case of the video still—with the narrative content of the image up for grabs and linked inextricably to the struggle for control over a larger narrative, of which the image is only a segment—one cannot be so sure. Pauleit is perhaps too quick to perceive in the video still a communal gaze—though this surely explains the discomfort that can be felt when any one person attempts to use such an image for his or her own purposes. Imagine the uproar, for example, if an album cover or an advertisement for a home security company (or indeed a scholarly publication) made use of the still we have been discussing.[82] In an age, however, when atrocities are performed before surveillance cameras—are *staged* with the surveillance apparatus in mind—one cannot expect the narrative structure of the image (its meaning, its emplotment, its ownership) *ever* to resolve cleanly. The third and, for our purposes, most relevant distinction therefore turns on the *intentional structure* of the image and the implications this has for ethical action. We evoke de Man's pivotal essay "Intentional Structure of the Romantic Image" on purpose: in that piece, de Man identifies the previous significant revolution in the nature of the image—around the turn of the nineteenth century. Romantic imagery, he writes, in contrast to the allegorical structures of the previous age,

> is grounded in the intrinsic ontological primacy of the natural object. Poetic language seems to originate in the desire to draw closer and closer to the ontological status of the object, and its growth and development are determined by this inclination. . . . This movement is essentially paradoxical and condemned in advance to failure. There can be flowers that "are" and poetic words that "originate," but no poetic words that "originate" as if they "were."[83]

For de Man, the fundamental orientation of the Romantic image is towards an object—a Grecian urn, let's say, or a field of daffodils—in the real world, and the desire that spurs the poetic act is ontological. We evoke Wordsworth on purpose as well: in the history that we have been tracing, the development of this kind of image was inseparable from the emergence of a new idea of individual autonomy rooted in privacy—the private, isolated individual providing a ground for the perceived object, and the reverse. That the act is fore-doomed by the referential nature of language is a conclusion that will be familiar to readers of de Man and the legions of critics influenced by him; language is "able to posit regardless of presence but, by the same token, unable to give a foundation to what it posits except as an intent of consciousness."[84] With much of the same attendant pathos, Barthes draws a similar conclusion about the photograph when he observes, "Reference . . . is the founding order of Photography."[85] The surveillant image, in pointed contrast, is not fundamentally ontological, it is not directed first and foremost towards the world of things: its primary referential orientation is temporal, a fact that, counterintuitively, pushes it back towards allegory of a very peculiar kind, one we have not yet encountered in this study.

This move from the problem of *presence* to the problem of *narrative* affects, finally, what we could term the *ethical structure of the image*. While a closed-circuit camera is not without purpose—someone obviously put it there with the intention of either dissuading criminals or catching them, though usually after the fact—the camera itself is powerless to intervene in the moment of recording, and, as we have seen, the persons watching are often distracted or unable to grasp what they're seeing. If anything, as we also have noted, the "purpose" of the image may be the work of the observed—a possibility that grows in proportion to the observed person's awareness of the recording apparatus. The photographer, on the other hand, is always confronted with a basic moral dilemma: to get involved or to snap that picture? This crisis is at the heart of Susan Sontag's early arguments about photography as "an act of non-intervention," her point that every photograph of a violent event is a record of the event being allowed to happen.[86] If, to conclude our experiment, the image from the Portland Jetport had in fact been a conventional photograph, one may be sure that the F.B.I. would have been interested in talking with the cameraman: what precisely had he or she found significant at that instant? And why had he or she failed to stop the two men or alert security?

That the video still is only the record of our impotence, however, does not rob it entirely of moral implications. Paradoxically, the ethically compromised position of the photographer *makes possible* the more detached, aesthetic experience of the viewer. That is to say: by the time a photograph reaches an audience in cold print, the immediate moral crisis it records has passed—and this opens the door for a more detached appreciation. When Barthes contrasts the *studium* (essentially, the meaning) of a photograph from its *punctum* (the aesthetic experience he gets from viewing it), he is recognizing this curiosity:

> [The *punctum* breaks] the *studium*. This time it is not I who seek
> it out (as I invest the field of the *studium* with my sovereign
> consciousness), it is this element which rises from the scene,
> shoots out of it like an arrow and pierces me. . . . A photograph's
> *punctum* is that accident which pricks me (but also bruises me,
> is poignant to me).[87]

The *punctum*, significantly, is random and most often in direct contradiction to the intended meaning of the image; for example, when looking at a sentimental photograph of New York's Little Italy, Barthes identifies the *punctum* as the bad teeth of one small child.[88] It is precisely this randomness and interpretive freedom, however, that the surveillant image restricts—indeed, it forecloses on the notion of a *punctum* altogether, as the entire work of isolating and then understanding the image is subsumed into the struggle over narrative content. When one views the video still from Portland, one's only *appropriate* reaction is "those are the men who will cause the 9/11 disaster"; if one experiences aesthetic delectation of some other kind—if one is "pricked" by, say, the color of the carpet—one has had a *perverse* reaction to the image. To put it another way: just as the ethical crisis of the photograph makes possible the aesthetic experience of the viewer, so the neutrality of the video still *displaces* the ethical crisis of the image—over its proper interpretation— *onto* the viewer, disallowing a freer aesthetic response. We may pause here, then, to observe some basic distinctions between the older and newer kinds of image:

ROMANTIC IMAGE (AFTER DE MAN)	SURVEILLANT IMAGE
The moment frozen in time	The moment isolated and selected in retrospect
Ontological Intention (Presence)	Temporal Orientation (Narrative)
Ethics of Intervention (the artist)	Ethics of Interpretation (the viewer)
Action	Inaction
Aesthetic detachment possible for viewer	Aesthetic response problematic
The Photograph	The Video Still
The Grecian Urn	The contents of the typist's bedroom

Admittedly, an analysis of the aesthetic image, as such, brings us only so close to our larger claim: that the experience of surveillance has effected a plenary change in the perception—or, one might say, the reading—of everyday reality and has caused certain moral side effects with which society has barely begun to grapple. The next reasonable question to ask, therefore, is: what is it like to exist in a *world* in which everyday objects feel more like "surveillant" than "Romantic" (or, for that matter, conventionally "realistic") images? In the last chapter, we observed the early twentieth-century return of allegorical structures, both in the tradition of progressive liberalism and, far more consequentially, in paranoid politics and art. In the latter, the organizing "singularity" was understood to be at once human and demonic, standing behind appearances and rendering empirical reality a sham. A "surveillant" reality, we would suggest, also has an allegorical quality—though, because of its temporal dimension, this quality is unlike any form of allegory we have encountered. If we return, by way of illustration, to the still from Portland: it was common, in the period following September 11, to look back on the years previous as coded with double meanings. Events that at the time had seemed innocuous, or were simply invisible (for example, an uncommonly high number of young Saudi Arabian men taking flying lessons), now assumed a sinister, if flattened, second sense as counters in a narrative of which no one—or only a few—had been aware, the organizing "singularity" lying in an unsuspected future. In retrospect, one recognized oneself as having lived, without violence to the term, *in* an allegory. But why stop at "having lived?" Wouldn't it be likely that the present was similarly riddled with the signs and tokens of a dire futurity, that we were all the barely adequate readers of submerged narratives that surrounded us on all sides—in short, that the present moment was an allegory without a key? The sheer ubiquity of images akin to the Portland still would only encourage the temptation to look upon the miscellaneous detritus of everyday life as similarly, if obscurely, freighted. The evident similarity to what we called, in chapter 4, "paranoid allegory" should not blind us to some fundamental distinctions. Where paranoid allegory is always present-directed (the unseen Enemy is always to be confronted *now*, his machinations unfolding as we speak), proleptic allegory looks to the future. Because of this, proleptic images escape the inadequacy that de Man and others saw as endemic both to the Romantic symbol and to all earlier forms of allegory. That is, where earlier allegorical systems, including those generated by paranoia, inevitably tottered on the patently artificial relation between tenor (a demonic enemy of near godlike power) and vehicle (the evidence of the senses), and where the Romantic image, because of its very status as discourse, inevitably failed to attain the ontological status of the object, the surveillant image was *always* adequate. But to what? Although paranoid systems inevitably foundered in contradiction, their prescriptions for action were unambiguous: once the enemy had been identified—the Jews, the masons, the liberals—a course of necessary, violent revenge was clear. With prolepsis, however, the singularity was always being deferred. Adequate to what, then? And what, finally, did the unanswerability of this last question mean for the possibility of action?

Pretrauma and Modernist Incompletion

> The best lack all conviction, while the worst
> Are full of passionate intensity.
>
> —W. B. Yeats, "The Second Coming"

Surprisingly, perhaps, it is on this score that literary Modernism comes to our aid; for a variety of reasons, this body of work—and the work of Eliot in particular—comprises the first sustained examination of the moral and intellectual consequences of a surveillant temporality. An analogy may be drawn to our earlier analysis of the development of privacy rights: as in the eighteenth century, when arguments about the self were first worked out *through* poetry, so much of the key thinking about problems of surveillant temporality first emerged *in* the literature of the early twentieth century. Again, this is not simply a case of literature "reflecting" or "expressing" the mood of the times, or of literature merely offering convenient examples of the phenomena under discussion; rather, the Modernists were the first to worry about the temporal problems we now associate with modern surveillance—and to explore their consequences in depth. Though the Modernists, finally, were not thinking primarily *about* surveillance as they worked through issues of prolepsis, they instinctively grasped the ways that these issues implied a monitoring perspective—and drew on the imagery of surveillance to explore them.[89] How, then, to return to the case with which we began the chapter, do we make sense of Tiresias, whose foreknowledge seems to render him culpable in the scene that he witnesses? The easy analogies fail: is he like a closed-circuit camera with foresight? Is he like those photographers who, during the siege of Sarajevo, would camp out at known hot spots waiting for innocent passersby to be shot? Is his inaction a symptom of anomie, an illustration of McLuhan's claim that "the price of eternal vigilance is indifference"?[90] Does he represent, as we wondered at the start, a more thorough breakdown in the relation between knowledge and action that Keenan and others see as an effect of omnipresent surveillance? In fact, we would argue, none of these scenarios quite works; rather, Tiresias's actions (or inactions) have something to do with the condition of being an artist during a time of social unrest and uncertainty—and are best understood as an exploration of the possibility of authority within the peculiar temporal logic we have been discussing. We will, presently, revisit Tiresias and his unwillingness or inability to avert a half-unsatisfying sexual encounter, but would suggest that the most expedient way into the problem is through the analysis of a distinctive *formal* effect of modern literature: incompletion.

Paul Valéry's comment that (in Auden's paraphrase) "a poem is never finished, only abandoned" would have sounded nonsensical to the eighteenth- or nineteenth-century mind; it is hard to imagine Pope, or even Keats (who abandoned as many poems as he finished), agreeing with the underlying sentiment that literary works are *by nature* beyond completion.[91] By the middle of the twentieth century, however, the truth of the comment was widely acknowledged, resulting in a single, basic gesture—"concluding" a work with tropes of unfinishability—that is so pervasive in Modern literature as to be practically invisible.[92] The most common (and commonsensical) explanation of this phenomenon is that, as Eliot would put it, contemporary history has been "an immense panorama of futility and anarchy."[93] Even more dramatically, Benjamin bewails the replacement of "older narration by information, [and] of information by sensation, [reflecting] an atrophy of experience."[94] Given such conditions, leaving a text unfinished becomes a conscious aesthetic, intellectual, and even moral strategy; the polished conclusion, by contrast, is a sign of dishonesty and inadequacy to the times.[95] The merit of this perspective, perhaps, is the way it preserves the stability of unresolved texts; to ascribe fragmentation and chaos solely to conscious experiment, however, risks reading purpose and intention into (what are possibly) profoundly unconscious processes. Not surprisingly, a powerful riposte to the formalist explanation of Modernist incompletion has been offered by contemporary trauma theory: persons who have experienced a catastrophic event compulsively revisit the experience in an attempt to grapple with the reality of death. The aggravating incident, Cathy Caruth observes, is not "fully assimilated as it occurs" but rather "repeats itself, exactly and unremittingly . . . in the nightmares and repetitive actions of the survivor."[96] The "unassimilated nature" of trauma, she continues, has ramifications for the structure of works written by an affected author: when one experiences something horrible (for the Modernists, World War I is but the most spectacular example), the experience can never fully be resolved. Thus, for this school of critics, trauma, as displayed in the unfinished elements of a text (fragmentation, for instance) is the natural result of an inability to bring closure to the past.

An excellent description, one might think, of the ending to *The Waste Land* (London bridge is falling down falling down / *Poi s'ascose nel foco che gli affina* / *Quando fiam uti chelidon*—O swallow swallow [etc.]). Fragments appearing out of any identifiable context, but with uncanny clarity; a numbness or flatness of affect that Freud, in *Beyond the Pleasure Principle*, considered a key symptom of the traumatic sufferer: it is not hard to see why *The Waste Land* has been diagnosed time and again as the work of a traumatized sensibility.[97] And yet—before we can write Eliot a prescription, as it were—something about his conclusion troubles our verdict: the poem's massive gestures of closure (shantih shantih shantih) are destabilized, not by the sense of an unresolved past but by appeals to a future event that will, retroactively, give coherence and shape to all that has passed before and, presumably, repair a fragmented world. "Shall I at least set my lands in order?"—the culminating event, the thunder gathering over Himavant and whatever it forebodes, is deferred to an instant *after* the poem has ended. To put it in terms we have been using, the narrative and temporal structure of Eliot's closing imagery seems to point towards a future perfect. This is an effect for which neither formalist nor psychoanalytic approaches are able to account, focused as they are, respectively, on the moment of the poem's writing and on the author's past.[98] Rather, one might hazard the following generalization: reacting to a series of disasters, of which World War I, again, is but the most spectacular instance, the Modernists essentially invented a new way of perceiving time—not by looking back, but by looking ahead. The present moment is understood to be meaningful only in the context of a profound event which has not yet occurred, the lineaments of which should be perceptible to the well-trained mind but which inevitably escape full certainty. This new temporal sense has certain concrete effects on literary form: images displaying the narrative and intentional structures we have already analyzed at length, a supplanting of hypotaxis by parataxis, and—above all—a sense that even the most aesthetically "complete" work cannot attain full closure in the present moment.[99]

At the risk of paradox, we might call our current condition, which finds this early expression in much Modern literature, *pretraumatic.* Looking back on the faded photos of volunteers waiting to enlist in the Great War, Philip Larkin would comment, "Never such innocence again."[100] The line has been read usually as a lament—and at worst as an exercise in maudlin self-pity—but surely, beyond that, we can hear a tone of steely resolve. Having endured catastrophe after catastrophe, the speaker is determined not to be caught by the next disaster with his pants down—though he cannot know to a certainty what that disaster will entail. In much the same mood, Frost looks towards "a night of dark intent" and concludes that "someone had better be prepared for rage."[101] Past upheavals have conditioned these writers to expect future "singularities"—and the present is imagined as an allegory in the making. The speakers of Eliot's poems of the teens and early twenties are typically feeble old men or anxious young ones, possessed of sensibilities infinitely susceptible to, but powerless before, the onslaughts of experience. In poems like "Gerontion" or "Rhapsody on a Windy Night," one may trace the replacement, as the basis for a poetic, of the Romantic imagination by something closer to mere consciousness. We instantly recognize the world of these poems—paratactic and de-realized, full of obscurely significant details—as akin to the landscapes of Spenser and Langland; as the projections, that is, of an ideology, rather than a naturalistic depiction of time and space.

> And now a gusty shower wraps
> The grimy scraps
> Of withered leaves about your feet
> And newspapers from vacant lots;
> The showers beat
> On broken blinds and chimney pots[102]

The same odd mixture of flatness and resonance is to be found in the contents of the typist's bedroom—or, indeed, in the characters who populate the vignette (properly speaking, the young man carbuncular should be capitalized, as he *would* be in Langland). Of course, Langland's ideological clarity, which might bestow meaning on these details and personages, is absent; if the speaker is to be taken as a figure for the poet, Eliot seems to be saying that in our day and age the best poetry can do is *record* the debris of life as it passes before the mind (or the eyes). As he puts it elsewhere, the poetic process is now a "passive attending upon the event," and the writerly faculty a "mechanism of sensibility," with poets differing from ordinary mortals only in the fineness of their mechanisms.[103]

But what, then, to do about Tiresias? While he suffers from the feebleness of Eliot's earlier narrators, Eliot endows him with prophetic foreknowledge. One suspects that this gesture is, in part, the poet's own recoiling from the implications of "Preludes," "Gerontion," and the rest: proleptic allegory, gesturing towards a *future* coherence that will *retroactively* confer meaning (quite possibly of a horrific kind), allows the Modernist writer to salvage at least a sense of knowingness and authority. The gesture brings with it, however, a perhaps unexpected moral side effect: however fictitious the claim of foreknowledge, it nevertheless carries, rhetorically at least, an acknowledgement of responsibility for what follows. (If one knows that in five minutes' time a toddler will waddle into a busy road and get hit by a car, one can't then simply let it happen.) Paradoxically, the attempt to retain some authority in the face of powerlessness leads to a seeming affirmation of inaction—a *choice* of inaction—as a response to atrocity. The sheer triviality of the tryst in *The Waste Land*, part 3 is indeed a misdirect, with Eliot perhaps trying to squirm out of the ethically impossible corner into which he's backed himself (imagine how differently the scene, and Tiresias's role in it, would read if the young man carbuncular *strangled* the typist). The scene's broader connotations *are* atrocious and thus, probably, the underlying reason for the horror our colleague's student felt. Behind the question *why doesn't Tiresias just do something* lies a sharper discomfort: why has Eliot insinuated into this scene a speaker whose very nature forecloses on any possibility of ethical action? As a surveiller, Tiresias is neither apathetic nor ignorant, nor is he confused by what he sees; rather, inaction seems to be the condition of his foreknowledge. In Eliot's own terms, this condition has turned him from a full-fledged "character" into a mere "spectator." Tiresias may be most interesting to critics of Modernism as a figure for the poet; but as such Eliot, the proleptic allegorist, has thought his way into a malaise, and a kind of moral stupidity, to which surveillance psychology is all too susceptible. In the event, "I, Tiresias" is not a mask Eliot cares to wear much longer. In his next attempt at prophecy, he flees to the group voice of "The Hollow Men," only regaining the first person singular with conversion and submission to an explicitly providential view of the future.

W. B. Yeats, another modern poet with a susceptibility to pretrauma, best indicates why proleptic allegory, as a state of mind or as an approach to reality, is difficult to sustain—unlike paranoia. It also begins to suggest the *limits* of the analogy we have drawn between Modernist poetics and the pretraumatic or proleptic characteristics of the present. For engaged intellects in a time of crisis these attitudes offer a position at once alluring and morally precarious; the awareness that something possibly awful is about to happen (from the "The Second Coming": "*Surely* some revelation is at hand") is undercut by a deeper ignorance ("Surely *some* revelation is at hand") that seemingly disallows conviction. From an artistic perspective, this ambiguity is not inherently despicable; in any case, it sometimes makes for good poems and novels. Indeed, it is in this willingness to accept a stance that disallows conviction—but permits good art—that the Modernists susceptible to pretrauma most clearly show their descent from the decadents. As we saw in chapter 4, by the last decades of the nineteenth century, the dialectical struggle between privacy and observation had resulted in some extreme positions—the ideology of absolute privacy, as articulated by Pater, undercutting communal participation of any kind. For writers invested in this idea of selfhood, in which autonomy implied solitude, but who also retained social commitments, the only "way out" was a kind of magical thinking: the symbolist claims, made by Yeats among others in the 1890s, that solipsistic withdrawal and immense worldly influence—the latter often expressed as fantasies of total surveillance—somehow went hand in hand. Against the failure of these fantasies in the early twentieth century, proleptic allegory could be seen as a retrenching maneuver. By postponing the catastrophic singularity to the future, it preserved the core inheritance of liberalism most important to the decadents: the autonomous individual as the interpretive center of experience. At the same time, through its fundamental ignorance and pervasive irony (the unknown future event ironizing all present actions), the mode was essentially apolitical and quietistic. Proleptic allegory can thus be distinguished from both rightist paranoia and the progressive liberal tradition: just as paranoia preserved the allegorical Will to Power at the expense of allegorical aesthetics, so prolepsis preserved the aesthetics while sacrificing the Will to Power; just as progressivism diminished individual autonomy in order to preserve liberalism's activist program, so prolepsis sacrificed an activist program in order to preserve individual autonomy.

Given the pressures, both moral and intellectual, *towards* conviction—and with it, action—pretrauma readily slides into easier, more reductive habits of thought, like (to be sure) paranoia. Even among those *not* susceptible to paranoia, pretrauma as a condition has fluctuated in appeal; the reason for this can be summed up by a single word: *certainty*. Not the manufactured certainty of paranoia, but a certainty derived from a clear view of where history is leading. With certainty about what lies ahead, narrative closure again becomes possible—one might say inevitable.

When proleptic allegory fades away in this sense, it can always be ascribed to local and limited causes; indeed, the same may happen in our own moment. Samuel Hynes has described a cohort of writers—Auden, Orwell, MacNeice—who came of age too late to participate in World War I, who saw that catastrophe as the defining event of modernity and, with a sense of having missed out, looked forward with an almost perverse excitement towards the next disaster.[104] By the early thirties, it was more or less clear what form that disaster would take, and with certainty, action of the most purposive kind again became possible—witness the participation of Auden, Orwell, and countless others in the Spanish Civil War, as well as a broader generational activism that Orwell, at least, viewed with a certain skepticism. As Hynes remarks, Evelyn Waugh "was the first English novelist to see his own time as a period *entre deux guerres*"—and indeed, *Vile Bodies*, written in 1930, ends with its hero on the field of battle, caught in a second Great War (we use that term advisedly):

> He took out a pipe, filled it, and began to smoke. The scene all round him was one of unrelieved desolation; a great expanse of mud in which every visible object was burnt or broken. Sounds of firing thundered from beyond the horizon, and somewhere above the grey clouds were aeroplanes. He had had no sleep for thirty-six hours. It was growing dark.[105]

The endless expanse, distant thunder, and incipient rain might well recall *The Waste Land*. The similarity in structure, however, only underlines the immense gap in sensibility between Eliot and Waugh: Waugh, for all the World War I iconography, is perfectly certain what to expect next—as is Auden, especially in his poems after 1935; as is Orwell in *Homage to Catalonia;* as is MacNeice at the end of *Autumn Journal*—and with that conviction, the complex dynamic between formal completion and conceptual incompletion, between rhetorical knowledge and practical inaction, comes itself to a close—at least for the period of High Modernism. By engaging with prolepsis on a more abstract plane, however, Eliot suggested the way its mechanisms could operate in the broader culture at any time—as they indeed *have* operated in recent decades. Prolepsis, in other words, was the way of the future.

LIBERAL READING

> Machines will be capable, within twenty years, of doing any work a
> man can do.
> —*Herbert Simon, 1965*[106]

> Watch it closely.
> —*Elizabeth Bishop, "The Monument"*

We began this chapter in a literature classroom; let us conclude there. Although over the course of this study we have engaged with a variety of disciplines, this has not *primarily* been a work of political theory, or sociology, or psychology; rather, taking as its foundational premise the idea that surveillance and literature, as kindred (if different) practices, have light to shed on each other—on each other's histories, modes of operation, ways of grappling, as it were, with the reality principle—it has been, above all, a literary study. Along the way, a second premise, or major claim, emerging from our argument has assumed a weight equal to the first: that the problems of surveillance and literature are mutually relevant to the fate of liberalism. Or at least to liberalism as we have defined it: as an art of instrumental agreements, perched between the equally unacceptable (though more logically consistent) alternatives of absolutism and anarchy, holding as its central values the autonomy of the individual, freedom of action, and mutual toleration. Concerned as they are with discovering the truth about other people, both literature and surveillance speak to these central values, suggesting the limits that may be imposed on them, the degrees to which they may be violated, but also the means by which they may be preserved. To these claims, we would now add—and finish with—a third, which has been only implicit in our argument to this point: that the habits of mind vital for both the survival of these liberal values and the effective practice of surveillance are best nurtured in the liberal arts classroom, if it is worthy of the name. To situate our argument in the broadest terms, then: what does surveillance *tell* literature? What does the study of literature *tell* surveillance?

Surveillant Reading

Surveillance, the monitoring of human activities for the purposes of anticipating or influencing future events, is not the same thing as literature. It does, however, share some of literature's interests (discovering the truth about other people) and is susceptible to some of the same temptations as literature—most notably, trying to coerce or create an inner truth when empathy (full, absolute empathy) inevitably fails. Where the two practices most differ, as human undertakings, is precisely in their relation to future events; and this is, not coincidentally, where surveillance offers its most timely corrective to literary analysis and to much literary theory in general. The proleptic qualities of the surveillant image—its peculiar temporal, narrative, ethical, and intentional structures—are well captured by some Modernist writing; beyond that, however, they are foreign, or even inimical, to ordinary literary practice. Most works of fiction or poetry, by mere virtue of having beginnings and endings, encourage the supposition that time can be arrested, or at least that chunks of time can be cordoned off from the flow and presented more or less intact. This supposition, though untrue, is a necessary first step in any text's production of meaning; to entertain the opposite view is to produce something like the open-ended transcripts of "Gerontion" and "Preludes" or (to a lesser extent) Tiresias's sections of *The Waste Land:* meticulously detailed but courting sheer meaninglessness. In a more fraught way, though for the same reason, the *analysis* of literature often embraces the same suppositions: any literary theory that is invested in hermeneutics will be drawn more to the synchronic, static, stable elements of a text than the ones that cannot be pinned down. This truism is relevant equally to the most conservative formalisms (with their appeals to the "verbal icon" or "well-wrought urn") and the ideologically invested theories that typically appeal to an extrinsic "nonverbal 'outside'" and present themselves as anti-formalist.[107] Theories of the latter sort, as Stanley Fish has put it, are "rhetorics whose usefulness is a function of contingent circumstances. It is ends . . . that rule the invocation of theories, not theories that determine goals and the means by which they can be reached."[108] Psychoanalytic readings of texts will turn those texts into allegories of the truths of psychoanalysis; Marxist readings will turn them into allegories of the class struggle; thus, too, many species of postcolonial, gender, new historicist (etc.) theory. Often enough, this allegorizing tendency is a legacy of the linguistic turn—the essentially static (and, indeed, monist) quality of Saussurean theory (the language frozen and laid open for structural analysis) in no way contradicted by the varieties of post-structuralism that emerged in response to it. Even theories that take historical process as a starting point typically need, in the service of an ideological reading, to embrace the static in order to generate meaning—for example the synchronic slices Raymond Williams recommends in order to reveal the residual or emergent structures of feeling in a given culture.[109]

If the world could actually be frozen in the manner explicitly or tacitly assumed by the kinds of theory under discussion, surveillance would not be necessary. Its eyes always on future actions, surveillance is interpretation in time. For this reason above all, Foucault's attempts to extrapolate from the conditions of the panopticon (in which future actions are controlled and largely predetermined) to a societal condition of "panopticism" could not have been further off the mark. Indeed, to look at the problem from the other direction, the temporal orientation of surveillance has a sizable effect on one's stance towards both interpretation and meaning in general. It is not too much to say, for example, that—whatever the firm lines of distinction we have drawn so far—*all* literary images, and not just the images employed by a handful of Modernist authors, partake *to some extent* of the temporal complexities (narrative, ethical, intentional) that we have associated with surveillant prolepsis. We do not mean to overstate the case: Modernist works foreground and interrogate these proleptic qualities, and the problems that come with them, in ways that other works simply do not; this is on account of historical reasons we have discussed at length. Nevertheless, the experience of surveillance assures us that meaning can never be isolated in any clean way—that it is *always* fluid and contested, a rebuke to the very idea of a single master narrative excluding all other interpretive centers. At the very least, meaning exists within a web of contesting motives and incongruent narratives, to which any one individual has only partial access at any time. To the extent that literary works are gestures made in time—which cannot, actually, be cordoned off from the rest of history—the temporal problems of surveillance, and their implications for interpretation, must apply to literature as well.

More fundamentally, however, surveillance has a tortured relationship with *meaning itself*—and this, too, has consequences for the interpretation of texts. Of the two principal tactics of surveillance—empathy and coercion—we would probably be correct to take empathy as the elder, in a prehistoric or precultural sense. In its empathetic aims, surveillance tries to capture the truth of lived experience, the inner beings of other people. Strictly speaking, this lived experience has no "meaning" at all: it simply *is*. Meaning, at this very early point, would only have become an over-riding concern of surveillance when the purest empathy (inevitably) failed; only at this point—let's call it the dawn of civilization—would *inter-pretation*, attempting to figure out the narratives of others (sympatheti-cally rather than empathetically), have entered the picture. It is also at this point that the more coercive imposition of the watcher's own meanings on the watched, a tendency we have repeatedly identified as allegorical, would have risen to prominence. But in any event, we do not need to construct just-so stories to explain what the histories of *both* surveillance and literature, especially *after* the fall of allegorical culture, have illus-trated with reasonable clarity. Throughout this book we have observed that surveillance and literature are linked most deeply on the *modal* level—and thus, too, the history of their dilemmas. Renaissance allegory, of both the literary and political kinds, had told the truth about other people, a truth consistent with absolute power. In a manner of speaking, it was unconflicted. By contrast, liberalism, with its high valuation of the autonomous individual and its belief in native human dignity, has had a much harder task—hedging itself, with varying success, against both anarchy and absolutism by means of contracts: instrumental agreements. Literature written in the liberal spirit, accordingly, has had the same trouble with meaning that surveillance has had—its deepest empathetic ambitions being essentially hostile to the idea of interpretation; the (inevi-table) failure of these ambitions leading to equally complex tactics and compromises, with allegory, and the imposition of meaning, as the demon in the system: liberalism's Other and constant temptation.

This quandary, in great measure, explains our own procedures: although the ambitions of this book have been theoretical, they have not, by and large, been *hermeneutic*. Our intention, that is to say, has not been to offer yet another *key* by means of which literature and culture might be unlocked, yet another way of allegorizing the social or aesthetic text. Such approaches have their place—we do not mean to dismiss them, and they certainly make possible productive analytical work by many people—but they conflict, finally, with our aim to identify and develop a distinctly liberal approach to reading. For us, this has meant paying attention to the

complex, if unspoken, instrumental agreements underlying the production of literature, and specifically the author/reader relation; it has meant,
too, taking account of the stakes each time those agreements have been
modified, stretched, betrayed—or fulfilled. On the face of things, this
method could seem quite close to rhetorical, reader-centered approaches
to literature (of a Stanley Fish, say)—yet, in their concern with authoritative interpretation (even the collective interpretations of communities),
such theories are no closer to our position than more overtly ideological
schools. Nor are we principled relativists— in the manner of the earlier
Fish. To throw the locus of meaning entirely on the reader is as far
from our intentions as submitting all meaning to a Mighty Explanation—
ideological and rhetorical theories echoing, in contemporary garb, the
age-old opponents of liberalism: absolute authority and pure chaos.

Rather, the complex agreements that underpin the author/reader
relation inevitably impose constraints upon interpretation—and the
violation or modification of these agreements carries both political and
moral weight. For this reason, our focus has ultimately been less on readerly perceptions (our greatest point of difference from the theoretical
school to which we are perhaps closest in feeling: the phenomenological
criticism of Wolfgang Iser and Hans Robert Jauss) than on *authorial
tactics:* how does literature, promising to make sense of the human experience, establish agreements with its readers and then work within or
flout those agreements? What are the consequences when literature
makes, keeps, or breaks an implicit promise? Over the course of this
book, this attention has produced a series of targeted and, in the exact
sense, historical analyses: our account of conventional realism and the
connections between empirical methods and readerly belief; the development of privacy theory through poetic arguments about autonomy; the
slow stretching of conventional realism to admit modalities essentially
foreign or hostile to it; the eruptions of the subgenres, often at the service
of reinvigorated allegorical thinking; the political ironies of the paranoid
uncanny; and so on. We would suggest, however, that liberal reading, of
the sort that we have outlined, is a generalizable method—albeit in a
less obvious way than a new hermeneutic or ideological theory
("Surveillancism") would be. Less *easy,* too: liberal reading does not begin
with conclusions and then search a cultural or literary text for confirming
details; instead, it involves determining and analyzing the parameters a

work of literature establishes as a condition of its own production, and accounting for the reasons why the work manages to live within those parameters, or not. In this sense, perhaps, the practical applications of liberal reading will always be "local." Though our own liberalism, by this point, should be fairly obvious, we would also suggest, finally, that our method has, at best, an ambiguous relation to judgment. Our conviction that liberalism, perched between the absolutism of enforced belief and the chaos of nihilism, is the "best" position—albeit a logically vulnerable one—does not necessarily imply a preference for the genres that hew most closely to those beliefs (realistic novels, say, or Wordsworthian lyric). It does not imply an aesthetic preference, at all events—and a moral preference, if one exists, goes no further than personal beliefs. It *does* imply, however, and most importantly, that all texts, as human documents, as salvos in the truth-finding, truth-making enterprise of life, require close watching—equally.

Readerly Surveillance

And so we end in the literature classroom, where that attention, one would hope, is paid more concertedly and rigorously than anywhere else. As should also be clear by now, it is also where we believe the training of minds adequate to grapple with the problems of contemporary surveillance is most likely to take place. So long as these problems, in both academic and journalistic discourses, continue to be presented as matters of efficiency, to be solved through better management, or as problems of technology, to be solved through better tools, the role of the liberal arts classroom will go unrecognized. Indeed, the great hope of "smart surveillance," as it has somewhat wishfully been dubbed, is the final engineering of objective, systematized data-recognition processes independent of human intelligence—the purest of pure sciences. Au courant buzzwords like "fuzzy logic," "strong AI," or "affective computing" evoke the idiosyncrasies of human thought precisely to exorcize them—even as the idiosyncrasies of the programmers are casually ignored. Meanwhile, the chief lines of critique or resistance to the worst excesses or misapplications of surveillance concede the logic in advance by largely adopting the same technocratic language; thus the promise of "affective computing," to detect untruth by distinguishing between eleven basic human emotions (as revealed by facial tics), is echoed by Gary Marx's helpful list of "eleven behavioral techniques of neutralization intended to subvert the collection of personal information" (for example, "distorting"—by sucking on a penny before taking a breathalyzer test).[110] Perhaps computers will finally determine a way of correlating head bumps to ambition or degeneracy— and the professional resisters find ways (involving plasticine, perhaps) to evade them. In our introduction, we wondered what place literary studies has in a field so configured—and our answer remains the same: none worth occupying, and so much the worse for the field.

Interpretation, narrative, readership, persona, motivation, discourse, character, close reading, empathy, authorship, intention, representation. Literary studies naturally lacks the purported objectivity of science; indeed, this is its strength, human thought being fundamentally ineffi- cient, disorderly, illogical—and susceptible to intuitive leaps for precisely those reasons. To the extent that both the initiators and the targets of surveillance remain human, the human arts will remain relevant to understanding the stakes in any surveillance situation: understanding what it means, as Bishop commands, to watch something "closely," to watch it well, and also to recognize the complexities of watching. These imperatives are of practical value—but, once again, we would not wish our contentions to be misunderstood: the humanities offer no magic key to either the problems faced by surveillance experts or the challenges of those under watch. Just as our literary-theoretical approach refuses alle- gorizations of the text, so the lessons of liberal reading do not point towards a new, infallible surveillance technology: no "Surveillancism," then—and no Literature-Inspired Surveillance Protocol either. Having, we hope, debunked certain naïve claims when made by the hard sciences, we will not commit the same error ourselves: reading T. S. Eliot will not help with tasks at which facial recognition software, "strong AI," or phrenology have failed.

Rather, the tasks and insights that literary study makes possible lie altogether elsewhere. Literary texts are, among other things, attempts to grapple with, without ever solving, the problem of being human—a problem with moral, ontological, political, ethnic, erotic, epistemic, (etc.) dimensions. While exposure to the humanities will not necessarily make one a better person (Stalin loved Mozart, Goebbels did his Ph.D. in eighteenth-century drama), *lack* of exposure will almost certainly leave one comparatively narrow; as a teacher, one hopes that one's students' experience of reading will nurture their capacities for empathy and the appreciation of difference, that it will leave them unafraid of ambiguity and of the questions of life that cannot, finally, be answered; that it will make them aware of the extent to which the world around them is a *human* world—the product of human thought, creativity, and effort—and thus awaiting their own contributions to it. The rhetorical devices and formal techniques that literature develops in its grappling with life are not "life itself"; all the same, the "metacognitive" capacities (to use the vogueish term) nurtured by careful attention to these devices and techniques are undoubtedly transferable outside the realm of the text. Just as a liberal reader, encountering a novel or poem, understands not merely *what* he or she is reading (a work's genre, its modality, its narrative structures, and so on) but also *how* the act of reading is embedded in a network of motives and agreements tacit or otherwise, so a reader thus trained can recognize the world itself as a play of representations and modalities, of conflicting narratives, some of them side plots, some major story lines. Such a knowledge is useful not only for the surveillance agent—who must not confuse his or her narration of any given situation for the narratives of those under watch, and who allegorizes the world at his or her own peril—but also for anyone charged with negotiating the manifold spheres of surveillance (systemic or otherwise) that constitute both civic and private life. Which is to say, everyone.

For reasons all too easy to apprehend, some of the loudest challenges to this view of the humanities as *practical* have come not from scientists (who, when not simply indifferent to the work of the humanities, are often its most fervent supporters), but from writers in fields immediately adjacent: next-door neighbors to the humanities, as it were—sometimes erstwhile or panicked humanists attempting to annex the supposed prestige of the sciences to their own work, sometimes social scientists who, with the best of intentions, perceive the brightest future hopes for the humanities to lie with the efficiencies of the market. Thus—an example of the first tendency, drawn from any number of like-minded pieces—a classicist turned expert on "new" media:

> One consequence of the networking of culture is the
> abandonment of the ideal of high culture (literature, music, the

fine arts) as a unifying force. . . . As our written culture becomes a vast hypertext, the reader is free to choose to explore one subnetwork or many, as he or she wishes. It is no longer convincing to say that one subject is more important than another. . . . The computer provides the only kind of unity now possible in our culture: unity at the operational level. . . . From this perspective, cultural literary [*sic*] does not require a knowledge of traditional texts; instead . . . this operational definition is now making cultural literacy synonymous with computer literacy. [In the future] there will be a large market for the electronic equivalents of how-to books and interactive romances, science fiction, and other genres. Small groups will read and write "serious" interactive fiction and non-fiction. Tiny networks of scholars will conduct esoteric studies in ancient and modern literature and languages [etc.].[111]

As with any work of speculation or prophecy, these contentions are non-falsifiable in the moment of their uttering (in this case, the early nineties). The fact, moreover, that several of these predictions have turned out to be demonstrably incorrect (the "hypertext" has not replaced older models of reading, and we are still, mercifully, awaiting those "interactive romances") in no way compromises the polemic: had the book been written today, it would doubtless make similar claims, equally impossible to disprove, on behalf of Facebook or YouTube.[112] Joining the chorus welcoming a "networked society," in which no subject "is more important than another," the author nevertheless concludes that the ancient role of art, already reduced to a set of "esoteric studies," "must now be abandoned"—the intellectual glibness fully exposed by the claim of necessity.[113] On consideration, this would mean "abandoning" quite a bit: in addition to losing a "cultural literacy" not subsumable under "computer literacy," it would also mean destroying the conditions under which empathetic readers and social participants are produced. It is the empathetic reader, finally, made aware of the way his or her actions occur within a "network" (to use our author's term of art) of narratives and motives, tacit and overt agreements, who is best suited to navigate a *human* world. In this light, it is telling that the author's early examples of "connected" groups and communities (MOOs, MUDs, etc.) have developed into what one might term "selfish" media: although Google+, Twitter, and the like are commonly referred to as "social," their appeal lies in facilitating the presentation of a painstakingly edited and compulsively updated version of the self to a large audience. Given that this version of the self is created within strictly controlled and coercively surveilled corporate parameters, the similarity of these outlets for self-expression to earlier expressive media (like poetry, say) can be overstated.[114] We suspect, in short, that "new media studies" will fall far short of its potential so long as close-minded and unthinkingly deterministic attitudes predominate. To the extent that "new" media come to satisfy the empathetic needs supplied by the "traditional" humanities, the role of art will (necessarily) *not* be redefined; contrarily, to the extent that "new" media do not satisfy these needs, "traditional" art will (necessarily) be anything but an "esoteric study."[115]

For the moment, in any case, the site where powers of attention and empathy are most rigorously nurtured and concentrated remains what it has been for more than a century: the humanities classroom. Indeed, it is hard to imagine the *kind* of intuitive leap experienced by our colleague's student, troubled by Tiresias's inaction, occurring in any other institutional context. The question going forward, unfortunately, is how much longer the pedagogy that encourages such thinking will be permitted to continue. Whatever the loud proclamations of the occasional lapsed humanist, the humanities face a far more severe, though quiet and subtle, challenge from the second locus of critique: the culture of assessment and quantifiable learning goals that has overspread the nation in recent decades. Against a backdrop of constant pressure to increase "STEM" funding, a fretting over the perceived paucity of students taking engineering or computer science courses, an alarmed concern over the rigor of Chinese high-school physics classes (and so on), the humanities are viewed as indulgences, impractical, useless. The only way to "save" the humanities, therefore, is to quantify their content in narrowly practical terms—usually defined as a set of concrete skills—and to make them pay. Lyotard caught these attitudes at an early stage and deftly identified their deepest motives:

> The performativity criterion has its "advantages." It excludes in
> principle adherence to a metaphysical discourse; it requires the

renunciation of fables; it demands clear minds and cold wills; it replaces the definition of essences with the calculation of interactions; it makes the "players" assume responsibility not only for the statements they propose, but also for the rules to which they submit those statements in order to make them acceptable. It brings the pragmatic functions of knowledge clearly to light, to the extent that they seem to relate to the criterion of efficiency: the pragmatics of argumentation, of the production of proof, of the transmission of learning, and of the apprenticeship of the imagination. . . . Such behavior [uses terror]. . . . By terror I mean the efficiency gained by eliminating, or threatening to eliminate, a player from the language game one shares with him. He is silenced or consents, not because he has been refuted, but because his ability to participate has been threatened. . . . The decision makers' arrogance . . . consists in the exercise of terror. It says: "Adapt your aspirations to our ends—or else."[116]

The culture of assessment (which adheres to what Lyotard would call the "performativity criterion") is ultimately in the interests of a society envisioned as managerial, bureaucratic, systemic—what progressivism is often accused of, but without progressive ideals—a society in which "efficiency" replaces "metaphysical discourses" (like those at the heart of liberalism: the autonomy of the individual, an abstract ideal of social justice, etc.). The path to such a society is all too clear—and is to be found in the fetishization of incessant testing and measuring, which has already taken over primary and secondary education in this country, and which the demands of accreditors and legislatures are now extending into higher academia. Within the terms that we have developed, the assessment culture—rooted, indeed, in a distinctly contemporary species of anti-liberalism (a.k.a. "neoliberalism")—is identifiable readily as systemic surveillance at its most authoritarian, allegorical, and involuntary: the educational system reimagined not as a source of autonomous free thinkers but as a "coercive testing regime" and generator of cogs in a well-functioning machine. It is a form of surveillance, ultimately, whose aim is to render the adequate critique of surveillance, or indeed of any aspect of the system, impossible. That the processes of incessant testing have only produced better test-takers, while severely hobbling students in most other respects, is, in this light, not a fault of assessment culture but its signal achievement.[117]

It is not, finally, in the interests of a liberal, democratic society to accede to this logic. The premises underlying humanities training are indeed "metaphysical"—one might even say that they are "fables." In any case, they are—like liberalism itself—articles of faith. In opposition to a political and national culture increasingly bent on the measurable, on the efficient, the humanities offer a promise that might seem quixotic: that the pursuit of intellectual interests not *obviously* practical will render students, not less, but *more* fit to recognize and therefore deal effectively with the complexities of the world. *A young woman, in her first year of college, takes a literature course, and there encounters a long twentieth-century poem that first baffles her, then disturbs her deeply, and finally leads her to a question about knowledge and action—a question unresolved by either the instructor's fumbling answers or the poet's own notoriously arcane attempts at (or satires of) explanation; a question, one would hope, undeterred by the smiles of her more polished classmates. Over against the content received from other courses this young woman may be taking to fulfill her Gen. Ed. require-ments—Intro to Stats, perhaps, or Personal Health—it is hard to make a case for the applicability of her question;* and yet there is no effective citizenship where such questions go unasked. To be a liberal citizen is to possess a readerly understanding of one's place in society: one's interpretive centrality balanced by empathetic generosity, a respect for other interpre-tations, and an ability to anticipate and respond to the thoughts of others. The truth about those other people may never be obtainable in full—a lesson that both surveillance and literature teach even as they forget or ignore their own wisdom. An act of forgetting that amounts to both a statement of belief and a practical imperative: to *see* liberally is finally to take the autonomy of others as a given, whatever (statistical) problems or conceptual paradoxes that leads to—not a Young Man Carbuncular, but a young man, carbuncular. A man driving to the airport . . .

NOTES

INTRODUCTION

1. The number of books on surveillance published recently is almost literally beyond counting. A selective bibliography might include, among studies from a sociological or political perspective (some intended for a broad audience, others more specialized): David Brin, *The Transparent Society: Will Technology Force Us to Choose Between Privacy and Freedom?* (Reading, MA: Addison-Wesley, 1998); Jeremy W. Crampton, *The Political Mapping of Cyberspace* (Chicago: University of Chicago Press, 2003); Amitai Etzioni, *The Limits of Privacy* (New York: Basic Books, 1999); Oscar Gandy, Jr., *The Panoptic Sort* (Boulder, CO: Westview Press, 1993); John Gilliom, *Overseers of the Poor: Surveillance, Resistance, and the Limits of Privacy* (Chicago: University of Chicago Press, 2001); Richard Hunter, *World without Secrets* (New York: John Wiley and Sons, 2002); David Lyon, *The Electronic Eye: The Rise of Surveillance Society* (Minneapolis: University of Minnesota Press, 1994); John Parker, *Total Surveillance: Investigating the Big Brother World of E-Spies, Eavesdroppers and CCTV* (London: Judy Piatkus, 2000); Charles J. Sykes, *The End of Privacy: Personal Rights in the Surveillance Society* (New York: St. Martin's Press, 1999); Reg Whitaker, *The End of Privacy: How Total Surveillance Is Becoming a Reality* (New York: New Press, 1999). Richard Blum's collection *Surveillance and Espionage in a Free Society* (New York: Praeger, 1972) is a classic political study. The humanities, excluding philosophy, are largely absent from the conversation. One notes, however, John McGrath's *Loving Big Brother: Performance, Privacy and Surveillance Space* (London: Routledge, 2004) and Ann Gaylin's *Eavesdropping in the Novel from Austen to Proust* (Cambridge: Cambridge University Press, 2002). The most important contribution to surveillance studies in art theory is surely Thomas Y. Levin,

Ursula Frohne, and Peter Weibel, eds., *CTRL [SPACE]: Rhetorics of Surveillance from Bentham to Big Brother* (Cambridge: MIT Press, 2002). Several essays from this collection are noted separately below. Among books devoted to the technical questions surrounding contemporary surveillance one notes: Joel McNamara, *Secrets of Computer Espionage* (Indianapolis: Wiley, 2003); Julie K. Petersen, *Understanding Surveillance Technologies* (Boca Raton: CRC Press, 2001); Bruce Schneier and David Banisar, eds. *The Electronic Privacy Papers: Documents on the Battle for Privacy in the Age of Surveillance* (New York: Wiley, 1997). Surveillance, of course, is a standby of the mass media, but the *New York Times Magazine* has been particularly invested, publishing several essays by the legal scholar Jeffrey Rosen (in, for example, the October 7, 2001, and April 14, 2002, issues) and devoting the entire December 3, 2006, issue to the problem.

2. Sykes, 69.

3. Thomas Y. Levin, "Rhetoric of the Temporal Index: Surveillant Narration and the Cinema of 'Real Time,'" in Levin, Frohne, and Weibel, eds., *CTRL [SPACE]*, 578–79.

4. *Enemy of the State*, directed by Tony Scott (Burbank, CA: Touchstone Films, 1998).

5. For detailed box office data, see http://www.boxofficemojo.com/movies/?id=enemyofthestate.htm.

6. A recent article in the *Chronicle of Higher Education* provides a good survey of the field as it presently stands: Peter Monaghan, "Watching the Watchers," *Chronicle of Higher Education*, March 17, 2006, A18–A25.

7. Carole Cadwalladr, "Singularity University: Meet the People Who Are Building Our Future," *Observer*, April 29, 2012.

8. While the panopticon was one of Jeremy Bentham's projects, he got the idea from his brother Samuel, who had come up with the model while staying in Russia. See, for example, Janet Semple, *Bentham's Prison: A Study of the Panopticon Penitentiary* (Oxford: Clarendon Press, 1993), 105.

9. Jeremy Bentham, "Panopticon; or, The Inspection House," in *Works of Jeremy Bentham*, ed. John Bowring, 11 vols. (Edinburgh: William Tait, 1843; rpt. New York: Russell and Russell, 1962), 4:39–40. Further references will be to this edition.

10. Michel Foucault, *Discipline and Punish*, trans. Alan Sheridan (New York: Vintage, 1977), 101. All future references are from this edition.

11. In a passage that addresses Bentham directly, Foucault summarizes the idea of internalization as he understands it: "Hence the major effect of the Panopticon: to induce in the inmate a sense of conscious and permanent visibility that assures the automatic functioning of power. . . . He who is subjected to a field of visibility, and who knows it, assumes responsibility for the constraints of power; he makes them play spontaneously upon himself; he inscribes in himself the power relations . . . he becomes the principle of his own subjection" (202–3).

12. Foucault comments: "On the whole, therefore, one can speak of the formation of a disciplinary society . . . that stretches from the enclosed disciplines . . .

to an indefinitely generalizable mechanism of 'panopticism.' . . . A few years after Bentham, Julius gave this society its birth certificate. . . . Speaking of the panoptic principle, he said that there was much more there than architectural ingenuity: it was an event in the 'history of the human mind.' . . . Julius saw as a fulfilled historical process that which Bentham had described as a technical programme. Our society is one not of spectacle, but of surveillance. [From the position of the centralized observer] 'no part of the Empire is without surveillance, no crime, no offence, no contravention that remains unpunished, and that the eye of the genius who can enlighten all embraces the whole of this vast machine, without, however, the slightest detail escaping his attention' " (216–17).

13. For example, Whitaker, 139–88, or Crampton, 171–88.

14. Consider the numerous articles in the *New York Times* that unconsciously borrow from Foucault's theory, e.g., John Schwartz, "Bombings in London: Surveillance; Cameras in Britain Record the Criminal and the Banal," *New York Times*, July 23, 2005; Iver Peterson, "Our Towns; City's Artists Are Its Pride, And a Pain," *New York Times*, May 23, 1999.

15. Zygmunt Bauman, *Society under Siege* (London: Polity, 2002), 40, 89.

16. Gilles Deleuze, "Postscript on Control Societies," in Levin, Frohne, and Weibel, eds., *CTRL [SPACE]*, 318.

17. Miran Božovič, Introduction, *Jeremy Bentham: The Panopticon Writings* (London: Verso, 1995), 2.

18. Peter Weibel, "Pleasure and the Panoptic Principle," in Levin, Frohne, and Weibel, eds., *CTRL [SPACE]*, 211.

19. Jean Baudrillard, "The Precession of Simulacra," in *Simulacra and Simulation*, trans. Sheila Faria Glaser (Ann Arbor: University of Michigan Press, 1994), 5–6.

20. To give one of many: http://www.whatreallyhappened.com/hijackers_video. html—where viewers are encouraged to analyze the footage with various conspiracy theories in mind.

21. See, for example, Timothy Druckrey, "Secreted Agents, Security Leaks, Immune Systems, Spore Wars," in Levin, Frohne, and Weibel, eds., *CTRL [SPACE]*, 151. Cf. also Parker, 65.

22. Druckrey, 152.

23. Bentham, "Panopticon," 66.

24. The case is cited by Jeffrey Rosen in "A Watchful State," *New York Times Magazine*, October 7, 2001.

25. Consider the future career of a rebel prisoner held in an actual panopticon prison from 1953–55: Fidel Castro. Castro was held in the Presidio Modelo on Isla de la Juventud/Isle of Pines, Cuba, which was built, in classic circular panoptic style with central observation tower, in 1928.

26. T. W. Adorno and Max Horkheimer, *Dialectic of Enlightenment*, trans. Edmund Jephcott (Stanford: Stanford University Press, 2002), esp. 1–63. Jürgen Habermas, *The Structural Transformation of the Public Sphere: An Inquiry into a Category of Bourgeois Society*, trans. Thomas Burger with the assistance of

Frederick Lawrence (Cambridge: MIT Press, 1989). Max Weber, *The Protestant Ethic and the Spirit of Capitalism*, trans. Talcott Parsons (London: Routledge, 1930).

27. Extended treatments of the theme of spectatorship in the work can be found in *Renoir at the Theatre: Looking at La Loge*, ed. Ernst Vegelin van Claerbergen and Barnaby Wright (London: Courtauld Gallery, 2008); Charles Harrison, *Painting the Difference: Sex and Spectator in Modern Art* (Chicago: University of Chicago Press, 2005), esp. 31ff.; Griselda Pollock, *Vision and Difference: Feminism, Femininity and Histories of Art* (London: Routledge, 1988), esp. 108ff.

28. Virginia Woolf, "Mr. Bennett and Mrs. Brown," in *The Captain's Death Bed and Other Essays* (New York: Harcourt Brace, 1950), 96.

CHAPTER I. THE RETREAT OF ALLEGORY

1. William Shakespeare, *Othello*, I.i.49–65. *Riverside Shakespeare*, 2d ed., ed. G. Blakemore Evans and J. J. M. Tobin (Boston: Houghton Mifflin, 1997), 1252. All future references are to this edition.

2. Cf. Lacey Baldwin Smith, *Treason in Tudor England: Politics and Paranoia* (Princeton: Princeton University Press, 1986), 67.

3. Stephen Greenblatt, *Renaissance Self-Fashioning from More to Shakespeare* (Chicago: University of Chicago Press, 1980), 236.

4. Angus Fletcher, *Allegory: The Theory of a Symbolic Mode* (Ithaca: Cornell University Press, 1960), 2. *Agoreuein*, which, as Fletcher explains, gives us the second half of the word allegory, connotes public, open, declarative speech. This sense is inverted by the prefix *allos*. Thus allegory is often called 'inversion.' E.g., ed. Thomas Cooper, in Thomas Elyot, *Bibliotheca Eliotae: Eliotes Dictionarie* (London, 1559): '*Allegoria*—a figure called inversion, where it is one in woordes, and an other in sentence or meaning.' "

5. Ibid.

6. Ibid., 120; See also Gordon Teskey, *Allegory and Violence* (Ithaca: Cornell University Press, 1996), 163.

7. Indeed, the book was first rejected by the Dial Press with the explanation that it was "impossible to sell animal stories in the U.S.A" (Orwell to Leonard Moore, *The Collected Essays, Journalism and Letters of George Orwell* [New York: Harcourt, 1968], 4:110).

8. C. S. Lewis, in *The Allegory of Love: A Study in Medieval Tradition* (Oxford: Oxford University Press, 1936), offers a classic articulation of this position: Chrétien "can hardly turn to the inner world without, at the same time, turning to allegory. . . . It would not surprise us if Chrétien found some difficulty in conceiving the inner world on any other terms. It is as if the insensible could not yet knock at the doors of poetic consciousness without transforming itself into the likeness of the sensible: as if men could not easily grasp the reality of moods and emotions without turning them into shadowy persons. . . . When Lancelot hesitates before mounting the cart, Chrétien represents his indecision

as a debate between *Reason* which forbids, and *Love* which urges him on. A later poet would have told us directly . . . what Lancelot was feeling: an earlier poet would not have attempted such a scene at all." Lewis, 1, 30.

9. See Lewis, 48.

10. Walter Benjamin, *The Origin of German Tragic Drama,* trans. John Osborne (London: NLB, 1977). The term "singularity" is deployed by Teskey: "A poetics of allegory can achieve stability only by grounding itself on an unambiguous determination of the 'other' in the word *allegory* as that to which the discourse refers, the ideal 'meaning.' This determination is formalized in poetics as what I call the *singularity,* the ineffable presence into which, it is supposed, everything in the allegorical work ultimately is drawn. The singularity operates in an allegory as does the vanishing point in a linear perspective: it is never visible itself, but everything that *is* visible directs the eye toward it." Teskey, 5.

11. In this sense, allegory is a more honest form of expression than symbolism, which pretends to adequacy: where the critic needs to deconstruct a symbolist poem, allegory obligingly deconstructs itself—thus foregrounding something true about discourse and the world. As J. Hillis Miller puts it: "What seems specific to allegory is a larger degree of manifest incompatibility between the tenor and the vehicle than we tend to expect in symbol, where the 'material' and 'spiritual' meaning are thrown together, as the name suggests, with some implication of overlapping, consubstantiality, or participation. In allegory the one does not directly suggest the other. . . . In allegory, writing and personification reveal . . . the eternal disjunction between the inscribed sign and its material embodiment." J. Hillis Miller, "The Two Allegories," *Allegory, Myth, and Symbol,* ed. Morton W. Bloomfield (Cambridge: Harvard University Press, 1981), 357, 365. See also Paul de Man, *Allegories of Reading* (New Haven: Yale University Press, 1979).

12. Fletcher, 22. Compare Maureen Quilligan, *The Language of Allegory: Defining the Genre* (Ithaca: Cornell University Press, 1979), 24 et passim.

13. Jacob Burckhardt, *The Civilization of the Renaissance in Italy,* trans. S. G. C. Middlemore (London: Penguin Books, 1990), 98.

14. See Frank Kermode, Introduction to *Othello* in *Riverside Shakespeare,* 1246.

15. We're borrowing the vocabulary and example, of course, from Thomas S. Kuhn. See *The Structure of Scientific Revolutions,* 2d ed., enlarged (Chicago: University of Chicago Press, 1970), 1–22.

16. S. K. Heninger, Jr., *The Subtext of Form in the English Renaissance: Proportion Poetical* (University Park: Pennsylvania State University Press, 1994), 22.

17. Wisdom of Solomon 1:6–7 (New American Bible). Smith, *Treason in Tudor England,* quotes verse 7.

18. Philippe Ariès, Introduction, *A History of Private Life,* vol. 3: *Passions of the Renaissance,* ed. Roger Chartier, trans. Arthur Goldhammer (Cambridge: Harvard University Press, 1989), 1–10.

19. Thomas Greene, "The Flexibility of the Self in Renaissance Literature," *The Disciplines of Criticism: Essays in Literary Theory, Interpretation, and History,*

ed. Peter Demetz, Thomas Greene, and Lowry Nelson, Jr. (New Haven: Yale University Press, 1968), 244–45.

20. *Everyman*, 281–99, in *Medieval Drama: An Anthology*, ed. Greg Walker (Oxford: Blackwell, 2000), 282, line 22.

21. Cf. Teskey's summary (Teskey, 83ff.); also Smith, *Treason in Tudor England*, 32–54.

22. The most entertaining books about Walsingham's counterespionage operation are by John Bossy (*Giordano Bruno and the Embassy Affair* [New Haven: Yale University Press, 1991] and *Under the Molehill: An Elizabethan Spy Story* [New Haven: Yale University Press, 2001]). See also Curtis C. Breight, *Surveillance, Militarism and Drama in the Elizabethan Era* (New York: St. Martin's Press, 1996).

23. That is to say, by the end of the play, even though he has not seen the incriminating handkerchief, he believes he has. From the beginning, Shakespeare is consistent about Othello's myopia (see I.ii.30), and in the crucial eavesdropping scene, he pointedly does not recognize Desdemona's handkerchief:
Iago. And did you see the Handkerchief?
Othello. Was that mine?
Iago. Yours, by this hand. (IV.i.173–75)
But at the end, his imagination has run away with him. Just before killing his wife, he comments:
Othello. By heaven, I saw my handkerchief in's hand . . .
I saw the handkerchief. (V.i.62–66)
It's a testament to Iago's power that many Shakespeare scholars repeat Othello's error and believe that he has seen the evidence. (See Katherine S. Stockholder, "Egregiously an Ass: Chance and Accident in Othello," *Studies in English Literature, 1500–1900* 13.2 [Spring 1973]: 270). Cf. also Verdi's version of the scene in *Otello*, act 3, in which Otello unambiguously sees the handkerchief.

24. James Scott, *Seeing Like a State: How Certain Schemes to Improve the Human Condition Have Failed* (New Haven: Yale University Press, 1998), 2. See also Witold Kula, *Measures and Men*, trans. R. Szreter (Princeton: Princeton University Press, 1986), 3–29.

25. Reported by Smith, *Treason in Tudor England*, 121.

26. Greene, 250.

27. Smith comments: "The sixteenth-century model for the fully self-fashioned individual remained highly medieval in one important particular: it was closer to a Platonic ideal, fixed, universal, and timeless, than to the nineteenth-century model of an inner-directed individual, who, contrary to Donne's dictum, is an island unto himself, and who justifies his actions solely on his own identity and integrity." Smith, *Treason in Tudor England*, 91–92.

28. Fletcher, 22–23, 120

29. This began to change shortly after the appearance of the Contarini-Rosselli map early in the century, though even the Sebastian Münster map of 1538 continues to show the influence of the idea.

30. Thomas More, *Utopia*, trans. Paul Turner (London: Penguin Books, 1965), 50. All further references are to this edition.

31. Robert J. Wenke, *Patterns in Prehistory: Humankind's First Three Million Years* (New York: Oxford University Press, 1990).

32. Greenblatt, 36

33. Paul Turner, Introduction to *Utopia*, by Thomas More (London: Penguin Books, 1965), ix–xiv.

34. Greenblatt, 38.

35. Ibid., 38, 33. "Utopian institutions are cunningly designed to reduce the scope of the ego: avenues of self-aggrandizement are blocked, individuation is sharply limited. . . . In Utopia, pride of possession and pride of place are obliterated" (39).

36. The debate about whether the Renaissance subject possessed genuine interiority is a lively one. Joining Greenblatt from the Lacanian perspective is Marshall Grossman, *The Story of All Things: Writing the Self in English Renaissance Narrative Poetry* (Durham: Duke University Press, 1998), 3 et passim. A detailed examination of Renaissance inwardness comes from Katherine Eisaman Maus in *Inwardness and Theater in the English Renaissance* (Chicago: University of Chicago Press, 1995).

37. Greenblatt, 32.

38. William Shakespeare, *The Tempest*, Riverside Shakespeare, 1667–68. All references are from this edition.

39. Smith, *Treason in Tudor England*, 32, 187. Smith is quoting Jean Kaulek, *Correspondance Politique de MM de Castillon et de Marillac, 1527–1542* (Paris, 1885), 211.

40. Smith, *Treason in Tudor England*, 132.

41. The classic study of this phenomenon is Ernst H. Kantorowicz, *The King's Two Bodies: A Study in Mediaeval Political Theology* (Princeton: Princeton University Press, 1957).

42. John M. Mucciolo traces the emergence and present dominance of the colonial reading in "Shakespeare's 'Colonialist' *Tempest*, 1975 to the Present Day," *Shakespearean International Yearbook* 1 (1999): 311–21. The reading is so common that Greenblatt could famously claim, "It is very difficult to argue that *The Tempest* is *not* about imperialism" ("The Best Way to Kill Our Literary Inheritance," *Chronicle of Higher Education*, June 12, 1991, B1).

43. We suggest that the image of a "ship of state" was precisely on Shakespeare's mind here. It is a favorite metaphor of Machiavelli—a singularly appropriate source text, given the passengers on the boat. Various critics have argued for Machiavelli as a major presence throughout Shakespeare's work (see, for example Hugh Grady, *Shakespeare, Machiavelli, and Montaigne: Power and Subjectivity from Richard II to Hamlet* (Oxford: Oxford University Press, 2002), and John Roe, *Shakespeare and Machiavelli* (Cambridge, Eng.: Brewer, 2002).

44. The most influential of the many recent articles written on the presence of *Utopia* in *The Tempest* has been David Norbrook, " 'What Cares These Roarers

for the Name of King?': Language and Utopia in *The Tempest*," in Jonathan Hope and Gordon McMullan, eds., *The Politics of Tragicomedy: Shakespeare and After* (London: Routledge, 1992), 21–54. We disagree, however, with Norbrook's notion that the play opens up "utopian possibilities which question complacent celebrations of a natural order" (38). See also John X. Evans, "The Tempest and Utopia," *Moreana: Bulletin Thomas More* 18, no. 69 (March 1981): 81–83.

45. Fletcher, 55.

46. In *The New Atlantis*, "Salomon's House," at the center of Bacon's utopian kingdom of Bensalem, is a kind of steroidal Royal Society—a clearing house for the latest inventions (and some technologies yet to be invented in the real world—e.g., "furnaces of great diversities and that keep great diversity of heats"). Prominent among these inventions are futuristic methods of surveillance: the island's scientists have constructed "perspective houses" and "sound houses," which see and hear all, providing the means to keep tabs on populations near and far. Though Bensalem is strictly off-limits to foreigners, and well hidden, the officers of Salomon's House keep close watch on the rest of the world, for the purposes of industrial and military espionage: "We have twelve that sail into foreign countries, under the names of other nations (for our own we conceal), who bring us the books and abstracts and patterns of experiments of all other parts. These we call Merchants of Light." *The New Atlantis, Francis Bacon: A Selection of His Works*, ed. Sidney Warhaft (New York: Macmillan, 1982), 452–55.

47. The most forceful presentation of the argument that the novel articulates social as well as literary changes remains Ian Watt's in *The Rise of the Novel*. In his yoking of the novel to the rise of the middle class and other movements, Watt also distinguishes the novel's social valence from that of earlier prose forms, including allegory.

48. Fletcher, 151.

49. *The Dunciad* [B text], 3:241–46 (*Twickenham Edition of the Poems of Alexander Pope*, ed. John Butt et al., 11 vols. [London: Methuen, 1939–69], 5:332).

50. Letter of November 26, 1725, in *The Correspondence of Jonathan Swift, D.D.*, ed. F. Elrington Ball, 6 vols. (London: G. Bell, 1912), 3:292.

51. Jonathan Swift, *Gulliver's Travels*, ed. Claude Rawson and Ian Higgins (New York: Oxford University Press, 2005), 20.

52. Swift, *Examiner*, 15, in *The Prose Works of Jonathan Swift*, ed. Herbert Davis, 13 vols. (Oxford: Basil Blackwell, 1939–68), 3:13.

CHAPTER 2. THE LIBERAL PANOPTICON

1. See Tony Law, "How Vegas Security Drives Surveillance Tech Everywhere" *Popular Mechanics*, January 7, 2010. The article's lead-in reads: "Las Vegas casinos are incubators of the world's most advanced surveillance tech. Here's how the spy gear that helps Sin City has taught everyone from government to big banks how to snoop more effectively."

2. For these anecdotes as well as other information in this section we thank the security personnel interviewed at various casinos in Reno and Las Vegas, especially Fitzgerald's Casino, the Silver Legacy, and the Eldorado.

3. Michel Foucault, *Discipline and Punish: The Birth of the Prison*, trans. Alan Sheridan, (New York: Vintage Books, 1977), 216. All further references are to this edition.

4. See, for example, Michael Ignatieff's *A Just Measure of Pain: The Penitentiary in the Industrial Revolution, 1750–1850* (New York: Pantheon, 1978), e.g., 109–13.

5. See, for example, D. J. Manning, *The Mind of Jeremy Bentham* (London: Longmans, 1968) or D. G. Long, *Bentham on Liberty: Jeremy Bentham's Idea of Liberty in Relation to His Utilitarianism* (Toronto: University of Toronto Press, 1977). Janet Semple in her introduction to *Bentham's Prison: A Study of the Panopticon Penitentiary* (Oxford: Clarendon Press, 1993) offers a good review of anti-Benthamite positions (1–16).

6. The most influential application of Bentham's theories to eighteenth-century literature has been John Bender's *Imagining the Penitentiary* (Chicago: University of Chicago Press, 1987), chapter 2, which is dedicated to *Moll Flanders* and *Robinson Crusoe*. Bender focuses particularly on how "Defoe's narratives record the onset of an epoch-making revision in men's exercise of final authority over one another" (64). For Mr. Spectator as panoptical agent, see Scott Paul Gordon, *The Power of the Passive Self in English Literature, 1640–1770* (Cambridge: Cambridge University Press, 2002), esp. 90–100.

7. Anthony Ashley Cooper, Earl of Shaftesbury, *Characteristicks of Men, Manners, Opinions, Times*, 3 vols. (London, 1711–14), 1:83–84.

8. For Habermas's position, see esp. *The Structural Transformation of the Public Sphere: An Inquiry into a Category of Bourgeois Society*, trans. Thomas Burger with the assistance of Frederick Lawrence (Cambridge: MIT Press, 1989), 43ff. All further references are to this edition. See also Erving Goffman, *Behavior in Public Places* (New York: Free Press, 1963), and *Relations in Public* (New York: Basic Books, 1971); and David Riesman, with Nathan Glazer and Reuel Denney, *The Lonely Crowd* (New Haven: Yale University Press, 1961).

9. Erving Goffman, *The Presentation of Self in Everyday Life*, rev. ed. (New York: Doubleday, 1959), 251. All further references are to this edition. We will not review here the numerous critical applications of Goffman's theories to literature (which have often focused on the question of role-playing in the novel); we will note, however, that queer theory has served as a sort of counterbalance, with numerous critics (Butler, Sedgwick, etc.) attempting to mark out an idea of "performativity" distinct from Goffman's. See, for example, Butler's "Performative Acts and Gender Constitution: An Essay in Phenomenology and Feminist Theory," *Theatre Journal* 40.4 (988): 519–31, in which she sets out her opposition to Goffman's position.

10. As it happens, both Goffman and Riesman were avid readers of, and engaged closely with, eighteenth-century texts. See Goffman, 213, notes 1 and 2; see

also Riesman, 92–93, 101. See also Charles W. Morris's discussion of Mead in Charles W. Morris, Introduction to *Mind, Self, and Society: From the Standpoint of a Social Behaviorist*, by George Herbert Mead (Chicago: University of Chicago Press, 1934), xxiv.

11. We are well aware that "sentimentalism" is a contested term. Michael Bell describes the "historical confusion lurking in the term" (*Sentimentalism, Ethics, and the Culture of Feeling* [Palgrave, 2000], 3), and Markman Ellis describes at length the anxiety over it (*The Politics of Sensibility* [Cambridge, 1996], esp. 5ff.). Suffice it to say that during the eighteenth century itself, even the most famous "critics" of sentimentalism (Goldsmith, Kant, etc.) were also deeply influenced by various aspects of the movement.

12. Habermas, 49.

13. Ibid., 28.

14. Bentham, in John Bowring, *Memoirs and Correspondence of John Bentham*, in *Works of Jeremy Bentham*, ed. Bowring, 11 vols. (Edinburgh: William Tait, 1843; rpt. New York: Russell and Russell, 1962), 10:21.

15. D. G. Long, *Bentham on Liberty: Jeremy Bentham's Idea of Liberty in Relation to His Utilitarianism* (Toronto: University of Toronto Press, 1977), 218. Critics who read *Clarissa* as anticipatory of modern ideas of imprisonment include Nancy Armstrong, *Desire and Domestic Fiction: A Political History of the Novel* (Oxford: Oxford University Press, 1989) and Daryl Ogden, *The Language of the Eyes* (Albany: SUNY Press, 2005), esp. 67ff. Work on *Clarissa* by a number of other critics, including Kristina Straub and Terry Eagleton, also reflects the deep influence of Foucault.

16. Samuel Richardson, *Pamela; or, Virtue Rewarded*, 6th ed., 4 vols. (London, 1742), 2:169, 2:29. Further references are to this edition.

17. Goffman, *Presentation of Self*, 8.

18. These responses included both critical replies and innumerable parodies, ranging from Eliza Haywood's full-length *Anti-Pamela; or, Feign'd Innocence Detected* (with its protagonist, Syrena Tricksy) to anonymous pamphlets. See Bernard Kreissman, *Pamela-Shamela: A Study of the Criticisms, Burlesques, Parodies, and Adaptations of Richardson's Pamela* (Lincoln: University of Nebraska Press, 1960).

19. Certainly, there is at least a rudimentary awareness of this problem in *Pamela*. After the heroine's fortunes have turned, for example, and her marriage with Mr. B. is arranged, Pamela's main concern is to assure the world that her actions have been sincere, that she hasn't simply been a calculating gold digger. This produces passages of remarkable nuance, as in her explanation to her father and Mr. B. about why she does not want to rush the wedding: "Sir, . . . were I too sudden, it would look as if I doubted whether you would hold in your Mind, and was not willing to give you Time for Reflection. But otherwise, to be sure, I ought to resign myself implicitly to your Will" (*Pamela*, 2:97).

20. Henry Fielding, *An Apology for the Life of Mrs. Shamela Andrews*, ed. Sheridan W. Baker, Jr. (Berkeley: University of California Press, 1953), 64.

21. This is not to say that Fielding is simply "anti-empirical," or "anti-Lockean." Locke's theories by this point were almost axiomatic: even Fielding's "reactionary" positions contained "echoes" of Locke (see J. A. Downie, *A Political Biography of Henry Fielding* [London: Pickering and Chatto, 2009], 5–7). Fielding, like his contemporaries, lived within Locke's philosophy, whatever his reservations: "Locke's thoughts on politics, education, and religion correspond so closely with [Fielding's] own that his influence appears to have been deep and pervasive, as indeed it was generally in the century" (Martin Battestin, *A Henry Fielding Companion* [Westport, CT: Greenwood Press, 2000], 91).

22. Adam Smith, *The Theory of Moral Sentiments*, ed. Knud Haakonssen (Cambridge: Cambridge University Press, 2002), 11–12. All further references are to this edition.

23. See Goffman, *Presentation of Self*, 48–49; see also Riesman, *Lonely Crowd*, 3–26, 114ff. For a contrasting view, see Alan Wolfe, "The Missing Pragmatic Revival in American Social Science," in *The Revival of Pragmatism*, ed. Morris Dickstein (Durham: Duke University Press, 1998), 199–206.

24. One of the key debates in present-day Richardson criticism—whether his work is merely an enormous rhetorical experiment or a portrayal of real characters experiencing real things—is beside the point. Richardson's mature idea of character in *Clarissa* fully takes into account the way that, for a sentimental reader, these two questions cannot be separated. This debate, which has its roots in the earliest responses to the novel, was given new life by the rise of post-structuralist readings of *Clarissa* (see William Beatty Warner, *Reading Clarissa* [New Haven: Yale University Press, 1979], Terry Castle, *Clarissa's Ciphers* [Ithaca: Cornell University Press, 1982], etc.) and the ensuing responses by those committed to exploring or celebrating the psychological reality of Clarissa herself (Eagleton, Gordon, etc.).

25. In *The Power of the Passive Self in English Literature, 1640–1770*, Scott Paul Gordon labels as "Mandevillian misreaders" those critics who see Clarissa as an insincere manipulator; to read her behavior as anything but entirely unaffected is to indulge in cynicism. See also Gordon's "Disinterested Selves: *Clarissa* and the Tactics of Sentiment," *ELH* 64 (1997): 473–502. Also Heather Zias, "Who Can Believe: Sentiment and Cynicism in Richardson's Clarissa," *Eighteenth-Century Life* 27.3 (2003): 99–123.

26. Several critics have pursued Robert Adams Day's suggestion that "the earliest English epistolary novels may have evolved from the drama" (*Told in Letters: Epistolary Fiction Before Richardson* [Ann Arbor: University of Michigan Press, 1966], 195). See esp. John Richetti, "Richardson's Dramatic Art in *Clarissa*," *British Theatre and the Other Arts, 1660–1800*, ed. Shirley Strum Kenny (Washington: Folger Shakespeare Library, 1983), 288–308. Clarissa consistently imagines moments in her life as "scenes": "May but my *closing* scene be happy!" *Clarissa*, 3d ed., 8 vols. (London, 1751; rpt. *The Clarissa Project*, gen. ed. Florian Stuber [New York: AMS, 1990]), 2:246. All further references are to this edition. Lovelace consistently imagines his life as a play he is writing, and famously

opens volume 5 with a dramatic relation of his interaction with Clarissa in Hampstead ("Scene: Hampstead Heath," etc.).

27. Smith's solution to the dilemma is to posit an ideal and impartial spectator, abstracted from our social interactions.

28. The idea that Clarissa's death is inherently performative is a unifying one: while Eagleton excoriates Warner as a misogynist out to ruin Clarissa's good name, his assertion that Clarissa's death is designed to identify her as "a saint and martyr" resembles Warner's claim that the death is Clarissa's attempt to exert "godlike authority" over those around her.

29. Henri Poincaré, *Science and Hypothesis*, trans. W. J. Greenstreet (London: Walter Scott Publishing, 1907), xxii.

30. Hobbes, *Leviathan*, ed. C. B. Macpherson (London: Penguin Books, 1968), 183, 5. Further references are to this edition. The Latin is to be found in Hobbes's Præfatio ad Lectores to *Elementa Philosophica De Cive* (Amsterdam, 1657), xxv.

31. The position that Locke was essentially a follower of Hobbes is most closely associated with Leo Strauss (see esp. *Natural Right and History* [Chicago: University of Chicago Press, 1954], 165 et passim). The argument has subsequently been taken up by, among others, Michael P. Zuckert in *Launching Liberalism: On Lockean Political Philosophy* (Lawrence: University of Kansas Press, 2002) and Peter C. Myers in *Our Only Star and Compass: Locke and the Struggle for Political Rationality* (Lanham, MD: Rowman and Littlefield, 1998). A refutation of Strauss may be found in Quentin Skinner, "Meaning and Understanding in the History of Ideas," *History and Theory* 8 (1969): 3–53. See also Ian Harris, *The Mind of John Locke: A Study of Political Theory in its Intellectual Setting* (Cambridge: Cambridge University Press, 1994), 2.

32. John Locke, *An Essay Concerning Human Understanding*, book 2, chap. 32, par. 15 (Amherst, NY: Prometheus Books, 1995), 310–11.

33. See, for example, John W. Yolton, *Locke and The Compass of Human Understanding: A Selective Commentary on the Essay* (London: Cambridge University Press, 1970), 136 and 222, and Michael Ayers, *Locke: Epistemology and Ontology* (New York: Routledge, 1993), vol. 1, 209.

34. Lukács's frame of reference, it should be pointed out, is not English. As he later comments, in a 1962 preface, "novelists such as Defoe, Fielding and Stendahl found no place in [the] schematic pattern" of his early *Theory of the Novel*. Georg Lukács, *The Theory of the Novel*, trans. Anna Bostock (Cambridge: MIT Press, 1971), 14.

35. For an interesting discussion of this connection, see Jack Holland Rose on "Nihilism and Absolutism" (in *The Development of the European Nations* [London: Putnam, 1905]). Rose suggests that the nihilist movement in Russia was a precursor to absolutist rule.

36. Cf. L. T. Hobhouse, *Liberalism* (London: Oxford University Press, 1919), 7. Thus Anthony Arblaster's (largely hostile) *The Rise and Decline of Western Liberalism* (Oxford: Basil Blackwell, 1984) begins: "as a distinctive, organized political tendency, liberalism in the late twentieth century survives only precariously"

(3). Similarly Richard Bellamy: "Twentieth-century liberalism has suffered the curious fate of steadily declining in most countries as an electoral force exclusive to a particular party, whilst prevailing and even growing as a background theory" (*Liberalism and Modern Society* [University Park: Pennsylvania State University Press, 1992], 1). See also Theodore Lowi, *The End of Liberalism* (New York: W. W. Norton, 1969, 1979).

37. Lionel Trilling, *The Liberal Imagination: Essays on Literature and Society* (New York: Viking Press, 1951), xi. Jeremy Waldron offers a good overview of the internal divisions within the term "liberalism" in "Theoretical Foundations of Liberalism," *Philosophical Quarterly* 37 (April 1987): 127–150. Isaiah Berlin famously draws a distinction between "positive" liberty (which he associates with the likes of Rousseau and Hegel) and "negative" liberty, in which State interference in the lives of citizens is less pervasive. (Berlin associates this view with Mill and espouses it, with qualifications, himself.) "Two Concepts of Liberty," *Liberty*, ed. Henry Hardy (Oxford: Oxford University Press, 1998), 166–217.

38. As Ashcraft argues, the second treatise was likely written just before Locke had to flee to the Continent, and espouses an insurrectionary politics. See Richard Ashcraft, "Revolutionary Politics and Locke's *Two Treatises of Government:* Radicalism and Lockean Political Theory," *Political Theory* 8 (1980): 429–86.

39. Locke, untitled poem on the Restoration of Charles II, *Political Essays*, ed. Mark Goldie (Cambridge: Cambridge University Press, 1997), 203. The poem was first published in *Britannia Rediviva* (Oxford 1660) and is one of several highly conventionalized poems celebrating the Restoration contributed by Oxford scholars.

40. Locke, "An Essay on Toleration," *Political Essays*, ed. Mark Goldie (Cambridge: Cambridge University Press, 1997), 136. Further references are to this edition. The train of thought we reproduce is clearest on page 142.

41. This is David Heyd's paraphrase of Bernard Williams. Heyd, Introduction, *Toleration: An Elusive Virtue* (Princeton: Princeton University Press, 1996), 5. Williams's discussion may be found in the same volume (18–27). Numerous essays in Heyd's collection address this paradoxical aspect of toleration, especially those by John Horton, Barbara Herman, and Will Kymlicka. See also Herbert Marcuse's discussion of the topic, in which toleration is associated with the tyranny of the majority—toleration being as much a prerogative of power as anything else, in Marcuse's view: "Repressive Tolerance," *A Critique of Pure Tolerance* (Boston: Beacon Press, 1969), 81–123.

42. Slavoj Žižek, "Tolerance as an Ideological Category," *Critical Inquiry* 34 (Summer 2008): 660–82. See esp. 665–66.

43. Locke traveled to Cleves in 1665 as part of a diplomatic mission; the duchy of Brandenburg at that time had substantial populations of Lutherans, Calvinists, Roman Catholics, and Anabaptists. Roger Woolhouse, *John Locke: A Biography* (Cambridge: Cambridge University Press, 2007), 60–66. Also H. R. Fox Bourne, *The Life of John Locke*, vol. 1 (New York: Harper and Brothers, 1876), 103–21. In his letters from the time Locke comments admiringly on the

freedom of worship afforded to different faiths, thus: "Three professions [are] publically allowed: the Calvinists are more than the Lutherans, and the Catholics more than both (but no papist bears any office). . . . But yet this distance in their churches gets not into their houses. They quietly permit each other to choose their way to heaven; for I cannot observe any quarrels or animosities amongst them upon the account of religion" (Letter to the Hon. Robert Boyle, 12/22 December, 1665).

Or again: "To be serious with you the Catholick religion is a different thing from what we beleive [sic] it in England. . . . I have not met with any soe good naturd people or soe civill as the Catholick priests, and I have received many courtesies from them which I shall always gratefully acknowledge" (Letter to John Strachey, 26 December, 1665/5 January 1666). John Locke, *The Correspondence of John Locke*, ed. E. S. de Beer (Oxford: Clarendon Press, 1976), 228, 246.

44. Locke, "Atlantis," in *Political Essays*, ed. Mark Goldie (Cambridge: Cambridge University Press, 1997), 254. The Atlantis papers share some characteristics with his work on *The Fundamental Constitutions of Carolina* but the emphasis on surveillance is unique.

45. Locke, "Essay on Toleration," 148.

46. Cf. Ian Shapiro, *The Evolution of Rights in Liberal Theory* (Cambridge: Cambridge University Press, 1986), 122.

47. For Montesquieu these problems were reason enough to favor the creation of small republics (where factions are more difficult to form and more easily recognized and contained) over large ones—a position seized upon by the Anti-Federalists (and modern-day states' rights enthusiasts). For Madison, in contrast, the solution was the installation of a republican (representative) system rather than pure democracy (the latter offering no protection from the whims and decisions of a majority faction). See *The Federalist*, No. 10.

48. Criticisms of the original contract and State of Nature go back at least to Hume, who pointed out their obvious fictionality. See, for example, "Of the Original Contract," *Essays Moral, Political and Literary*, ed. Eugene F. Miller (Indianapolis: Liberty Fund, 1985), 465–87. Taking up the defense, Mark Goldie comments that for Locke, the State of Nature is "the state we naturally *are* in, not *were* in." As to the contract, Goldie argues that, "In part, Locke [is operating] in the spirit of modern theorists of consent, who offer a pure 'thought experiment': the contract is an act of political imagination in which we place ourselves in an 'original position' and ask what kind of society it would be rational to choose" (Introduction to Locke, *Two Treatises of Government* [London: Everyman, 1993], xxiv, xxviii).

49. Locke, "Essay on Toleration," 156–57.

50. Hobbes, *Leviathan*, I:1–6, 81–118.

51. Locke, *Essay Concerning Human Understanding* (book 2, chap. 27, par. 15, 27), 251, 256–57.

52. John Locke, *The Second Treatise of Government*, ed. Mark Goldie (London: Everyman, 1993), 129–30.

53. Something of this assertion survives in the contemporary debate. See, for example, Ronald Dworkin, "Liberalism," *Public and Private Morality*, ed. Stuart Hampshire (Cambridge: Cambridge University Press, 1978), 128–29.

54. Shapiro, 124–25. Other writers who recognize the theistic underpinnings of Locke's politics include J. B. Schneewind in "Locke's Moral Philosophy," *The Cambridge Companion to John Locke* (Cambridge University Press, 1994), 206–8, 220; J. W. Gough in *Locke's Political Philosophy* (Oxford: Clarendon Press, 1973), esp. 10–11; John Gray in *Liberalism* (Minneapolis: University of Minnesota Press, 1986), 12; and A. John Simmons in *The Lockean Theory of Rights* (Princeton: Princeton University Press, 1992), 14–67. See also Zuckert, 26.

55. George Mead, *George Mead on Social Psychology*, ed. Anselm Strauss (Chicago: University of Chicago Press, 1964), 39.

56. Michael Seidel, "Crusoe in Exile," *PMLA* 96 (1981): 363–74. See esp. 366–67. See also Seidel, *Robinson Crusoe: Island Myths and the Novel* (Boston: Twayne Publishers, 1991), 46–53.

57. Daniel Defoe, *Robinson Crusoe* (New York: W. W. Norton, 1975), 6. Further references are to this edition.

58. See Watt, *The Rise of the Novel*, esp. 89–92; see also Pat Rogers, *Robinson Crusoe* (London: George Allen and Unwin, 1979), 85–90. Seidel puts a more political spin on the idea, connecting it to a meditation on "sovereignty" (*Exile and the Narrative Imagination* [New Haven: Yale University Press, 1986]); he complicates his earlier argument (and Watt's basic position) in "*Robinson Crusoe*: Varieties of Fictional Experience," *The Cambridge Companion to Daniel Defoe*, ed. John Richetti (Cambridge: Cambridge University Press, 2008), 182–99, esp. 195ff.

59. For an interesting argument about Crusoe's motives, see Barbara Benedict, *Curiosity* (Chicago: University of Chicago Press, 2001), 108–10.

60. Besides Watts's discussions on Locke and Defoe, see also Isaac Kramnick, *Bolingbroke and His Circle* (Cambridge: Harvard University Press, 1968), esp. 188–200.

61. Of course Watt's theories, though wildly influential, have been disputed or dismissed by many (see, for example, Michael Boyd, *The Reflexive Novel: Fiction as Critique* [Lewisburg PA: Bucknell University Press, 1983]); many others have attempted to replace or refine Watt's realism-centered definitions (Paul Hunter suggests that "realism" can mean "unlikely" as well as "plausible" action in *Before Novels* [W. W. Norton, 1992]). See also Elizabeth Deeds Ermarth, *Realism and Consensus in the English Novel* (Edinburgh: Edinburgh University Press, 1998), esp. 33ff.

62. Watt, 12.

63. Ibid., 32.

64. We might note, too, that certain theories of realism, such as Auerbach's, would privilege the "biblical" realism of *The Faerie Queene* over the "rhetorical" realism of Defoe (in that the former work, oriented toward "truth" rather than perfect

accuracy, is not as oppressed by the responsibility of assembling irrelevant realistic details). See also Barthes on shifting standards of realism (and indeed of "the real") (e.g., "Literature Today," *Critical Essays*, trans. Richard Howard [Evanston: Northwestern University Press, 1972], 159ff.).

65. McKeon recognizes both the novel's slow development out of previous forms and its gradual consolidation as a genre, at least until 1740, when he imagines the dialectic which formed the novel as coming to a close (*The Origins of the English Novel, 1600–1740* [Baltimore: Johns Hopkins University Press, 1987], 19 et passim).

66. Cf. Hume's use of the terms "history" and "romance" in book 1, part 3 of *A Treatise of Human Nature*, 2 vols., ed. David Fate Norton and Mary J. Norton (Oxford: Clarendon Press, 2007).

67. Henry Fielding, *The History of the Adventures of Joseph Andrews*, Preface (Oxford: Oxford University Press, 1980), 4.

68. The first volume begins with a preface, in which "the Editor believes the thing to be a just History of Fact; neither is there any Appearance of Fiction in it" (3), while volume 3 ups the ante with a preface by the "author" himself: "I, *Robinson Crusoe*, being at this Time in perfect and sound Mind and Memory . . . do affirm, that the Story [is] Historical. . . . Farther, that there is a Man Alive, and well known too, the actions of whose Life are the Subject of these Volumes, and to whom all or most Part of the Story most directly alludes, this may be depended upon for Truth, and to this I set my Name" (260).

69. This is, perhaps, part of the reason theorists of the novel since Watt have been increasingly cautious about identifying the novel as the chosen vehicle of empiricism. Thus McKeon, for example, suggests that the novel is motivated not by a dialectic between empiricism and skepticism but between "naïve empiricism" and "extreme skepticism" (*Origins of the Novel*, 48); nevertheless, to create this opposition, McKeon must insist that empiricists and skeptics were recognized as such, and as presenting "coherent, autonomous and alternative" positions (22). We suggest, rather, that most "naïve empiricists" were anything but naïve about the difficulties of empiricism.

70. See Shklovsky's "Tristram Shandy Sterna i teoriya romana" (1921), published in several versions in English (usually as "Sterne's *Tristram Shandy*: Stylistic Commentary" or "The Novel as Parody" but under other titles as well).

71. William Wordsworth *The Prelude* (1805 version), ed. Jonathan Wordsworth, M. H. Abrams and Stephen Gill (New York: W. W. Norton, 1979), 258.

72. Richardson's work further increased the popularity of the subgenre, which was at its peak between the appearance of "The Adventures of a Valet" (1752) and John Macdonald's *Travels* (1790) (republished in 1927 as "The Memoirs of an Eighteenth-Century Footman"). The idea of a servant in possession of damaging information of course also forms the backbone of Godwin's *Caleb Williams* (1794).

73. As Ashcraft notes, Locke "was an avid reader of the anthropological reports contained in the voyage and travel literature of the seventeenth century."

Richard Ashcraft, "Locke's Political Philosophy," *The Cambridge Companion to John Locke* (Cambridge University Press, 1994), 238. Some historians of anthropology point to Locke's *Essay Concerning Human Understanding* as itself the founding text of the modern field (in that the notion of the tabula rasa makes modern anthropological theory possible) (see Marvin Harris, *The Rise of Anthropological Theory* [1968; rev. ed. London: Altamira, 2001], 11ff.).

74. David Hume, *An Enquiry Concerning the Principles of Morals*, ed. J. B. Schneewind (Indianapolis: Hackett, 1983), 49.

75. 6 Geo. I.c.6, "An Act to Prevent Delays in Writs of Error and for the Further Amendment of the Law."

76. John Stuart Mill, *On Liberty*, ed. Mary Warnock (New York: Meridian, 1962), 190.

77. Smith, *Theory of Moral Sentiments*, 67–68.

78. The most prominent critical voices on the subject of the difficulties of first-person narration are those of Dorrit Cohn (especially her discussion of consonant and dissonant effects in first-person narratives in *Transparent Minds* [Princeton: Princeton University Press, 1978]) and Wayne Booth (especially his discussion of the unreliable narrator in *The Rhetoric of Fiction* and the expanded discussion of first-person narration generally in the 1983 edition of that work).

79. Some, like Joe Bray and Ruth Perry, see epistolary novels as something like early attempts at stream-of-consciousness. Bray, in particular, argues for them as psychologically sophisticated and determinative of later novels' attempts to penetrate the inner self. (*The Epistolary Novel: Representations of Consciousness* [London: Routledge, 2003]; see also Perry, *Women, Letters, and the Novel* [New York: AMS, 1980].)

80. Locke, *Some Thoughts Concerning Education*, ed. John W. and Jean S. Yolton (Oxford: Clarendon, 1989), 243.

81. For an analysis of this innocence, see Gary Schneider's discussion of the "validity" of the letter, the "authenticity [of its] ability to transmit . . . emotion" (*The Culture of Epistolarity* [Newark: University of Delaware Press, 2005], 109ff.).

82. For some background to the ensuing discussion, see A. M. Ogilvie, "The Rise of the English Post Office," *Economic Journal* 3.11 (1893): 443–57; Philip Beale, *History of the Post in England* (Aldershot: Ashgate, 1998); H. W. Dickinson, *Sir Samuel Morland: Diplomat and Inventor, 1625–95* (Cambridge: Cambridge University Press, 1970); Foster W. Bond, "Samuel Morland and the Secret Opening of Letters," *Postal History Society Bulletin* 79 (1955): 26–28; Peter Fraser, *The Intelligence of the Secretaries of State and Their Monopoly of Licensed News, 1660–88* (Cambridge: Cambridge University Press, 1956), esp. 25; Susan Whyman, "A Passion for the Post," *History Today* 59.12 (2009). The levels of cynicism vary. For F. M. L. Thompson, the postman is a kind of counter to the Victorian policeman, "a friendly, unassuming, unobtrusive official; a member of the working class himself" (*The Rise of Respectable Society* [London: Fontana Press, 1988], 359); Eileen Cleere, on the other hand, has a more cynical (and narrowly Foucauldian) view of the institution (*Avuncularism* [Stanford: Stanford University Press, 2004], 182–83).

83. Cromwell, qtd. in James Rees, "Footprints of a Letter Carrier" (Philadelphia, 1866), 62–63. See a discussion of this passage in John Doran, *Memories of Our Great Towns* (London: Chatto and Windus, 1882), 26–27.

84. Dickinson, 14.

85. The Foreign Secretary also created "plant" letters for foreign courts and agents.

86. Dickinson, 96. Certainly early on, far from feeling any compunction about opening private correspondence, state agents were quite proud of how well they did it. Charles II went to the secret room himself and saw "the opening . . . [of] all manner of seals, as well in wafer as in wax, and then closing and sealing them up again, so as never to be discovered by the most curious eye" (Dickinson, 99). A whole little industry developed around creating the "secret engines" of postal surveillance (there was, for example, a special machine for opening seals). (See Howard Robinson, *Britain's Post Office: A History of Development from the Beginnings to the Present Day* [Oxford: Oxford University Press, 1953], 54, 97; see also Gary Schneider, *The Culture of Epistolarity: Vernacular Letters and Letter Writing in Early Modern England, 1500–1700* [Newark: University of Delaware Press, 2005], esp. 75–108.)

87. See, for example, *Valuable Secrets Concerning Arts and Trades* (London, 1775). Chapter 10, "Secrets relative to the making of curious and useful sorts of Ink" contains two invisible ink recipes. Of course, invisible ink was its own open secret, and the Foreign Secretary began to treat suspicious letters with special "liquors" designed to reveal invisible writing. Nevertheless, invisible ink was used by those we might expect (George Washington) and many whom we might not: one letter writer tells his female friend to hold up a page to the heat ("Beyond this I dare not trouble you"). The writer was John Locke (see Cranston, *John Locke: A Biography* [London: Longman, 1957], 35; Wayne Glausser, *Locke and Blake* [Miami: University Press of Florida, 1998], 16).

88. A healthy number of letters (Defoe's, most famously) wove encoded political reports into otherwise mundane passages. The government simply responded by employing more and better-trained code breakers, usually from the Deciphering Branch, a part of the Secret Department that specialized in cryptography and translation. (For all this, see Kenneth Ellis, *The Post Office in the Eighteenth Century* [Oxford: Oxford University Press, 1958], 60ff.)

89. August 2, 1731, *The Correspondence of Jonathan Swift*, ed. Harold Williams (Oxford: Clarendon, 1963), 3:490–91.

90. Dr. King to Mrs. Whiteway, June 24, 1737, in *Correspondence of Jonathan Swift*, 5:53.

91. For instance Habermas describes writers "unfolding" themselves in letters—but also how those same letters were always audience-oriented and often intended for publication (as in the case of Goethe). See also *Letter Writing as a Social Practice*, ed. David Barton and Nigel Hall (Philadelphia: John Benjamins, 2000), esp. Konstantin Dierks, "The Familiar Letter and Social Refinement in America, 1750–1800," 31–41.

92. Barton and Hall, *Letter Writing as a Social Practice*. See also Carol Poster and Linda C. Mitchell, eds. *Letter-Writing Manuals and Instruction from Antiquity to the Present*, and Eve Tavor Bannet, *Empire of Letters* (Cambridge: Cambridge University Press, 2005).

93. The most influential examination of the novel's embrace of earlier forms of discourse and narrative remains Bakhtin's, especially that presented in "From the Prehistory of Novelistic Discourse." M. M. Bakhtin, *The Dialogic Imagination: Four Essays by M. M. Bakhtin*, trans. Caryl Emerson and Michael Holquist (Austin: University of Texas Press, 1981), 41–83.

94. We leave to Richardson scholars the fraught question of when, if ever, Pamela starts writing letters with Mr. B.'s surveillance in mind and whether her style ever changes to meet or anticipate his expectations. The general trend of Richardson criticism for the past fifty years or so has been to defend Pamela against any charges of hypocrisy or manipulativeness that might come her way. Margaret Anne Doody, for example, indicates that Pamela's language changes halfway through the novel but suggests it is only because she is growing up (*A Natural Passion: A Study of the Novels of Samuel Richardson* [Oxford: Clarendon Press, 1974], 61ff.). An influential early effort in this type of defense is A. M. Kearney's "Richardson's *Pamela:* The Aesthetic Case," *Review of English Literature* 8 (1966): 78–90.

95. The most famous treatment of this development is found in Barthes, though his description of the "reality effect" imagines it as more of a modern phenomenon (Flaubert, etc.), and a departure from the traditional forms of "verisimilitude" that had held sway since classical times.

96. Again, the first panopticon was actually designed and constructed by Samuel Bentham (Jeremy's brother) on Potemkin's estate in Russia. See Samuel Werrett's discussion in "Potemkin and the Panopticon: Samuel Bentham and the Architecture of Absolutism in Eighteenth Century Russia," *Journal of Bentham Studies* 2 (1999): 1–24.

97. We would like to thank Dan Mitchell and the staff of Special Collections at University College London for access to Bentham's currently unpublished materials. The UCL Bentham Project aims to publish a new edition of all the works and correspondence of Bentham. Twenty-six volumes (of an estimated seventy) have so far appeared.

98. Indeed, Bentham's place in the contemporary, largely Christian effort to create more humane prison conditions in order to encourage reflection (led by Jonas Hanway, William Blackburn, and others) is often underestimated.

99. Habermas, 86.

100. Smith, *Theory of Moral Sentiments*, 27.

101. *Idler* 38 (January 6, 1759) in *The Idler and the Adventurer*, ed. W. J. Bate and others, vol. 2 in the *Yale Edition of the Works of Samuel Johnson*, 23 vols. (New Haven: Yale University Press, 1958–), 120.

102. Bentham, "Postscript," in "Panopticon," in *Works of Jeremy Bentham*, 4:71–72.

103. Ibid., 79.

104. Ibid., 66.

105. Anna Howe refers to the "inmost recesses of your heart" (1:255); Lovelace speaks of his desire to trace human nature "thro' its most secret recesses" (5:213).

CHAPTER 3. INVIOLATE PERSONALITY

1. Public figures whose "secret" weddings have drawn exhaustive press coverage over the past few years include everyone from Beyoncé to Nicolas Sarkozy; wedding companies now offer "secret wedding" packages for the average couple. For the Kidman-Urban wedding, see Sophie Tedmanson and Nick Leys, "International Paparazzi at the Ready for Nicole and Keith Show," *Australian*, June 1, 2006.

2. William Congreve, *Complete Plays of William Congreve*, ed. Herbert Davis (Chicago: University of Chicago Press, 1967). Famously, Mirabell's footman in *The Way of the World* describes couples lined up at Pancras Church, a notorious spot for unlicensed ceremonies, "as 'twere in a Country Dance" (1.i.114).

3. Patricia Meyer Spacks, *Privacy: Concealing the Eighteenth-Century Self* (Chicago: University of Chicago Press, 2003), 8. In addition, numerous literary works make this a thematic concern. In *Cecilia* (1782), Frances Burney shows her heroine "thunderstruck" after Mortimer, the man she loves, suggests a private marriage. *Cecilia, or Memoirs of an Heiress*, ed. Peter Sabor and Margaret Anne Doody (New York: Oxford University Press, 1988), 555.

4. This is true not only of purely historical work (including the most comprehensive history of privacy, Philippe Ariès's and Georges Duby's *A History of Private Life*, trans. Arthur Goldhammer (Cambridge: Belknap Press of Harvard University Press, 1991), but also of literary history. The dividing line in the American literary-critical consideration of privacy is roughly 1989— the year in which the English translation of Habermas appeared. Important cultural studies of privacy in the eighteenth century preceding this date include Christina Marsden Gillis's *The Paradox of Privacy: Epistolary Form in Clarissa* (Gainesville: University of Florida Press, 1984). The vast majority of studies since 1990 are Habermasian to some extent: this includes even those works which do not engage with Habermas explicitly (e.g., Tita Chico, *Designing Women: The Dressing Room in Eighteenth-Century Literature and Culture* [Lewisburg PA: Bucknell University Press, 2005]), as well as those which make Habermas a central concern (above all Michael McKeon's formidable *The Secret History of Domesticity* [Baltimore: Johns Hopkins University Press, 2005]; see also, for example, Thomas O. Beebee's "Publicity, Privacy and the Power of Fiction in the Gunning Letters," *Eighteenth-Century Fiction* 20.1 [2007]: 61–88). The several critics who have alluded to Warren and Brandeis within literary studies are also, by and large, Habermasian (e.g., Milette Shamir, "Hawthorne's Romance and the Right to Privacy," *American Quarterly* 49.4 [1997]: 746–79).

5. To repeat a line we quoted in the previous chapter: "The innermost core of the private was always oriented towards an audience" (Habermas, 49).

6. Charles O. Gregory and Harry Kalven, Jr., *Cases and Materials on Torts* (Boston: Little, Brown, 1959), 883. In a similar spirit, Kalven deems Warren-Brandeis the "most influential law review article of all" in "Privacy in Tort Law: Were Warren and Brandeis Wrong?" *Law and Contemporary Problems* 31.2 (1966): 326–41, 327.

7. A precedent is: Thomas M. Cooley, *A Treatise on the Law of Torts*, 2d ed. (Chicago: Callaghan, 1888), 29.

8. Warren and Brandeis, "The Right to Privacy," *Philosophical Dimensions of Privacy: An Anthology*, ed. Ferdinand Schoeman (Cambridge: Cambridge University Press, 75–103), 76–77. Future references will be cited parenthetically in the text.

9. Though some legal scholars have sought to distinguish "confidentiality law," which arguably preexists Warren and Brandeis, from "privacy law." See, for example, Neil M. Richards and Daniel J. Solove, "Privacy's Other Path: Recovering the Law of Confidentiality," *Georgetown Law Journal* 96.1 (2000): 123.

10. The tactic of breaking down the right to privacy into already existing rights is associated most closely with William L. Prosser, who argued that it could be analyzed into four separate categories, not one of them concerned with the health of one's "personality": freedom from intrusion, from the disclosure of private facts, from the presentation of one's character in a false light, and from the wrongful appropriation of one's name or image. Prosser, "Privacy," *California Law Review* 48 (1960): 383–423; 389. This position was later echoed in its essentials by Judith Jarvis Thomson ("The Right to Privacy," *Philosophy and Public Affairs* 4.4 [1975]: 295–314), and Solove, who suggests that "the problems [that go under the name 'privacy'] are not related by a common denominator or core element. Instead, each problem has elements in common with others, yet not necessarily the same element. . . . We label the whole cluster 'privacy,' but this term is useful primarily as a shorthand way of describing the cluster. Beyond that, it is more fruitful to discuss and analyze each type of problem specifically." Daniel Solove, *Understanding Privacy* (Cambridge: Harvard University Press, 2008), 171–72.

11. Kalven, "Privacy in Tort Law," 328–29. Thus also Alan F. Westin: "The movement begun by . . . Warren and Brandeis was essentially a protest by spokesmen for patrician values against the rise of the political and cultural values of 'mass society.'" Westin, *Privacy and Freedom* (New York: Atheneum, 1967), 348. In a recent book, Lawrence M. Friedman has argued that modern privacy rights arose as part of a "Victorian Compromise," a complex web of legal developments aimed at protecting social elites from exposure. Lawrence M. Friedman, *Guarding Life's Dark Secrets: Legal and Social Controls over Reputation, Propriety, and Privacy* (Stanford: Stanford University Press, 2007).

12. Both hostile and supportive critics mention the style of the essay. Don R. Pember speaks of its "verbal overkill" (*Privacy and the Press: The Law, the Mass Media, and the First Amendment* [Seattle: University of Washington Press, 1972], 41); Jeffrey Rosen its "touching," "ringing" language (*The Unwanted Gaze: The Destruction of Privacy in America* [New York: Random House, 2000], 43, 44). Edward Bloustein, in "Privacy as an Aspect of Human Dignity: An Answer to Dean Prosser" (*New York University Law Review* 39 [1964]: 962–1007, 1001), meanwhile, reminds us that Brandeis had "a touch of the prophet's vision and the poet's tongue."

13. The first and last quotations are from David M. O'Brien, *Privacy, Law, and Public Policy* (New York: Praeger Publishers, 1979), 5. The middle two are from Solove, 18. Several others describe the phrase as "vague" (e.g., Walter F. Pratt, *Privacy in Britain* [Lewisburg PA: Bucknell University Press, 1979], 59).

14. It is easy to see why subsequent commentators would have trouble turning "The Right to Privacy" into workable law. How can one distinguish, for example, between the mere annoyances of life and intrusions sufficiently powerful to injure the self? Surely different people are affected by intrusion differently. Still more perplexing, how can one prove that *harm* has actually occurred, even in the most egregious cases of violated privacy? For a discussion of this problem, see Judith Wagner DeCew, *In Pursuit of Privacy: Law, Ethics and the Rise of Technology* (Ithaca: Cornell University Press, 1997), 4, at 15. The problem is central to the recent decision in *Doe v. Chao*, 540 U.S. 614 (2004). Most commentators pose the last question simply as a practical matter (for example, physical injuries are easy to identify but mental suffering is not—and is easy to lie about), and several indeed have deemed it unanswerable. In the words of Marc Rotenberg, director of the Electronic Privacy Information Center: "Proving actual harm in a privacy case will remain very difficult." "Prepared Statement of Marc Rotenberg, Executive Director, Electronic Privacy Information Center," 36–39 in *S.2201 Online Personal Privacy Act. Hearing before the Committee on Commerce, Science and Transportation. U.S. Senate, 107th Cong., 2d sess., April 25, 2002* (Washington, DC: U.S. Government Printing Office, 2006), 38. Kalven, not surprisingly, is among the skeptics ("I suspect . . . that the achievement of the new tort remedy has been primarily to breed nuisance claims" [Kalven, 339]), yet even the tort's defenders have found these problems difficult to answer.

15. *Olmstead v. United States*, 277 U.S. 438, 478 (1928).

16. See Richard Posner, "An Economic Theory of Privacy," *Regulation* (1978): 19–26; Bloustein's "Privacy as an Aspect of Human Dignity: An Answer to Dean Prosser"; and Robert Gerstein, "Intimacy and Privacy," *Ethics* 89 (1978): 76–81. Ronald Dworkin has referred to the case (or at least its reputation) in several places as a "brilliant fraud" (for instance, in *Taking Rights Seriously*, rev. ed. [Cambridge: Harvard University Press, 1979], 119).

17. All page references are to Habermas. Compare Edward Shils, who presents a similar idea (not, however, from a Marxist perspective), in "Privacy: Its Constitution and Vicissitudes," *Law and Contemporary Problems* 31/2 (1966): 290–96.

18. See Habermas, 19, 24, 51.

19. Ibid., 28. For the critique of autonomy see esp. 46–47. Not all writers influenced by Habermas are willing to follow him this far; McKeon's *The Secret History of Domesticity* is a vast application of, and expansion on, Habermas's work on the public sphere and goes a long way towards complicating some of that book's more reductive conclusions. Nevertheless, to the extent that McKeon shares Habermas's materialist and economic premises, most importantly that the public and private constitute each other, the idea of privacy in the sense urged by Warren and Brandeis is never seriously entertained.

20. Adam Smith, *The Theory of Moral Sentiments*, ed. Knud Haakonssen (Cambridge: Cambridge University Press, 2002), 100.

21. See "Estimates of the Population of London, 1550–1801," Appendix 1a in Francis Sheppard, *London: A History* (Oxford: Oxford University Press, 2000). The consensus estimate is that London's population was just short of 1 million at the turn of the century.

22. Joseph Addison, *The Spectator*, ed. Donald F. Bond, 5 vols. (Oxford: Clarendon Press, 1965), 3:506.

23. See Samuel Johnson, *Rambler*, No. 148, in *The Yale Edition of the Works of Samuel Johnson*, ed. W. J. Bate and Albrecht B. Strauss, 14 vols. (New Haven: Yale University Press, 1958–), 5:21.

24. "London," in *Poems*, vol. 6 of *The Yale Edition of the Works of Samuel Johnson*, ed. E. L. McAdam, Jr., and G. Milne (New Haven: Yale University Press, 1964), 6:55, lines 136–39.

25. Smith, *Theory of Moral Sentiments*, 67–68.

26. Johnson, in James Boswell, *Life of Johnson*, 2d ed., 6 vols., ed. George Birkbeck Hill and Lawrence Powell (Oxford: Clarendon Press, 1964), 4:308–9.

27. Even as Burke, in much the same mood, admitted that "temporary solitude . . . is itself agreeable," he also held that "absolute and entire solitude . . . is as great a positive pain as can almost be conceived." Burke, *Philosophical Enquiry into the Origin of Our Ideas of the Sublime and Beautiful* (1757), 1:220.

28. Thus William Cowper's advice on attending to "the interior self" in *The Task* (in *The Poems of William Cowper*, ed. John D. Baird and William Ryskamp, 3 vols. [New York: Oxford University Press, 1980–95], 3:279–82):
    A life all turbulence and noise, may seem
    To him that leads it, wise and to be prais'd;
    But wisdom is a pearl with most success
    Sought in still water, and beneath clear skies.

29. See Spacks, 24 et passim.

30. Classic accounts of this problem can be found in Basil Willey, *The Seventeenth Century Background* (London: Chatto and Windus, 1934), 298ff., and in M. H. Abrams, *The Mirror and the Lamp: Romantic Theory and the Critical Tradition* (New York: Oxford University Press, 1953), 5 et passim.

31. *William Wordsworth: The Poems*, 2 vols., ed. John O. Hayden (Harmondsworth: Penguin, 1977; reprint 1981), 2:38, lines 19–23. All future references are to this edition.

32. Warren's family in particular had a deep interest in the poet; indeed, Warren's brother Edward (Ned) was the subject of an intervention of sorts when his family became concerned that he was reading too much Wilde and not enough Wordsworth. See Martin Burgess Green, *The Mount Vernon Street Warrens: A Boston Story, 1860–1910* (New York: Scribner's, 1989), 73. Brandeis, for his part, had been moved to hear Emerson (a friend and champion of Wordsworth) lecture on poetry and education and filled notebooks with his favorite passages from Romantic and Victorian poets. See Philippa Strum, *Louis Brandeis: Justice for the People* (Cambridge: Harvard University Press, 1984), 20. We thank the staff of the Robert D. Farber University Archives and Special Collections Department at Brandeis University for access to these materials.

33. Thus Locke had established that identity depends upon our consciousness of past actions ("As far as this consciousness can be extended backwards to any past action or thought, so far reaches the identity of that *person.*" *An Essay Concerning Human Understanding* [book 2, chap. 27, par. 9], 247). To give Locke's infamous example: "Let him once find himself conscious of any of the Actions of *Nestor,* he then finds himself the same Person with *Nestor*" (340). In *Observations on Man* (1749), David Hartley pursues Locke's arguments on a more biological level, arguing that "vibrations" associated with different stimuli help to create memories, which in turn form the foundation of personal identity. Neither Hartley nor Locke, it should be noted, drew any strong conclusions about the relevance of this psychological model for privacy.

34. The line is Bacon's; as Locke put it in the *Essay,* true solitude is a "burden too heavy for human sufferance" (book 2, chap. 28, par. 12; 282–83).

35. Wordsworth's transition from a solipsist to, as David Bromwich puts it, a "pious communitarian" has been told elsewhere: as he aged, he settled into a conservative politics, rejecting along the way many of his deepest insights about privacy. David Bromwich, *A Choice of Inheritance: Self and Community from Edmund Burke to Robert Frost* (Cambridge: Harvard University Press, 1989), 62–63. The standard view is that Wordsworth shifted from radical to arch-conservative during the middle part of his career; in *Wordsworth's Second Nature: a Study of the Poetry and Politics* (University of Chicago Press, 1984), James K. Chandler, while not disagreeing with the increased conservatism of the later works, nevertheless cautions that the early Wordsworth's positions were often more conservative than we recognize (e.g., xviii). As far as privacy goes, however, there is a marked, noticeable turn later in Wordsworth's life away from his early celebration of it.

36. It was not long before the market attempted to rectify this problem: Thomas Cook helped initiate mass tourism as we know it with a series of organized tours during the 1840s, including trips to the Lake District. Thomas Cook tours and "Wordsworth's Lake District" grew in popularity together: by 1891, "Publisher's Circular" could review David Douglas's guidebook *The English Lake District as Interpreted in the Poems of Wordsworth* immediately after a review of the Thomas Cook Co.'s *The Business of Travel: A Fifty Year Record of Progress* (*Publishers'*

Circular 1306 [July 11, 1891], 39). The irony, of course, is that Wordsworth was hardly advocating mass organized tourism as a way to get in touch with the private self.

37. *The Prelude*, book 7, "Residence in London," 1805 version, lines 722–28.

38. See, for example, Hille Koskela, "'Cam Era'—the contemporary urban Panopticon," *Surveillance and Society* 1.3 (2003).

39. This comment was made in conversation by a senior officer in the Metropolitan Police (New Scotland Yard office) in 2009. We withhold his name by request.

40. This stature, admittedly, would begin to decline soon enough (see Hans Aarsleff, "Locke's Reputation in Nineteenth-Century England" in *John Locke: Critical Assessments*, ed. Richard Ashcraft [New York: Routledge, 1991]). Nevertheless, for the first decade or two of the century his name remained a talismanic one: even as determined a critic as Coleridge had to admit that "no parson preaches, no Judge speechifies, no Counsellor babbles against Deism but the great Mr. Locke's name is discharged against the infidels, Mr. Locke, that greatest of philosophers" (*Collected Letters of Samuel Taylor Coleridge*, ed. Earl Leslie Griggs [Oxford: Oxford University Press, 1956, rpt. 2002], 2:702).

41. See, for example, Christopher Dandeker, *Surveillance, Power and Modernity: Bureaucracy and Discipline from 1700 to the Present Day* (Cambridge: Polity Press, 1994).

42. A fact not lost on a host of critics: see, for example, Mark Seltzer, "The Princess Casamassima: Realism and the Fantasy of Surveillance," *Nineteenth-Century Fiction* 35 (1980–81): 506–34, 516–17. See also John Pickles, *A History of Spaces: Cartographic Reason, Mapping, and the Geo-Coded World*, esp. 131ff. (e.g., "cartographic truth [is] an example of the exercise of power, linked to the will to dominate and control"; he cites Foucault). For Foucault and cartography more generally, see Jeremy W. Crampton and Stuart Elden, *Space, Knowledge and Power: Foucault and Geography* [Aldershot: Ashgate, 2007] esp. 223ff.); Thomas J. Bassett, "Cartography and Empire Building in Nineteenth-Century West Africa," *Geographical Review* 84. 3 (1994): 316. For an account of the limitations of State cartography, see James Scott, *Seeing Like a State: How Certain Schemes to Improve the Human Condition Have Failed* (New Haven: Yale University Press, 1998).

43. Numbering of houses began during the eighteenth century and was mandated in 1765; the *Post Office Directory of London*, listing people's home addresses, was first published in 1799; and so on. The first widespread house-numbering system appeared in France in 1768, a system designed to facilitate the location of troops housed in civilian homes. Home delivery began in America in 1863. See Reuben S. Rose-Redwood, "Indexing the Great Ledger of the Community: Urban House Numbering, City Directories, and the Production of Spatial Legibility," *Journal of Historical Geography* 34.2 (2008): 286–310.

44. Charles Booth, *Life and Labour of the People in London*, 17 vols. (London: Macmillan, 1902), 17:142.

45. Franco Moretti, among others, has seen value in Booth, contrasting the poverty patterns in Booth's maps with the crime locations in the Sherlock Holmes

stories, for example. He also talks about the mutual attempt in Booth and the novel to make the "confusion" of the city seem "legible." (*Altas of the European Novel* [London: Verso, 1998], 77ff.)

46. *Times*, October 18, 1850, 4c. Other signs of the times: in 1836, the General Register Office was established, and registration of births and deaths was centralized and made a state concern (before it had been left to parish churches); in 1853, registration of births with the government became obligatory. By 1874 the Births and Deaths Registration Act punished failure to register a birth with a fine. See Goldman, "Statistics and the Science of Society in Early Victorian Britain: An Intellectual Context for the General Register Office," *Society for the Social History of Medicine* 4.3 (1991): 415–34.

47. For example: the formation of the Metropolitan Police Service in 1829; the passing of the Poor Law Amendment Act in 1834 (and the replacing of Outdoor Relief with the new, mandatory workhouse system); the passing of the Land Tax Act of 1834 and the establishment of central tax collection inspectorates over the ensuing decades.

48. Johann Gottlieb Fichte, *The Science of Rights*, trans. Adolph Ernst Kroeger (Philadelphia: J. B. Lippincott, 1869), 378–79. Isaiah Berlin identifies Fichte as one of the "six enemies of human liberty" in *Freedom and Its Betrayal* (Princeton: Princeton University Press, 2003), 50ff.

49. "Of the Stationary State," book 4, chapter 6 of *Principles of Political Economy* (*The Collected Works of John Stuart Mill*, ed. J. M. Robson, 33 vols. [Toronto: University of Toronto Press, 1965], 3:755). Mill, it should be remembered, survived an early emotional breakdown largely by reading Wordsworth, "a medicine for my state of mind." John Stuart Mill, *Autobiography*, ed. Jack Stillinger (Boston: Houghton Mifflin, 969), 88–89.

50. John Stuart Mill, *On Liberty*, ed. Mary Warnock (New York: Meridian, 1962), 135. Of course Mill's work can be viewed in different lights: for every critic who has taken him as an apostle of complete freedom and permissiveness, there is another who sees him as a secret prophet of order and control. Our own dialectical understanding of privacy and surveillance means that it is unsurprising that an advocate of one might be drawn also to the other. The view of Mill as an advocate of control has been made recently by Joseph Hamburger: "While Mill did value liberty and individuality, there is evidence—a great deal of it, I believe—that he also advocated placing quite a few limitations on liberty and many encroachments on individuality [etc.]." *John Stuart Mill on Liberty and Control* (Princeton: Princeton University Press, 2001), xi.

51. Thus Sir William Harcourt in an 1873 speech delivered at Oxford: "Liberty does not consist in making others do what you think right; but liberty is a negative phrase, and public expediency is the primary object of legislation." Quoted (or possibly paraphrased) in *Saturday Review of Politics, Literature, Science and Art* 35 (January 4, 1873): 3.

52. The lack of privacy produces persons (not "individuals") unable to perceive what has been taken from them, and so not obviously in need of restitution. Post is

perhaps the most articulate in a long line of theorists attempting to save the principle of "inviolate personality" through recourse to social-constructionist thinking generally and the work of Goffman in particular. Robert F. Murphy, examining privacy from an anthropological perspective, is perhaps the first writer to discuss the value of Goffman for understanding the problem. See Robert F. Murphy, "Social Distance and the Veil," *American Anthropologist* 66 (1964): 1257–74. See also Westin, 33–35. In the 1970s especially, a series of writers came to see privacy as one way of regulating Goffman's "information game" and thus shaping the formation of the self. See, for example, Gerstein, 23, and Robert C. Post, "The Social Foundations of Privacy: Self and Community in the Common Law Tort," *California Law Review* 77 (1989): 957–1010, but also Charles Fried, "Privacy," *Yale Law Journal* 77 (1968): 475–93; James Rachels, "Why Privacy Is Important," *Philosophy and Public Affairs* 4.4 (1975): 323–33; and Jeffrey H. Reiman, "Privacy, Intimacy, and Personhood," *Philosophy and Public Affairs* 6.1 (1976): 26–44.

53. Joseph Conrad, *The Secret Agent* (New York: Penguin, 1984), 53.
54. Friedrich Engels, *The Condition of the Working Class in England*, trans. W. O. Henderson and W. H. Chaloner (Stanford: Stanford University Press, 1968), 31.
55. As Peter Melville Logan puts it, "In the Report, the residences of the working class become true domestic spaces only when they are ventilated, drained, and opened up to the surveillance of the middle class" (*Nerves and Narratives: A Cultural History of Hysteria in Nineteenth-Century British Prose*). See also Mary Poovey, *Making a Social Body: British Cultural Formation, 1830–1864 (Chicago: University of Chicago Press, 1995)*, esp. chapter 2.
56. Metropolitan Police Act of 1829, 10 Geo. IV. c.44.
57. Ammunition, doubtless, for the Foucauldian argument that "the law" is one smoothly operating machine, with each department blurring into the next. Each department, too, is internally consistent, so that the police are omnipresent, continuous, coordinated. Typically, though, the claim is pushed beyond plausibility, thus Foucault: "The police state establishes an administrative continuum that, from the general law to the particular measure, makes the public authorities and the injunctions they give one and the same type of principle, according it one and the same type of coercive value" (*The Birth of Biopolitcs: Lectures at the College de France, 1978–1979*, ed. Michel Senellart, trans. Graham Burchell [London: Palgrave Macmillan, 2008], 168ff.).
58. Charles Dickens, *Bleak House*, ed. George Ford and Sylvere Monod (New York: W. W. Norton, 1977), 134.
59. In *Oliver Twist*, by contrast, the predecessors of the Metropolitan Police are notable for their youthful inefficiency (the Bow Street runners fail where Mr. Brownlow, a private individual, succeeds).
60. "On Duty with Inspector Field," *Works of Charles Dickens*, Riverside Edition (Cambridge: Riverside Press, 1869), 225. Quotations in the following paragraphs are from this edition.
61. George Orwell, "England Your England," in *A Collection of Essays* (New York, Harcourt Brace, 1946), 271.

62. As numerous commentators have pointed out, the police occupy a special
position within the spectrum of Victorian fiction and cut to something at the
core of the ideological work performed by the novel. Preeminently, D. A. Miller,
in *The Novel and the Police* (Berkeley: University of California Press, 1988) has
suggested that fiction effectively internalized the disciplinary work of the law,
carrying out (while simultaneously concealing the fact that it was doing so)
the enforcement of social norms by other means. This line of reasoning relies
on its own highly reductive view of police work and, in exposing the covert,
occasionally misses the obvious. It has little to say about the immense burden
of desire invested, quite explicitly, both by the author and (for very different
reasons) by segments of the public, in figures like Field. Still more to the point,
it has little to say about the genuine despair of passages like Dickens's "solemn
consideration" at the start of chapter 3: the failure of empirical observation—
which Dickens recognized as the death knell of the realistic novel—did not
spare the police. In any case, Miller's Foucauldian work was such a landmark
that much of the work on literature and the police since has positioned itself
as complicating his arguments. Marie-Christine Leps suggests that Miller's
arguments are reductive (*Apprehending the Criminal: The Production of Deviance
in Nineteenth-Century Discourse* [Durham: Duke University Press, 1992] e.g.,
134); Caroline Reitz introduces her study of the police and the detective novel as
taking up Lauren Goodlad's call to move away from the strict Foucauldianism
that had dominated Victorian studies and in particular treatments of the police
and the law (Reitz, *Detecting the Nation: Fictions of Detection and the Imperial
Venture* [Columbus: Ohio State University Press, 2004], xx). Other critics
have embraced the analogy between law enforcement and novel writing more
enthusiastically, with many positing a one-to-one relation between the two—
enough that we might refer to them collectively as the police/prison critics.
Critics in this vein include John Bender, who argues that free indirect discourse
in the novel is a parallel device to the panoptic prison; Mark Seltzer, who in
his discussion of the "panoptic eye of . . . narration," suggests that "techniques
of narrative seeing and point of view reproduce social modes of surveillance
and supervision . . . the realist project operates through a comprehensive
surveillance and policing of the real"; and a host of others (Bender, *Imagining
the Penitentiary* [Chicago: University of Chicago Press, 1987], 203; Seltzer, *Henry
James and the Art of Power*, 24, 18). See also McKnight, Jaffe, etc. Dorrit Cohn
critiques the school in "Optics and Power in the Novel," *New Literary History*
26.1 (1995): 3–10, and in a response to Bender's and Seltzer's objections later in
the same issue (35–37).

63. "Edgar Allan Poe, "The Man of the Crowd," *Collected Works of Edgar Allan Poe*,
3 vols., ed. Thomas Ollive Mabbott (Cambridge: Belknap Press of Harvard
University Press, 1978), 2:507–9. Future references are to this edition.

64. Thus Walter Benjamin: "The people in ["The Man of the Crowd"] behave
as if they could no longer express themselves through anything but a reflex
action."

65. Physiognomy has ancient origins; by the seventeenth century Browne is defending the practice in *Religio Medici:* "For there are mystically in our faces certain Characters which carry in them the motto of our Souls, wherein he that cannot read A. B. C. may read our natures." The most prominent eighteenth-century physiognomist, Johann Lavater, argued that "as are the features, so will be the mind" (280) and provided silhouettes with which to practice. Each silhouette was described in terms of the personality it conveyed, e.g., "A man of business. Undoubtedly possessed of talents, punctual honesty, love of order, and deliberation. An acute inspector of men; a calm, dry, determined judge. To the middle of the mouth is an advancing trait, which speaks superiority in common affairs." Or: "Such the nose, such is all."

66. Samuel Roberts Wells, *New Physiognomy, or Signs of Character . . .* (New York, 1871). See also James W. Redfield, *Comparative Physiognomy: or, Resemblances between Men and Animals* (New York, 1866).

67. Poe, "The Fall of the House of Usher," in *Collected Works*, 2:401–2; "Ligeia," *Collected Works*, 2:312.

68. In theater, too, an entire language was developed for actors based upon postures and gestures. John Walker, in the influential *Elements of Elocution* (1799), describes a "system," by which emotions are recognizable through "external appearance of countenance and gesture" (331). "Tranquility," for example, is shown by "the countenance open, the forehead smooth, the eyebrows arched, the mouth just not shut, and the eyes passing with an easy motion from object to object, but not dwelling long upon any one" (333). Illustrated guides were popular, particularly Henry Siddons's *Practical Illustrations of Rhetorical Gesture* (1822). Dozens of such poses were designed, memorized, and implemented, in full faith that the inner life could be expressed in clear physical terms. For Siddons, postures and looks are a window into the soul—whether or not one wishes them to be: "The man who wishes to conceal the predominant passions of his soul ought to guard, above all things, against allowing them to fix in his *eyes*" (23).

69. Alexander Bain, *On the Study of Character, Including an Estimate of Phrenology* (1861); see also Samuel Bailey, *Letters on the Philosophy of the Human Mind*, 2d ser. (1858), 206–15: "At the outset it may be admitted that the connexion thus shown to exist between the size of a certain part of the skull, and an excessive manifestation (say) of fear might be usefully employed in aiding us to regulate our intercourse with our fellow-men, to select individuals for particular offices, to choose professions for young people . . . and, in a word, to appreciate the character of both ourselves and others."

70. Walt Whitman, *Leaves of Grass: The First (1855) Edition* (New York: Penguin, 1959), 13.

71. Ibid., 37.

72. Ibid., 15.

73. Melville's own image for this recurring character, from *Pierre*, is the empty sarcophagus: "By vast pains we mine into the pyramid; by horrible gropings we come to the central room; with joy we espy the sarcophagus; but we lift the

lid—and no body is there!—appallingly vacant as vast is the soul of a man."
Herman Melville, *Pierre; or, The Ambiguities* (Evanston: Northwestern University
Press, 1971), 285.

74. "Benito Cereno," in *The Piazza Tales and Other Prose Pieces, 1839–1860,* vol. 9 of
The Writings of Herman Melville, ed. Harrison Hayford, Alma A. MacDougall,
and G. Thomas Tanselle (Evanston: Northwestern University Press, 1987), 46.
All further references are to this edition.

75. For a reading of "Benito Cereno" as ironic depiction of the blinding effects of
liberal ideology, see J. H. Kavanagh, "That Hive of Subtlety: 'Benito Cereno' as
Ideological Critique," *Bucknell Review* 28 (1984): 127–57.

76. An example of misinformation: "There is something in the negro which, in
a peculiar way, fits him for avocations about one's person. Most negroes are
natural valets and hair-dressers, taking to the comb and brush congenially as
to the castanets." This is part of a description of Babo seemingly tending to
Cereno. Either the narrator is not omniscient (and thus lying to us indirectly) or
lying to us outright (83).

77. Fredric Jameson, *The Political Unconscious: Narrative as a Socially Symbolic Act*
(Ithaca: Cornell University Press, 1981), 206.

78. Horkheimer's and Adorno's attack on mass culture receives its best known
treatment in "The Culture Industry: Enlightenment as Mass Deception," in
Dialectic of Enlightenment: Philosophical Fragments, trans. Edmund Jephcott
(Stanford: Stanford University Press, 2002); Adorno's argument for high
modernist abstraction may be found in "Cultural Criticism and Society" and
"Arnold Schoenberg, 1874–1951." These last two may be found in *Prisms,* trans.
Samuel and Sherry Weber (Cambridge: MIT Press, 1967). Peter Bürger mounts
the attack on high culture, especially art for art's sake in *Theory of the Avant-
Garde,* trans. Michael Shaw (Minneapolis: University of Minnesota Press, 1984).
Pierre Bourdieu's nuanced account of the motives behind the "field of art's"
establishment of its autonomy vis-à-vis the "field of power" may be found in
The Rules of Art: Genesis and Structure of the Literary Field, trans. Susan Emanuel
(Stanford: Stanford University Press, 1995), 47–112.

79. The idea that elite literature (or "authentic art") forced open the divide is
one pushed most effectively by the Frankfurt School. For the "Great Divide"
generally, see Andreas Huyssen, who argues in *After the Great Divide:
Modernism, Mass Culture, Postmodernism* (Bloomington: Indiana University
Press, 1986) that "attempts to destabilize the high/low opposition not only
"have never had lasting effects" but have actually added "new strength and
vitality to the old dichotomy" (vii).

80. For a discussion of the critical tendency towards seeing detective fiction as
a "re-affirmation of social order" designed to numb readers to the rise of
surveillance, see Ralph Willett, *The Naked City: Urban Crime Fiction in the
USA* (Manchester, UK: Manchester University Press, 1996), 7; for the "textual
Panopticon" and relation to the bourgeois reading public, see John Scaggs,
Crime Fiction (New York: Routledge, 2005), 45ff.

81. This is a focus of Miller's *The Novel and the Police*, esp. 33ff., where he distinguishes between police "vision" and detective "super-vision" (e.g., "If one were to speak of an ideology borne in the form of the detective story, here would be one of its major sites: in the perception of everyday life as fundamentally 'outside' the network of policing power" [36–37]).

82. See J. L. Mackie, *Persons and Values*, ed. Joan Mackie and Penelope Mackie (Oxford: Clarendon Press, 1985), 46ff. For an examination of the relevance of *mens rea* to literature, see Lisa Rodensky, *The Crime in Mind: Criminal Responsibility and the Victorian Novel* (Oxford, 2003), in particular the discussion of the increased importance of *mens rea* as a theme after John Austin rethinks English jurisprudence in the 1830s.

83. Wilkie Collins is the most famous example of the lawyer-novelist who worries the *mens rea* question. The challenge of determining one's frame of mind at the moment of a criminal act gave birth to an entire vocabulary of "voluntary muscular contractions" and "mechanical acts" and led to legal scholars grappling in all seriousness with Johnson's quip that Garrick (an early proponent of method acting) could have legally been hanged after his performance of *Richard III* (after all, he was thinking the same criminal thoughts as his subject). The situation became problematic enough that during the late part of the century new categories of crimes were defined in which *mens rea* did not need to be shown ("strict liability" offenses). For a thorough history of nineteenth-century case law on the question of drunkenness and *mens rea*, see Douglas Aikenhead Stroud, *Mens Rea or Imputability under the Law of England* (London, 1914), 98ff.

84. Conan Doyle has Sherlock Holmes, in the first of the Holmes stories, mock this device: "Sherlock Holmes rose and lit his pipe. 'No doubt you think you are complimenting me in comparing me to Dupin,' he observed. 'Now, in my opinion, Dupin was a very inferior fellow. That trick of his breaking in on his friends' thoughts with an apropos remark after a quarter of an hour's silence is really very showy and superficial. He had some analytical genius, no doubt; but he was by no means such a phenomenon as Poe seemed to imagine.'" In subsequent stories, Holmes performs the same "trick." "A Study in Scarlet," *The Complete Sherlock Holmes*, 2 vols. (New York: Barnes and Noble Classics, 2003), 1:18–19. Further references to this edition.

85. Arthur Conan Doyle, "The Sign of Four," *The Complete Sherlock Holmes*, 1:160.

86. Thus, too, many of his numerous successors; Poirot, for example, purposefully induces a fatal heart attack in one suspect he particularly dislikes and ends his career by murdering another.

87. See Leps, *Apprehending the Criminal*, 193ff.

88. Not that everyone and his uncle haven't tried. A persistent theme in the criticism of this story is the need to assign meaning to (i.e., to allegorize) the ape. Thus, the orangutan represents the id; it represents African Americans; it represents the "servile" class; it represents capitalism; it represents his mother's illicit lover, the father of Rosalie Poe; it represents the infant's entry into signification, etc., etc.

89. Henry James's connections with the Warren family are recounted by Brook Thomas in *American Literary Realism and the Failed Promise of Contract* (Berkeley: University of California Press, 1997). As Thomas writes, "Henry James . . . knew Bayard's daughter, having met her on a visit to Washington, D.C., in 1882. Impressed by her charm, he wrote to his mother that she and her friends were 'such as one ought to marry, if one were marrying'" (57). In the event, Mabel Bayard married Samuel Warren the next year.

90. Henry James, Introduction, *The Novels and Tales of Henry James, New York Edition*, vol. 13 (New York: Charles Scribner's Sons, 1908), x.

91. See *Boston Globe*, November 16, 1890. Other variations on the theme included "Stage and Platform Gossip" and "Newsy Notes Concerning Actors" (e.g., August 7, 1892). There were sports-related versions as well, including the baseball-themed "Newsy Items about Local Leaguers" (April 2, 1888).

92. William H. Bushnell, "Journalistic Barbarism" (1886), qtd. in Hazel Dicken-Garcia, *Journalistic Standards in Nineteenth-Century America* (Madison: University of Wisconsin Press, 1989), 192ff.

93. For a discussion of the speech, see Don R. Pember, *Privacy and the Press: The Law, the Mass Media, and the First Amendment* (Seattle, University of Washington Press, 1972), 13. Cleveland particularly admired Wordsworth's "Happy Warrior."

94. Henry James, *The Reverberator, The Novels and Tales of Henry James, New York Edition*, vol. 13 (New York: Charles Scribner's Sons, 1908), 166, 199. Further references are to this edition.

95. Ibid., 144.

96. It is worth noting here that some of the most articulate critics of privacy rights indeed approach the issue from a feminist perspective; in this view, privacy is merely a shield for abuses within the home. This position is most closely associated with Catherine MacKinnon in *Toward a Feminist Theory of the State* (Cambridge: Harvard University Press, 1989), but see also Patricia Boling, *Privacy and the Politics of Intimate Life* (Ithaca: Cornell University Press, 1996), 8–10 and 85–87.

97. For the origin of the story: William L. Prosser, "Privacy," 383. The source Prosser cites, incorrectly, is Alpheus Thomas Mason, *Brandeis: A Free Man's Life* (New York: Viking Press, 1946), 70. A more recent article casts doubt on the Warrens' social life as an aggravating factor at all (cf. Brook Thomas, "The Construction of Privacy in and around *The Bostonians*" [*American Literature* 64.4 (1992): 719–47]).

98. It is also a testament, perhaps, to Prosser's overwhelming authority at midcentury that numerous authors simply accepted the story at face value. These include Samuel H. Hofstadter and George Horowitz, *The Right of Privacy* (New York: Central Book Company, 1964); Ellen Alderman and Caroline Kennedy, *The Right to Privacy* (New York: Alfred A. Knopf, 1995); and Harry Kalven, Jr., "Privacy in Tort Law." Jeffrey Rosen even embellishes the tale: "What outraged Brandeis and Warren was a mild society item in the Boston *Saturday Evening Gazette* that described a lavish breakfast party Warren himself had

put on for his daughter's wedding." Rosen, *The Unwanted Gaze*, 7. Pember has established that Warren's eldest daughter was in fact married in 1905. See *Privacy and the Press*, 24.

CHAPTER 4. THE RETURN OF ALLEGORY

1. Henry James, "The Private Life," *The Novels and Tales of Henry James*, vol. 17 (New York: Charles Scribner's Sons, 1909), 217–66.
2. Ibid., 219. James's identification of Robert Browning as his inspiration for Clare Vawdrey is to be found on page xv of his introduction to the New York Edition.
3. Ibid., xiv.
4. When the New Hampshire Supreme Court, for example, heard the case of *Hamberger v. Eastman* (1964), in which a husband and wife sued their landlord for installing listening devices in their bedroom, the justices readily found for the plaintiffs on the grounds of mental suffering, even though the couple could not prove that the landlord had ever "listened or overheard any sounds or voices originating from [their] bedroom" (106 N.H. 107, 112 [1964]). Reviewing the case, which marked the New Hampshire court's first acknowledgment of the invasion of privacy tort, Robert C. Post approvingly notes the *impersonality* of this decision. In Post's view, an "intense and narrow focus on the actual mental suffering of specific individuals" does not make good law; and indeed, the *Eastman* court did not reach its decision "merely because the plaintiffs were in fact discomfited, but rather because the installation of the device was 'offensive to any person of ordinary sensibilities'" (Post, "Social Foundations of Privacy," 960). Drawing on the language of the second *Restatement of Torts* (1977), Post concludes that, in adjudicating cases of privacy invasion, it is beside the point either to ask whether actual suffering has occurred or to consider the broad variability in the way different people react to intrusion. The *Restatement* reads as follows: "One who intentionally intrudes, physically or otherwise, upon the solitude or seclusion of another or his private affairs or concerns, is subject to liability to the other for invasion of his privacy, if the intrusion would be highly offensive to a reasonable person" (*Restatement [Second] of Torts* § 652B). By placing the question in the hands of "any person of ordinary sensibilities" (an ancestor of the *Restatement*'s "reasonable person"), the New Hampshire court correctly recognized that, in privacy cases, community standards are always at issue: it isn't the individual, but the putative "'reasonable person' who suffers" (Post, 961). It is an elegant argument, which perhaps resolves the central difficulty in Warren and Brandeis—but it is also devastating to their aims.
5. Glenn Negley, "Philosophical Views on the Value of Privacy," *Law and Contemporary Problems* 31.2 (1966): 321. See also Elizabeth Price Foley, *Liberty for All: Reclaiming Individual Privacy in a New Era of Public Morality* (New Haven: Yale University Press, 2006), 3–10. Foley's position is libertarian. A good example of this view of law, from the 1800s, seeing the coercive aspects of law in a positive light is James Fitzjames Stephen, *Liberty, Equality, Fraternity*, ed. R. J. White (Cambridge: Cambridge University Press, 1967), 60–61.

6. Stephen, 241.
7. Walter Pater, *The Renaissance: Studies in Art and Poetry*, in *Walter Pater: Three Major Texts*, ed. William E. Butler (New York: New York University Press, 1986), 218–19.
8. Hume, *Treatise of Human Nature*, book 1, part 4, section 6 (1:165).
9. Pater, 219.
10. Yeats, "Who Goes with Fergus?" *The Collected Works of W. B. Yeats: The Poems*, ed. Richard J. Finneran and George Harper (New York: Macmillan, 1989), 43, line 6; Symons, "The Absinthe-Drinker," *Poems: Volume One* (London: Martin Secker, 1924), 124, lines 1, 14.
11. This clear-eyed rejection of worldly commitments has long supplied ammunition to the argument that decadence not only undermined liberal society but aided and encouraged liberalism's enemies, with the hermetic withdrawal we see in Pater, Symons—or, rather, their Continental counterparts Mallarmé, Stefan George, and others—culminating in a toxic aestheticization of politics itself by the likes of Goebbels and Mussolini. See esp. Peter Bürger, *Theory of the Avant-Garde*, and also Andreas Huyssen, *After the Great Divide: Modernism, Mass Culture, Postmodernism*. Andrew Hewitt extends Bürger's conclusions in *Fascist Modernism: Aesthetics, Politics and the Avant-Garde* (Stanford: Stanford University Press, 1993). For Bürger, whose account is probably the best known and most influential, decadence marked the culminating moment in a long process, spanning most of the nineteenth century, in which the field of aesthetic production severed itself from the culture at large; indeed, in Bürger's view, this separation was the inevitable fate of art under the conditions of bourgeois liberalism (23). In a useful insight, Bürger draws a distinction between the individual work of art and art as an institution: even as the field moved into greater autonomy, it remained possible for individual works to exercise political influence "that [militated] against the autonomy of the institution" (26). Full autonomy became possible only when the contents of art "[lost] their political character, and art [wanted] to be nothing other than art . . . a stage reached . . . in Aestheticism" (27). This description accords particularly well with German and French decadent lyrics, in which the escape from life is figured as both exquisite and stagnant—a kind of beautiful living death. The inertia so vividly depicted in, say, George's "Mein Garten," is, for Bürger, a necessary precondition for the avant-garde's repoliticization of art; it also leaves the Aesthetic vulnerable to appropriation by the far right (a point on which Bürger and Benjamin agree, though their accounts of this process differ in specifics); it is an argument encouraged, certainly, by George's own flirtation with Nazism in later life. See Robert E. Norton, *Secret Germany: Stefan George and His Circle* (Ithaca: Cornell University Press, 2002), 723ff.
12. Indeed, it is worth recalling that many decadents on both sides of the channel, in possible contradiction to their art, were engaged in radical politics. The socialist John Barlas, whose career suffered a mild setback after his arrest for opening fire on the House of Commons (Wilde bailed him out), was also

capable of minor decadent gems like "Beauty's Anadems" and "The Dancing Girl." See Christopher S. Nassaar's headnote to Barlas in *The English Literary Decadence: An Anthology* (Lanham, MD: University Press of America, 1999), 127.

13. "The Symbolism of Poetry," *W. B. Yeats: Early Essays,* ed. George Bornstein and Richard J. Finneran, vol. 4 of *The Collected Works of W. B. Yeats* (New York: Scribner, 2007), 116–17.

14. "Vivre? les serviteurs feront cela pour nous" (*Axel*, in "L'Option Supreme" in part 4, "Le Monde Passionel").

15. Arthur Symons, "In Bohemia," *Silhouettes,* 2d ed. (London: Smithers, 1896), 23.

16. Indeed, withdrawal can in the British tradition be viewed, paradoxically, as a *precondition* of social engagement. This line of thinking, which goes back at least to Matthew Arnold, can be seen most clearly, perhaps, in Wilde's aesthetes, who always turn out to be capable of decisive action when more conventional sticks-in-the-mud are paralyzed. Lord Goring in *An Ideal Husband,* to cite a ready example, is an unlikely embodiment of disinterestedness, the condition which, in Arnoldian liberalism, makes the rational exercise of power possible.

17. Borges published "El Aleph" in 1945. See *The Aleph and Other Stories, 1933–1969,* trans. Norman Thomas di Giovanni (New York: E. P. Dutton, 1970).

18. Symons in "The Decadent Movement in Literature." This 1883 essay reads like a dry run for his better-known work on symbolism six years later and is notable for perceiving lines of affinity between artistic trends usually kept separate: "The latest movement in European literature has been called by many names, none of them quite exact or comprehensive—Decadence, Symbolism, Impressionism, for instance. . . . Taken frankly as epithets which express their own meaning, both Impressionism and Symbolism convey some notion of that new kind of Literature which is perhaps more broadly characterized by the word Decadence" (223–24). Though most critics distinguish between Decadence and Symbolism, we intentionally follow Symons's suggestion that these distinctions were less clear to the decadents themselves.

19. The second, and worst, of the Dupin stories, "The Mystery of Marie Roget," in which Poe endeavored to solve an *actual* New York murder, is perhaps the oddest iteration of this paradoxical mix of hermeticism and worldly influence. In the earlier Holmes stories, moreover, Holmes's connections to the decadent lifestyle (most evident in his drug use and in Conan Doyle's frequent descriptions of his behavior as "languid") is fairly overt. It is striking to think that *The Sign of Four* and *The Picture of Dorian Gray* were commissioned at the same London dinner party. See Shafquat Towheed, Introduction, *The Sign of Four,* by Arthur Conan Doyle (Peterborough, Ontario: Broadview Press, 2010), 9–10.

20. James apparently came to know Brandeis via Brandeis's sister-in-law, Pauline Goldmark, with whom he had a sentimental relationship. Thus a letter from 1906 reads: "went to the Brandeises. . . . Very pleasant & very beautiful. After my nap, found Brandeis sitting with Henry [William's son]. . . . Brandeis I like." William James, letter to Alice Howe Gibbens James, August 30, 1906,

The Correspondence of William James, vol. 11 April 1905–March 1908, ed. Ignas K. Skrupskelis and Elizabeth M. Berkeley (Charlottesville: University of Virginia Press, 2003), 263. The editors comment on James's possible romantic attachment to Pauline Goldmark on xli–xlii.

21. Examining recent work by (mostly German) experimental psychologists, James comments that "the English writers have in the main contented themselves with . . . introspection. [But while] the works of Locke, Hume, . . . Hartley [and the Mills] will always be classics in this line, . . . psychology is passing into a less simple phase." The Germans, he continues, have undertaken a study of "the *elements* of mental life, dissecting them out from the gross results in which they are embedded, and as far as possible reducing them to quantitative scales." William James, *The Principles of Psychology*, vol. 1 (New York: Henry Holt, 1890), 192. All further citations are from this edition. Ruth Anna Putnam has observed that during James's lifetime the disciplines of psychology became independent of one another, and James contributed decisively to this separation—in no small part through this experimental focus. Ruth Anna Putnam, Introduction, *The Cambridge Companion to William James*, ed. Ruth Anna Putnam (Cambridge: Cambridge University Press, 1997), 1–2.

22. Perhaps most famously, James was deeply influenced by Locke's memory-theory of identity, and his conclusion that "the same brain may subserve many conscious selves, either alternate or switching," is almost entirely Lockean. See Richard M. Gale, *The Divided Self of William James* (Cambridge: Cambridge University Press, 1999), 350; see also Gerald E. Myers, *William James: His Life and Thought* (New Haven: Yale University Press, 2001), 363ff.

23. James is referring to both James and John Stuart Mill.

24. Cf. James's extended discussion of the "Soul-Substance" in *Principles*, 1:342–50.

25. The more familiar, expanded version of the novel was published in book form in 1891.

26. Ruth Anna Putnam discusses James's hostility to aestheticism in "Some of Life's Ideals," *Cambridge Companion to William James*, 286.

27. See also discussion in Myers, *William James*, 144.

28. "Lecture VII: The Continuity of Experience," 756–67, in *A Pluralistic Universe*, 625–819, in *William James: Writings, 1902–1910*, Library of America Edition, ed. Bruck Kuklick (New York: Literary Classics of the United States, 1987), 759–60.

29. Thomas Hobbes, *Leviathan*, ed. C. B. Macpherson (London: Penguin Books, 1968), 161.

30. Robert B. Westbrook, "Pragmatism and Democracy: Reconstructing the Logic of John Dewey's Faith," in *The Revival of Pragmatism: New Essays on Social Thought, Law, and Culture*, ed. Morris Dickstein (Durham: Duke University Press, 1998), 131.

31. This was the focus of attack by several English critics who, early on, perceived James's theory of truth to be vulnerable. See, for example, G. E. Moore, "William James's 'Pragmatism,'" *Proceedings of the Aristotelian Society* 8 (1908): 33–77, and

Bertrand Russell, "William James's Conception of Truth," *Philosophical Essays* (London: Longmans, Green, 1910), 127–49.

32. Cf. James Conant, "The James/Royce Dispute and the Development of James's 'Solution,'" in *Cambridge Companion to William James*, ed. Putnam, 186–213, esp. 193–95.

33. Ellen Kappy Suckiel, "William James," 30–43 in *A Companion to Pragmatism*, ed. John R. Shook and Joseph Margolis (Oxford: Wiley-Blackwell, 2006), 34. Similarly Richard Rorty: "James never was sure how to avoid the counterintuitive consequence that what is true for one person or group may not be true for another." Rorty, "Religious Faith, Intellectual Responsibility, and Romance," in *Cambridge Companion to William James*, 85.

34. His analysis of Locke recalls, specifically, the theistic underpinnings of liberalism. "Our personal identity," James writes, "consists, for Locke, solely in pragmatically definable particulars. Whether, apart from these verifiable facts, it also inheres in a spiritual principle, is a merely spurious speculation. Locke, compromiser that he was, passively tolerated the belief in a substantial soul behind our consciousness." William James, *Pragmatism* (Indianapolis, Hackett, 1981), 45.

35. Other books had used the halftone here and there, but Riis's was the first to exploit the technology in an "extensive" way. See Martin Parr and Gerry Badger, *The Photobook: A History*, vol. 1 (London: Phaidon, 2004), 53.

36. J. A. Hobson, *The Crisis of Liberalism: New Issues of Democracy* (London: King and Son, 1909).

37. The characteristic text of the latter position is Sumner's 1883 diatribe *What Social Classes Owe to Each Other*, which manages to move through almost every known cliché about the "brutish" and lazy masses, concluding that society has always had and will always have "its advance-guard, its rear-guard, and its stragglers" (rpt. Caldwell, ID: Caxton Printers, 1952, page 61). We might also contrast the liberal position with the more hard-nosed conservatism of a Christopher Tiedeman, who lamented that "governmental interference is proclaimed and demanded everywhere as a sufficient panacea for every social evil which threaten [sic] the prosperity of society" and argued that the state has no right to "protect the weak against the shrewdness of the stronger" (*The Limitations of Police Power* [St. Louis: F. H. Thomas, 1886], vi).

38. "State coercion" is one of Spencer's central concerns. In the 1870s and 1880s Gladstonian politicians such as Sir William Harcourt continued to argue that liberalism should refuse to compel morality. Hobhouse, himself firmly on the statist side of things, would defend against charges of "coercion" in equally liberal terms: "It is not possible to compel morality because morality is the act or character of a free agent, but . . . it is possible to create the conditions under which morality can develop, and among these not the least important is freedom from compulsion by others" (*Liberalism* [London: Oxford University Press, 1942], 143). Hobhouse is replying to Bagehot's famous claim that one cannot make a man good by act of Parliament; Bernard Shaw provided a

simpler response: "We now know that you cannot make them good in any other way."

39. Ross Posnock provides a cogent account of James's legacy amongst the progressives, also detailing the way some James acolytes, like Lippmann, went far beyond James's prescriptions in their advocacy of State control. Ross Posnock, "The Influence of William James on American Culture," *Cambridge Companion to William James*, ed. Putnam, 322–42.

40. We are not, it should be clarified, claiming a single origin for progressivism in pragmatism. A convenient overview of the numerous, non-philosophical sources of the movement is provided by Staley P. Caine in "The Origins of Progressivism," *The Progressive Era*, ed. Lewis L. Gold (Syracuse: Syracuse University Press, 1974), 11–34. See also David Marcell, *Progress and Prgmatism* (Westport, CT: Greenwood Press, 1974), 93–145, in which Marcell discusses the influence of evolutionary theory on progressivism.

41. See, for example, Reinhold Niebuhr, Arthur Schlesinger (e.g., "Liberalism in America"), and the Agrarian critiques, (e.g., Lyle Lanier, "A Critique of the Philosophy of Social Progress"). When Robert Penn Warren took an anti-segregation position in an early essay, Donald Davidson dismissed it as having "'progressive' implications" (see Hugh Ruppersburg, *Robert Penn Warren and the American Imagination* [Athens: University of Georgia Press, 1990], 30). Such uses of the word remain standard in the right-wing media, as we see in Glenn Beck's "declaration of war" on the "progressive movement" and his recent pronouncement that "the progressive movement . . . is the cancer that is inside both parties" (*Glenn Beck Program*, June 8, 2009).

42. Consider, for example, how various prominent progressivists worried away at the ideas of complete "autonomy" and unrestricted "individualism." Richard Ely was one of many to see unfettered, anarchistic autonomy as "individualism gone mad" (*Recent American Socialism* [Baltimore: Johns Hopkins University Press, 1885], 258); E. A. Ross suggested that unrestricted autonomy creates amoral lawlessness and pointed to the "decadents" as an example of "profoundly anti-social individualism" (*Social Control: A Survey of the Foundations of Order* [New York: Macmillan, 1901], 269).

43. John B. Watson, *Behaviorism*, rev. ed. (Chicago: University of Chicago, 1930 [1924]), 104. The Little Albert experiments, in which a fear of rats was induced in a nine-month old boy (by making loud noises whenever the baby touched a rat), were carried out by Watson and his partner in 1920.

44. Jeremy Bentham, *Panopticon; or, The Inspection House*, Letter 21.

45. In like manner, too, the progressivists supported the "efficiency" movement, with its concepts of automatic action, calculated management of the individual, and consolidation of bureaucratic power. Indeed, the man who coined the efficiency movement's catchphrase—"scientific management"—was the same one who enshrined privacy as a legal right: Louis Brandeis. Frederick Winslow Taylor, the guru of "scientific management" (e.g., *The Principles of Scientific Management* [1911]), got the phrase from a 1910 decision by Brandeis (see Oscar

Kraines, "Brandeis' Philosophy of Scientific Management," *Western Political Quarterly* 13.1 [1960]: 191–201).

46. The most notorious example is B. F. Skinner's *Walden Two*, which describes a community designed to create a more practical and efficient moral code and a pattern of behavior which supports it. Since behavior is most easily molded at younger ages, a "Manager of Play" is dutifully installed. Various indignities follow—from forbidden lollipops covered in powdered sugar to detect the tongue prints of the weak, up to the program of increasingly painful electric shocks delivered to children to "build up a tolerance to . . . annoying situation[s]" (*Walden Two* [New York: Macmillan, 1976], 72). Suffice it to say that Skinner's vision of a society based on a "Technology of Human Behavior" represents the purest articulation of a certain totalitarianism seen by many as the inevitable outcome of state management.

47. John Stuart Mill, *On Liberty*, ed. Mary Warnock (New York: Meridian, 1962), 195.

48. "The Search for the Great Community," in *The Later Works of John Dewey, 1925–1953*, vol. 2, *1925–1927, Essays, Reviews, Miscellany, and The Public and Its Problems* (Carbondale: Southern Illinois University Press, 2008), 329.

49. Ibid.

50. Possibly the most frequently quoted lines from Weber, noting how bureaucracy, generated by societies to promote social goods, has often turned into a trap. The modern economic order "is now bound to the technical and economic conditions of machine production which to-day determine the lives of all the individuals who are born into this mechanism. . . . In Baxter's view the care for external goods should only lie on the shoulders of the 'saint like a light cloak, which can be thrown aside at any moment.' But fate decreed that the cloak should become an iron cage." Max Weber, *The Protestant Ethic and the Sprit of Capitalism*, trans. Talcott Parsons (London: Routledge Classics, 1992), 123.

51. William James, "The Social Value of the College-Bred," *William James: Writings, 1902–1910*, Library of America Edition, ed. Bruce Kuklick (New York: Literary Classics of the United States, 1987), 1246.

52. Walter Lippmann, *The Phantom Public* (New York: Harcourt Brace, 1925), 13.

53. Ibid., 155.

54. Green discusses "positive freedom" in "Liberal Legislation and Freedom of Contract" (1881). Real-world policies rooted in this argument begin to appear first and foremost in the field of law, giving rise to the "legal realism" movement: the idea that the state existed to manipulate the law, with an eye towards individual freedom. The patron saint of the movement was Holmes, with his sensitivity to liberal worries that liberalism was becoming a cover for corporate exploitation of the individual. Holmes: "The life of the law has not been logic; it has been experience. The felt necessities of the time, the prevalent moral and political theories . . . have had a good deal more to do than the syllogism in determining the rules by which men should be governed. The law

embodies the story of a nation's development through many centuries, and it cannot be dealt with as if it contained only the axioms and corollaries of a book of mathematics" (*The Common Law* [Cambridge: Harvard University Press, 1963], 5). Holmes's dissent in *Lochner v. New York*—the high-water mark of pro-corporate laissez-faireism—articulated the liberal battle lines: "The Fourteenth Amendment does not enact Mr. Herbert Spencer's Social Statics." See also Morton J. Horwitz, *The Transformation of American Law, 1870–1960: The Crisis of Legal Orthodoxy* (New York: Oxford University Press, 1992).

55. John Dewey, *Democracy and Education: An Introduction to the Philosophy of Education* (New York: Macmillan, 1961), 357. For an account of Dewey's dispute with Lippmann over the proper limits of State control, see Robert B. Westbrook, "Liberal Democracy," in *Companion to Pragmatism*, 290–300.

56. Richard Wright, *Black Boy* (New York, Meridian: 1980), 273.

57. H. G. Wells, *A Modern Utopia* (London: Chapman and Hall, 1905), 9. Future references are to this edition.

58. Brandeis's infatuation with Taylorism has become a fashionable subject recently. A good summary of his enthusiasm can be found in Melvin Urofsky, *Louis Brandeis: A Life*, 294ff.; a less academic summary of recent scholarship on the matter is Jill Lepore's "Not So Fast," *New Yorker* (October 12, 2009). An article that connects this enthusiasm to surveillance (and the panopticon specifically) is Robert Sprague's "From Taylorism to the Omnipticon: Expanding Employee Surveillance beyond the Workplace," *John Marshall Journal of Computer and Information Law* 25 (Winter 2007), 1.

59. A trend bemoaned as early as 1984, fittingly enough, by Paul Schlueter in "Trends in Orwell Criticism: 1968–1983," *College Literature* 11.1 (1984): 94–112—though ironically, that same issue offered its own example of the Huxley-Orwell-Zamyatin combination, in Gorman Beauchamp's "1984: Oceania as Ideal State," 1–12; 1. Recent entries in this tradition include Richard Posner, "Orwell versus Huxley: Economics, Technology, Privacy, Satire," *Philosophy and Literature* 24.1 (April 2000): 1–33; and Leonidas Donskis, *Power and Imagination: Studies in Politics and Literature* (New York: Peter Lang, 2008), esp. in the section "The Coming of the Machine: Zamyatin, Huxley, and Orwell," 104ff.

60. George Orwell, "Freedom and Happiness," *Complete Works* (London: Secker and Warburg, 1998), 18:13ff. The review appeared in the *Tribune*, January 4, 1946. Orwell had, after considerable effort, procured a French translation of *We* (*"Nous Autres"*); no English edition was available at the time, to his dismay (he urged publishers to reissue the older edition).

61. Orwell, as ever exhibiting the anxiety of influence, comments that Huxley was obviously indebted to Zamyatin: "The first thing anyone would notice about *We* is the fact—never pointed out, I believe—that Aldous Huxley's *Brave New World* must be partly derived from it" (18:14). Huxley denied this, and though his "plagiarism" has become a popular canard, it indeed seems highly unlikely. Orwell's own indebtedness is undeniable—he admits in a letter to Gleb Struve

that *We* inspired him to attempt "that kind of work" himself (*Complete Works*, 16:99).

62. Orwell, "Freedom and Happiness," 18:15.

63. Aldous Huxley, Foreword, *Brave New World* (New York: HarperPerennial, 1989), xv. Subsequent references are to this edition.

64. Ibid., 65.

65. Huxley's brother was a eugenicist and Huxley himself was enthusiastic about eugenics well into the 1930s.

66. His first name is taken from Hermann von Helmholtz, the German physicist. A recent discussion of the significance of the name is in Jerome Meckier, "Onomastic Satire: Names and Naming in *Brave New World*," in *Aldous Huxley: Modern Satirical Novelist of Ideas* (Berlin: LIT Verlag Munster, 2006), 196.

67. At least in *this* novel; in 1962 he did imagine existence on the islands as utopian, in his final novel *Island*.

68. George Orwell, "You and the Atom Bomb," *Tribune*, October 19, 1945, in *Complete Works*, 17:320–21.

69. Orwell, "Freedom and Happiness," 18:15.

70. H. Rider Haggard, *King Solomon's Mines* (New York: Barnes and Noble Classics, 2004), 108.

71. Ibid., 109–10.

72. Jeffrey Meyers, *Orwell: Life and Art* (Champaign: University of Illinois Press, 2010), 178. The term "witch-hunt" is Haggard's coinage; the *OED* identifies Orwell's *Homage to Catalonia* (1938) as first using the term in its modern political sense: "2. a. A single-minded and uncompromising campaign against a group of people with unacceptable views or behavior."

73. Jean-Jacques Rousseau, *The Social Contract*, trans. G. D. H. Cole, revised and augmented by J. H. Brumfitt and John C. Hall (London: Everyman's Library, 1973), 191. Berlin's distinction between positive and negative liberty is to be found in "Two Concepts of Liberty," *The Proper Study of Mankind: An Anthology of Essays*, ed. Henry Hardy and Roger Hausheer (New York: Farrar, Straus and Giroux, 1998), 191–242. For the critique of Rousseau, see esp. 219–20, 233.

74. Rousseau, 194, Berlin, 206.

75. Noyes, who founded the Oneida community, published *History of American Socialisms* in 1870.

76. Morris himself had been a supporter of the Liberal Party before his socialist conversion—and the largely agrarian paradise he imagines is patently an attempt to produce liberal ends by communitarian means (for his liberal loyalties, see 421ff. in Fiona MacCarthy, *William Morris: A Life for Our Time* [London: Faber and Faber, 1994]). "State socialism" is indeed criticized in *News from Nowhere*, with the central government having largely been abolished. Privacy is recognized as a virtue: the "crowded" city has been replaced by a kind of medieval garden-suburb, with green spaces where dense neighborhoods used to be. People can choose to live and work alone; schools have been replaced

by private, unguided reading; many spend their summers in remote forests
or the "northern wastes." There is no civil law, no police force, no "criminal
class"—crime itself, in a confirmation of the work's minimalist (or Blakean)
logic, having conveniently disappeared when the laws defining it were scrapped.
That this paradise was made possible by a bloody overthrow of the English
government is treated as a charming historical anecdote—the narrator literally
sleeps through the revolution, and the question of how the new, stable State
will be maintained, should disgruntled groups ever emerge, is swept under the
rug. The more coercive aspects of (especially) Continental socialism are thus
almost wholly absent. Resting as it did on both a psychological sleight of hand
and a determined political naïveté, *News from Nowhere* came under the harshest
criticism from leftist writers taking issue with Morris's view of human nature
(Engels, Wells, etc.).

77. *Selections from the Works of Fourier*, trans. Julia Franklin (London: Swan
Sonnenschein, 1901), 96.

78. William James, "The Moral Equivalent of War," *William James: Writings, 1902–
1910*, 1287.

79. The State has complete control of the law, education, and industry—the last
now reorganized into a "national army"—and Bellamy's protagonist (a visitor
from the nineteenth century) is repeatedly faulted for his outmoded belief in
"self-support."

80. Thus: "But for all men, since man is a social creature, the play of will must fall
short of absolute freedom. . . . In an organised state each one of us has a more
or less elaborate code of what he may do to others and to himself, and what
others may do to him. He limits others by his rights, and is limited by the
rights of others, and by considerations affecting the welfare of the community
as a whole" (32). All of which demolishes the minimalism of a Morris:
"It does not follow, as these people would have us believe, that a man is
more free where there is least law and more restricted where there is most
law" (33).

81. Wells, *Modern Utopia*, 31ff. On privacy, Wells continues: "The desire for absolute
personal privacy is perhaps never a very strong or persistent craving. In the
great majority of human beings, the gregarious instinct is sufficiently powerful
to render any but the most temporary isolations not simply disagreeable, but
painful. . . . [I]t is only a scarce and complex modern type that finds comfort and
refreshment in quite lonely places and quite solitary occupations. . . . [U]nder
the Utopian conditions to which we shall come when presently we strike yonder
road, [the desire for privacy] may be reduced to quite manageable dimensions"
(37). Wells goes on to suggest that to satisfy the modern demand, "Privacy
beyond the house might be made a privilege to be paid for in proportion to the
area occupied."

82. Wells, 172. The heart of the system is the "Great Index": "The effectual indexing
of [everyone in the world], the record of their movement hither and thither,
the entry of various material facts, such as marriage, parentage, criminal

convictions and the like, the entry of the new-born and the elimination of the dead, colossal task though it would be, is still not [impossible]. . . . The classification of thumb-marks and of inalterable physical characteristics goes on steadily, and there is every reason for assuming it possible that each human being could be given a distinct formula, a number or "scientific name," under which he or she could be docketed. . . . A little army of attendants would be at work upon this index day and night. From sub-stations constantly engaged in checking back thumb-marks and numbers, an incessant stream of information would come, of births, of deaths, of arrivals at inns, of applications to post-offices for letters, of tickets taken for long journeys, of criminal convictions, marriages, applications for public doles and the like. A filter of offices would sort the stream, and all day and all night for ever a swarm of clerks would go to and fro correcting this central register, and photographing copies of its entries for transmission to the subordinate local stations, in response to their inquiries. So the inventory of the State would watch its every man and the wide world write its history as the fabric of its destiny flowed on" (165).

83. "But the mildly incompetent, the spiritless and dull, the poorer sort who are ill, do not exhaust our Utopian problem. There remain idiots and lunatics, there remain perverse and incompetent persons, there are people of weak character who become drunkards, drug takers, and the like. . . . All these people spoil the world for others. . . and with most of them there is manifestly nothing to be done but to seclude them from the great body of the population. You must resort to a kind of social surgery" (143). In 1901, Wells had recommended euthanasia for those social outcasts. H. G. Wells, *Anticipations of the Reaction of Mechanical and Scientific Progress upon Human Life and Thought* (London: Harper and Brothers, 1901), 323–24.

84. H. G. Wells, *The War of the Worlds* (Racine, WI: Golden Press, 1964), 11.

85. Most recent discussions of paranoia as a political formation are influenced to some extent by Richard Hofstadter's essay "The Paranoid Style in American Politics," in *The Paranoid Style in American Politics and Other Essays* (New York: Vintage Books, 1965), 3–40.

86. Ibid., 4.

87. The "sham" quotation is from Mark Fenster, *Conspiracy Theories: Secrecy and Power in American Culture* (Minneapolis: University of Minnesota Press, 1999), 23; the block quotation is Hofstadter, 29.

88. Hannah Arendt, *The Origins of Totalitarianism*, new ed. (New York: Harcourt, Brace, and World, 1966), 352. The *locus classicus* in the psychoanalytic discussion of paranoia remains Freud's analysis of Daniel Paul Schreber (Freud, *The Schreber Case*, trans. Andrew Webber [New York: Penguin, 2003]).

89. Most notably John Farrell. As Farrell puts it, the premodern world had "struck a balance between the recognition of sinfulness and the power to act rightly, [aiding believers in their] attempts to be faithful to the ideal" and compensating for their inability to do so; by contrast, paranoia is modern society's "means of

coping with the inevitable discrepancy between the way its occupants feel things ought to be and the way they are." *Paranoia and Modernity: Cervantes to Rousseau* (Ithaca: Cornell University Press, 2006), 21–22, 18. For a contrasting account tracing paranoia to the Enlightenment, see Cynthia Hendershot, who argues that paranoia was generated by the totalizing claims of Newtonian science. These claims "haunt" our increasingly skeptical and nontotalizing worldviews. (Hendershot, "Paranoia and the Delusion of the Total System," *American Imago* 54.1, p. 16).

90. Or, as Eric Hoffer put it, "Mass movements can rise and spread without a belief in God, but never without a belief in a devil" (*The True Believer: Thoughts on the Nature of Mass Movements* [New York: Harper and Row, 1951], 89).

91. Working within a German context, Fritz Stern remains the key analyst of the proto-Fascist's hatred for liberalism. The German tradition has some significant differences from the Anglo-American, but the basic psychology is similar enough. See Fritz Stern, *The Politics of Cultural Despair: A Study in the Rise of the Germanic Ideology* (Berkeley: University of California Press, 1961), xii–xxi. For homegrown American Fascists, Hofstadter observes, the New Deal and Progressivism were reliable sources of anxiety. Hofstadter, 25.

92. The formulation—a clinical one—is Eugen Bleuler's in 1911, quoted by Jerrold M. Post and Robert S. Robins, *Political Paranoia: The Psychopolitics of Hatred* (New Haven: Yale University Press, 1997), 4.

93. Arendt, 351–52.

94. "With keen attention to detail, the paranoid interprets away (often with great ingenuity) facts that do not fit in with his delusions and seeks clues and 'real meanings' in every event and comment" (Robins and Post, 8).

95. T. W. Adorno, "Qualitative Studies of Ideology," in *The Authoritarian Personality*, by T. W. Adorno, Else Frenkel-Brunswik, Daniel J. Levinson, R. Nevitt Sanford (New York: Harper and Row, 1950), 612–13.

96. Fenster, 95.

97. Hofstadter, 31.

98. The notion of preemptive revenge is associated most closely with Arendt. See 429.

99. Robins and Post, 7ff.

100. On the eradication of private and public in Fascist states, see George L. Mosse, "Toward a General Theory of Fascism," *Comparative Fascist Studies: New Perspectives*, ed. Constantin Iordachi (New York: Routledge, 2010), 65.

101. Arendt makes the (ultimately Durkheimian) argument about the break-up of traditional communities, producing a large population susceptible to massive explanatory ideologies. Arendt 352–53. See also Stern.

102. Weber's analysis of bureaucracy may be found in the last chapter of *The Protestant Ethic* and, in a far more developed way, in the third part of *Wirtschaft und Gesellschaft*. Harold Perkin's *The Rise of Professional Society: England since*

1880 remains the classic account of the growth of a professional class in late
nineteenth-century Britain (London: Routledge, 1989). Although Perkin
outlines the wide ramifications of this development—in the welfare state,
in both leftist and rightist politics—David Trotter extends Perkin's insights
specifically into a study of political paranoia. See *Paranoid Modernism: Literary
Experiment, Psychosis, and the Professionalization of English Society* (New York:
Oxford University Press, 2001), 6–15, 82–84.

103. See esp. Brantlinger's discussion of the "imperial gothic" in *Rule of Darkness:
British Literature and Imperialism, 1830–1914* (Ithaca: Cornell University Press,
1980), 227ff.

104. One of the best discussions of Chesney is to be found in I. F. Clarke, *Voices
Prophesying War: Future Wars, 1763–3749* (New York: Oxford University Press,
1992), 1–40. For a discussion of "invasion fictions," see Anthony Masters,
Literary Agents: The Novelist as Spy (Oxford: Basil Blackwell, 986), 1–15.
Among other genres involved, we would note the enormous boom in moral
guidebooks and children's literature of a certain corrective stripe. The extreme
desire to clarify the moral landscape led many of these authors to grasp any
clarifying ideologies that were to hand. To give one example: Baden Powell,
worried that the loss of empire was being accelerated by moral naïveté back
home, used his Boy Scout platform to train boys to "read" the good vs. the
bad; his language was phrenological: "The shape of the face gives a guide to
the man's character" (*Scouting for Boys: A Handbook for Instruction in Good
Citizenship*, ed. Elleke Boehmer [Oxford: Oxford University Press, 2005], 69).

105. Arthur Conan Doyle, "The Final Problem," *The Complete Sherlock Holmes*, 2
vols. (New York: Barnes and Noble Classics, 2003), 1:558.

106. Ibid., 559.

107. Auden draws this distinction in his essay "The Guilty Vicarage: Notes on the
Detective Story by an Addict," *The Complete Works of W. H. Auden, Prose*, vol.
2, *1939–1948*, ed. Edward Mendelson (Princeton: Princeton University Press,
2002), 261–69.

108. Conan Doyle, "His Last Bow," *The Complete Sherlock Holmes*, 2:480–49.
Holmes, who begins his career as a decadent, drugging himself, is at the end
chloroforming enemies of the State.

109. John Buchan, *The Thirty-Nine Steps* (New York: Dover, 1994), 22–23. All further
references will be to this edition.

110. The distinction between two main types of spy novel has been made repeatedly.
See, for example, John G. Cawelti and Bruce A. Rosenberg, *The Spy Story*
(Chicago: University of Chicago Press, 1987), 19–20. Cawelti and Rosenberg
distinguish between a "heroic" tradition and a "complex" tradition. See also
John Atkins, *The British Spy Novel: Styles in Treachery* (London: John Calder,
1984), 16–17.

111. *The Secret Agent* offers Buchan a template fully formed: London is menaced
by a "subterranean" conspiracy, consisting of both "educated anarchists"
and the agents of foreign governments; against this threat Conrad poses a

surprisingly efficient English police force and, even more important, in the
Assistant Commissioner, a brave and assured hero, able to pierce the veil with
ease. At points, one feels that episodes and characters have been lifted entire.
For example, Conrad's chief authority figure, the Home Secretary Sir Ethelred,
is primarily a figure of fun; possessing a massive and "rustic" physiognomy,
he's described more than once as resembling a tree. In much the same way,
Buchan's equivalent character, Sir Walter Bullivant, is initially described as
"a huge man . . . with a canvas bag slung over his shoulder" (59). The chief
inheritance, however, is to be found in Buchan's hero. Like the Assistant
Commissioner, Hannay feels displaced amongst the English: of Scottish
descent (like his fictional successor James Bond, as well as Buchan himself),
he has an outsider's perspective developed during his career in the colonies—
and when we first meet him is disgusted with the capital: "the talk of the
ordinary Englishman made me sick," etc. (1).

112. Joel Hopkins, "An Interview with Eric Ambler," *Journal of Popular Culture* 9.2
(Fall 1975): 290.

113. A notable element of this tradition is the whipping up of suspicion and
resentment against immigrants, as in Walter Wood's *Enemy in Our Midst*
(1906), where German immigrants take over London: "Soho was riddled with
them. There, as in Stepney, entire streets were held by aliens" (see Martin
Priestman, *Cambridge Companion to Crime Fiction* [Cambridge: Cambridge
University Press, 2003], 117). Le Queux likewise reveals great numbers
of German immigrants to be "spies." Very much the same sentiment
pervades the Bond books, with Fleming regularly imagining mixed races
and immigrants as criminal fifth columns (e.g., "Chigroes" in *Dr. No*). For
a description of some of the earliest, and most xenophobic, spy writers, see
LeRoy L. Panek, *The Special Branch: The British Spy Novel, 1890–1980* (Bowling
Green, OH: Bowling Green University Popular Press, 1980), 1–84.

114. Farrell, 5.

115. Conan Doyle, "A Case of Identity," *The Complete Sherlock Holmes*, 1:225.

116. See related discussion in Farrell, 136.

117. Patrick O'Donnell suggests that "paranoia [is] a kind of narrative work or
operation that articulates the 'individual's' relation to the symbolic order: the
stories that emerge from this are narratives of identification with the cultural
imaginary" (*Latent Destinies: Cultural Paranoia and Contemporary U.S. Narrative*
[Durham: Duke University Press, 2000], 14).

118. In the eyes of certain literary-minded critics, paranoia is nothing more than
a crisis of interpretation. Leo Bersani sees paranoia as linked to "interpretive
distress" (*Culture of Redemption* [Cambridge: Harvard University Press, 1990],
179); Bran Nicol goes one step further and sees it *as* interpretive distress:
"Paranoia itself, as the psychoanalytic definitions of the condition indicate,
is essentially a crisis in interpretation. . . . The classic symptoms of paranoia,
in other words, involve making false sense of the world. . . . The paranoiac
looks "behind" the ostensible meaning of language to an alternative one. At

the heart of paranoia, then, is a battle to understand/impose meaning" (Nicol, "Reading Paranoia: Paranoia, Epistemophilia, and the Postmodern Crisis of Interpretation," *Literature and Psychology* 45 [1999]: 44–46).

119. That is to say: the mental suspension Hannay experiences can be related to similar moments in Conrad where the mind lags behind the senses—most famously the death of the helmsman in *Heart of Darkness*.

120. Jacques Berthoud, "The Secret Agent," in *The Cambridge Companion to Joseph Conrad* (Cambridge: Cambridge University Press, 1996), 100–121; 106.

121. Kaczynski, who had read *The Secret Agent* at least a dozen times, sometimes used "Conrad" as an alias. Parallels between his rhetoric and that of the Professor encouraged the FBI to recruit Conrad scholars in their search for a suspect. Kaczynski also used the initials "FC" in his letters as a tribute to the anarchists' "FP" signature in *The Secret Agent*. See "Unabomber Case Very Conrad-esque," *Washington Post*, July 9, 1996.

122. Joseph Conrad, *Under Western Eyes* (Oxford: Oxford World Classics, 2003), 46, 54.

123. Ibid., 138.

124. Disputing a good many readers who saw the works as unremittingly cynical, Mann was among the first to observe that *The Secret Agent* "is an anti-Russian story, plainly enough, anti-Russian in a very British sense and spirit. Its background consists in politics on the large scale, in the whole conflict between the British and Russian political ideology—[and in] the Pole's passionate love of England." Thomas Mann, *Past Masters and Other Papers*, trans. H. T. Lowe-Porter (New York: Alfred A. Knopf, 1933), 234–35.

125. We take Conrad's (and Ford's) impressionism, as outlined in the former's preface to *The Nigger of the Narcissus* and in the latter's "On Impressionism," as an extension of realistic techniques rather than a rejection of them.

126. The phrase "Orwell was right" has become a popular Internet meme and graffiti tag. For Orwell being "prophetic," see, for example, Ruth Ann Lief, *Homage to Oceania: The Prophetic Vision of George Orwell* (Columbus: Ohio State University Press, 1969) and Irving Howe, who suggests that any stylistic awkwardness in the book is a consequence of its "urgencies of prophetic expression" ("Orwell: History as Nightmare," *American Scholar* [Spring 1956]: 193–207). The trope is well established on the conspiratist right as well (e.g., Mark Dice's *Big Brother: The Orwellian Nightmare Come True* [2011]).

127. Orwell preferred Swift's attack, in book 3 of *Gulliver's Travels*, "on what would now be called totalitarianism": "He has an extraordinary clear prevision of the spy-haunted 'police State,' with its endless heresy-hunts and treason trials, all really designed to neutralize popular discontent by changing it into war hysteria." ("Politics vs. Literature: An Examination of *Gulliver's Travels*," in *Complete Works*, 18:417–31; 423).

128. The TLS was confident that "this is not a work which many adults will read through more than once" (*Times Literary Supplement*, November 25, 1955). The *Observer* review, by Edwin Muir, noted that Tolkien's "good people are

consistently good, his evil figures immovably evil" (August 22, 1954). See also Michael Moorcock, "Epic Pooh" (e.g., "The Lord of the Rings is much more deep-rooted in its infantilism than a good many of the more obviously juvenile books it influenced").

129. Wilson pays special attention to the cardboard allegory of the work, noting that "what we get is a simple confrontation—in more or less the traditional terms of British melodrama—of the Forces of Evil with the Forces of Good" (*The Nation*, April 14, 1956). J. W. Lambert in the *Sunday Times* noted in bewilderment that "Ariosto, Malory and Spenser are evoked" and suggested that "it may be more helpful to suggest that those who enjoyed, say, the Brothers Grimm, . . . *The Wind in the Willows* or T. H. White's *Sword in the Stone* will find this bizarre enterprise very much to their taste"; it is, he concludes in a phrase we encounter in reviews of spy literature, "a book for bright children" (August 8, 1954).

130. *The Two Towers*, in *The Lord of the Rings* (New York: Houghton Mifflin, 1994), 688. Future quotations from this edition.

131. *Paradise Lost*, 4.198–203. *John Milton: Complete Poems and Major Prose*, ed. Merritt Y. Hughes (New York: Odyssey Press, 1957), 282.

132. *Nineteen Eighty-Four*, in *Complete Works*, 9:175; 9:112; 9:29; 9:240; 9:84, etc. Future references as *1984*.

133. *Homage to Catalonia*, in *Complete Works*, 6:168–69.

134. See, for example, Norman Podhoretz, "If Orwell Were Alive Today," *Harper's* (January 1983), 30–37; Christopher Hitchens, in much the same spirit, insists that Orwell always had Stalin in mind, in more or less everything he ever wrote (see *Why Orwell Matters* [New York: Basic Books, 2002], esp. chapter 4, "Orwell and the Left").

135. "London Letter, 3 January 1941" (*Partisan Review*, March–April 1941), in *Complete Works*, 12:352–53.

136. "A Letter from England, 3 January 1943" (*Partisan Review*, March–April 1943), in *Complete Works*, 14:293.

137. "London Letter" (*Partisan Review*, Winter 1944–45), in *Complete Works*, 16:411–12.

138. "London Letter, 5 June 1945" (*Partisan Review*, Summer 1945), in *Complete Works*, 17:163. It would seem at first that additional precedent might be found in the regular descriptions of the sheer dirtiness and simpleminded credulity of the working classes in *The Road to Wigan Pier* (e.g., his depiction of the Brookers in the opening chapter [*Complete Works*, 5:5ff]). And yet the notorious "lower classes smell" sequence in *Wigan Pier* (5:119ff) is in fact a refutation of sorts, and the book is suffused with a sentimental love for the workers: the real critique is largely aimed at the middle classes. There is no precedent in *Wigan Pier* for *1984*.

139. Ibid., 17:164.

140. "The belief that nothing exists outside your own mind—surely there must be some way of demonstrating that it was false? Had it not been exposed long ago as a fallacy? There was even a name for it, which he had forgotten. A faint

smile twitched the corners of O'Brien's mouth as he looked down at him. 'I told you, Winston,' he said, 'that metaphysics is not your strong point. The word you are trying to think of is solipsism.' "

141. See John Rodden's discussion in "Orwell on Religion: The Catholic and Jewish Questions," *College Literature* 2.1 (1984): 48–50.

142. "Review of *The Spirit of Catholicism*" (*New English Weekly*, June 9, 1932) in *Complete Works*, 10:248. The real-life proof is found, he argues elsewhere, in the way the Catholic writer always supports Catholic countries ("just as the Communist feels that he must in all circumstances support the U.S.S.R.") ("As I Please," 30, in *Complete Works*, 16:263).

143. *1984*, 9:218.

144. Ibid., 9:266 ("priest," 9:257; "priests of power," 9:276).

145. Ibid., 9:282.

146. Orwell's conviction that religious logic was a contradiction in terms is, of course, inescapable in his writings: "Few thinking people now believe in life after death, and the number of those who do is probably diminishing" ("Arthur Koestler," in *Complete Works*, 16:391–402; 16:399).

147. "As I Please," 59 (*Tribune*, February 16, 1945), in *Complete Works*, 17:50–51. And in "As I Please," 76 (March 7, 1947): "One of the great faults of the present government is its failure to tell the people what is happening and why. . . . However, with the wartime machinery of propaganda largely scrapped . . . it is not easy for the government to publicise itself. . . . The most obvious means of publicity is the radio" (*Complete Works*, 19:67).

148. Barzun, "Meditations on the Literature of Spying," *American Scholar* 34 (Spring 1965): 167–78; 172–73.

149. Reviewing *Our Game* in the *New Yorker*, John Updike took the opportunity to evaluate "Cold War thrillers" as a group: "When I peeked into these evidently absorbing tomes I got a suffocating gray impression of armaments catalogues and code nerds and excessively factual dialogue elucidating how every double-cross had another behind it and all roads led to a vast distrust. . . . [T]here is something of boyish daydream about 'Our Game.' [Its] questing adventures take us back to . . . Victorian times, when the great, multicolored globe existed as a vast playing field on which truehearted Englishmen could chase their personal rainbows while the picturesque heathen cheered."

In less dignified terms, Salman Rushdie, furious over a speech in which le Carré suggested that Rushdie should not have been surprised by the fatwa, initiated a vicious spat in the editorial pages of the *Guardian*. Rushdie declared le Carré "a pompous ass" and a "philistine"; amidst the storm of invective, Rushdie's parting shot stands out: " 'Ignorant' and 'semi-literate' are dunces' caps he has skillfully fitted on his own head. I wouldn't dream of removing them. Le Carré's habit of giving himself good reviews . . . was no doubt developed because, well, somebody has to write them. . . . A novel, Mr. le Carré, [is] not a gibe. You know what a novel is, don't you, John?" Behind Updike's and Rushdie's rhetoric lies a single accusation: the spy novel is not serious literature.

150. This border-policing, it is worth noting, is mutual—witness Ambler's jaundiced remark about "respectability" or Greene's careful segregating of his output into novels (*The End of the Affair, The Power and the Glory*) and "entertainments" (*Our Man in Havana*).

151. As in Woolf's attacks on Galsworthy and Bennett in "Modern Fiction" and elsewhere. See Virginia Woolf, "Modern Fiction," *The Common Reader: First Series* (London: Hogarth Press, 1925), 184–95.

152. W. Somerset Maugham, *Ashenden* (London: Vintage Classics, 2000), viii. Future references are to this edition.

153. Barzun, "Meditations," 176.

154. Hoggart, *Auden: An Introductory Essay* (London: Chatto and Windus, 1951), 20.

155. See, for example, Mendelson's discussion in *Early Auden* (New York: Viking Press, 1981), 3–17. Also Samuel Hynes, *The Auden Generation: Literature and Politics in England in the 1930s* (New York: Viking Press, 1977), 9–97.

CHAPTER 5. TOWARDS A THEORY OF LIBERAL READING

1. *The Waste Land* ("III. The Fire Sermon"), lines 215–48, in *Collected Poems, 1909–1962* (New York: Harcourt Brace, 1963), 51–76.

2. Ibid., 73.

3. The idea is central enough to Socrates that Plato returns to it a number of times (in the *Apology, Meno, Protagoras*, etc.); Aristotle responds in the *Nicomachean Ethics*, book 7, chapter 2.

4. Thomas Keenan, "Publicity and Indifference: Media, Surveillance, 'Humanitarian Intervention,'" *PMLA* 117.1 (January 2002): 112.

5. Levin, Frohne, and Weibel, eds., *CTRL [SPACE]*, 10.

6. Louise Amoore, "Governing by Identity," in Colin J. Bennett and David Lyon, eds. *Playing the Identity Card* (New York: Routledge, 2008), 33.

7. Midori Ogasawara, "A Tale of the Colonial Age, or the Banner of New Tyranny? National Identification Card Systems in Japan," in ibid., 108.

8. Parker, 294.

9. Discussed in Sykes, 39.

10. A position discussed, with considerable skepticism, by David Will: "The existing model of identity is . . . open to abuse. Terrorists and criminals misuse multiple identities to leach [*sic*] off society, and even kill us. A single identifier is needed to prove who you are, or that you are who you say you are. . . . The notion of identity at play in [this] ID discourse is an identity mediated, managed, protected and legitimated through the state (broadly conceived of course). . . . The government gains a number of benefits (crime prevention, less drain on resources, etc.) while the individual gets his identity protected from external threats." ("The United Kingdom Identity Card Scheme: Shifting Motivations, Static Technologies" [*Playing the Identity Card*, 176]).

11. For an example of the former tendency, one might turn to Henri Lefebvre: "The state is consolidating on a world scale. It weighs down on society (on all societies) in full force; it plans and organizes 'rationally,' with the help of knowledge and technology, imposing analogous, if not homologous, measures irrespective of political ideology, historical background, or the class origins of those in power. The state crushes time by reducing differences to repetitions of circularities. . . . The violence of power is answered by the violence of subversion. . . . State-imposed normality makes permanent transgression inevitable. As for time and negativity, whenever they emerge, as they must, they do so explosively" (*Production of Space*, 23).

12. "The Visible Man: Ethics in a World without Secrets," *Harper's*, August 2011, 36.

13. Lyon, Introduction to *Surveillance, Privacy, and the Globalization of Personal Information*, ed. Elia Zureik, L. Lynda Harling Stalker, Emily Smith, David Lyon and Yolande E. Chan (Montreal: McGill–Queen's University Press: 2010), 1.

14. Staff at Scotland Yard, in interviews with the authors, energetically testified to the sheer amount of paperwork required to access most private and commercial security cameras.

15. Baudrillard, "Precession of Simulacra," *Simulacra and Simulation*, 76. In similar fashion, Baurdillard discusses the "eye of TV" (e.g., 29). The phrase "the eye of television" has indeed become an oddly prevalent trope in much media criticism.

16. Lyon in *Surveillance, Privacy and the Globalization of Personal Information*, 3. The idea that privacy has "vanished," worryingly, is one we have heard almost without fail in the question and conversation periods following lectures we have delivered on various campuses.

17. See Kantorowicz, *The King's Two Bodies*. Foucault draws on Kantorowicz in his discussion of the idea in *Discipline and Punish*.

18. Parsons of course admitted to the existence of subsystems and "boundaries" (between two corporations, say), but such divisions did not interfere with his belief (explored especially in and after *The Social System* [1951] and during the construction of the AGIL paradigm) that a grand theory could be developed to describe universal social functions. Luhmann is just as committed to providing a "general theory," though he is far more committed to the differentiation and to some extent independence of systems.

19. We refer specifically to Luhmann's distinction between the biological individual, who is irrelevant to society, and the social individual, who is understood as a unit in a communications system; Luhmann argues, consequently, that society does not really consist of concrete, autonomous individuals. For Lyotard, see *The Postmodern Condition: A Report on Knowledge*, trans. Geoff Bennington and Brian Massumi (Minneapolis: University of Minnesota Press, 1984), 11–12. Future references are to this edition. Habermas has leveled variations of this charge since his public debate with Luhmann began in *Theory of Society or Social Technology* in 1971.

20. Habermas, *Faktizität und Geltung*, 181–87. The English translation is *Between Facts and Norms: Contributions to a Discourse Theory of Law and Democracy* (Cambridge: MIT Press, 1996).
21. Habermas tries to reconcile the two by viewing them as "equi-primordial" (ibid.), a stance which does not diminish the basic quality of opposition between the two.
22. Lyotard, 35.
23. This is of course Berlin's project in "Two Concepts of Liberty."
24. Lyotard, 37.
25. This is obviously *not* the path that Habermas goes down; he diagnoses precisely these problems in his attempt to save the liberal tradition while nevertheless clinging to Rousseauvian ideas of consensus.
26. Locke's entire discussion of "society" is profoundly complicated by his Christianity and specifically his Protestantism (his insistence on the importance of Christian charity and caring for the poor, for example, and his early withholding of toleration from Catholics and atheists). Modern-day "libertarians" who claim Locke as their spiritual father tend to ignore these elements of his thought.
27. Locke's one appearance: "Locke: 'In the beginning all was America.'" Giorgio Agamben, *Homo Sacer: Sovereign Power and Bare Life*, trans. Daniel Heller-Roazen (Stanford: Stanford University Press, 1998), 36.
28. Ibid., 1–2.
29. Ibid., 7–8.
30. The most tangible result of this data collection is the constant reorganization of the layout of shopping environments: shelving practices, aisle layout, etc. Supermarkets lead the way in this area.
31. Deleuze, "Postscript on Control Societies," in *Negotiations, 1972–1990* (New York: Columbia University Press, 1995), 182.
32. Timothy Druckrey, "Secreted Agents, Security Leaks, Immune Systems, Spore Wars," in Levin, Frohne, and Weibel, eds., *CTRL [SPACE]*, 151.
33. For Parsons (in his early work, particularly), the quest for "efficiency" is simply proof of the individual's rationality (e.g., *The Structure of Social Action* [1937; New York: Free Press, 1968], 1:19); Lyotard, on the other hand, argues that "efficiency" is the means by which power legitimates certain systems (e.g., *Postmodern Condition*, 47).
34. Deleuze, 178.
35. Michel de Certeau, *The Practice of Everyday Life*, trans. Steven Rendall (Berkeley: University of California Press, 1984), 91–92
36. Ibid., 95. In their revisions of Foucault, Deleuze and Bauman shift their focus from the purported "center" of disciplinary power to the discrete consumers who allow the system to run. The extent to which this revises Foucault at all is highly debatable—but in any case: "Capitalism," Deleuze claims, is "no longer directed toward production, but toward products, that is, toward sales or markets. . . . The sales department becomes a business center or 'soul'" (320).

Foucault is at least as interested in the dispersal of power on the local level; something his revisers tend to ignore. As a Jesuit, de Certeau is perhaps closest in sensibility to Tolkien, whose panoptic tower-dweller Sauron has similar fantasies of transparency, which come to a sorry end.

37. Ibid., 96.

38. So, for example, products are used in unanticipated ways, whether illegal (cold medicine and antifreeze as ingredients in illicit drugs) or legal (baking soda is just as likely today to be used in household cleaning, or to cure acne, or to deodorize a refrigerator as it is in baking).

39. Scott, *Seeing Like a State*, 6–7. See also John Gilliom's study of welfare recipients in Appalachia. He suggests that "everyday tactics of subterfuge, evasion and concealment" are becoming a "defining form of politics in the surveillance society." The recipients are under close bureaucratic watch, and have little or no privacy to speak of—but this does not particularly concern them or hamper their ability to game the system (*Overseers of the Poor: Surveillance, Resistance, and the Limits of Privacy* [Chicago: University of Chicago Press, 2001], 101).

40. Scott, 7.

41. Lyotard, 48.

42. Adam Smith, *Theory of Moral Sentiments*, 151.

43. Slavoj Žižek, *Enjoy Your Symptom! Jacques Lacan in Hollywood and Out* (New York: Routledge, 2001), 203.

44. The most extensive meditation on this topic is probably Lyon's *Surveillance and Social Sorting: Privacy, Risk, and Digital Discrimination* (London: Routledge, 2003).

45. Eli Pariser, *The Filter Bubble* (New York: Penguin, 2011). For his discussion of "font size" as one of the fifty-seven signals, see http://blogs.westword.com/ showandtell/2011/06/we_talk_with_moveon_board_pres.php?page=2.

46. Scott, 22, 6.

47. *CTRL [SPACE]*, 12.

48. The school is indeed a salutary example: in a democratic state, the school system is preferably not designed so as to produce group-thinking drones. The allegorical pressures should instead be low, given that a free society needs an intellectually diverse population of autonomous individuals to survive. Indeed, if there is one group most sensitive to oppressive, coercive surveillance in the classroom, it is teachers themselves (who reacted with outrage, for example, when Bill Gates and others suggested that classes be recorded and analyzed to evaluate student and teacher ability). Teachers in Britain denounced a similar plan as "Big Brotherish"; one student commented, "Cameras can be useful, but also they are an invasion of your privacy and sometimes they make me feel uncomfortable because I don't know when someone could be watching me." (Graeme Patton, "Teachers Condemn 'Big Brother' Spy Cameras in Schools," *The Telegraph*, July 21, 2009).

49. See, for example, Nelson Arteaga Botello, "Privacy and Surveillance in Mexico and Brazil: A Cross-National Analysis," in *Surveillance, Privacy, and the*

Globalization of Personal Information, ed. Elia Zureik et al. (Montreal: McGill–
Queens University Press, 2010), 212ff. As Zureik summarizes, Botello shows
that in Mexico "personal security is regarded as a precondition for privacy,
leading to support for surveillance devices such as closed circuit television." See
also Botello, "Security Metamorphosis in Latin America," in *Surveillance and
Everyday Life*, ed. Vida Bajc and Willem de Lint (New York: Routledge, 2011),
236–57. For the Indian villager, see Lydia Polgreen, "Scanning 2.4 Billion Eyes,
India Tries to Connect Poor to Growth": "[Registering in the Indian national
computer database] will give me an identity. . . . It will show that I am a human
being, that I am alive, that I live on this planet" (*New York Times*, September 2,
201).

50. Cf. Keenan, 114–15.

51. By 2006, facial recognition technology had improved "a hundredfold since
1995" (see Mark Williams, "Better Face-Recognition Software," *Technology
Review*, May 30, 2007; online at http://www.technologyreview.com/
Infotech/18796/?a=f). Most work on "pattern matching" has moved to "string
matching" and related "fast matching" strategies.

52. Louise Amoore, "Algorithmic War: Everyday Geographies of the War on Terror,"
Antipode 41.1 (2009): 49–69.

53. Amoore (ibid.) points out that what started out as a commercial endeavor on the
part of IBM has entered general use by governments.

54. This remark was made in an interview with the then-head of surveillance and
security (who remains anonymous at his request) at Fitzgerald's Casino, Reno,
Nevada, date withheld; it was later repeated in its essentials (the acronym in
particular) by several people working in surveillance at Nevada casinos.

55. Coppola's decision actually to change the soundtrack (i.e., the actor actually does
say the line differently the last time around, and this new track is dubbed in
over the original) has been the subject of debate among film scholars and movie
buffs for decades. For our purposes, the decision is simply a canny decision on
Coppola's part, given the psychology involved.

56. By using this language, we should clarify, we are not echoing the claims of the
U.S. Supreme Court in the Citizens United decision; there, corporations were
declared "citizens," with the same legal rights as a human individual—a rather
different phenomenon.

57. Louise Amoore and Marieke de Goede, "Transactions after 9/11: The Banal Face
of the Preemptive Strike," *Transactions of the Institute of British Geographers* 33. 2
(April 2008): 173–85; 175.

58. Amoore and de Goede assure us that "this example is drawn from the
documented experiences of a participant in 'London in a Time of Terror,'
Birkbeck College, London, 8 December 2006" (183, n2).

59. Near the end of the hunt, Ratliff was taking on high-visibility "challenges" (go
to the fiftieth floor of a building, attend a book reading, etc.) set for him by his
editors—and announced to trackers via clues in the *New York Times* crossword
puzzle.

60. Fredric Jameson, *Postmodernism, or, the Cultural Logic of Late Capitalism* (Durham: Duke University Press, 1991), 6.

61. Baudrillard, 2. Theodor W. Adorno and Max Horkheimer, *Dialectic of Enlightenment*, trans. John Cumming (New York: Verso, 1979), 126. See also Guy Debord, *The Society of the Spectacle*, trans. Donald Nicholson-Smith (New York: Zone Books, 1995).

62. Agamben, *The Coming Community*, trans. Michael Hardt (Minneapolis: University of Minnesota, 1993), 82. Jameson, "Postmodernism and Consumer Society," in *The Anti-Aesthetic: Essays on Postmodern Culture*, ed. Hal Foster (Port Townsend, WA: Bay Press, 1983), 125.

63. Eco, *Travels in Hyper-reality: Essays* (New York: Houghton Mifflin, 1986), 44.

64. Jameson, *Postmodernism*, 20; for Baudrillard on Lascaux, see *Simulation and Simulacra*, 9.

65. Weibel, in *CTRL [SPACE]*, 210.

66. De Certeau, 96.

67. Baudrillard, 6.

68. Ibid., 15.

69. A depressing endpoint of several analyses of "reality TV." The classic example is surely Baudrillard's analysis of the Louds in the documentary *An American Family:* "This family was already hyperreal by the very nature of its selection: a typical ideal American family, California home, three garages, five children, assured social and professional status, decorative housewife, upper-middle-class" (etc., etc.). Even correcting for the characteristic hyperbole, this is typical of the way paranoid thought reduces real people into empty figments. Baudrillard, 30–32.

70. Pynchon, *V.* (New York: Harper and Row, 1986), 454.

71. David Foster Wallace, "*E Unibus Pluram:* Television and US Fiction," *Review of Contemporary Fiction* 13.2 (1993): 151–94.

72. Lyotard, xxiii and 31.

73. Ibid., xxiii.

74. Ibid., 16–17.

75. Ibid., xxv. Goffman gets a footnote on 90.

76. Lyotard, 10, 21.

77. Lyotard establishes his post-structuralist (Lacanian, Foucauldian) bona fides by disavowing the idea of the subject. Ibid., 15.

78. Winfried Pauleit, "Video Surveillance and Postmodern Subjects: The Effects of the Photographesomenon," in Levin, Frohne, and Weibel, eds., *CTRL [SPACE]*, 469.

79. Roland Barthes, *Camera Lucida*, trans. Richard Howard (New York: Farrar, Straus and Giroux, 1981), 96.

80. Jameson, "Postmodernism and Consumer Society," 125. Baudrillard, "History: A Retro Scenario," in *Simulacra and Simulation*, 43.

81. Baudrillard, *Simulacra*, 1.

82. Pauleit cites as an example of this phenomenon the Bulger case. In 1993, James Bulger, a two-year-old from Liverpool, was murdered by two other children.

The video surveillance, from a Liverpool mall, of Bulger being lead away by
his killers was subsequently used by the British artist Jamie Wagg, causing
widespread outrage. Pauleit, 470–74.

83. Paul de Man, *The Rhetoric of Romanticism* (New York: Columbia University
Press, 1984), 7.

84. Ibid., 6.

85. Barthes, 77.

86. Sontag, *On Photography* (New York: Dell, 1977), 11 et passim.

87. Barthes, 26–27.

88. Ibid., 44–45.

89. The monitoring perspective appears regularly throughout Modernist
literature; we might mention, as among the most famous examples, that
of Woolf in *The Years* or the implied aerial perspective of "Wandering Rocks"
in *Ulysses*.

90. Marshall McLuhan, *Understanding Media* (New York: McGraw-Hill,
1964), 30.

91. W. H. Auden, 1965 Foreword, *Collected Poems*, ed. Edward Mendelson (New
York: Vintage Books, 1976), xxvi. Much has been written on the Romantic
fragment—one might start with Marjorie Levinson's authoritative book on the
subject: Marjorie Levinson, *The Romantic Fragment Poem: A Critique of a Form*
(Chapel Hill: University of North Carolina Press, 1986).

92. One need only consider, for example, the final gesture of Joyce's *Portrait*, the
concluding lines of *Between the Acts*, or, indeed, almost anything by Samuel
Beckett. In contrast to literally unfinished works like *The Cantos* or *The Trial*, that
is to say, these pieces are aesthetically "finished" while nonetheless conceiving
of themselves as incomplete.

93. T. S. Eliot, "Ulysses, Order, and Myth," *Selected Prose of T. S. Eliot*, ed. Frank
Kermode (New York: Harcourt, Brace, 1975), 175.

94. Walter Benjamin, "On Some Motifs in Baudelaire," *Illuminations*, ed. and intro.
Hannah Arendt (New York: Schocken, 1968), 159.

95. Thus, in her influential book on *Poetic Closure*, Barbara Herrnstein Smith
comments that, "In 'the age of suspicion' . . . where conviction is seen as
self-delusion, and all last words are lies, the only resolution may be in the
affirmation of irresolution." According to this position, influenced by the New
Criticism, Modernist poems embrace the unfinished as a way of challenging
the meaning of literature—and indeed, of human production generally. (*Poetic
Closure: A Study of How Poems End* [Chicago: University of Chicago Press, 1968],
240–41.)

96. Cathy Caruth, *Unclaimed Experience: Trauma, Narrative, and History* (Baltimore:
Johns Hopkins University Press, 1996), 5–6.

97. To the point that a recent collection about clinical trauma begins with an
epigraph from *The Waste Land* (*Broken Images, Broken Selves: Dissociative
Narratives in Clinical Practice*, ed. Stanley Krippner and Susan Marie Powers
[New York: Routledge, 1997], ix).

98. Nor, it might be added, is this quality to be explained by reading modern literature within an explicitly providential context, as in the work of Benjamin. Or, more recently, Balachandra Rajan. See, for example, *The Form of the Unfinished*, (Princeton: Princeton University Press, 1985), esp. 250ff.

99. The proleptic quality in Modernist literature, we should make clear, has not gone entirely unnoticed—witness Robert Spoo's justly famous reading of the "Nestor" episode in *Ulysses*. As Spoo points out, Stephen's hour in Dalkey is suffused with imagery of the Great War: while he and his students are palpably bored by the lesson of the day (Pyrrhus's futile struggle against the Romans), *we* cannot help but hear the pre-echoes of a war to come. Spoo moves beyond the idea of trauma as determined entirely by the past. In *Ulysses*, he argues, "The narrative present . . . [is] saturated with the past and the future, in some cases over-determined by them." The school boys' field-hockey game is at once ordinary play and an allegory for their "potential victimization." " 'Nestor' and the Nightmare: The Presence of the Great War in *Ulysses*," *Twentieth Century Literature* 32.2 (1986): 137–54; 145. A clear instance of prolepsis—and yet just as clearly distinguishable from the problem we are discussing: by setting his novel more than a decade in the past, Joyce is able to point forward to a "future" catastrophe with which his audience is already quite familiar. This familiarity, in turn, allows for a stable allegory (the students, for example, representing the doomed thousands). Similar recursive structures can be detected in any number of prewar novels. In *Nostromo*, to pick a striking instance, Don Vincente Ribiera's splendid entry into Sulaco (in chapter 8) is colored by the reader's knowledge that, eventually, he will need to flee for his life "like a rabbit"; the ignominious exit having already been recounted in chapter 2.

100. Philip Larkin, "MCMXIV," in *Collected Poems*, ed. Anthony Thwaite (London: Faber, 1988), 127–28.

101. Robert Frost, "Once by the Pacific," in *Complete Poems of Robert Frost* (New York: Holt, Rinehart and Winston, 1964), 314; lines 10–11, 12.

102. Eliot, "Preludes," in *Collected Poems, 1909–1962*, 13.

103. Eliot, "The Metaphysical Poets," in *Selected Prose of T. S. Eliot*, ed. Frank Kermode (New York: Harcourt, Brace, 1975), 64.

104. Samuel Hynes, *The Auden Generation: Literature and Politics in England in the 1930s* (New York, Viking Press, 1972), 17–35.

105. Evelyn Waugh, *Vile Bodies* (Boston: Little, Brown, 1930), 315–16.

106. Herbert Simon, *The Shape of Automation for Men and Management* (New York: Harper and Row), 96.

107. The language is de Man's, in "Semiology and Rhetoric" (in *Allegories of Reading*, 3).

108. Fish, "Rhetoric," in *Critical Terms for Literary Study*, ed. Frank Lentricchia and Thomas McLaughlin (Chicago: University of Chicago Press, 1990), 217.

109. The terminology is to be found in Williams, "Marxism and Literature" (Oxford: Oxford University Press, 1977).

110. For the eleven basic emotions, see Paul Ekman, "Basic Emotions," in *Handbook of Cognition and Emotion*, ed. T. Dalgleish and M. Power (Sussex, UK: John Wiley and Sons, 1999). Marx, "A Tack in the Shoe: Neutralizing and Resisting the New Surveillance," *Journal of Social Issues* 59 (2), (2003): 369–90.

111. Jay David Bolter, *Writing Space: The Computer, Hypertext, and the History of Writing* (Hillsdale, NJ: Lawrence Erlbaum, 1991), 233–37. Other examples abound. Thus, in a recent Op-Ed piece, a philosopher proclaiming himself a "naturalist":

    "Can science and naturalistic philosophy do without [history and literary theory]? This is a different question from whether people, as consumers of human narratives and enjoyers of literature, can do without them. The question naturalism faces is whether disciplines like literary theory provide real understanding? [*sic*] . . . If semiotics, existentialism, hermeneutics, formalism, structuralism, post-structuralism, deconstruction and post-modernism transparently flout science's standards of objectivity, or if they seek arbitrarily to limit the reach of scientific methods, then naturalism can't take them seriously as knowledge. That doesn't mean anyone should stop doing literary criticism any more than forgoing fiction. Naturalism treats both as fun, but neither as knowledge" (Alex Rosenberg, "Why I Am a Naturalist," *New York Times*, September 17, 2011; online at http://opinionator.blogs.nytimes.com/2011/09/17/why-i-am-a-naturalist/).

112. Indeed, the second, revised edition of the book (2001), while quietly dropping several of the predictions of the first, replaces them with a new but related set of claims, just as non-falsifiable; notable is the suggestion that we may now be in "the late age of prose itself" (2d ed., 213).

113. Bolter, 237.

114. "MUDS" are "Multi-User Domains" (originally "Multi-User Dungeons"); "MOOS" are a subset: "MUDS, Object Oriented." Both are, essentially, text-based, multi-user, online environments.

115. One last example, from a religious studies scholar trying his hand at academic administration: "As departments fragment, research and publication become more and more about less and less. Each academic becomes the trustee not of a branch of the sciences, but of limited knowledge that all too often is irrelevant for genuinely important problems. . . . [Therefore we should] abolish permanent departments, even for undergraduate education, and create problem-focused programs. These constantly evolving programs would have sunset clauses, and every seven years each one should be evaluated and either abolished, continued or significantly changed. . . . A Water program would bring together people in the humanities, arts, social and natural sciences with representatives from professional schools like medicine, law, business, engineering, social work, theology and architecture. Through the intersection of multiple perspectives and approaches, new theoretical insights will develop and unexpected practical solutions will emerge."

Awakening late in life to the "impractical" nature of the humanities, this writer hopes to reinvent the humanities as a kind of court jester for the sciences, and proposes interdisciplinary approaches to (pseudo-scientific) problems; he would also, puzzlingly, eliminate the disciplines themselves (Mark Taylor, "End the University as We Know It," *New York Times*, April 26, 2009).

116. Lyotard, 62–64.

117. For "coercive testing regime," see David Brooks's Op-Ed piece "Testing the Teachers" (*New York Times*, April 19, 2012): "Colleges have to test more to find out how they're doing. . . . There has to be some way to reward schools that actually do provide learning and punish schools that don't. There has to be a better way to get data. . . . The challenge is not getting educators to embrace the idea of assessment. It's mobilizing them to actually enact it in a way that's real and transparent to outsiders. . . . Should we impose a coercive testing regime that would reward and punish schools based on results?"

INDEX

Page numbers in *italics* refer to illustrations.